Introduction to

STATISTICAL METHOD

by

B. C. Brookes, M.A.
Reader in Information Studies in the University of London

and

W. F. L. Dick, M.A.
Technical Officer, Imperial Chemical Industries

Second Edition

HEINEMANN·LONDON

Heinemann Educational Books Ltd
LONDON EDINBURGH MELBOURNE TORONTO
AUCKLAND SINGAPORE JOHANNESBURG
HONG KONG NAIROBI IBADAN

Cased Edition SBN 435 53123 9, Paperback SBN 435 53124 7
Part One only SBN 435 53121 2
Second edition © B. C. Brookes and W. F. L. Dick 1969

First published 1951
Reprinted with corrections 1953
Reprinted 1955, 1958, 1960, 1961, 1963,
1965, 1966, 1967
Second Edition 1969
Reprinted 1969

Published by Heinemann Educational Books Ltd
48 Charles Street, London W1X 8AH
Printed in Great Britain by Butler and Tanner Ltd
Frome and London

Preface to Second Edition

IN this new edition of our book we have introduced some additional material which we hope will make the book more useful to many readers. In Chapter VII there are now sections describing the use of confidence limits for both the mean and standard deviation. The use of confidence limits as a means of expressing the reliability of these statistical parameters occurs frequently in many fields of science. Again, in Chapter VII the use of Fisher's approximation to the z-test has been replaced by the more convenient variance ratio or F-test. Tables of F at the 5% and 1% significance levels have been added in Appendix II.

A new chapter has been added at the end dealing with some aspects of statistical theory which involve rather more mathematical expertise than is required for the main body of the book. We hope that this short survey of a number of statistical techniques will point the way to further applications which are beyond the scope of this book.

Finally, a set of miscellaneous exercises has been added which covers the whole field of applications described in the book. These exercises are not arranged in any particular order. As far as possible, they are constructed so that arithmetical manipulation is not excessive and the reader's attention can be focussed on the statistical content of the problem.

We have also incorporated a number of corrections and amendments. Here we should like to take this opportunity of thanking the many readers who have written to us since the book was first published. Their comments, suggestions and corrections have been of great value to us in preparing this new edition.

B. C. B.
W. F. L. D.

January 1969

Preface to First Edition

WE hope that this book will provide an introduction to statistical methods for those who may find them useful in the specialist study of branches of science such as physics, chemistry, biology, psychology and economics. A knowledge of the elementary principles and techniques of statistics is becoming a necessary part of a well-balanced education. As the basic ideas are not inherently difficult, and as they are certainly not beyond the grasp of any secondary school sixth form pupil, it is hoped that this useful branch of applied mathematics will find an increasingly important place in the school curriculum.

Teachers of mathematics who would like to introduce statistics into the school curriculum are faced with several difficulties. The first is the lack of suitable text-books; the authors hope that this book will help to remedy this defect. The second difficulty has been the lack of ready-made exercises and worked-out examples. Here it is necessary to emphasise that the exercises provided in this book are intended only to illustrate techniques; they must be supplemented by exercises on data collected by the student. It is important that the student should learn how to tabulate and analyse data that he has himself collected. No text-book can provide both the figures and the background information which will make the exercises of "live" statistical interest. A text-book example is necessarily "dead" however elaborately it may be dressed.

A disadvantage of statistics is that the exercises normally involve much arithmetical computation. This is unavoidable; until schools can afford to add a computing machine to the equipment of the mathematical laboratory, the difficulty will have to be faced. Some may suggest that the arithmetic of the exercises could be reduced, for example, by increasing the class-intervals and reducing the frequencies of a distribution; but it has to be remembered that, as many of the basic statistical ideas are applicable only to large samples, it would be misleading and possibly erroneous to simplify the exercises too much. In some of the exercises derived from actual published results little will be lost by "rounding off" or otherwise adjusting the published data to reduce the labour of computation. Another way of surmounting the difficulty is to allow students to work in small groups so that they share the work. It should be noted that the data of many of the exercises are used for more than one exercise; if the calculations are carefully filed, the student can save himself unnecessary repetition of work already done.

The scope of the book has not been determined by any examination syllabus. It provides more than is necessary at present to cover the optional statistics syllabuses of the General Certificate examining bodies, and it covers the methodological part of the Certificate Examination of the Royal Statistical Society. It has not been written for students specialising in mathematics; the reader who is capable of attaining the Ordinary Standard in Mathematics in the General Certificate should have no mathematical difficulties. The "Mathematical Notes" and "Mathematical Exercises" can be omitted by those who find them too difficult.

ACKNOWLEDGMENTS

We have to thank Professor G. A. Barnard of Imperial College for his kind and helpful criticisms of the manuscript. Though we have tried to incorporate his many suggestions, we realise that we have not always succeeded.

Messrs. D. J. Bartholomew. W. A. Twyman, S. Webb and J. G. Woodruff of the Science Upper Bench at Bedford Modern School have given great assistance in the tedious task of checking answers to the exercises.

Our thanks are due to Imperial Chemical Industries, Ltd., Messrs. Oliver and Boyd, and the Editors of *Biometrika*, for the material appearing in Tables XXVI, XXX, and XXXIX, which was taken from *Statistical Methods in Research and Production* (Oliver and Boyd).

Finally we have to thank Mr. Alan Hill of Messrs. Heinemann, and the staff of the Windmill Press, for their unfailing help with the technical details of publication.

November 1950.

B. C. B.
W. F. L. D.

PUBLISHER'S NOTE

This book is available in three editions: (*a*) Part One only, (*b*) Complete edition (cased) and (*c*) Complete edition (paperback).

Contents

PART ONE

ix

PART TWO

Introduction to
STATISTICAL METHOD

Part One

Part One

Introduction

The Origin of Statistics

The systematic collection of official statistics originated in Germany towards the end of the eighteenth century. In its earliest form it was an attempt to assess, for political purposes, the relative strengths of the German states by comparing such things as population, industrial and agricultural output. In England, Statistics is a legacy of the Napoleonic wars. In order to raise the new taxes that the cost of the war demanded, it was found necessary to begin that systematic collection of numerical data which would enable government departments to base their expectations of revenues and expenditures with more precision than had hitherto been required. The age of form-filling had begun, and with it began the development of that branch of applied mathematics which provides us with systematic methods of analysing large numbers of related numerical facts.

As its name implies, the word "statistics" was originally applied only to such data as the State required for its official purposes. The word has since acquired a wider meaning, so that it now embraces any set of quantitative data relating to a particular measurement, whether that data is of interest to the State or not. The same word is also used, not only for the material which is analysed, but also for the methods applied in its analysis. A third meaning is given to the word in the singular, i.e., to the noun, "statistic". A "statistic" is a measure of some property of a set of numerical data, e.g., a cricketer's average is a statistic of his scores. The particular meaning attached to the word is usually made clear by its context.

The theoretical development of the subject is founded on the work of many famous mathematicians of whom it is possible to mention only a few. Pascal (1623–1662) investigated the properties of the coefficients of binomial expansions and invented a mechanical computing machine. James Bernouilli (1654–1705) was the author of possibly the first treatise on the theory of probability, a subject to which later members of the Bernouilli family made further important contributions. De Moivre (1667–1754) who is best known for his theorem in trigonometry wrote on probability and on annuities. Laplace (1749–1827) also developed the theory of probability, but perhaps the greatest and most original of these earlier writers on statistical subjects was Gauss (1777–1855). The method of least squares and the properties of the "Normal" curve are two of the subjects he studied. In more recent times statistics has continued to

1

develop largely through the work of British statisticians among whom
Francis Galton, Karl Pearson, R. A. Fisher and G. U. Yule are
perhaps the best known. To the mathematical graduate the theory
and application of statistics offer interesting and fruitful fields of
research.

The Application of Statistics

Most readers of this book will already have had some experience
of the elementary treatment of numerical data in school work. If
you have ever calculated the average of several results in your
laboratory experiments, or if you have used columnar representation
of rainfall to show the difference between two types of climate in
your geography classes, or have shown by graph or diagram some
aspect of the growth of industrial activity in your history course,
then you have already been introduced to the science of Statistics.
Outside the class-room you have probably been a keen observer of
the statistics displayed in the results tables of the county cricket
championships, of the associated football league tables, or of some
other form of organised sport. At home you must have enjoyed
games of cards or dice and have had to make some simple application
of the theory of probability. Statistics is by no means remote from
everyday affairs.

On leaving the seclusion of your school or university you will
become, in the eyes of the official statisticians, a new self-maintaining,
and therefore taxable, unit in the community. You will then find,
whatever your attitude to the subject may be, that Statistics
insistently intrudes into your daily life. Your net income and your
standard of life are seriously affected by the expenditure, contributed
by you in rates and taxes, which is needed for defence, health services,
education, roads, and the many other services for which Parliament
and local governments are now responsible. All this expenditure, and
your share of the cost, is based on the interpretation of the statistics
made available to the departments concerned. Some understanding
of "figures" by the general public is therefore essential, and is even
more necessary in those who are responsible for our welfare.

In the nineteenth century economic theory gave strong support to
the policy of *laissez-faire*, claiming that the supply of goods and
services would automatically follow demands as they arose, and that
economic and social progress was best achieved by allowing un-
restricted competition in all fields of industry and commerce. To-day
we live in a period of transition; economic activities are being more
and more closely directed to the production of such goods, and the
provision of such services, as the government may decide to be most
urgently required. The political arguments involved are irrelevant
to the purpose of this book, but the facts to be realised are that our

future is very largely being *planned*, and that this planning, to be successful, must be soundly based on the correct analysis of complex statistical data. A cursory inspection of a copy of the *Annual Abstract of Statistics* published by H.M. Stationery Office will give the reader a clear impression of the interest that is taken in all forms of production by Government departments.

Besides these more obvious intrusions of statistics into the economic, social and political affairs which concern everyone, there are many narrower fields of human activity in which statistical methods are now applied. For example, in production engineering there are manufactured many small but composite pieces of mechanism that depend for their correct functioning on some dimensions of the components being maintained within very narrow limits of accuracy. The mass production of such components used to continue almost automatically until, because of wear in the machine, some batch of components failed to reach the required degree of accuracy in a critical dimension and were therefore useless and relegated to the scrap-heap. By the time this had been discovered, and the defect remedied, many more of the faulty components had been produced. Mass production of this kind, in which precision is required, is therefore now usually subjected to what is termed "Quality Control", which is a kind of sampling, a very important aspect of Statistics. The introduction of Quality Control into engineering was somewhat delayed by the suspicious and the hostile attitude that the practical man frequently displays when he is confronted with "impractical figure-mongers". The application of Quality Control received a great impetus, however, during the War, when its adoption in one factory after another was accompanied by fewer breakdowns of the assembly line and demonstrable decreases of material waste in the form of unusable manufactured components; and all this was achieved at little extra cost.

Most large industrial and commercial enterprises now employ research workers trained in the application of statistical method. Such statisticians may be engaged in Market Research for example. This work requires the analysis of data obtained from either the firms and sales organisations or by direct enquiry of the public, in order to find the best way of presenting the firms' products to the public. The work of the Listener Research organisation of the British Broadcasting Corporation is of this kind.

Statisticians may also be required to trace a batch of products through the manufacturing processes in order to determine the source and cause of variations from the standard of quality required, e.g., in the manufacture of steel, textiles, optical glass, etc. Such problems as arise in the arrangement of typewriter and similar keyboards, the design of the automatic telephone exchange systems, the compilation of railway time-tables for sections of the line carrying a high traffic density, all fall within the scope of the statistician. Recently one of our most eminent statisticians has applied his science to the analysis of literary vocabulary and has developed methods which help in identifying the origin of literary works of disputed authorship.*

Like other sciences, too, it can be put to less constructive uses. It is rumoured that, before delivering a speech, a certain American politician made a statistical survey of public opinion and used the information so obtained to make his speech agreeable to the greatest possible proportion of his audience. In war, it is used to assist the tactician to combine maximum destruction with minimum effort; it is also the basis of "Logistics", which is the planning of the movement and supply of military forces.

For the research worker in any field that is concerned with quantitative results a knowledge of statistical methods is useful. It is specially valuable when his work is concerned with material that *lives* and which is therefore not subject to the rigid control which the physicist and chemist can usually apply in their experimental work, e.g., in psychology, public health, education, biology, agriculture. However, apart from the particular needs of the specialist, enough has been said to show that any person who claims to be educated, any good citizen, should have some understanding of elementary statistical methods. Ignorance of the higher branches of mathematics is sometimes made an excuse for ignorance of statistics, but for an appreciation of the value and the limitations of the subject no more is required than accuracy in arithmetic and some common-sense.

The Limitations of Statistics

The remark can still sometimes be heard that "Statistics (or figures) can prove anything!", but it will always be found that people who say this know nothing of the subject, and that the statement is usually the opening defensive move in anticipation of an attack on a favourite prejudice. Statisticians, you will find, only very rarely claim to prove anything, and, even if they do, it is usually something unrelated to statistics. In his training the statistician is taught to examine the reliability of his data and the justification of his conclusion with the utmost suspicion, and the beginner will usually be surprised to find with what reserve the statisticians view results which are said to be "obvious to the meanest intelligence". If in an enthusiastic moment, a statistician does go so far as to say that a positive conclusion may be drawn from a set of results, then you will find that while few things are certain, the statistician has usually taken care that the odds that his statement is correct are at least

* YULE, G. U. *A Statistical Study of Literary Vocabulary.* (Cambridge, 1944.)

20 to 1, and furthermore, that his conclusion will be supported by other statisticians who have examined the data.

Again, no one is more aware of the limitations of applied Statistics than the statistician. He regards the subject as a gardener regards a sieve, or the mechanic regards a box-spanner; that is, as an *implement* which has a useful, particular and limited function. The sieve by itself will not produce orchids, but it will help the gardener to prepare a suitable compost; the box-spanner by itself will not construct an aircraft engine, but its use will speed up the assembly of the components. Similarly with Statistics: it will assist in the orderly arrangement of the data to which it is applied, and give added precision to any conclusion that may be inferred. Moreover, if you give a sieve and some earth to any man and ask him for orchids you will be lucky to get them unless he is also a gardener; if you hope to enjoy your flying it would be as well to ensure that your engines were assembled, not only by a man provided with a box of tools, but by a trained mechanic. Similarly, if you are asked as a statistician to compare, let us say, the value of Fertiliser A with that of Fertiliser B when applied to turnips, you must first learn all you can about fertilisers in general, about the application of fertilisers, about the growing of turnips, and many other associated subjects. In fact, you must be an agricultural expert, at least as far as fertilisers and turnips are concerned. In general, therefore, you will find that the practical statistician is in the first place a physicist, an engineer, a biologist, an economist, or some other specialist, and that he has a sound background of knowledge of the field in which he is carrying out his investigations.

CHAPTER I
The Representation of Numerical Data

1.1 Introduction

Whatever may be the nature of the material to be analysed, it is usually found to be in a disorderly form in its primary state. The first need is therefore to reduce the data to some kind of order. When this has been done the exact relation between the quantities considered may be immediately obvious, but this happens only rarely. It is therefore usually profitable to illustrate the relation between the quantities being examined by some kind of diagram, since a pictorial representation usually makes a clearer impression on the mind than columns of figures, and more readily suggests what should be the next step in the analysis. In this chapter some methods of arranging data and of presenting them diagrammatically will be described.

1.2 Tabulation and the Drawing of Diagrams

The practical work required of readers of this book necessitates considerable practice in the tabulation of statistical data. It must be emphasised from the start that neat and careful setting out of the primary data is essential for efficient statistical calculation. Neatness and care not only reward the individual doing the work by making the necessary constant checking of results easier to do, but beginners should also realise that the work they carry out, particularly any original experimental work, may be of interest to others, however trivial it may appear to them. All work done on a given problem or experiment must therefore be set out neatly and compactly so that the whole of the working can be rapidly examined by anyone interested in it. Neatness and orderliness are therefore the first requirements.

All tables should be given titles, and the origin of the data should be mentioned. Each column should be given a heading, and if a symbol is used for it, its significance should be explained. Consideration should be given to the layout of the columns before commencing the table, to ensure that no cramping of the figures will be required. Totals and other important results should be underlined and set out so as to be obvious to any one looking for them.

All diagrams and graphs should be given titles. The significance of the abscissæ and the ordinates should be explained and the scales should be chosen so as to demonstrate the important features of the graph as clearly as possible, remembering that the scales used need not start at zero.

Any relaxation of these rules will be regretted since it will inevitably lead to waste of time and futile effort. In most of the examples provided the data will already be reduced to order, but it is strongly recommended that the reader should carry out the practical work suggested and thereby practise the arrangement of data himself.

1.3 Variables

It is first necessary to explain some of the common statistical terms.

A **variable** is a feature characteristic of any member of a group, yet differing in quantity or quality from member to member. For example, a cricket team consists of a group of chosen players. A feature which they have in common is their individual batting average, which will usually differ from one player to another. The batting average is a variable differing in quantity. Another feature which they have in common is a pair of eyes, the colour of which may differ from one player to another. This differing quality of eye-colour is also a variable.

A variable can be either *continuous* or *discrete*. In elementary mathematics and physics the variables met with are usually continuous. Boyle's Law, which states that the relation between the pressure (P) and the volume (V) of an enclosed mass of gas at a given temperature is determined by the relation $PV = K$, a constant, provides an example. If the pressure be changed from one value, P_1, to another, P_2, the volume will change in accordance with the law, and the differences in pressure and volume can be made as small as we like, or, at least, as we can measure. For a given range of pressure the corresponding volumes are said to constitute a continuous variable. In biology, we more frequently meet discrete variables. For example, the number of peas in a pod can only take certain small integral values such as 3, 4, 5, 6, etc. The number of peas in a pod is limited to certain possible values and is therefore a discrete or discontinuous variable.

In practical measurements, even if the variables being measured are by nature continuous, we do in fact treat them as though they were discrete, since all measurements are read "correct to the nearest" unit or sub-unit. For example, the height of a boy at various ages is a continuous variable. As the boy grows from 4 ft. to 5 ft. his height passes through all possible values between these limits. It is usually sufficient, however, to measure his height correct to the nearest half-inch, and we thereby limit the variable to a number of values, namely twenty-five. This variable is therefore treated as though it were discrete. The material with which we shall deal in this book is mostly of this type.

1.4 Frequency Distributions with Discrete Variables

The preliminary treatment of numerical data depends to some extent on whether the variable is continuous or discrete. Since discrete variables are the easier to deal with, a simple example will be considered first.

Experiment I. 1.—A set of 10 cards numbered 1 to 10 (e.g., a suit from a pack of playing cards) is shuffled, and three cards are drawn at random.* Examine the value of this sum for a large number of drawings, and comment.

In this experiment the variable, which we will denote by x, is the sum of three integers, the maximum value of which will be $10 + 9 + 8 = 27$, and the minimum value $1 + 2 + 3 = 6$. The value of x can therefore only be any whole number between these extremes. It is therefore possible to classify the values of x as they arise. This can best be done by using graph paper, marking off along the "x-axis" the values $6, 7, 8, \ldots 26, 27$, at equal intervals, and noting the occurrence of a given value of x by making a cross or dot on the corresponding ordinate. The number of occurrences, or *frequency*, of any value of x can then be quickly summed.

Typical results of such an experiment in which 600 card drawings were made are given in Table I. In this table

x = observed sum of three cards.

n = number, or frequency of cards with this sum, x, obtained in the experiment.

ν = the expected or theoretical number or frequency which would be obtained in 600 trials.

A table of this kind is called a *frequency distribution*.

Examination of Table I shows the salient features of the distribution. The most frequent values of x are 14, 15, 16 and 17. A much clearer impression is, however, given by Fig. 1 which is the type of diagram obtained when the data are recorded as suggested above. This is an example of a frequency diagram. The diagram shows more clearly than the Table the symmetry of the distribution.

Mathematical Note. The values of ν can be calculated by considering the number of ways in which each value of x can be partitioned into three different integers. Thus,

$$6 = 1 + 2 + 3$$
$$7 = 1 + 2 + 4$$
$$8 = 1 + 2 + 5 = 1 + 3 + 4$$
$$9 = 1 + 2 + 6 = 1 + 3 + 5 = 2 + 3 + 4$$
etc,

The relative values of ν for 6, 7, 8 and 9 are therefore 1, 1, 2, and 3 respectively.

* The significance of the term "at random" will be considered more fully later, but a working knowledge of it is assumed for the present.

*Experiment I.*2. Shuffle together 3 sets of 10 cards numbered 1 to 10. Draw 3 cards and note their sum. (It will range from 3 to 30.) Repeat at least 500 times.

TABLE I

DISTRIBUTION OF RESULTS IN CARD-DRAWING EXPERIMENT

Observed Sum x	Exptl. Freq. n	Theor. Freq. ν	Observed Sum x	Exptl. Freq. n	Theor. Freq. ν
6	2	5	17	51	50
7	6	5	18	43	50
8	10	10	19	44	45
9	22	15	20	40	40
10	12	20	21	30	35
11	19	25	22	24	25
12	45	35	23	16	20
13	36	40	24	17	15
14	50	45	25	11	10
15	54	50	26	5	5
16	53	50	27	10	5
			Totals	600	600

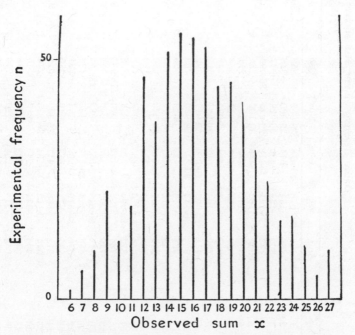

FIG. 1. Diagram of the results of the card-drawing experiment.

TABLE II

DAILY READING OF THE BAROMETRIC HEIGHT (INS.) AT WORTHING

Date	Aug.	Sept.	Oct.	Nov.	Dec.	Jan.	Feb.	Mar.	Apr.	May	June	July
1	30·196	30·078	30·656	30·059	29·859	30·247	29·652	29·756	30·234	29·931	30·419	30·376
2	·268	·164	·674	29·960	·846	·413	·443	·788	·252	·859	29·424	·087
3	·300	·128	·630	30·029	·967	·583	·483	·704	·193	·964	·810	·027
4	·173	·121	·410	29·995	30·093	·404	·652	·682	·039	30·210	30·057	29·794
5	29·946	·162	·456	30·100	·135	·182	·989	·776	·046	·162	29·805	·924
6	·895	·279	·485	·424	·274	·115	30·005	·877	·486	·028	·952	30·330
7	·928	·295	·486	·411	·344	·150	·150	·950	·440	29·998	30·114	·346
8	·867	·114	·484	·075	·542	29·954	29·860	·920	·225	30·149	29·846	·484
9	·882	·105	·023	29·971	·430	·726	30·091	·973	·265	·165	30·003	·458
10	·745	29·996	29·985	30·017	·382	·675	29·933	·989	·429	·083	29·575	·411
11	·904	30·233	30·245	29·973	·408	·826	30·357	·984	·339	·079	·952	·263
12	·938	·246	·432	·972	·525	·976	·317	·688	·062	·025	·986	·075
13	·969	29·912	·480	·972	·175	30·673	·459	·503	·082	29·786	30·217	29·869
14	·914	·871	·445	30·076	·320	·816	·671	·748	·186	·803	·175	·846
15	·839	·952	·391	·148	·103	·919	·761	30·035	·036	·932	29·974	·879
16	30·044	30·616	·385	·078	29·778	·735	·670	·340	·118	·932	·949	·884
17	29·877	29·996	·246	·060	·258	·480	·535	·348	·040	·954	·970	·674
18	·784	·789	·132	·076	28·983	29·996	·350	·359	·043	·954	·894	·745
19	·779	·792	·136	·052	·783	30·068	·146	·338	·471	·909	·899	·870
20	·777	30·640	·033	·082	29·558	·336	29·944	·166	·442	·892	30·108	·974
21	·586	·124	29·817	·158	·474	·358	30·125	·147	·389	·921	·330	·960
22	·570	29·879	·859	·194	·384	·318	·186	29·649	·502	30·112	·436	·986
23	·897	·873	·689	·042	·280	·055	29·475	30·105	·272	·151	·285	30·207
24	·912	·866	·411	29·999	·021	·441	·941	·215	29·924	29·941	·045	29·896
25	30·014	30·152	·531	30·235	·218	·265	·943	·308	·609	·753	·047	30·166
26	·206	·334	·246	·215	·646	·027	·745	·353	·603	·627	29·850	29·933
27	·084	·259	·663	·354	·856	·099	·868	·404	·558	·642	30·125	30·010
28	29·954	·218	·285	·229	·710	·085	·791	·297	·466	·694	·127	·018
29	·891	·443	·500	29·997	·760	29·849	—	·202	·522	·777	·228	·010
30	·901	·586	·962	30·026	30·104	·542	—	·345	·797	·797	·289	·042
31	30·088	—	30·076	—	·257	30·069	—	·271	—	·699	—	·065

In Experiment I. 1 described above, the results are separated into classes, each class containing the number of occurrences of some number between 6 and 27. The number of classes is therefore equal to the number of possible values of the variable, and the *class interval*, i.e., the difference of the value of x corresponding to adjacent intervals, is unity. In many cases it is not necessary to record the frequency of each individual value of the variable. It may be profitable to increase the size of the class interval and to record only the corresponding "grouped" frequencies. For example, in Table II (p. 10) there are 365 readings of the daily barometric height at Worthing. These readings are correct to five significant figures over a range of approximately $28\cdot500''$ to $31\cdot000''$, so there are about 2500 possible values of the reading and very few repeated values. If we are interested in the annual general distribution of barometric pressures rather than in the day-to-day variation it is hardly necessary to consider the readings in such detail. It saves time and labour if the readings are first collected into broader classes. The data of Table II could be grouped into classes with equal intervals of $0\cdot01''$. The number of classes would then be reduced from about 2500 to about 250. Suitable limits for these classes would be $28\cdot755''-28\cdot765''$, $28\cdot765''-28\cdot775''$, and so on. Though a reading such as $28\cdot756''$ is clearly a member of the class $28\cdot755''-28\cdot765''$, what is to be done about a reading such as $28\cdot855''$, which falls exactly on the dividing line between two adjacent classes? The convention is to allot $\frac{1}{2}$ to each of the frequencies of the two adjacent classes.

Though the number of classes has now been reduced from 2500 to 250, we still have a number which is inconveniently large for any analysis involving calculations. With negligible loss of accuracy we can reduce the 250 classes to 25 by increasing the class interval from $0\cdot01''$ to $0\cdot1''$. The corresponding classes would now be $28\cdot75''-28\cdot85''$, $28\cdot85''-28\cdot95''$, etc. A further reduction to class intervals of $1''$ gives at most four classes, and the grouping is then too coarse to show clearly anything but the most obvious features of the distribution. The three groupings are illustrated in Fig. 2 by a method which will be described in the next section. It can be seen, however, that of the three diagrams the first is too detailed and the third is too coarse. The second diagram, based on 22 classes, shows the main features of the distribution in reasonable detail.

For normal purposes a maximum of about 25 classes shows the main characteristics of a frequency distribution as clearly as any greater number could do. In the analysis of examination results, in which the possible mark usually varies from 0 to 100, class intervals of 5 marks are usually taken. Apart from the considerations already mentioned it is unreasonable, knowing the difficulties of assessing scripts, to take a difference of less than 5, or even 10, marks as

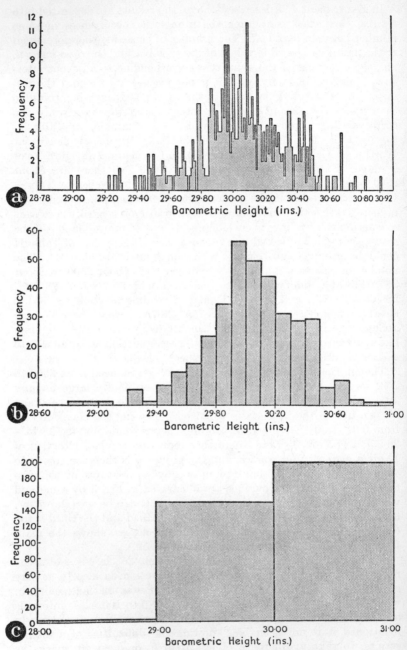

FIG. 2.   The effect of grouping the data of Table II.

indicating any appreciable difference of attainment even in so precise a subject as Arithmetic. Knowledge of the precision with which the data under examination has been attained helps the statistician to determine a sensible class interval.

1.5 Histograms

The figures below are the marks obtained in a school arithmetic examination by 130 boys taking the same paper, the marks being given in the alphabetical order of the boys' names, and the highest possible mark being 80. Taking a class interval of 5 marks let us construct a frequency diagram.

The marks are:

22	76	46	54	56	41	55	42	27	9	22	46	31
43	17	44	51	13	15	52	63	48	18	3	65	67
46	1	68	48	21	27	38	15	13	33	10	56	63
34	29	41	26	16	25	60	33	36	10	53	24	63
50	51	22	26	54	19	14	78	36	43	47	61	18
65	43	25	41	70	37	21	72	33	49	71	42	54
68	35	42	25	68	47	18	28	56	57	25	58	68
17	38	10	57	33	31	67	24	74	3	12	16	48
15	71	26	50	54	29	27	27	28	55	59	50	58
74	54	35	67	59	61	59	26	56	43	58	3	62

The class intervals adopted will be 1–5, 6–10, 11–15, 16–20, etc. The frequency distribution is obtained by counting and tabulating the number in each class, e.g., the class 1–5 contains the marks 1, 3, 3, 3, giving a frequency of 4; the class 6–10 contains the marks 10, 9, 10, 10, again giving a frequency of 4. The complete distribution may then be set out as in Table III. The total of the frequency

TABLE III

FREQUENCY DISTRIBUTION OF MARKS IN AN ARITHMETIC EXAMINATION

Class	Frequency	Class	Frequency
1–5	4	41–45	11
6–10	4	46–50	12
11–15	7	51–55	11
16–20	8	56–60	13
21–25	11	61–65	8
26–30	12	66–70	8
31–35	9	71–75	5
36–40	5	76–80	2
		Total	130

column is found. This must be equal to the number of observations. To illustrate this distribution diagrammatically it is usual to draw the column type of frequency diagram we used for the barometric data, called a *histogram*. The area of each column is proportional to the frequency of the corresponding class. In the present example the class intervals are all equal and therefore the columns all have the same width. It follows in this special case that the *heights* as well as the *areas* of the columns are proportional to the corresponding frequencies.

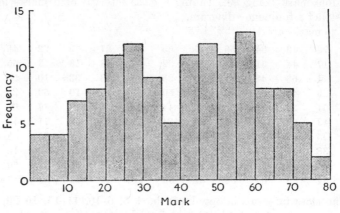

FIG. 3.   Histogram of marks.

This histogram (Fig. 3) shows clearly an unusual feature. Examination marks in large groups usually show a steady increase to a maximum followed by a steady decrease, i.e., they give "one-humped" histograms (Fig. 4). The low frequencies in the 30–35, 36–40 classes divide the histogram of Fig. 3 into two humps. Why has this occurred? It is not possible to give an answer without knowledge of the examination paper set, the method of marking, the students who took the paper, etc. Actually the marks were obtained from four parallel forms and the results confirmed, what had already been ascertained in other ways, that two of the forms were comparatively backward. It must be emphasised that we can draw no conclusion whatever from the data we have examined here. The example has been chosen partly to show that the diagrammatic representation of sets of numbers often makes more apparent the deviations from what is expected. Questions and research may then follow.

An example of this kind of problem arose during the war. It was noticed that when the final scores of trained air-gunners were diagrammatically represented a two-humped histogram was unexpectedly obtained instead of a one-humped histogram (Fig. 4). How did this arise? It was suggested that the two humps might occur if there were two distinct types of gunner, one type being naturally better marksmen than the other. If this were true, then it would be important to find some means of identifying each gunner (they might be found to have blue eyes, a scientific education, flat feet, etc.) and hence a method of selecting them. In such a case it is necessary to examine, first of all, the way in which the scores are obtained. Before we look for the super-marksman let us be sure he exists. Examination

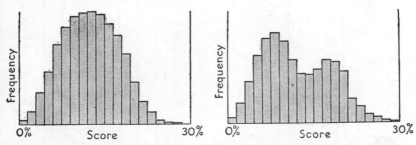

FIG. 4. One- and two-humped distributions.

showed that the two-humped curve was inherent in the scoring system adopted. The super-marksman did not exist.

1.6 Unequal Class Intervals

Sometimes we find that the data presented for analysis have already been classified though the classification may not be in the form best suited for further analysis. Class intervals which are *unequal* are sometimes used, particularly with distributions which have a long "tail", in order to express the main features of the distribution as concisely as possible. Table IV (a) shows a distribution in which the class intervals are unequal; it provides all the information required for many administrative purposes, e.g., the 2–4 year old children are "infants", the children of the next group are "primary school pupils", and so on. Table IV (b) is a distribution of incomes in which the class intervals increase as the frequencies rapidly diminish. The last class interval, moreover, is open; it has no upper limit. How can such data be represented by a histogram?

The important point to remember is that in the histogram the frequency of any class is proportional to the *area* of the corresponding column. If the class interval is increased then the width of the corresponding column is increased proportionally. The height of the column must therefore be *decreased* in the same proportion.

The distribution of the school pupils of Table IV (a) is represented by the histogram of Fig. 5 (a). It will be seen that the *area* of each column is proportional to the frequency of the corresponding range

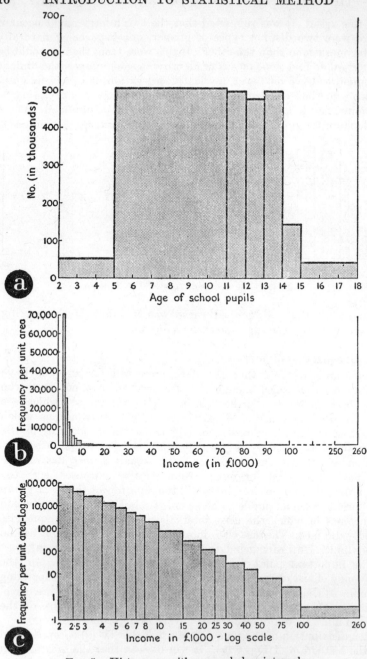

FIG. 5.   Histograms with unequal class-intervals.
(a) Histogram of data with unequal class-intervals.
(b) A very asymmetrical distribution (Data of Table IV (b)).
(c) Use of logarithmic scales (Data of Table IV (b)).

of the variable. The method of calculating the *heights* of the columns is shown in the table.

The distribution of Table IV (*b*) provides further problems of presentation. The problem of deciding the width to be allotted to the last class is less important than at first sight appears as its height is

TABLE IV (a)

NUMBER OF PUPILS ON THE REGISTERS OF MAINTAINED AND ASSISTED PRIMARY AND SECONDARY SCHOOLS IN ENGLAND AND WALES IN JANUARY, 1946. (*Annual Abstract, No.* 84.)

Age	Number (*thousands*)	Height of Column
2–4 +	164	55
5–10 +	3064	511
11 +	497	497
12 +	477	477
13 +	496	496
14 +	143	143
15–18 +	162	41

TABLE IV (b)

THE DISTRIBUTION OF INCOMES LIABLE TO SURTAX IN THE FINANCIAL YEAR ENDED 5TH APRIL, 1945. (*Annual Abstract, No.* 84.)

Income (in £1,000)		Frequency	Height of Column
Exceeding	*Not exceeding*		
2·0	2·5	35,148	70,296
2·5	3·0	23,809	47,618
3·0	4	25,519	25,519
4	5	12,920	12,920
5	6	7,646	7,646
6	7	4,940	4,940
7	8	3,339	3,339
8	10	4,117	2,058
10	15	4,289	858
15	20	1,559	312
20	25	657	131
25	30	351	70
30	40	301	30
40	50	155	15·5
50	75	141	5·6
75	100	60	2·4
100	—	50	0·3

almost negligible. From the data it can be surmised that the height of the last column is probably less than that of the preceding one, but that is all. Sometimes further information may help to decide the appropriate class interval. For the year considered it is known that the surtax payers whose incomes were over £100,000 had a total income of £9,000,000. The average income was therefore about £180,000. It is not unreasonable to regard the last few incomes as spread evenly over the range £100,000 to £260,000 to give the required average of £180,000. Having decided on the width of this class interval, the height of the column can be calculated since we know that the area of the column is to be 50 units on the area scale. If, in other cases, the further information such as we have used in this example is not available, then only a judicious guess is possible.

Having calculated the heights of the columns for the data of Table IV (b) it will be found that it is not possible to represent this distribution effectively by a histogram. It has a very high peak at one end and falls rapidly to a long flat tail. The outline of Fig. 5 (b) follows the axes so closely that little detail is observable. In cases of extreme asymmetry like this the numerical values of the variable and the frequency are sometimes replaced by their logarithms. The work of drawing diagrams to logarithmic scales is simplified by using specially ruled graph paper. Diagrams based on logarithmic scales should not, however, be used to represent data to those who may not appreciate the effect of the logarithmic transformation on the original distribution. They are used only to suggest further steps in the statistical analysis of the data. In this example it becomes apparent from the use of logarithmic scales in Fig. 5 (c) that the relation between log (Income) and log (Frequency) is almost linear.

Finally, it must be emphasised again that the fundamental property of the columns of a histogram is their *areas*, not their heights. If equal intervals are used throughout then the areas are proportional to the heights, but this is merely a special case.

1.7   Frequency Curves

In the previous section we considered the effect of increasing the span of the class intervals of a distribution using the Worthing barometric data as an illustration. Suppose that we start again with the 365 readings and construct a histogram with class intervals of 0·001″. We should obtain a histogram with about 300 columns separated by gaps of various widths and representing frequencies of 1, 2, 3 and perhaps 4. If we continued the readings day by day for a second year, adding to the histogram a unit of area to the column corresponding to each reading, some of the gaps would be occupied, some of the columns increased. If this process were continued year after year for many years all the gaps would eventually be filled. The columns in the centre of the histogram would gradually become inconveniently long, so it would be necessary to scale down the unit area from time to time. Eventually we should expect to arrive at a histogram rather like that of Fig. 6, in which the columns show a gradual change in height from one to the next.

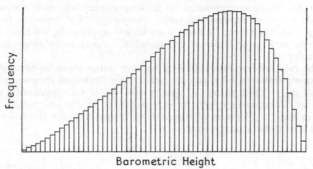

Barometric Height

Fig. 6.   Histogram with small class-intervals and a very large population.

Now suppose we improved our technique of measuring the barometric height so that we could easily measure it correct to 0·0001″ and, further, increased the number of readings from one per day to one per hour. A histogram of such a distribution would approximate to the same general shape as the first one, but, as the class intervals are decreased to one-tenth of their former value, we should find that the steps from one column to the next are proportionally smaller. Using the same scales, both histograms would have the same area for equal numbers of readings. If in the second histogram we now increased the number of readings tenfold, its area would also be increased tenfold. By reducing the frequency scale to one-tenth, the area scale is reduced in the same ratio. The area under the second histogram would again be equal to that under the first histogram, but the second histogram would have a smoother outline.

If this triple process of decreasing the class interval, increasing the number of readings, and reducing the area scale could be continued indefinitely, the steps of the histograms would become smaller and smaller and its outline would approach more and more closely to a smooth curve. The limiting curve to which the histogram approaches under these conditions is an abstraction of great importance in statistics. It is called a *frequency curve*.

Frequency distributions with finite class intervals are discontinuous functions of the variable and require rather cumbersome methods of calculation in their analysis. Frequency curves, however, are usually continuous functions of the variable and their properties can be investigated by the methods of the calculus. Later in this book some frequency distributions are regarded as finite samples of infinite populations which are distributed according to certain laws. The histograms of the samples are regarded as approximations to the known frequency curves of these infinite populations.

Mathematical Note. The frequency curve has an important property concerning its area which is analogous to the fundamental property of the histogram. Since it represents an infinite population with a continuous variable we must replace the term "frequency" by "relative frequency density", and the term "class" is no longer applicable; we have to state the upper and lower limits of the variable for any interval we may need to consider.

If the relative frequency density for any value x can be expressed as a continuous function of x, say $f(x)$, then the "relative frequency" in the interval $x_1 - \frac{1}{2}\delta x$ to $x_1 + \frac{1}{2}\delta x$ where δx is infinitesimally small is $f(x_1) . \delta x$. This product $f(x) . \delta x$ is represented by the shaded area of the curve in Fig. 7. The sum of the relative frequencies for the whole distribution is obviously unity, so that

$$\int_a^b f(x)dx = 1$$

where a and b are respectively the least and greatest values of the variable. The relative frequency in any interval is therefore equal to the area under the curve lying between the ordinates which bound the interval. This area property of the frequency curve is of fundamental importance in the theory of sampling.

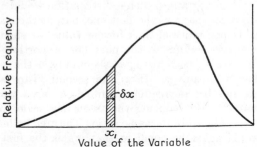

FIG. 7.   Area property of the frequency curve.

EXERCISES I

(Number, file and keep any exercises done; reference may be made to them in later exercises.)

1. The table shows the results of counting the number of stigmata on capsules of the Shirley Poppy [Enfield II (1902). *Biometrika*, **2**, 8b.] Illustrate the distribution.

Number	7	8	9	10	11	12	13	14	15	16	17	18
Frequency	1	7	27	88	182	254	278	222	124	41	15	5

2. A count of the number of tentacles in *Hydra vulgaris Pallas* gave the following distribution for a sample of 869 individuals [Liu and Chang (1946). *Nature*, **157**, 728.] Draw a diagram to illustrate the data.

Number	3	4	5	6	7	8	9
Frequency	1	2	61	646	132	24	3

3. In an experiment Buffon and De Morgan tossed a coin repeatedly and counted the length and number of "runs", i.e., sequences of heads or tails. The experimental results are given in the table. [Quoted by Pearse (1928). *Biometrika*, **20A**, 325.] Draw the histogram as far as your scale permits the tail to be shown.

Length of run	1	2	3	4	5	6	7	8	9	10	11–15
Frequency	4,165	2,028	982	480	266	132	71	36	17	9	6

4. In an analysis of sentence length as a criterion of literary style the number of words in each of 600 sentences of G. K. Chesterton's *Shorter History of England* were counted. The results are summarised in the table. [Condensed from data of Williams (1939), *Biometrika*, **31**, 357.] Draw a histogram.

No. of words	1–5	6–10	11–15	16–20	21–25	26–30
Frequency	3	27	71	113	107	109
No. of words	31–35	36–40	41–45	46–50	51–60	61–100
Frequency	68	41	28	18	12	3

The following examples are intended to give practice in the collection and arrangement as well as in the representation of the data. It is recommended that they be done by co-operative effort, e.g., students can often work in pairs, one as observer and the other as recorder. These examples are suggestions only; they should be adapted to the particular interests of the students. Any original data that is collected should be carefully filed for further analysis later in the course.

5. Count the frequencies of occurrence of the digits 1, 2, 3 . . . 9, 0, in four-figure logarithm tables of the numbers 1·00 to 9·99. Illustrate your answer by means of a histogram and comment on the results.

6. Choose an author in whom you are interested and find the distribution of sentence length of a sample of his work. The sample should contain several hundred sentences. Compare your histogram with that representing

    (a) the data of Ex. 4,

    (b) a second sample from the same author.

Comment on your results.

7. Construct frequency distributions of any sets of examination marks that are of interest, selecting a scheme of grouping that is appropriate. Draw the histograms and comment on the results.

8. Obtain the frequency distributions of individual cricket scores obtained in the county cricket championship, ignoring unfinished innings. Compare your histogram with that illustrating the data of the table below, which gives the distribution for the year 1931. [Martin, *Biometrika*, 26, 47.]

Runs	0	1, 2	3, 4	5, 6	7, 8	9, 10	11–20
Frequency	701	627	470	374	335	303	895

Runs	21–30	31–40	41–50	51–60	61–70	71–80	81–90
Frequency	524	330	170	105	83	56	35

Runs	91–100	101–120	121–140	141–200	Above 200
Frequency	22	36	18	11	1

9. Find the frequencies of occurrence of the letters *e*, *b* and *q* in lines of printed text. Draw histograms to illustrate the differences in the distributions.

10. Visit your local reference library to obtain data from which you can draw histograms to illustrate the following distributions:

(a) Parliamentary divisions in the U.K. according to numbers of electors,

(b) Families in Great Britain according to the numbers of members,

(c) Population of Great Britain according to age.

MATHEMATICAL

11. The relative frequency density of a continuous distribution is given by $f(x) = \dfrac{6x\,(a-x)}{a^3}$ where x ranges from 0 to a. Show that the relative frequency in the interval $x = 0$ to $x = \frac{1}{4}a$ is $\dfrac{5}{32}$. Sketch the frequency curve.

12. In a continuous distribution the variable x ranges from $-b$ to $+b$ and the relative frequency density is known to be proportional to $\dfrac{1}{a^2 + x^2}$. Show that the equation of the frequency curve is $y = \dfrac{1}{k\,(a^2 + x^2)}$ where $k = \dfrac{2}{a}\tan^{-1}\dfrac{b}{a}$. Sketch the curve for the cases in which (i) $b = 2a$, (ii) $b = 4a$.

1.8 Frequency Polygons

A second method of representing frequency distributions is to join the middle points of the top of the columns of the histograms by straight lines to give a broken curve. The data represented by the histogram in Fig. 3 is represented by such a diagram—called a *frequency polygon*—in Fig. 8.

We have seen that the area under any column of the histogram is exactly proportional to the corresponding frequency; in the frequency polygon, however, the area under any part of the broken curve is

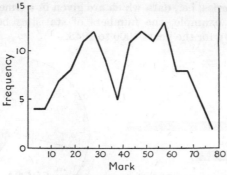

FIG. 8.   Frequency polygon of marks.

only approximately proportional to the corresponding frequency. Because of this loss of accuracy the frequency polygon is not recommended as a means of illustrating distributions. If it is used sometimes in preference to a histogram it is because it gives a spurious appearance of continuity suggesting a completeness of data that may be unwarranted. Its use should therefore be regarded with suspicion.

In general the histogram should always be used in preference to the frequency polygon. A possible exception to this rule occurs only when, for the sake of comparison, two rather similar distributions are to be represented on the same diagram. If the distributions overlap there may be less confusion if they are represented by frequency polygons.

1.9   Other Representations of Numerical Data

For statisticians the construction of a frequency diagram is usually only a first step in the analysis of the numerical data, but in many everyday activities the effective presentation of the data is the end of the matter. This presentation can usually be made more effective if the data can be represented in some simple diagrammatic form. Types of diagram other than those already described can frequently be seen in the daily papers and in advertisements. Most of these diagrammatic devices are well suited to their purpose, but some may be misleading to those who do not also appreciate the underlying figures. We shall therefore briefly describe and comment on the most popular types of diagram.

Apart from frequency distributions there are two other main types of statistical data which may be represented by simple diagrams:

(a) Categorical data, i.e., data which relates to categories or classes, such as a list, for example, giving the countries of origin and corresponding numbers of alien tourists visiting Britain.

(b) Time series, i.e., data which are given in a time sequence such as, for example, the numbers of statistics books published annually for the years 1900 to 1948.

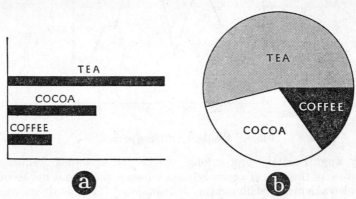

Fig. 9.   Charts of categorical data.
(a) Bar-chart.   (b) Pie-chart.

Categorical data are usually represented by *bar-charts* or *pie-charts*. The data of Table V, col. (a) are represented in these two ways in Fig. 9 (a) and Fig. 9 (b) respectively. The bars are of equal width and their lengths, shown in col. (b) of Table V, are proportional to the numbers they represent. Sometimes the bars are broken up into separated unit lengths; sometimes these unit lengths are replaced by simple pictograms. In Fig. 9 (b) the separate items are represented by slices of the pie. The angles of the slices are proportional to the corresponding figures; the method by which these angles are calculated should be apparent in column (c) of Table V. Pie-chart blanks are obtainable with the circle already divided into 100 parts so that percentages can be drawn in without further calculation.

TABLE V

WEEKLY AVERAGE CONSUMPTION OF TEA, COCOA AND COFFEE IN THE U.K. FOR JULY, 1948.   (*Monthly Digest of Statistics*, 32.)

	(a)	(b)	(c)
Tea	3,260 *tons*	1·63 *ins.*	$195° \left(= 3{,}260 \times \dfrac{360°}{6{,}010} \right)$
Cocoa	1,850 *tons*	0·92 *ins.*	111°
Coffee	900 *tons*	0·45 *ins.*	54°
Total	6,010 *tons*		360°

As the eye is perhaps better trained to assess ratios of lengths than of angles, the bar-chart and its modifications are probably preferable for general use, though the pie-chart shows more clearly the ratios of the parts to the whole. Both of these methods give true representa-

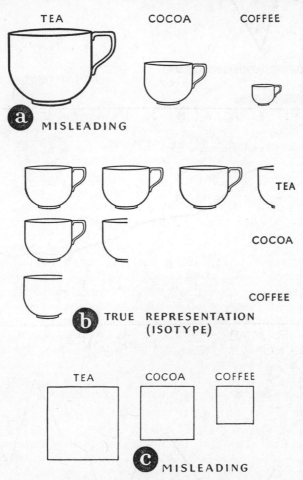

Fig. 10.   Further charts of categorical data.

tions of categorical statistics, and these are easily appreciated if the number of categories is not greater than about 10; if the number of categories in a list is greater than 10 some judicious grouping of the data is required.

There are, however, methods which may lead to ambiguous or misleading interpretations; they are frequently used deliberately to

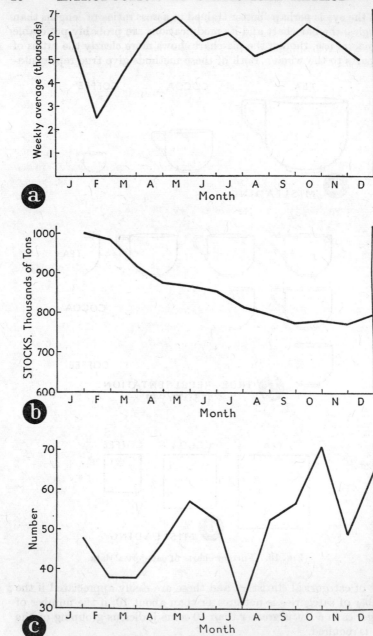

Fig. 11.   Charts with time-bases.

(a) Production of passenger cars—weekly average.
(b) Stocks of steel—end of month.
(c) Production of main-line locomotives—end of month.

exaggerate the differences they are intended to describe. For example the data of Table V are represented again in Fig. 10. In Fig. 10 (a) the relative consumption of tea has been exaggerated by suggesting a volumetric representation based on proportions which are true only in lengths. In Fig. 10 (b) the relative consumptions are fairly represented by the unit cups, but an unscrupulous advocate of cocoa-drinking might well bring psychology to his aid and distort the true picture by colouring the tea cups a bilious yellow, the coffee cups a dirty brown and the cocoa cups a warm and rosy red. In Fig. 10 (c) the relative consumption of coffee has been slightly exaggerated; the *areas* are proportional to the actual consumptions. Since this fact is not stated in the diagram this ambiguity may arise: Are the lengths or are the areas to be compared? In such a case most people form an impression to which comparisons of both length and area have contributed; and this compromise here flatters the smaller of any pair being compared

Time series are usually represented by graphs. Time is conventionally measured from left to right, i.e., along the x-axis in the positive direction; the second variable is measured along the y-axis, and corresponding values of the two variables are plotted. The points are then joined by *straight lines* to form broken curves.

There are, however, some differences of detail in the plotting of time series, depending on whether the second variable is primarily:

TABLE VI

SOME DATA RELATING TO STEEL FOR THE YEAR 1947.
(*Monthly Digest of Statistics*, 32.)

Month	(a) Production of Passenger Cars (weekly average) (*number*)	(b) Stocks of Steel (end of period) (*thousand tons*)	(c) Production of Main Line Locomotives (*number*)
Jan.	6,251	1,001	48
Feb.	2,480	983	38
Mar.	4,415	915	38
Apr.	6,058	871	47
May	6,874	866	58
June	5,854	855	53
July	6,226	815	31
Aug.	5,214	799	53
Sept.	5,689	782	57
Oct.	6,559	789	71
Nov.	5,894	775	49
Dec.	4,999	797	65

(a) an average, e.g., index number, the mean daily temperature;

(b) a level, e.g., stock of a commodity, the midday barometer reading;

or (c) a total, e.g., the week's output of coal, the day's rainfall.

Averages, for obvious reasons, are plotted to correspond with the centre of the period to which they refer; levels, to correspond with the time of the reading; totals, to correspond with the end of the appropriate period. The data of Table VI have been plotted in Fig. 11 to illustrate these differences.

In setting out charts it is not always necessary to measure the variables from zero. Very often the purpose of a chart may be to demonstrate small but important changes in large totals. The levels from which the variables are measured should be clearly marked and the space available for the chart should be used to display the significant features of the data as effectively as possible.

An alternative method of representing totals in time series is sometimes used, particularly for meteorological data. Fig. 12 shows the use of bar-charts to indicate the differences of the rainfall characteristics of two climatic regions. Though these charts are similar in appearance to histograms, and indeed have similar area properties, the word "histogram" will be used in this book to refer only to *frequency* distributions.

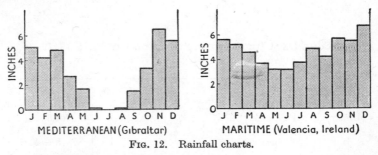

MEDITERRANEAN (Gibraltar)   MARITIME (Valencia, Ireland)

Fig. 12.   Rainfall charts.

Finally, whenever diagrams are used to present statistical data, the following rules should be observed:

(1) The diagrams should be simpler to understand and to appreciate than the tables of figures they represent.

(2) They should be free from ambiguities, i.e., magnitudes should be represented only by lengths or by angles.

(3) The diagrams should carry all information necessary to their appreciation, i.e., they should be given adequate legends and titles

Table VII

Daily Readings of Percentage Humidity (Worthing)

Date	Aug.	Sept.	Oct.	Nov.	Dec.	Jan.	Feb.	Mar.	Apr.	May	June	July
1	71	83	71	81	83	83	86	80	75	56	78	95
2	64	82	77	91	93	97	82	70	69	76	73	84
3	81	94	71	97	92	84	98	54	54	49	70	95
4	75	94	81	88	90	77	95	79	69	64	90	95
5	59	86	60	100	69	87	80	95	95	62	87	79
6	63	60	86	92	81	92	96	84	62	65	81	70
7	62	77	86	92	80	89	94	80	83	70	73	58
8	90	77	87	93	50	98	52	50	91	91	83	70
9	77	73	76	77	90	89	57	79	64	68	75	77
10	70	75	82	84	90	88	94	70	58	60	88	68
11	75	99	88	77	96	100	80	82	67	69	69	80
12	71	95	71	83	81	91	86	41	69	78	87	66
13	88	78	88	84	77	77	99	65	84	73	70	71
14	83	88	82	92	91	70	98	73	68	62	55	78
15	95	88	96	84	86	76	82	69	61	62	90	47
16	75	98	94	72	94	84	88	78	71	83	95	91
17	76	89	94	72	73	78	88	69	91	68	77	78
18	75	81	87	77	79	84	79	86	93	79	64	95
19	72	80	88	97	86	87	90	91	72	94	87	81
20	75	85	85	100	100	70	89	72	79	85	77	68
21	92	89	100	100	59	92	92	92	74	85	70	78
22	74	81	86	100	88	82	55	97	54	80	67	78
23	63	61	82	92	92	81	69	91	68	92	81	95
24	88	75	90	92	91	86	82	93	86	83	82	95
25	96	70	86	89	94	95	58	79	98	72	77	80
26	66	73	64	84	97	94	79	77	93	88	92	69
27	70	94	70	81	91	94	98	69	75	95	75	71
28	47	93	82	90	86	69	88	68	74	96	78	74
29	89	82	93	84	93	75	62	76	90	94	79	73
30	86	68	93	65	84	86	—	75	81	92	88	71
31	78	—	94	—	96	84	—	52	—	89	—	92

SUMMARY OF CHAPTER I

1. The main types of statistical data are:
  (a) Frequency distributions,
  (b) Categorical data,
  (c) Time series.

2. Frequency distributions are represented by histograms or frequency polygons; continuous distributions by frequency curves.

3. Categorical data are represented by charts, e.g., bar-charts and pie-charts.

4. Time series are usually represented by straight-line graphs; exceptions occur.

5. Diagrams representing numerical data should be simple, unambiguous, true, and adequately labelled.

EXERCISES II

1. Draw histograms of the data from which Table III is derived using different class intervals, e.g., 4, 8 and 10 marks. Comment on the change of appearance of the histogram as the class interval is increased.

2. What would be the effect on the frequency distribution of Table III and the histogram representing it if the maximum possible mark were raised from 80 to 100,
  (a) by adding 20 to each mark,
  (b) by multiplying each mark by 1·25,
  (c) by multiplying each mark by 1·1 and then adding 12?

3. Draw a histogram of the data of Table II. Comment on the result.

4. Frequency distributions are required of the sets of data of which the maximum and minimum values of the variable are given below. Suggest suitable class divisions and intervals, all intervals to be equal.

		Max.	Min.
(a)	Daily sunshine	13·6 hrs.	0 hrs.
(b)	Examination marks	937	259
(c)	Life of electric bulbs	3,675 hrs.	12·8 hrs.
(d)	Period of telephone calls	37·5 min.	0·12 min.
(e)	Weight of "1 lb." shop weights	1·0223 lb.	0·9871 lb.
(f)	Circulation of a daily paper	879,637	765,292

5. The figures given in Table VII are the daily readings of the percentage humidity for one year at Worthing. Tabulate the figures in the form of a frequency distribution and construct the corresponding histogram.

6. Construct a chart to show simultaneously the daily readings of the percentage humidity (Table VII) and the barometric height (Table II) for the month of August. Comment on the result.

7. How would you illustrate by diagram the following kinds of numerical data? Give brief reasons for your choice.

(a) Average yield per acre of wheat in Great Britain for each of the last 10 years.

(b) The harvest yields of the main cereal crops, wheat, oats, barley, rye, maize, rice in the U.S.A. for a given year.

(c) The number of deaths in road accidents in Great Britain for each month of the last two years.

(d) The frequency distribution of the sizes of boots issued to Army conscripts during a given period.

(e) The proportion of time spent in school on each of the subjects taught.

8. Construct diagrams to illustrate the following data. (*Annual Abstract, No.* 84.)

Compare the data of (*b*), (*c*), (*d*), (*h*) and (*j*) with the most up-to-date comparable data available to you: draw a second diagram in each case and comment on the changes that have occurred.

Extend the data of (*f*), (*g*) and (*k*) by reference to the latest statistical abstracts available to you.

(a) *Average number of frosty days at Cambridge.*

Month	Jan.	Feb.	Mar.	Apr.	May	June
No.	13·3	12·6	12·2	6·2	1·3	0·1

Month	July	Aug.	Sept.	Oct.	Nov.	Dec.
No.	—	—	0·3	3·8	8·3	12·3

(b) *Age distribution of the population of the U.K. in the year* 1946. (The numbers given are thousands.)

Age group	0–4	5–9	10–14	15–19	20–24	25–29
Male	1,954	1,701	1,659	1,743	1,828	1,813
Female	1,864	1,644	1,613	1,723	1,871	1,827

Age group	30–34	35–39	40–44	45–49	50–54	55–59
Male	1,916	1,945	1,844	1,574	1,353	1,237
Female	1,950	1,998	1,913	1,757	1,620	1,481

Age group	60–64	65–69	70–74	75 and over.
Male	1,070	892	651	616
Female	1,333	1,128	840	960

(Demographic data of this type are usually represented by a "pyramid", i.e.. a histogram in which age is measured along the ordinate and the corresponding frequencies of male and female are measured to the left and the right respectively.) Consider carefully what you propose to do about the last entry in the table in which the class interval is unknown.

(c) *Number of men killed underground in coal-mining, Great Britain, 1948, and causes.*

Explosions	24	Haulage	136
Falls of ground	277	Miscellaneous	45
Shaft accidents	11	*Total*	493

(d) *Analysis of population employed in manufacturing industries in England and Wales, 1931.* (Some further grouping may be desirable.)

	No. (Thousands)		No. (Thousands)
Bricks, pottery, glass	171	Textile goods	1,050
Chemicals, paints, oils	133	Food	337
Metals	1,575	Drinks	108
Textiles	1,174	Tobacco	31
Leather, etc.	87	Woodwork	242
Paper, etc.	285	Building, etc.	861
		Miscellaneous	129

(e) *Deaths in the United Kingdom analysed by age, for the years 1932 and 1946.* (Numbers in thousands.)

Age in years	1st year	2nd year	2–4	5–14	15–24	25–34
1932	50	11	10	13	21	25
1946	40	2	3	7	10	15

Age in years	35–44	45–54	55–64	65–74	75 and over.
1932	31	54	89	127	137
1946	24	46	87	148	186

Comment on the changes that these figures show.

(f) *Sales of electricity for public lighting in Great Britain.* (Million units.)

Year	1935	1936	1937	1938	1939	1940
No.	268	298	339	367	248	17
Year	1941	1942	1943	1944	1945	1946
No.	18	20	20	28	177	260

Comment on these figures.

(g) *Deaths from motor-vehicle accidents for England and Wales.*

Year	1935	1936	1937	1938	1939	1940
No. killed	5,240	5,354	5,463	5,474	6,638	6,018
Year		1941	1942	1943	1944	1945
No. killed		6,392	4,632	3,575	3,994	3,598

(h) *Distribution by age of single males and females in the United Kingdom in 1931.* (See note to Ex. (b).) The numbers are in thousands.

Age	0–14	15–19	20–24	25–34	35–44
Male	4,808	1,705	1,463	1,079	315
Female	4,712	1,694	1,332	1,105	573

Age	45–54	55–64	65–74	75 and over.
Male	250	181	88	22
Female	431	306	187	74

(j)   Analysis of schools by size in England and Wales, 1946.

No. of pupils	0–50	51–100	101–150	151–200	201–250
No. of schools	5,736	4,552	3,936	3,480	3,194
No. of pupils		251–300	301–400	401–500	Over 500
No. of schools		2,586	3,018	1,172	683

(k)   Stocks of natural rubber in thousands of tons (end of period).

Year	1935	1936	1937	1938	1939	1940
Stock	209	103	80	105	52	96
Year	1941	1942	1943	1944	1945	1946
Stock	99	62	60	47	52	181

PRACTICAL

(Each member of the class should be allotted a task of day-to-day recording. The data collected by this means should be summarised from time to time and filed for further analysis later in the course.)

9. Collect exceptionally good and bad examples of diagrammatic representation from the press, magazines, etc. Display them with appropriate comments.

10. In collaboration with the geography department collect, record and analyse the local day-to-day meteorological data.

11. In collaboration with the biology department measure and record data on
  (a)   rate of growth of plants,
  (b)   yield of plants.

12. Keep day-to-day records of the prices of Government securities and selected industrial shares.

MATHEMATICAL

13. The relative frequency density of a continuous distribution is e^{-x} where x ranges from 0 to infinity. Show that the relative frequencies of the intervals in which x ranges between (i) 0 and 0·288, (ii) 0·288 and 0·693, (iii) 0·693 and 1·39, (iv) 1·39 and infinity, are each equal to $\frac{1}{4}$. Sketch the curve and show the first three intervals.

CHAPTER II
Measures of Position

2.1 Introduction

It has been shown in Chapter I how the main characteristics of a frequency distribution can be demonstrated visually. In the comparison of two or more sets of data, however, it is usually desirable to be able to make a quantitative as well as a qualitative comparison. Hence the following questions arise:

(a) What are the principal characteristics of a frequency distribution?

(b) How can they be measured?

The first requirement in comparing two distributions of the same variable is to know their relative *positions*. For example, if we were to compare the marks of a good set of candidates against those of a weaker set taking the same examination we should find that, on the whole, the marks of the better set were higher than those of the weaker set. If the frequency distribution of the two sets were represented by histograms on the same scale we should find two histograms of roughly the same shape but in different positions along the axis which represents the marks, as in Fig. 13. It is necessary to find some method of expressing this difference in position numerically. The measures of position used are the *mode*, the *median* and various forms of the *mean* or *average*. These will now be considered in turn.

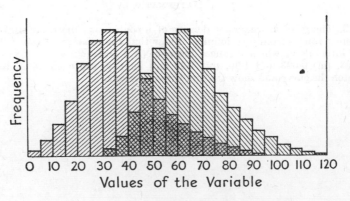

Fig. 13. Two distributions differing in position.

2.2 The Mode

The histograms of Fig. 13, which are of similar shape, can be located by the value of the variable corresponding to the maximum ordinate or highest column of each of the histograms; the maximum ordinates occur for the groups 30–35 and 60–65. These values of x are called the *modes* of the distributions. The mode of a distribution is therefore the most frequent or most "popular" value of the variable.

In distributions of discrete variables it is possible to determine the mode by examining the frequency distribution. For example, in the distribution given below the mode is 14, since this is the value of x corresponding to the highest frequency.

x	f	x	f
12	3	16	15
13	37	17	8
14	53	18	5
15	27	19	1

While the mode thus provides a very easy and accurate measure for locating distributions which are simple in form and closely similar, it is of little use if the distributions are dissimilar or if they have two or more maxima. The two histograms shown in Fig. 14 have the same mode but curve B, on the whole, occupies a different position from A.

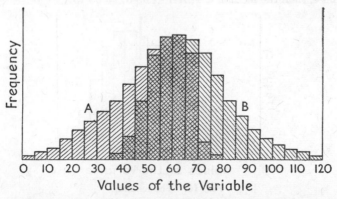

FIG. 14. Dissimilar distributions with the same modal groups.

Furthermore, comparatively few statistical distributions are of discrete variables with unit class intervals. When the class interval has a span of more than one unit the highest frequency might depend on the class-boundaries selected or on the width of the span. It would also have to be decided at what point of the most frequent class interval the mode should be located, a decision which is not easy to make if the frequency diagram is not symmetrical. As a practical measure of position the mode is therefore of limited use, but in suitable cases it is useful because of its simplicity.

2.3   The Median

The median is defined as that value of the variable for which there are equal numbers of frequencies of greater and smaller values; in other words, if the observations are arranged in order of magnitude, the median is the middle observation. For a continuous distribution it is the value corresponding to the ordinate which divides the area under the frequency curve into two equal parts.

In some kinds of distribution the median is easy to find. If the variable is discrete, and the frequency of every individual value of the variable is known, it is only necessary to arrange the values in order of magnitude and count them. The value corresponding to the middle term is the median. If the distribution consists of an even number of observations it is not possible to apply the definition precisely as there are two middle terms. It is usual in such cases to take as median the value of the variable half way between the two middle values. For example, if there are 151 observations in a distribution and the 75th, 76th and 77th are respectively 22·371, 22·373 and 22·374, then the median is 22·373. If the 80th and 81st observations in a distribution of 160 members are respectively 67·7 and 68·6, then the median is $\frac{1}{2}(67·7 + 68·6) = 68·15$.

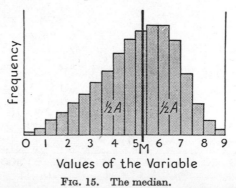

Values of the Variable

FIG. 15.   The median.

If the distribution consists of a large population spread over comparatively few values of the variable the middle value can be determined by constructing a *cumulative frequency table* for the distribution. Corresponding to each group of the distribution we find the frequency of occurrence of values of the variable which are equal to or less than that of the group. The last entry in the cumulative table, that corresponding to the greatest value of the variable, should therefore be N, the total of the population. The group which contains $\frac{1}{2}N$ is then the median group. The method of deriving the cumulative frequency table is illustrated by the following example.

Example. As part of an experiment to compare the yield of two types A and B of broad bean, some pods of each type were opened and the number of beans in each were counted. Compare the two types of bean given the data of Table VIII.

TABLE VIII

FREQUENCY DISTRIBUTIONS OF THE NUMBER OF BEANS PER POD IN TWO TYPES OF BROAD BEAN

No. of Beans Per Pod	Frequency Type A	Frequency Type B	Cumulative Freq. A	Cumulative Freq. B
1	17	4	17	4
2	29	28	46	32
3	36	41	82	73
4	16	35	98	108
5	0	4	—	112
6	0	3	—	115
Total	98	115		

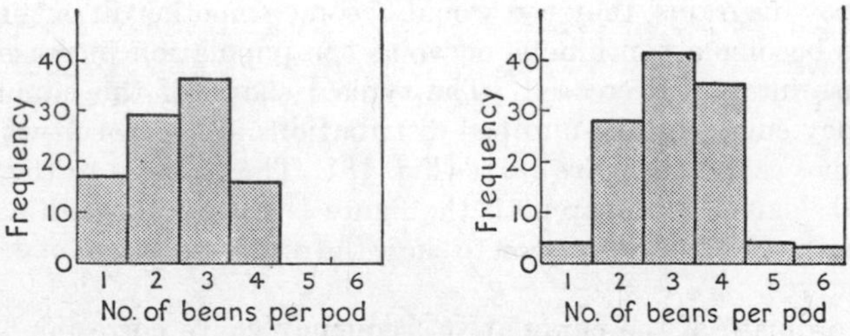

FIG. 16.   Histograms of bean distributions.

The frequency diagrams of these distributions are shown in Fig. 16 and the cumulative frequency diagrams in Fig. 17. The middle values of the type A distribution, the 49th and 50th, both lie in the group which contains three beans per pod, since this group contains the 47th to the 82nd values when they are placed in order of magnitude. The middle value of the type B distribution, the 58th, also lies in the same group, since this group contains the 33rd to the 73rd values. The median value is therefore 3 for both groups.

It is clear from the frequency diagrams that on the whole type B contains more beans per pod than type A, and this fact should be made apparent by the measure of position. Neither the mode, which is also 3 for both groups, nor the median succeeds in discriminating between these two distributions.

If, as is commonly the case, only *grouped* frequencies have been recorded, then the median *group* only can be determined by the

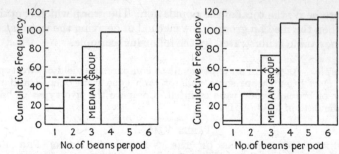

FIG. 17.   Cumulative frequency diagrams of bean distributions.

method used in the above example. By means of a graph, however, a more or less accurate estimate of the median value can be obtained. The graphical method depends on a property of the *cumulative frequency curve* which we will now describe.

In Section 1.7 the frequency curve was defined as the limiting form of the histogram of a distribution when its population is increased without limit and all values of the variable lying between the two extreme values are possible. If at all stages of the process, and using the same scales as for the histograms, we draw the cumulative frequency diagrams, they too would become smoother in outline and tend to become a continuous curve as the population increased and the class interval decreased. The typical shape of the cumulative frequency curve for one-humped distributions is the reason why it is sometimes called the *ogive curve* (Fig. 18). The likeness to the architectural "ogive" is apparent if the figure is turned through a right-angle in the clockwise direction to show the original method of drawing these curves.

The ordinate of the cumulative frequency curve corresponding to the value x of the variable represents the cumulative relative frequency of the frequency curve up to the value x. The maximum ordinate of the cumulative frequency curve is therefore unity. The

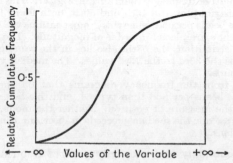

FIG. 18.   The cumulative frequency or ogive curve.

value of x corresponding to a cumulative relative frequency of $\frac{1}{2}$ is the middle value of x, i.e., it is the median of the distribution. In the frequency curve the ordinate at the median value divides the frequency curve into equal parts each of area $\frac{1}{2}$.

Mathematical Note. For a continuous distribution with a relative frequency density of $f(x)$ and range a to b, the ordinate of the cumulative frequency curve for the value x is $\int_a^x f(x)dx$. For m, the median value of x the ordinate is $\frac{1}{2}$ so the median is given by $\int_a^m f(x)dx = \frac{1}{2}$.

Just as the histogram of a finite grouped distribution is sometimes considered to be an approximation to an abstract smooth curve representing the infinite population of which the grouped distribution is a sample, so the cumulative frequency diagram may be considered as an approximation to the corresponding cumulative frequency curve. The graphical method of estimating the median of a grouped distribution is based on this idea. It will be illustrated by reference to the data of Table IX.

TABLE IX

ESTIMATES OF THE TOTAL POPULATION DISTRIBUTIONS IN THE U.S.S.R. FOR THE YEARS 1940 AND 1970. (Notestein et al., 1944.) (*In millions.*)

Age	1940		1970	
	f	cf	f	cf
0–5	23·6	23·6	22·3	22·3
5–10	17·7	41·3	21·9	44·2
10–15	21·2	62·5	21·6	65·8
15–20	16·6	79·1	21·7	87·5
20–25	14·5	93·6	21·9	109·4
25–30	16·6	110·2	21·9	131·3
30–35	13·9	124·1	20·6	151·9
35–40	11·9	136·0	15·8	167·7
40–45	8·6	144·6	18·7	186·4
45–50	6·9	151·5	14·2	200·6
50–55	6·0	157·5	12·0	212·6
55–60	5·0	162·5	13·0	225·6
60–65	4·1	166·6	10·0	235·6
65–70	3·1	169·7	7·4	243·0
70–75	2·1	171·8	4·3	247·3
75–80	1·3	173·1	2·4	249·7
80–85	0·5	173·6	1·1	250·8
85+	0·2	173·8	0·4	251·2
Totals	173·8		251·2	

The columns headed by *cf* give the cumulative frequencies of the two distributions. The histograms and cumulative frequency diagrams are shown in Fig. 19, in which the last intervals of the distributions have been taken to be 10 years. To estimate the median, smooth curves are drawn through the right hand corners of the columns as approximations to the ideal cumulative frequency curves. The median values are then obtained by finding the values of x corresponding to $\frac{1}{2}N$ for each curve. They are found to be 22·7 years and 28·7 years for the 1940 and 1970 distributions respectively.

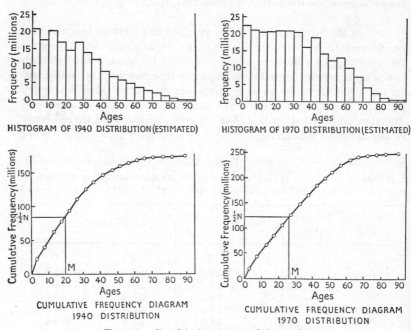

HISTOGRAM OF 1940 DISTRIBUTION(ESTIMATED)   HISTOGRAM OF 1970 DISTRIBUTION(ESTIMATED)

CUMULATIVE FREQUENCY DIAGRAM
1940 DISTRIBUTION

CUMULATIVE FREQUENCY DIAGRAM
1970 DISTRIBUTION

FIG. 19.   Graphical estimate of the median.

This graphical method of estimating the approximate value of the median should be used only for grouped data, that is, data for which the middle value cannot be determined with precision by more direct means. If all the actual values of the variable are precisely known then it is possible to determine the median exactly by putting the values in order of magnitude and noting the middle value.

EXERCISES III

MODES AND MEDIANS

1. Find the medians of the distributions of (*a*) Ex. I, 1, (*b*) Ex. I, 2.

2. Find the modes and medians of the two distributions of Ex. II, 8 (b). Show that for these distributions the median is the better measure of location.

3. By reference to the data of Ex. I, 3, show that neither the mode nor the median is a satisfactory measure of location for very asymmetrical distributions.

4. Find by the graphical method estimates of the medians of the two distributions of Ex. II, 8 (h), omitting the first group, and comment on your results.

5. Use the data of Ex. II, 8 (j) to find an estimate of the median size of school to be found in England and Wales in 1946.

MATHEMATICAL

6. The cumulative relative frequency function of a continuous distribution is x^2, where x takes all values from 0 to 1. Show that the median value of x in the frequency curve is 0·79.

7. The relative frequency density of a continuous distribution is given by $f(x) = \dfrac{1}{\pi} \cdot x \sin x$, and x varies from 0 to π. Find the equation of the cumulative relative frequency curve. Obtain an estimate of the median value of x by the use of a graphical method.

2.4 The "Sigma" Notation

The Greek capital letter, Σ, sigma, is used in algebra to denote "the sum of all terms like . . ."; it is a convenient shorthand frequently used in statistics.

Suppose we are dealing with the four quantities a, b, c and d. Then we could write the expressions

$$a + b + c + d \text{ as } \Sigma a,$$
$$\text{or } (ab + ac + ad + bc + bd + cd) \text{ as } \Sigma ab.$$

It must be emphasised that the expression Σab includes all terms like ab.

Similarly, $a^3 + b^3 + c^3 + d^3$ could be written Σa^3.

It is also convenient to use letters with suffixes attached to them to represent the individual members of a group, e.g., $a_1, a_2, a_3, \ldots$; $x_1, x_2, x_3 \ldots$

Using the sigma notation the sum

$$a_1 + a_2 + a_3 + \ldots + a_{28}$$

can be written more shortly as $\overset{28}{\Sigma_1} a_r$. This shorthand expression is read as "the sum of all terms like a_r, where r takes, in turn, all the integral values $1, 2, 3, \ldots$ to 28".

EXERCISES IV

1. Evaluate the following expressions:

$$\Sigma_1^5 r, \Sigma_1^5 r^2, (\Sigma_1^5 r)^2, \Sigma_1^5 2^r.$$

2. Verify the following identities by expanding the Σ terms:

(a) $\Sigma_1^n k x_r = k \Sigma_1^n x_r$, if k is a constant,

(b) $\Sigma_1^n (x_r + y_r)^2 = \Sigma_1^n x_r^2 + 2 \Sigma_1^n x_r y_r + \Sigma_1^n y_r^2$

(c) $\Sigma_1^n (2r - 1) = 1 + 3 + 5 + \ldots + (2n - 1) = n^2$

(d) $\Sigma_1^n x_r - \Sigma_2^{n+1} x_r = x_1 - x_{n+1}$

(e) $\Sigma_1^n (x_r^2 - x_{r+1}^2) = x_1^2 - x_{n+1}^2$

3. Given that $\Sigma_1^n r^2 = \frac{1}{6} n (n + 1) (2n + 1)$ show that

$$\Sigma_{n+1}^{2n} r^2 = \frac{1}{6} n (2n + 1) (7n + 1).$$

2.5 The Arithmetic Mean or Average

If the values of a variable are represented by $x_1, x_2, x_3, \ldots x_n$, then the arithmetic mean, or average, denoted by $\bar{x}$, is defined by the relation

$$\bar{x} = \frac{1}{n}(x_1 + x_2 + \ldots + x_n) = \frac{1}{n} \Sigma x$$

If the value x_1 occurs f_1 times, and x_2 occurs f_2 times, etc., then

$$\bar{x} = \frac{1}{N}(f_1 x_1 + f_2 x_2 + \ldots + f_n x_n) = \frac{1}{N} \Sigma f x$$

where $N = f_1 + f_2 + \ldots + f_n = \Sigma f$

When N is small the calculation is carried out in the usual way, e.g., the average of the five numbers 33, 37, 38, 42, 47 is

$$\frac{1}{5}(33 + 37 + 38 + 42 + 47) = 39 \cdot 4$$

If n is large, however, it would be very laborious to perform the calculation in the same way; the application of two simple algebraic ideas can appreciably reduce the computation. These may be represented by the identities:

$$\frac{1}{n} \Sigma_1^n (a + x_r) = a + \frac{1}{n} \Sigma_1^n x_r \tag{i}$$

and $$\frac{1}{n} \Sigma_1^n C x_r = C \cdot \frac{1}{n} \cdot \Sigma_1^n x_r \tag{ii}$$

where a and C are constants.

Arithmetical examples are:

$$\tfrac{1}{5}\,(943 + 947 + 948 + 952 + 957)$$
$$= 950 + \tfrac{1}{5}\,(-7 - 3 - 2 + 2 + 7) = 950 - 0{\cdot}6$$
$$= 949{\cdot}4$$

and
$$\tfrac{1}{6}\,(75 + 175 + 225 + 150 + 375 + 275)$$
$$= 25 \,.\, \tfrac{1}{6} \,.\, (3 + 7 + 9 + 6 + 15 + 11)$$
$$= 212{\cdot}5$$

The computation and check of the arithmetic mean of a frequency distribution is shown in Table X. The procedure is summarised below:

(a) Arrange the data as a frequency distribution with equal class-intervals (cols. 1 and 2).

(b) Estimate as accurately as you can the class which contains the average value. It does not matter if the estimate is incorrect, but the better your guess the less computation you will have to do. Note the middle value of the class you have selected.

In Table X it was estimated that the class 51–55 contained the average value. The middle of this class is 53, and therefore this value will be taken as the *working mean*, denoted by a. (Using identity (i).)

(c) In column 3, corresponding to the class 51–55, is entered the number 0, to show that the middle value of this class is the working mean. All the centres of the other class intervals are now measured from 53, the unit being the span of the class interval. (Using identity (ii).) The centre of the class 21–25, for example, is 23, and the difference between 23 marks and 53 marks is $- 30$ marks, which is -6×5 or $- 6$ intervals.

The figures of column 3 will normally run from 0 to $- 1$, $- 2$, $- 3$, etc., upwards and from 0 to 1, 2, 3, etc., downwards and in sequence, unless some intervals have zero frequency and are omitted. These numbers are called the *deviations* of the classes from the working mean, and are denoted by d.

(d) In each row of column 4 the product fd is calculated, i.e., the frequency of each class is multiplied by the corresponding deviation with the appropriate sign attached. These are summed.

(e) Columns 5 and 6 provide a very useful check which should be completed as a matter of habit. Column 5 is made up by adding 1 to the corresponding number of column 3, and column 6 is obtained by multiplying together the corresponding numbers of columns 2 and 5. The check consists of subtracting the sum of column 4 from that of column 6. If the arithmetic is correct it will be found that

$$\Sigma f(d + 1) - \Sigma fd = \Sigma(fd + f - fd) = \Sigma f,$$

which is the total of column 2.

(f) Having thus indirectly checked column 4, the total of that column is multiplied by the span of the class interval, i.e., 5 (denoted by C), and divided by the number of observations which is 661 (denoted by N). Taking regard of its sign this quotient is then added to the working mean to give the required arithmetic mean.

TABLE X

COMPUTATION OF THE ARITHMETIC MEAN

The percentage marks obtained by 661 candidates in an examination are classified by intervals of 5 marks. The classes are set out in col. 1, and the corresponding frequencies in col. 2.

1	2	3	4	5	6
x	f	d	fd	$(d + 1)$	$f(d + 1)$
11–15	8	−8	−64	−7	−56
16–20	15	−7	−105	−6	−90
21–25	39	−6	−234	−5	−195
26–30	47	−5	−235	−4	−188
31–35	52	−4	−208	−3	−156
36–40	53	−3	−159	−2	−106
41–45	54	−2	−108	−1	−54
46–50	56	−1	−56	0	−845
51–55	59	0	−1,169	1	59
56–60	53	1	53	2	106
61–65	48	2	96	3	144
66–70	45	3	135	4	180
71–75	39	4	156	5	195
76–80	32	5	160	6	192
81–85	23	6	138	7	161
86–90	17	7	119	8	136
91–95	13	8	104	9	117
96–100	8	9	72	10	80
	661		1,033		1,370
		Total	− 136	*Total*	+ 525

Check $\Sigma f(d + 1) - \Sigma fd = 525 - (- 136)$
$$= 661$$
$$= N$$
$$Mean = a + C \cdot \frac{1}{N} \cdot \Sigma fd$$
$$= 53 + 5 \cdot \frac{1}{661} \cdot (- 136)$$
$$= 53 - 1 \cdot 03$$
$$= 51 \cdot 97$$

The algebraic verification of this procedure is as follows:

The deviation, $\qquad d = \dfrac{x - a}{C}$

and therefore $\qquad x = a + Cd$

Multiplying by f, $\qquad fx = fa + fCd$

By definition, $\qquad \bar{x} = \dfrac{1}{N} \Sigma fx$

$$= \frac{1}{N} \Sigma fa + \frac{1}{N} \Sigma fCd$$

$$= a + \frac{C}{N} \Sigma fd$$

since $\Sigma f = N$.

Compared with the mode or median as a measure of the position of a distribution, the arithmetic mean has several advantages. In the first place it is better known and understood. In most practical cases it is also a better discriminant, that is, it locates a distribution with greater precision and it is more widely applicable. While the calculation of the arithmetic mean requires more computation, it is necessary in any case to do this work if the distribution is to be analysed further. The algebraic form of the mean is also much more convenient to manipulate than those of the mode and median, and because of this fact it has become a quantity of fundamental importance in the theoretical development of statistics. Because of their simplicity, however, the mode and median are still of use in suitable cases.

The calculation of the mean is closely analogous to the finding of the x-coordinate of the centre of gravity of a plane lamina of the same shape as the histogram of the distribution, and hence the mean is sometimes called the *first moment* of the distribution.

Mathematical Note. For a continuous distribution the mean is given by

$$\bar{x} = \int_a^b xf(x)dx$$

where $f(x)$ is the relative frequency density, and a and b are the lower and upper limits of x respectively.

2.6 The Weighted Mean

The arithmetic mean of a frequency distribution has been defined as

$$\bar{x} = \frac{1}{N} \Sigma fx = \frac{f_1 x_1 + f_2 x_2 + \ldots + f_n x_n}{f_1 + f_2 + \ldots + f_n}$$

where $f_1, f_2, \ldots f_n$ are the frequencies of $x_1, x_2, \ldots x_n$. The term "frequency" is sometimes given a wider interpretation than we have used so far, particularly in economics, and is often replaced by the term "weight".

The *weighted mean* is defined as

$$\bar{x}_w = \frac{w_1 x_1 + w_2 x_2 + \ldots + w_n x_n}{w_1 + w_2 + \ldots + w_n} = \frac{\Sigma wx}{\Sigma w}$$

where the weights $w_1, w_2, \ldots w_n$, are numerical coefficients assigned to the variables $x_1, x_2, \ldots x_n$. These coefficients may be frequencies, numbers proportional to frequencies, estimates of frequencies, or may have no relation to frequencies at all, as illustrated by the following simple examples.

(a) A car manufacturer produces 3 models, which he sells at £900, £1,100 and £1,300. To take £1,100 as the average price of the cars he sells takes no account of the relative numbers of each. If the relative numbers of each are 10, 4 and 1 respectively, then the weighted mean is

$$£\frac{900 \times 10 + 1,100 \times 4 + 1,300 \times 1}{10 + 4 + 1}$$

$$= £980$$

This is a better representation of what is understood by the "average price" than the simple mean.

(b) A candidate obtains the following percentages in an examination: Latin, 75; Mathematics, 84; French, 56; English, 78; Science, 57; History, 54; Geography, 47. It is agreed to give double weight to the marks in English, Mathematics and Latin. What is his weighted mean?

$$= \frac{75 \times 2 + 84 \times 2 + 56 + 78 \times 2 + 57 + 54 + 47}{2 + 2 + 1 + 2 + 1 + 1 + 1}$$

$$= 68\cdot8$$

His unweighted mean would have been 64·4.

It has been possible to work out the simple examples given above by direct application of the definition. For more complex cases the calculation may be done as for a frequency distribution with the frequencies replaced by the weights.

EXERCISES V

1. The frequency table below gives de Vries' data on buttercup petals (quoted by Pearse, *Biometrika* **20A**, 325). Find the mean.

Number per flower	5	6	7	8	9	10
Frequency	133	55	23	7	2	2

2. Find the means of the distributions of (a) Ex. I, 1, (b) Ex. I, 2.

3. Calculate the mean age of the male and female populations of the United Kingdom for the year 1946 using the data of Ex. II, 8 (b). Refer to Ex. III, 2 and compare the median and the mean as effective measures of location for this type of data.

4. Use the data of Ex. I, 4 to show that the mean length of sentence in the sample of G. K. Chesterton's writing is of 25·8 words.

5. Find the mean size of school given by the data of Ex. II, 8 (*j*). Assume that the schools of over 500 pupils have an average of 600 pupils.

6. (*a*) An examination candidate's percentages are: English, 73; French, 82; Mathematics, 57; Science, 62; History, 60. Find the candidate's weighted mean if weights of 4, 3, 3, 1, 1 respectively are allotted to the subjects.

    (*b*) The average percentages for the same examination were 57, 52, 48, 55, 50 for the above subjects respectively. Find the weighted mean for the whole examination.

7. The element tin consists of a mixture of 10 isotopes which have atomic weights ranging from 112 to 124. The proportions in which the isotopes occur in the element are given in the table. Calculate the mean atomic weight of the mixture.

Isotope A.W.	112	114	115	116	117	118	119	120	122	124
Percentage	1·1	0·8	0·4	15·5	9·1	22·5	9·8	28·5	5·5	6·8

8. The table gives the sunshine records for the months of the two years 1943 and 1946 over England and Wales. The figures are percentages of the corresponding monthly means (hours per day) for the period 1909–1933. Show that the sunshine totals for each of the two years 1943, 1946, are 107% and 96% respectively of the mean for the period 1909–1933.

	J	F	M	A	M	J
Mean	1·50	2·35	3·61	4·95	6·09	6·60
1943	92	129	115	111	125	102
1946	99	114	93	126	105	88

	J	A	S	O	N	D
Mean	5·71	5·40	4·65	3·35	2·04	1·28
1943	109	91	99	98	111	111
1946	103	84	77	76	63	149

2.7 Index Numbers

One of the best known examples of a weighted mean is the cost-of-living index. It is one of the most important index numbers used in economic statistics, but the construction of a satisfactory cost-of-living index is a very complex problem. Firstly, its purpose must be decided, because this helps to determine the particular meaning of the vague term "cost of living" which the proposed index is required to measure. Then, how is this cost-of-living to be measured? What items are to be included? Since, for example, the cost of coal may vary according to the distance from the pit-head, how are the costs of the selected items to be assessed? What weights should be assigned to the items? All these and many other problems have to be solved before the purely arithmetical part of the process is reached.

In the United Kingdom it was decided in 1947 to suspend the publication of the cost-of-living index which was based on the everyday expenses of the year 1904, because the index no longer corresponded with the expenditure of the average household. An index of retail prices was substituted. This index was the arithmetic mean of eight other price index numbers weighted as follows:

Food,	348	Clothing,	97
Rent and rates,	88	Fuel and light,	65
Household durable goods,	71	Services,	79
Miscellaneous goods,	35	Drink and tobacco,	217

In 1964 this index was again revised to meet the ever-changing pattern of average family expenditure. This index is the arithmetic mean of ten other indexes weighted thus:

Food,	314	Household durable goods,	62
Alcoholic drink,	63	Clothing and footwear,	95
Tobacco,	74	Transport and vehicles,	100
Housing,	107	Miscellaneous goods,	63
Fuel and lighting,	66	Services,	56

The cost-of-living indexes of different countries are based on the costs of different commodities and on different weights, so that these indexes are not strictly comparable. In all economic statistics it is particularly necessary to examine most carefully the sources of all data that may be required as the basis of a logical argument. It is essential to ensure that any data being compared are *homogeneous*, that is, that they refer to precisely the same class of things and have been found by precisely the same method of enumeration. A glance at the footnotes which accompany any reliable table of economic data may serve as a warning of the kind of thing that may affect the homogeneity of statistics. For example at the bottom of Table on Coal Productivity in the *Monthly Digest of Statistics* we find the following notes included among others:

(i) "The introduction of a revised form of return resulted in a net increase of about 1,250 in the total wage-earners in 1943."

(ii) "From the end of 1942 certain additional categories were included as workers at the coal face. On the old basis the figure for 1943 was 2·86." (On the new basis the figure is 2·75.)

(iii) "Owing to the varying practice by collieries in recording men on colliery books, a standard method of recording wage-earners was adopted as from the beginning of 1946. The effect of this was to reduce the number on colliery books by approximately 2,500 and absenteeism by 0·30%."

These notes indicate how easily large apparent variations may be due merely to modifications in the method of counting or to a redefinition of the category that is enumerated.

Most index numbers are weighted arithmetic means but for some purposes other types of weighted means may be more convenient or may give better representations of the variations they are used to describe. The *geometric* mean is occasionally used in economic statistics; it may be preferable to the arithmetic mean if the variations the index is required to describe are ratios rather than differences, e.g., a rise of an index from 120 points to 180 points may be considered to be an increase either of 50% or of 60 points. In the first case an equivalent increase of the index would be from 80 points to 120 points; in the second case, from 80 points to 140 points; the appropriate index numbers should be based on the geometric and arithmetic means respectively.

The geometric mean, g, of two numbers a and b is such that $\dfrac{a}{g} = \dfrac{g}{b}$ or $g = \sqrt{ab}$, so that $\log g = \frac{1}{2}(\log a + \log b)$, i.e., log (geometric mean) = arithmetic mean of $\log a$ and $\log b$.

This definition of the geometric mean can be extended to any number of terms, so that the geometric mean, g, of $x_1, x_2 \ldots x_n$ is given by

$$n \cdot \log g = \Sigma_1^n \cdot \log x_r$$

If the terms are to be weighted, by weights, $w_1, w_2 \ldots w_n$, respectively, then the weighted geometric mean is given by

$$(\Sigma_1^n w_r) \cdot \log g = \Sigma_1^n (w_r \cdot \log x_r).$$

Example. A composite index number is to be constructed from the following index numbers and weights.

Index No.	133	141	125	173	182
Weight	5	4	7	1	3

Calculate the index number as (a) an arithmetic mean, (b) a geometric mean.

(a) Taking 140 as the working mean the calculation may be tabulated:

Deviation	Weight	Wt. × Dev.
−7	5	−35
+1	4	+4
−15	7	−105
+33	1	+33
+42	3	126
	20	163 − 140 = 23

Index number $= 140 + \dfrac{1}{20} \times 23 = 141$, correct to the nearest whole number.

(b) The working mean of the logarithms is 2·0000; the calculation may be tabulated:

Index No.	Log (Index)	Dev.	Wt.	Wt. × Dev.
133	2·1239	0·1239	5	0·6195
141	2·1492	0·1492	4	0·5968
125	2·0969	0·0969	7	0·6783
173	2·2380	0·2380	1	0·2380
182	2·2601	0·2601	3	0·7803
			20	2·7429

$$\text{Log (Index)} = 2 \cdot 0000 + \frac{1}{20} \cdot 2 \cdot 7429$$
$$= 2 \cdot 1371$$

Index $= 137$ to the nearest whole number.

Index numbers are being increasingly used in the presentation of economic statistics and an understanding of their construction, their uses and their limitations is essential to any student of economics. For further information, however, the references listed in the bibliography should be consulted.

2.8 Moving Averages

Many business firms record their achievements in profit, turnover or production in some graphical form as the significance of those achievements can usually be more rapidly appreciated as graphs than as lists of numbers. The progress of a company, however, is rarely one of uniformly increasing prosperity such as would be represented by a smoothly rising line on the graph. Apart from trade "booms" and "slumps" there may be seasonal or other periodic variations and random fluctuations of many kinds. The graphical representation of irregular data of this kind may be difficult to interpret unless some method of "smoothing" the minor irregularities is devised. One such method is provided by the use of the *moving average*, which is defined as the average of a consecutive set of n observations, where n is some convenient number. The smoother graph of the moving average may give a better idea of "trends" than the unmodified record.

The value of the moving average for the first n observations will be

$$m_1 = \frac{1}{n} \Sigma_1^n x$$

The next value of the moving average will be

$$m_2 = \frac{1}{n} \Sigma_2^{n+1} x,$$

and in general the rth value will be

$$m_r = \frac{1}{n} \Sigma_r^{n+r-1} x$$

Any value of the moving average can be obtained from the preceding values by the relations:

$$m_2 = m_1 + \frac{x_{n+1} - x_1}{n},$$

$$m_3 = m_2 + \frac{x_{n+2} - x_2}{n},$$

and, in general,

$$m_{r+1} = m_r + \frac{x_{n+r} - x_r}{n}$$

Since each moving average represents the mean of several readings it is usual to mark it on the graph, in time, at the middle of the time interval it covers; for example, if a moving average covers the years 1901–1910, it would be plotted against the year 1905.

A practical difficulty is the selection of a suitable value for the span of n. The greater n is made the smoother becomes the graph, but the smaller is the indication of a change of trend. It is also desirable to choose n so that the moving average is not affected by any periodic variations; n must therefore be a multiple of the number of observations that constitute a period.

The data of Table XI are represented by the graph joining the crosses in Fig. 20. The method of calculating 10-year moving averages is shown below and the moving averages themselves are marked by circles on the graph. The graph of the moving average indicates that the circulation of the library steadily increased, paused and then increased again at a slower rate.

TABLE XI

ANNUAL CIRCULATION OF A LIBRARY (THOUSANDS OF ISSUES) AND THE CALCULATION OF A 10-YEAR MOVING AVERAGE FOR THE YEARS 1921–1945.

Data. (Tabulate the data in n columns, where n is the span.)

Year	0	1	2	3	4	5	6	7	8	9
192–	—	14·5	17·6	18·9	19·3	22·7	25·8	26·7	26·5	28·3
193–	29·9	33·5	32·3	31·4	28·9	29·0	27·3	29·1	33·5	37·0
194–	39·8	39·6	38·3	37·1	36·0	35·3				

C

Differences.   (Top row from second, second row from third.)

| — | 19·0 | 14·7 | 12·5 | 9·6 | 6·3 | 1·5 | 2·4 | 7·0 | 8·7 |
| 10·9 | 6·1 | 6·0 | 5·7 | 7·1 | 6·3 | — | — | — | — |

The differences are now divided by the span (in this case 10) and are added successively to the average for the first 10 years, 1921–1930, which is 23·02.

Average of years 1921–1930   = 23·02

Average of years 1922–1931 = 23·02 + 1·90 = 24·92

Average of years 1923–1932 = 24·92 + 1·47 = 26·39, etc.

The average of the years 1921–1930 is plotted in the middle of that period, and the successive averages at one year intervals.

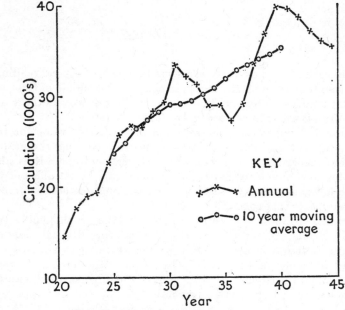

Fig. 20.   Time chart with moving average.

The effect of changing the span of a moving average when the variable exhibits a periodic fluctuation is illustrated in Fig. 21. The data are the mean daily air temperatures at sea-level for England and Wales over a period of 40 months, and have been chosen because we already know that we can expect a fluctuation with a 12-month period with a fairly steady average from year to year. The 12-month moving average is seen to be almost a straight line; as the temperature reading of any month in one year is discarded the temperature in the same month of the next year is added; the difference is usually

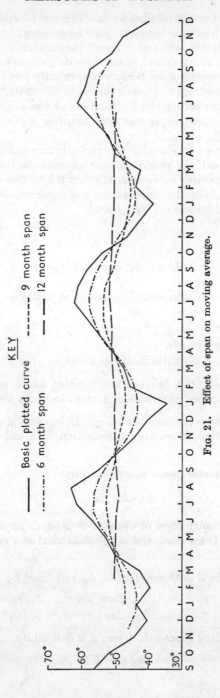

KEY

Basic plotted curve

6 month span

9 month span

12 month span

Fig. 21. Effect of span on moving average.

small, and even this is divided by 12. There is no appreciable steady change of temperature from one year to another, and therefore the straight line obtained is roughly parallel to the time axis.

The 9-month and 6-month spans show deviations from the straight line of the 12-month span because the months that are added and subtracted at each move are not the same months of the year. Both moving averages reflect the fluctuations of the original graph, but the amplitude increases as the span number diverges from 12 (or multiples of 12).

If it is required to examine the periodic fluctuations rather than the general trend, the procedure, in this example, would be first to find the average value for each month, but the further analysis of time series in which periodic fluctuations are superimposed on a steady trend is beyond the scope of this book.

SUMMARY OF CHAPTER II

1. The three most important measures of position of a distribution are:

    (a) The mode,

    (b) The median,

    (c) The arithmetic mean, or average.

2. The mode is the value of the variable which occurs most frequently. In grouped distributions ambiguities may arise.

3. The median is the middle reading. It depends on all the members of the distribution; in grouped distributions it is usually determined graphically.

4. The arithmetic mean, $\bar{x}$, is defined by

$$\bar{x} = \frac{1}{n} \cdot \Sigma x.$$

It is the best known form of average; it depends on all the readings; its calculation is the first step in the statistical analysis of numerical distributions.

5. The weighted arithmetic mean, $\bar{x}_w$, is defined by

$$\bar{x}_w = \frac{\Sigma w x}{\Sigma w}$$

6. The weighted geometric mean, g, is defined by

$$(\Sigma w) \cdot \log g = \Sigma (w \cdot \log x).$$

7. Index numbers are used in economic statistics to indicate changes in prices, production, etc.; they are usually weighted means.

8. Moving averages are used to smooth time series.

EXERCISES VI

INDEX NUMBERS

1. Calculate to the nearest integer the "interim index of retail prices" for January 13th, 1948, and June 15th, 1948, from the price relatives given in the table. The index is a weighted arithmetic mean. (*Monthly Digest of Statistics*.)

	Weights	January 13th	June 15th
Food	348	103·6	113·5
Rent and rates	88	100·1	99·2
Clothing	97	102·7	108·5
Fuel and light	65	109·2	110·4
Household durable goods	71	107·5	107·5
Miscellaneous goods	35	111·1	109·3
Services	79	103·5	104·8
Drink and tobacco	217	104·1	110·8

2. Calculate to the nearest integer the "interim index of industrial production" for (a) January 1946, (b) January 1947, (c) January 1948. Index numbers of production are listed in the table below, together with the corresponding weights. The index is the weighted arithmetic mean. (*Monthly Digest of Statistics*.)

Group	Weight	Jan. 1946	Jan. 1947	Jan. 1948
Mining and quarrying	78	94	105	118
China and earthenware	4	81	107	143
Glass	6	88	109	116
Bricks, cement, etc.	21	59	120	153
Metals, vehicles, etc.	381	86	108	123
Chemicals	65	96	100	123
Textiles and clothing	93	92	105	117
Leather, fur	6	85	102	100
Food, drink, tobacco	107	104	94	103
Wood and cork	25	87	104	109
Paper and printing	39	88	110	111
Other manufactures	19	80	118	148
Building	92	71	93	111
Gas, electricity, etc.	64	113	121	121

3. A certain total wholesale price index number is the weighted geometric mean of the wholesale price index numbers of (a) food and tobacco,

(b) industrial materials and manufactures, (c) building materials. Calculate this total index for the four years for which data are given below:

	Weights	1960	1962	1964	1966
(a)	6	136	161	162	163
(b)	13	134	155	165	178
(c)	1	117	139	147	167

MOVING AVERAGES

4. Draw graphs to show, for any selected month, the variations of the barometric height and percentage humidity at Worthing using the data of Tables II and VI. Add the graphs of 10-day moving averages.

5. The world's annual production of silver is tabulated below for the years 1904–1941. The units are millions of ounces. Draw the graph of this data and of the 10-year moving average. Briefly describe the trend. (Condensed from the data of *The Statist*.)

Year	0	1	2	3	4	5	6	7	8	9
190–	—	—	—	—	164	172	165	184	203	212
191–	222	226	224	224	168	184	169	174	197	174
192–	175	171	213	246	239	245	254	254	257	262
193–	248	196	165	190	221	254	274	268	266	272
194–	263	—	—	—	—	—	—	—	—	—

6. The monthly rainfall in Scotland for the years 1942–1946 is given in the table. Illustrate the data by a graph and add the 12-month moving average. Draw a second graph based on this data to show the average rainfall for the 12 months of the year. Comment on your results. (*Annual Abstract*, No. 84.)

	Jan.	Feb.	Mar.	Apr.	May	June
1942	6·7	3·0	2·7	2·2	3·3	2·0
1943	5·7	4·9	2·7	4·0	4·2	3·6
1944	6·0	2·7	2·0	3·2	3·7	4·4
1945	6·1	5·9	3·2	2·3	4·6	4·3
1946	5·6	4·0	2·9	2·0	1·7	4·1

	July	Aug.	Sept.	Oct.	Nov.	Dec.
1942	4·1	5·0	6·2	6·7	1·7	6·7
1943	3·1	5·9	4·5	7·3	4·3	3·1
1944	2·9	3·3	5·4	6·0	7·4	6·0
1945	3·6	3·2	5·7	5·3	1·1	5·7
1946	5·4	4·6	6·6	0·7	7·2	5·2

7. The table gives (in thousands) the number of insured workers in Great Britain registered as unemployed each month for the years 1938–1942. Draw a graph of this data and of the 12-month moving average. Briefly relate the trend, as shown by your graph, to your knowledge of the events of this period. (*Annual Abstract*, No. 84.)

	Jan.	Feb.	Mar.	Apr.	May	June
1938	1,904	1,888	1,829	1,818	1,846	1,885
1939	2,032	1,890	1,728	1,626	1,478	1,342
1940	1,471	1,466	1,083	931	843	709
1941	653	528	391	343	317	252
1942	162	161	137	119	114	106

	July	Aug.	Sept.	Oct.	Nov.	Dec.
1938	1,871	1,836	1,865	1,855	1,904	1,912
1939	1,251	1,203	1,261	1,327	1,322	1,305
1940	755	721	789	797	768	683
1941	234	214	178	171	159	151
1942	103	115	109	100	104	100

8. The annual average price index of merino wool for the years 1900–1938 is tabulated below. Draw a graph of this data and then superimpose on it the graph of a 5-year moving average. Briefly describe the trend. (Blau, *Journal Royal Stat. Soc.*, **109**, 231.)

	0	1	2	3	4	5	6	7	8	9
190–	79	72	87	93	92	98	101	100	88	101
191–	101	94	98	105	109	131	187	252	249	393
192–	364	157	185	210	273	204	179	190	181	134
193–	91	76	69	96	92	93	117	122	83	—

9. Draw a graph to illustrate the United Kingdom production of steel together with a 10-year moving average for the years 1900–1946. The units are millions of ingot tons. (Condensed from data of Shone, *Journal Royal Stat. Soc.*, **110**, 284.)

	0	1	2	3	4	5	6	7	8	9
190–	4·9	4·9	4·9	5·0	5·0	5·8	6·5	6·5	5·3	5·9
191–	6·4	6·5	6·8	7·7	7·8	8·6	9·0	9·7	9·5	7·9
192–	9·1	3·7	5·9	8·5	8·2	7·4	3·6	9·1	8·5	9·6
193–	7·3	5·2	5·3	7·0	8·8	9·9	11·8	13·0	10·4	13·2
194–	13·0	12·3	12·9	13·0	12·1	11·8	12·7	—	—	—

ALGEBRAIC

10. Show that if $\bar{x}$ is the arithmetic mean of the quantities $x_1, x_2, \ldots x_r, \ldots x_n$, then

(a) $\sum_1^n (x - \bar{x}) = 0$

(b) $\sum_1^n (x - \bar{x})^2 = \sum_1^n x^2 - n\bar{x}^2$

and verify these identities when $x = 2r + 1$, and $r = 1, 2, 3, 4, 5$.

11. Show that the arithmetic mean of an arithmetic progression is equal to the mean of its first and last terms.

12. The arithmetic mean of n numbers of a series is $\bar{x}$. The sum of the first $(n - 1)$ numbers is S. Show that the nth number is $n\bar{x} - S$.

13. Distributions A and B have a total frequency of F_1 and F_2, and arithmetic means $\bar{x}$ and $\bar{y}$ respectively. Show that the arithmetic mean or the distribution obtained by combining A and B is

$$\frac{F_1\bar{x} + F_2\bar{y}}{F_1 + F_2}$$

Generalise this result for n combined distributions.

14. State and prove results for geometric means which are analogous to those of the previous question

15. A distribution $x_1, x_2, \ldots x_r, \ldots x_n$, with frequencies $f_1, f_2, \ldots f_r, \ldots f_n$, is transformed into the distribution $X_1, X_2, \ldots X_n$ with the same corresponding frequencies by the relation $X_r = ax_r + b$, where a and b are constants. Show that the mean, mode and median of the new distribution are given in terms of those of the first distribution by the same transformation.

16. In calculating a cost-of-living index, $w_1, w_2, \ldots w_r, \ldots w_n$, are the weights attached to price index numbers $x_1, x_2, \ldots x_r, \ldots x_n$, respectively. Show that the percentage increase in the cost-of-living index (an arithmetic mean), is $\dfrac{\Sigma wxp}{\Sigma wx}$ where $p_r\%$ is the increase in x_r.

17. Draw graphs of the following sequences:

    (a)   1, 2, 3, 4, 3, 2, 1, 2, 3, 4, 3, 2, 1, 2, etc., together with moving averages of 3-, 4-, 5-, 6-, and 10-unit spans.

    (b)   8, 11, 12, 13, 16, 19, 20, 21, 24, 27, 28, 29, 32, 35, 36, 37, 40, 43, together with moving averages of 4-, 5-, 6-, and 8-unit spans.

Comment on the results.

18. The "moving average" of a continuous function $y = f(x)$ may be defined as $\dfrac{1}{s}\displaystyle\int_x^{x+s} y\,dx$ where s is the "span". Investigate the behaviour of this function when $f(x) = ax + \sin x$ and $s = \frac{1}{2}\pi$, π and 2π in turn. Illustrate your results by diagrams.

MISCELLANEOUS NUMERICAL

19. Find the mode, median and arithmetic mean of each of the distributions A, B, and C and mark them on the frequency diagrams.

    A: Marks in a general knowledge test.

Mark	1	2	3	4	5	6	7	8	9	10
Frequency	2	7	17	29	38	41	40	30	17	6

    B: Weight of a crop of shallots (to nearest 0·1 oz.).

Weight	1	2	3	4	5	6	7	8	9	10	11	12	13	14
Frequency	52	81	63	54	30	22	14	10	6	3	1	2	1	2

C: Population of Great Britain according to size of family, 1931 (thousands).

No. in family	1	2	3	4	5	6
No. of families	689	2,240	2,460	1,980	1,271	747

No. in family	7	8	9	10 or more.		
No. of families	422	214	112	98		

(Take mean of last group as 12·0.)

20. Use the data of the table below to find the average age of U.K. and Colonial merchant shipping for each of the two given dates. Illustrate the distributions by a suitable diagram. The average of the last group may be taken as 30 years. (*Annual Abstract*, No. 84.)

Age (years)	0–5	5–10	10–15	15–20	20–25	Over 25
Sept. 1939	500	275	707	579	370	296
Dec. 1946	658	337	140	273	220	397

21. Find the average of the cricket score distribution given in Ex. I, 8.

22. Illustrate by suitable diagrams the data of the following tables:

(a) *Exports of non-ferrous metals and manufactures* (1,000 *tons*).

	Aluminium	Copper	Brass	Nickel	Tin
1935	7·9	39·0	22·6	11·7	23·0
1946	28·1	73·4	75·3	8·5	20·6

(b) *Monetary circulation in the United Kingdom* (*end of period*).

Year	1937	38	39	40	41	42	43	44	45	46	47
£1,000 m.	0·46	0·46	0·50	0·56	0·70	0·87	1·03	1·20	1·34	1·38	1·33

23. In a study of the wild carrot plant a count of the number of bracts per cluster in plants from Michigan and from Indiana gave the distributions of the table. Calculate the means and illustrate the two distributions by frequency diagrams. [Baten (1934), *Biometrika*, **26**, 443.]

Bracts per cluster	5	6	7	8	9	10	11	12	13	14	15	16
Michigan frequency	10	9	94	318	253	153	92	40	26	4	0	1
Indiana „	0	0	0	98	143	159	205	201	189	3	2	0

24. Do brains shrink with age? The weights of the brains of one particular group of persons divided into old and young sets, gave the following distributions: [Lesser (1933), *Biometrika*, **25**, 197.]

Weight in grams	800– 949	950– 1,049	1,050– 1,099	1,100– 1,149	1,150– 1,199	1,200– 1,249
Frequency, Old	3	6	8	19	11	14
Young	—	2	14	22	45	54

Weight in grams	1,250– 1,299	1,300– 1,349	1,350– 1,399	1,400– 1,449	Totals
Frequency, Old	14	3	6	1	85
Young	55	23	13	10	238

Compare the medians and the arithmetic means of these two distributions and comment on your results.

25. Find the average ages of men and women blood donors from the following data: [Fraser Roberts (1948), *Annals of Eugenics*, **14**, 115.]

Age, years	10–19	20–29	30–39	40–49	50–59
Frequency, women	7,845	16,008	13,107	9,685	6,374
men	3,016	6,894	9,229	5,714	3,575

Age, years	60–69	70–79	80–89	90 and over.
Frequency, women	2,137	173	9	—
men	1,492	170	9	1

26. The distributions of incomes liable to surtax for the years 1937–38 and 1944–45 (provisional) are tabulated below. Draw a diagram to illustrate the differences of the two distributions and calculate their means. The average income of the last group of the table may be taken as £180,000 per annum. (*Annual Abstract*, No. 84.)

Income in £1,000's					
Exceeding	2·0	2·5	3·0	4·0	5·0
Not exceeding	2·5	3·0	4·0	5·0	6·0
Frequency 1937–38	28,716	18,414	21,059	11,584	6,988
1944–45	35,148	23,809	25,519	12,920	7,646

Income in £1,000's					
Exceeding	6·0	7·0	8·0	10	15
Not exceeding	7·0	8·0	10·0	15	20
Frequency 1937–38	4,520	3,130	3,990	4,419	1,652
1944–45	4,940	3,339	4,117	4,289	1,559

Income in £1,000's					
Exceeding	20	25	30	40	50
Not exceeding	25	30	40	50	75
Frequency 1937–38	823	439	456	180	242
1944–45	657	351	301	155	141

Income in £1,000's		
Exceeding	75	Over
Not exceeding	100	100
Frequency 1937–38	96	108
1944–45	60	50

27. The age distribution of the population of the U.K. in 1940, and estimates of this distribution for 1970 are tabulated below (in millions). Compare the means of these distributions. Illustrate the data by constructing a demographic "pyramid". [Notestein et al. (1944).]

Age	0–4	5–9	10–14	15–19	20–24	25–29	30–34
1940	3·58	3·58	3·83	4·08	4·00	4·15	4·06
1970	1·96	2·18	2·41	2·63	2·94	3·20	3·38

Age	35–39	40–44	45–49	50–54	55–59	60–64	65–69
1940	3·81	3·47	3·15	2·93	2·72	2·38	1·88
1970	3·40	3·60	3·76	3·59	3·53	3·21	2·66

Age			70–74	75–79	80–84	85+	*Totals*
1940			1·32	0·80	0·37	0·15	50·26
1970			1·97	1·29	0·69	0·37	46·77

28. Briefly describe three measures of location for frequency distributions. What factors affect your choice of a measure of location when two or more distributions are to be compared?

29. Explain how to calculate the mean of a grouped frequency distribution.

30. Describe a method of smoothing time series. How can seasonal fluctuations in the time series be eliminated in the trend line?

31. What are index numbers and how are they constructed? Give the details of construction of some index number used in the *Monthly Digest*.

32. Describe, with references to data of your own selection, how to determine the median of a grouped frequency distribution.

PRACTICAL

33. Note the use (and misuse) of statistics in the correspondence columns of the daily newspapers. When it is possible confirm the statistics that are quoted, compared, or contrasted, and examine them for homogeneity.

34. Scan the general notes of any new issues of the *Monthly Digest*, *U.N. Monthly Bulletin, Annual Abstract*, etc., that are available in your local reference library. Note the details of construction of newly introduced index numbers.

CHAPTER III
Measures of Dispersion

3.1 Introduction

The second main characteristic of a distribution is its *dispersion* or *spread*, which is the degree of scatter or of variation of the variables about a central value such as the median or the average. Referring to Fig. 22, the distribution represented by the curve A is more widely scattered than that represented by the curve B, though their positions as measured by their averages are the same. How can this difference be measured? As with measures of position there are several possibilities, the choice of any particular one depending on the type of distribution and the degree of precision required. We shall consider the *range*, the *semi-interquartile range*, the *mean deviation from the median* and the *standard deviation*.

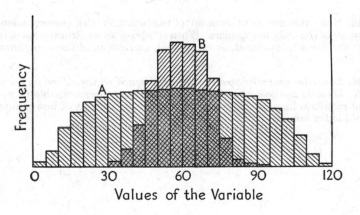

FIG. 22. Distributions with different dispersions.

3.2 The Range

The *range*, defined as the difference between the extreme values of the variable, is the simplest measure of dispersion. The ranges of the two distributions A and B of Fig. 22 would be $120 - 0 = 120$ units, and $95 - 30 = 65$ units, respectively. The range is thus a measure which is very easy to determine and use.

On the other hand it has some serious disadvantages, one of the most important of which is illustrated in Fig. 23. Each of the distributions represented by the curves C and D has a range of 120 units, but the curve D represents a distribution which, *on the whole*, has a wider scatter of the variable than has the distribution represented by *C*. The range may therefore fail to discriminate if the distributions are of different types.

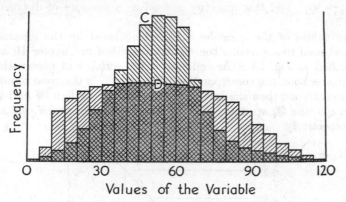

FIG. 23. Distributions with equal ranges.

If small populations, with similar distributions, are being compared the range may give a good indication of the spread; but the range depends only on the extreme values of the variable, and in nearly all types of distribution these occur least frequently and are therefore the least typical members of the distribution.

Because of its simplicity, however, the range may be used when suitable occasions arise.

3.3 The Semi-Interquartile Range

The *quartiles* are closely related to the median, which it will be remembered, divides a distribution into two parts in each of which there are equal numbers of observations. The quartiles divide each of these two halves into two further equal parts, so that between the

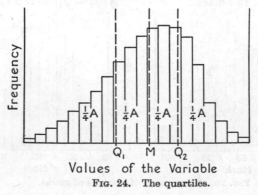

Values of the Variable

FIG. 24. The quartiles.

two quartiles there lies the middle half of the observations. If the values of the variable corresponding to the lower and upper quartiles be Q_1 and Q_2 respectively, then the *semi-interquartile range* is $\frac{1}{2}(Q_2 - Q_1)$, and this quantity is used as a measure of dispersion (Fig. 24).

The values of the quartiles are best obtained by the graphical method used to determine the median described in Chapter II, and illustrated in Fig. 25. The ordinate is the number of observations not greater than the corresponding value of x; N is the total number of observations; then the lower quartile Q_1, the median M and the upper quartile Q_2 are the values of x corresponding to $\frac{1}{4}N$, $\frac{1}{2}N$ and $\frac{3}{4}N$ respectively.

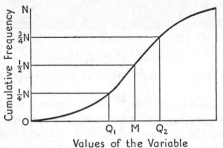

FIG. 25.   Graphical determination of the quartiles.

Applying this method to the data of Table XII, of which histograms are given in Fig. 26 we find that:

For distribution A.	*For distribution B.*
$Q_1 = 35 \cdot 5$ marks.	$Q_1 = 36 \cdot 6$ marks.
$M = 50 \cdot 5$ marks.	$M = 48 \cdot 0$ marks.
$Q_2 = 66 \cdot 3$ marks.	$Q_2 = 60 \cdot 4$ marks.
$M - Q_1 = 15 \cdot 0$ marks.	$M - Q_1 = 12 \cdot 4$ marks.
$Q_2 - M = 15 \cdot 8$ marks.	$Q_2 - M = 11 \cdot 4$ marks.
$\frac{1}{2}(Q_2 - Q_1) = 15 \cdot 4$ marks.	$\frac{1}{2}(Q_2 - Q_1) = 11 \cdot 9$ marks.

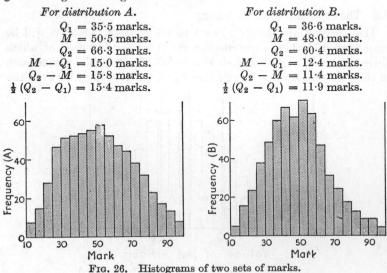

FIG. 26.   Histograms of two sets of marks.

It is apparent from the histograms that distribution A is more dispersed than distribution B although the ranges are equal. The semi-interquartile ranges, 15·4 and 11·9 marks, do however quantitatively discriminate between the two dispersions. The fact that $(M - Q_1) \gtreqless (Q_2 - M)$ in both cases shows that the distributions are not symmetrical; this difference between $(M - Q_1)$ and $(Q_2 - M)$ is sometimes used as a measure of asymmetry.

Statistical data are sometimes presented graphically in the form shown in Fig. 25, i.e., as ogive or cumulative frequency curves, but with the total frequency divided into 100 equal parts called *percentiles* (Fig. 27). The median, the upper and lower quartiles may therefore be regarded as the 50-, 75- and 25-percentiles respectively.

The use of percentiles in the analysis of examination marks is illustrated by the histograms (Fig. 26) and cumulative frequency diagrams (Fig. 27) representing the data of Table XII. Note that the cumulative frequencies are plotted against the upper class-limit values.

TABLE XII

FREQUENCY DISTRIBUTIONS OF MARKS IN TWO EXAMINATION PAPERS

Class	Frequency		Cumulative Frequency	
	A	*B*	*A*	*B*
11–15	8	5	8	5
16–20	15	16	23	21
21–25	39	24	62	45
26–30	47	39	109	84
31–35	52	50	161	134
36–40	53	61	214	195
41–45	54	68	268	263
46–50	56	63	324	326
51–55	59	72	383	398
56–60	53	65	436	463
61–65	48	48	484	511
66–70	45	32	529	543
71–75	39	25	568	568
76–80	32	18	600	586
81–85	23	13	623	599
86–90	17	9	640	608
91–95	13	9	653	617
96–100	8	5	661	622
	Total 661	622		

For A.

$Q_1 = \dfrac{661}{4}$ th variate value $= 35.5 + \left[\dfrac{165 \cdot 25 - 161}{214 - 161}\right] 5$

$= 35.90$

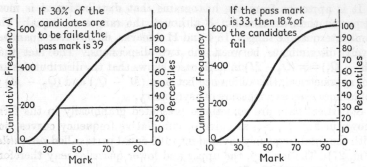

FIG. 27.   Cumulative frequency diagram of mark distributions.

3.4   The Mean Deviation

In the previous use of the deviation we have taken regard of the sign, e.g., in the case of deviations measured from the mean, some deviations are positive and some are negative, and the algebraic sum of these deviations from the mean is zero. If, however, the negative signs were disregarded the mean of the arithmetic values of these deviations from the mean would be a measure of the dispersion.

In Table XIII the deviations from the centre for the two simple symmetrical distributions are calculated. The symbol "d" stands for the deviation, and "$|d|$" (which is pronounced "mod. d") indicates that it is to be measured positively in all cases. The total deviations are found to be 10 and 14. These numbers could be used as measures of dispersion but it is usual to find the *mean deviations*, i.e., $\dfrac{10}{13}$ and $\dfrac{14}{13}$, so that the dispersion of distributions of different total frequencies may be compared. The two answers indicate, as would be expected, that the values of the first distribution are the more closely grouped about the centre. The mean is usually the most convenient centre

TABLE XIII

MEAN DEVIATION AS A MEASURE OF DISPERSION

x	f_1	f_2	$|d|$	$|f_1 d|$	$|f_2 d|$
9	1	2	2	2	4
10	3	3	1	3	3
11	5	3	0	0	0
12	3	3	1	3	3
13	1	2	2	2	4
Totals 13	13			10	14

from which to measure the deviation. It can be shown, however, that the mean deviation of a distribution is least when the deviations are measured from the median. It is therefore more logical to use the median rather than the mean. The proof in general terms that the mean deviation about the median is a minimum is cumbersome, and will not be given here.

TABLE XIV

CALCULATION OF THE MEAN DEVIATION ABOUT THE MEDIAN

Median of the distribution = 50·5 marks

x	f	$|d|$	$f|d|$
11–15	8	8	64
16–20	15	7	105
21–25	39	6	234
26–30	47	5	235
31–35	52	4	2(8
36–40	53	3	159
41–45	54	2	108
46–50	56	1	56
51–55	59	0	0
56–60	53	1	53
61–65	48	2	96
66–70	45	3	135
71–75	39	4	156
76–80	32	5	160
81–85	23	6	138
86–90	17	7	119
91–95	13	8	104
96–100	8	9	72
Totals 661			2,202

In Table XIV the method of calculating the mean deviation of distribution *A* of Table XII is shown for the cases in which the deviations are measured from the median. The deviations are first calculated in terms of class-intervals measured from the class-interval containing the median and then converted to marks. The result, 16·6 marks, should strictly be corrected for the fact that the deviations are calculated not from 50·5, the value of the median determined graphically, but from 53·0, the centre of the class-interval. This correction is small, however, and its application would suggest that the median is more accurately determinate than is in fact possible. Total deviation = 2,202 class intervals = 11,010 marks.

$$\text{Mean deviation about the median} = \frac{11,010}{661}$$
$$= 16\cdot6 \text{ marks.}$$

Using the mean deviation to compare the dispersions of distributions A and B of Table XII we have:

Mean deviation about the median
$$\text{Distribution } A = 16\cdot6 \text{ marks.}$$
$$\text{,,} \qquad B = 14\cdot0 \text{ marks.}$$

Mean deviation about the mean
$$\text{Distribution } A = 16\cdot8 \text{ marks.}$$
$$\text{,,} \qquad B = 14\cdot1 \text{ marks.}$$

The mean deviation about either the median or the mean as a measure of dispersion is seen to be both discriminating and easily computed.

EXERCISES VII

1. Combine distributions A and B of Table XII and prepare a graph from which can be read the percentage of candidates who reach any given mark. Find to the nearest whole mark the limiting marks that have to be reached if 10% are to be classified as "very good"; the next 25% as "passing with credit"; the next 40% as "passes" and the last 25% as "failures".

2. Confirm that the semi-interquartile range of distribution B of Table XII is 12·1 marks.

3. Show that the semi-interquartile ranges of the simple distributions C and D represented by the continuous and dotted straight lines of the figure are in the ratio of 2·42 : 1.

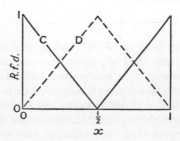

4. Calculate $\Sigma|fd|$ for each of the distributions P and Q, measuring the deviation in turn from each value of x. Plot a graph to show how $\Sigma|fd|$ varies with the origin of the measurements.

x	1	2	3	4	5	6	7	8	9
P: f	1	3	6	10	15	10	6	3	1
Q: f	15	10	6	3	1	3	6	10	15

5. A car manufacturer tested two types of speedometer by checking them for percentage error at 30 m.p.h. The results were:

% error	-5	-4	-3	-2	-1	0
Type X: f	3	6	10	14	13	11
Type Y: f	5	9	12	14	12	15

% error	$+1$	$+2$	$+3$	$+4$	$+5$	Total
Type X: f	14	8	2	2	0	83
Type Y: f	12	13	6	4	4	106

Find the mean error of each type.

6. Devise a simple measure of the "changeability" of the weather in your locality using the maximum daily temperature as the weather index.

MATHEMATICAL

7. Find, by a graphical method, the semi-interquartile ranges of the continuous distributions for which the range of x is O to π and the relative frequency functions are (a) $\dfrac{1}{\pi} \cdot x \sin x$, (b) $\dfrac{2}{\pi} \cdot \sin^2 x$.

8. Show that the mean deviation about the value x_1 for a continuous distribution with relative frequency density $f(x)$ and range a to b may be expressed as

$$\int_a^{x_1} (x_1 - x)f(x)dx + \int_{x_1}^b (x - x_1)f(x)dx$$

Use this result to verify the general rule that the mean deviation is a minimum when x_1 is the median, in the case for which $f(x) = 3x^2$.

3.5 The Standard Deviation

In the previous section the signs of negative deviations were ignored in finding the total deviation, but only at the expense of complicating the corresponding algebraic summations. This difficulty of signs may also be overcome by *squaring* the deviations. The mean of the squared deviations of a distribution about the mean is called the *variance*, but the direct use of the variance as a measure of dispersion has one major disadvantage. All the other measures of dispersion we have considered had the dimensions of the variable. To bring the new measure into line with this convention we therefore take the positive square root of the variance. The *standard deviation*, as it is now called, is denoted by s, and is therefore defined by

$$s = \sqrt{\frac{\Sigma fd^2}{N}}$$

where d = deviation from the mean,

N = total number of observations.

TABLE XV

CALCULATION OF THE STANDARD DEVIATION

1	2	3	4	5	6	7	8
x	f	d_1	fd_1	fd_1^2	(d_1+1)	$f(d_1+1)$	$f(d_1+1)^2$
11–15	8	−8	−64	512	−7	−56	392
16–20	15	−7	−105	735	−6	−90	540
21–25	39	−6	−234	1,404	−5	−195	975
26–30	47	−5	−235	1,175	−4	−188	752
31–35	52	−4	−208	832	−3	−156	468
36–40	53	−3	−159	477	−2	−106	212
41–45	54	−2	−108	216	−1	−54	54
46–50	56	−1	−56	56	0	−845	0
51–55	59	0	−1,169	0	1	59	59
56–60	53	1	53	53	2	106	212
61–65	48	2	96	192	3	144	432
66–70	45	3	135	405	4	180	720
71–75	39	4	156	624	5	195	975
76–80	32	5	160	800	6	192	1,152
81–85	23	6	138	828	7	161	1,127
86–90	17	7	119	833	8	136	1,088
91–95	13	8	104	832	9	117	1,053
96–100	8	9	72	648	10	80	800
	661		1,033	10,622		1,370	11,011
			Total −136			Total +525	

Check

$$\Sigma f(d_1+1)^2 - \Sigma fd_1^2 - 2\Sigma fd_1 = 11,011 - 10,622 + 2 \times 136$$
$$= 661 \text{ as required.}$$

Calculation

$$s^2 = \frac{C^2}{N} \left\{ \Sigma fd_1^2 - N(\Sigma fd_1/N)^2 \right\} = \frac{25}{661} \left\{ 10,622 - 661 \times \left(\frac{-136}{661} \right)^2 \right\}$$
$$= 400 \cdot 5$$
$$s = 20 \cdot 0 \text{ marks.}$$

The calculation of the standard deviation is explained with reference to the worked example in Table XV. The data is Distribution A of Table XII. The procedure is as follows:

(a) The frequency distribution is tabulated and the arithmetic mean and its check are worked out in the usual way in cols. 1, 2, 3, 4, 6 and 7.

(b) Col. 5 contains the products fd_1^2 obtained by multiplying the numbers of col. 4 by the corresponding numbers of col. 3. The sum of this column is found.

(c) Col. 8 contains the products $f(d_1 + 1)^2$, obtained from cols. 6 and 7. This column is also summed. It is required as a check on the correctness of the sum of col. 5. Since

$$\Sigma f(d_1 + 1)^2 - \Sigma fd_1^2 - 2\Sigma fd_1 = \Sigma f(d_1^2 + 2d_1 + 1 - d_1^2 - 2d_1)$$
$$= \Sigma f$$

it should be found that

Sum of col. 8 − sum of col. 5 − 2 × sum of col. 4 = sum of col. 2.

This checks the correctness of Σfd_1^2 and should always be carried out.

To prove the formula used in the calculation, let

d_1 = deviation from the working mean,

d = deviation from the arithmetic mean,

$\bar{x}$ = arithmetic mean,

x_0 = working mean,

C = class interval,

$N = \Sigma f$, the total number of observations,

$a = \bar{x} - x_0 = C\Sigma fd_1/N$

Then $d_1 = \dfrac{x - x_0}{C}$, from which

$$Cd_1 = x - x_0 = (x - \bar{x}) + (\bar{x} - x_0)$$
$$= d + a$$

Squaring, $C^2d_1^2 = d^2 + 2ad + a^2$

Multiplying by f, and summing for the whole distribution,

$$\Sigma fC^2d_1^2 = \Sigma fd^2 + \Sigma 2afd + \Sigma fa^2$$
$$= \Sigma fd^2 + 2a\Sigma fd + a^2N$$

since $\Sigma f = N$.

Note also that Σfd = sum of deviations about the mean, which is zero.

Therefore $\qquad \Sigma fC^2d_1^2 = \Sigma fd^2 + a^2N$

or $\Sigma fd^2 = C^2\Sigma fd_1^2 - a^2N$

Hence, $\qquad s^2 = \dfrac{1}{N}\Sigma fd^2 = \dfrac{C^2}{N}\left\{\Sigma fd_1^2 - N(\Sigma fd_1/N)^2\right\}$

from which s can be found.

The standard deviation of distribution A of Table XII is shown in Table XV to be 20·0. Similarly it may be shown that for distribution B, $s = 17\cdot0$.

The standard deviation has been of fundamental importance in the development of statistical theory. It is the measure of dispersion which is most frequently used in statistics.

Note that $|\Sigma fd|$ is a minimum when d is measured from the median; Σfd^2 is a minimum when, as in the standard deviation, d is measured from the mean.

The calculation of the variance is closely analogous to the finding of the moment of inertia of a plane lamina of the same shape as the histogram of the distribution about the axis in the plane through the centre of gravity. The variance is therefore sometimes called the *second moment* of the distribution. The standard deviation is analogous to the radius of gyration of the lamina.

Mathematical Note. For a continuous distribution the variance is given by

$$\sigma^2 = \int_a^b (x - \bar{x})^2 f(x)dx$$

$$= \int_a^b x^2 f(x)dx - 2\bar{x}\int_a^b xf(x)dx + \bar{x}^2\int_a^b f(x)dx$$

Since $\displaystyle\int_a^b xf(x)dx = \bar{x}$ and $\displaystyle\int_a^b f(x)dx = 1,$

we have $\displaystyle\sigma^2 = \int_a^b x^2 f(x)dx - \bar{x}^2.$

3.6 Comparison of Dispersions

To compare the dispersions of two distributions with different means it is sometimes useful to express the dispersions in a dimensionless form. This may be done by dividing the standard deviation by the mean, which also has the dimensions of the variable. The ratio $s/\bar{x}$ is therefore a number suitable for the required purpose. This quantity is known as the *Coefficient of Variation*.

Example. For the heights of mature black pine, $\bar{x} = 85$ft., $s = 10 \cdot 6$ ft.; for mature common spruce, $\bar{x} = 110$ ft., $s = 12 \cdot 2$ ft. Compare the variation of the two types of tree.

For the black pine $s/\bar{x} = 10 \cdot 6/85 = 0 \cdot 125$

For the common spruce, $s/\bar{x} = 12 \cdot 2/110 = 0 \cdot 111$

The black pine has therefore the larger coefficient of variation.

SUMMARY OF CHAPTER III

The four measures of dispersion are:

(a) The Range, which is equal to $x_n - x_1$,

(b) The Semi-interquartile Range, which is equal to $\frac{1}{2}(Q_2 - Q_1)$ and is determined graphically.

(c) The Mean Deviation from the Mean or from the Median, equal to $\frac{1}{N} \cdot \Sigma|fd|$.

(d) The Standard Deviation, s, which is the square root of the Variance. It is defined by $s^2 = \frac{1}{N} \cdot \Sigma fd^2$ where d is the deviation from the mean.

All these measures have the same dimensions as the variable.

EXERCISES VIII

STANDARD DEVIATION

1. One hundred rounds of each of two types of ammunition are fired from a clamped 0·22 in. rifle at a target 100 yds. distant. The height of the "strike" above a fixed line is measured to the nearest $\frac{1}{4}$ in. and the results are set out below:

Height ($\frac{1}{4}$ ins.)	8	9	10	11	12	13	14	15
Type P: $f =$	2	2	8	7	12	10	15	14
Type Q: $f =$	0	0	4	9	11	12	11	14

Height ($\frac{1}{4}$ ins.)	16	17	18	19	20	21	22
Type P: $f =$	12	8	7	2	0	1	0
Type Q: $f =$	13	10	8	2	1	3	2

Find the standard deviations of the vertical "spread" of the two types of ammunition.

2. The arithmetic mean and the standard deviation of a distribution are 32·3 and 15·7 units respectively. What is the mean square of the deviation measured from 36 units?

3. Find the standard deviation of the frequency distribution of 100 cricket scores collected by yourself.

4. Calculate the standard deviations of the data of (a) Table II; (b) Table VII.

5. Recalculate the arithmetic mean and standard deviation of distribution of Table XV after increasing the size of the class-interval (a) to 10 marks; (b) to 15 marks and compare your results with each other and with the results of Table XV.

6. In industry A the average weekly wage is 399·0 shillings with a standard deviation of 46·8 shillings. In industry B the corresponding figures are 314·1 shillings and 38·4 shillings. In which industry is the greater relative variation of wage found?

7. Using the data of Ex. XXXIV, 12, compare the relative variation of the lengths and breadths of beans.

ALGEBRAIC

8. Two distributions, with standard deviations s_1, s_2, means $\bar{x}_1$, $\bar{x}_2$ and populations N_1 and N_2 respectively, are combined. Show that the variance of the combined distribution is given by

$$(N_1 + N_2)\, s^2 = N_1 s_1^2 + N_2 s_2^2 + \frac{N_1 N_2}{N_1 + N_2}\, (\bar{x}_2 - \bar{x}_1)^2$$

Comment on this result when $\bar{x}_1 = \bar{x}_2$.
Find the standard deviation of the distribution $(A + B)$ using the values of s, $\bar{x}$ and N for the separate distributions given in Table XII.

9. Show that the standard deviation of the arithmetic progression $a, a + d, a + 2d, \ldots a + 2nd$, is greater than its mean deviation from the mean.

10. The deviation of a distribution is measured from a value differing from the mean of the distribution by x. Show that if x is plotted against the corresponding mean square deviation the points lie on a parabola.

11. If δ = mean square deviation about x, σ = standard deviation and $x - \bar{x} = a$, then it has been shown that

$$\delta^2 = \sigma^2 + a^2$$

State an analogous theorem from the theory of the dynamics of a rigid body.

12. Show that if a variable has the values 0, 1, 2 ... 9, and frequencies $^9C_0, {}^9C_1, {}^9C_2 \ldots {}^9C_9$ respectively, then $\sigma = 1\cdot5$.

MISCELLANEOUS NUMERICAL

13. Find the dispersions of the data of Table VIII, using all four measures of dispersion. Comment on the results obtained and state which is the most suitable measure to use.

14. Use the standard deviation as a measure of the dispersions of the two distributions of Ex. VI, 23.

15. Compare the horizontal and vertical dispersions of a machine-gun which, in firing a total of 1,000 rounds, gave the following distributions on a target marked in foot squares numbered in the two directions from a corner:

Square No.	1	2	3	4	5	6	7	8	9	10	11
Horizontal	1	35	47	98	206	219	187	155	45	6	1
Vertical	4	12	66	176	231	189	111	98	85	23	5

16. Find the mean deviation from the mean and the semi-interquartile range for each of the two distributions of Ex. VI, 25.

17. Calculate the standard deviations of Woo's measurements of the left and right frontal bones. The distributions are the totals of those given in Ex. XXXIV, 10.

18. The triangulation errors of two surveyors A and B are noted after all systematic corrections have been made. Calculate the standard deviations of the error distributions and hence compare the accuracy of the two surveyors.

Error (secs.)	−6	−5	−4	−3	−2	−1	0
A	3	4	6	8	4	10	29
B	2	1	4	7	9	12	33

Error (secs.)	1	2	3	4	5	6	Totals
A	5	9	7	6	6	3	100
B	8	4	12	5	1	2	100

19. Draw histograms of the distributions A, B and C. Calculate the standard deviations of A and B and hence obtain that of C. Explain your method and verify your result by direct calculation.

x	1	2	3	4	5	6	7	8	9	10
A	5	4	3	2	1	1	2	3	4	5
B	6	6	6	6	6	6	6	6	6	6
C	1	2	3	4	5	5	4	3	2	1

20. Three distributions each of 100 members and standard deviation 4·5 units are located with their arithmetic means at 12·1, 17·1 and 22·1 units respectively. Find the standard deviation of the distribution obtained by combining the three.

GENERAL

21. Describe how you would compare the accuracy of two types of ammunition which, when fired from the same clamped rifle, give roughly circular patterns of hits on a fixed target.

22. Briefly describe three methods of measuring the spread of frequency distributions. Comment on the uses and limitations of these methods.

23. The frequency polygon of a distribution of population N, mean $\bar{x}$ and standard deviation s, is shown in the diagram.

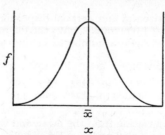

Copy the diagram and add sketches of the frequency polygons of two other distributions X and Y, each also of population N and mean $\bar{x}$, but with standard deviations of $\frac{1}{2}s$ and $2s$ respectively.

On a second copy of the diagram add sketches of two distributions P and Q, each of mean $\bar{x}$ and standard deviation s but with populations of $\frac{1}{2}N$ and $2N$ respectively.

24. A frequency distribution has values $x_1, x_2, \ldots x_n$ with frequencies $f_1, f_2, \ldots f_n$ respectively; it has arithmetic mean $\bar{x}$ and standard deviation s. Examine the distribution which has values $\mu_1, \mu_2 \ldots \mu_n$ with frequencies $f_1, f_2 \ldots f_n$ respectively where $\mu_r = \dfrac{x_r - \bar{x}}{s}$

Show that its mean is zero and its variance unity. Explain how distributions in different populations may be compared in form by transforming them to this dimensionless "standard measure".

MATHEMATICAL

25. Show that the standard deviation of the frequency curve $y = ae^{-ax}$ where x takes all values from 0 to ∞ is $1/a$.

26. Find the variances of the frequency curves (a) $y = \dfrac{1}{\pi} x . \sin x$ $(0 \leqslant x \leqslant \pi)$; (b) $y = \dfrac{2}{\pi} . \sin^2 x$ $(0 \leqslant x \leqslant \pi)$.

27. A continuous distribution has the frequency density function $\dfrac{k}{a^2 + x^2}$ where k is a constant and $a\sqrt{3} \geqslant x \geqslant -a$. Find k, $\bar{x}$ and σ when $a = 7\pi$.

CHAPTER IV

Probability

4.1 Introduction

The theory of probability plays a very important part in the methods used to arrange and analyse statistical data. Before some of the essential ideas about probability are discussed it is necessary to note certain results from the algebra of permutations and combinations which are used later.

THEOREM. If an event can take place in n_1 ways and, when this event has happened, a second event can take place in n_2 ways then the number of ways in which the two events can take place is $n_1 \times n_2$.

PROOF. When the first event has happened the second can occur in n_2 ways. But the first event can happen in n_1 ways with each of which the second event can be associated in n_2 ways. Therefore the number of ways in which the two events can take place is $n_1 \times n_2$.

Example 1. A French and an English interpreter are selected from a group of 8 people consisting of 5 French and 3 English interpreters. In how many different ways may the pair be chosen?

The French interpreter can be picked in 5 different ways and the English interpreter in 3. Therefore the number of different pairs which can be chosen is 5×3 or 15.

Example 2. Five competitors enter a race. In how many different ways may the first and second prizes be allotted?

The race may be won by any of the 5 competitors so there are 5 ways in which the first prize may be awarded. When the race has been won by 1 competitor the second place may be taken by any of the 4 remaining competitors. Therefore the number of ways in which the first and second prizes may be allotted is 5×4 or 20.

Corollary 1. If r events take place in order and the first event can happen in n_1 ways, and then the second event can happen in n_2 ways, and finally the last event can happen in n_r ways, then the total number of ways in which the r events can take place is

$$n_1 \times n_2 \ldots \times n_r.$$

Example 3. Four new pupils arrive at a school in which there are 5 houses. In how many ways may the pupils be appointed to a house so that they are all in different houses?

One pupil may be appointed to a house in 5 different ways. A second pupil may then be appointed to a house in 4 ways since he cannot go to the same house as the first pupil. Similarly a third pupil may be appointed in 3 ways and the fourth and last in 2 ways. Therefore the total number of ways in which the pupils can be placed in different houses is 5 × 4 × 3 × 2 or 120.

Corollary 2. If *r* events can each take place in order in *n* ways the total number of ways in which the *r* events can take place is n^r. This can be obtained immediately from Corollary 1 by putting

$$n_1 = n_2 \ldots = n_r = n.$$

Example 4. A coin is tossed 5 times. How many different sequences of heads and tails can be obtained?

There are 5 events and each can happen in 2 ways, either a head or a tail. The number of different sequences is therefore 2^5 or 32.

Example 5. About 1950, car registration numbers changed to 3 letters and 3 figures whereas formerly 2 letters and 4 figures were used. Assuming that all letters from *A* to *Z* and all numbers from 0 to 9 are employed show that the new method of registration allowed for approximately 2·6 the number of cars covered by the old method.

A single number can be chosen from 0 to 9 in 10 ways and so 3 numbers allowed for can be chosen in 10^3 ways. From these the number 000 must be excluded so that there are $10^3 - 1$ different combinations of numbers.

A single letter can be chosen in 26 ways and so there are 26^3 combinations of 3 letters each of which is associated with $10^3 - 1$ combinations of numbers so that with the new method there are altogether $26^3 \times (10^3 - 1)$ registration numbers.

Similarly it can be shown that with the old method there are $26^2 \times (10^4 - 1)$ possible registration numbers.

Therefore the ratio of new to old possible registration numbers is

$$\frac{26^3 \times 999}{26^2 \times 9999} = \frac{26 \times 111}{1111} \text{ or approximately 2·6.}$$

EXERCISES IX

1. A fiction and a non-fiction book are selected from a bookshelf containing 12 fiction and 30 non-fiction books. In how many ways can the choice be made?

2. In Example 2 of Section 4.1 call the competitors *A*, *B*, *C*, *D* and *E*. Write down the 20 possible ways in which the first and second prizes may be awarded.

3. There are 4 candidates for a classical, 3 for a mathematical and 8 for a history scholarship. In how many ways may the scholarships be awarded?

4. A change is rung with 7 bells, each bell being rung once. How many possible changes can be rung?

5. How may combinations of number, consonant and vowel can be made from "20 Players"? Write out all the possible combinations, e.g., 2, *y*, *a*; 0, *s*, *a*; etc.

6. In a throw of 2 dice how many ways can they fall? Write down all the possible results.

7. The result of a game may be either a win, a loss or a draw. How many possible series of results are there for a series of 6 matches?

8. In how many ways can 4 prizes be awarded to 3 boys when each boy is eligible for all the prizes?

9. A number lock has 4 rings each with 10 different numbers (0–9). How many attempts may be made to open the lock by a person ignorant of the combination?

10. A country issues state registration cards with 4 letters followed by a number of exactly 3 figures, e.g., *SBAL*/239. The figures 0 and 1 are not to be used and no letter beyond *T*. How many cards can be prepared?

11. A six-sided die is rolled 4 times. How many possible sequences of numbers can be obtained?

12. In a family of 5 each member decides to register with a different doctor under the National Health Scheme. There are 9 doctors available. How many possible ways may this family register?

4.2 ^nC_r, the Number of Combinations of n Things r at a Time

Four tickets are lettered a, b, c and d. Two tickets may be chosen from them in 4×3 or 12 ways which can be written as

ab	ba	ca	da
ac	bc	cb	db
ad	bd	cd	dc

If the order of the letters is not significant in the sense that drawing a and then b is not distinguishable from drawing b and then a, then ab is the same event as ba. In the table above it can be seen that there are 6 such events. The number of different combinations of 4 things taken 2 at a time is therefore 6.

Another way of expressing this is to say that 6 is the number of ways of choosing two tickets from four so that no pair contains the same tickets as any other pair. The conventional short hand notation for this is $^4C_2$ so that $^4C_2 = 6$.

THEOREM. ^nC_r, the number of combinations of n things taken r at a time is given by

$$^nC_r = n(n-1)(n-2)...(n-r+1)/r(r-1)(r-2)...3 \times 2 \times 1$$

PROOF. Suppose n tickets are numbered $1, 2, 3 ... n$. A number of tickets, r, is to be drawn.

The first ticket can be drawn in n ways.
A second ticket can then be drawn in $(n-1)$ ways.
A third ticket can then be drawn in $(n-2)$ ways and, finally,
the rth ticket can then be drawn in $(n-r+1)$ ways.

Therefore using Corollary 1 the total number of ways in which r tickets can be chosen is given by

$$N = n(n-1)(n-2)\ldots(n-r+1)$$

Consider now any set of r tickets occurring in the N sets say, for simplicity, the tickets which are numbered $1, 2, 3 \ldots r$. Every possible arrangement of this set is included in N and again using Corollary 1 the number of all possible arrangements is

$$r(r-1)(r-2)\ldots 3 \times 2 \times 1.$$

so that (^nC_r, the number of combinations of n tickets taken r at a time) $\times$ (the number of possible arrangements of a single set of r tickets) = (the total number of ways in which r tickets may be chosen from n) or

$$^nC_r \times r(r-1)(r-2)\ldots 3.2.1 =$$
$$n(n-1)(n-2)\ldots(n-r+1) \quad . \quad . \quad (1)$$

THE FACTORIAL NOTATION

It is customary to write

$$n! \text{ for } n(n-1)\ldots 3 \times 2 \times 1$$
$$r! \text{ for } r(r-1)\ldots 3 \times 2 \times 1, \text{etc.}$$

For example $5! = 5 \times 4 \times 3 \times 2 \times 1 = 120$.

Using this notation a convenient expression can be found for $n(n-1)\ldots(n-r+1)$,

since $n! = n(n-1)\ldots(n-r+1)(n-r)(n-r-1)\ldots 3 \times 2 \times 1$
$$= n(n-1)\ldots(n-r+1)(n-r)!$$

or $n(n-1)\ldots(n-r+1) = n!/(n-r)!$

Referring to equation (1) ^nC_r can now be written

$$^nC_r = n!/(n-r)!\, r!$$

Example 1.—There are three similar vacancies for which there are five applicants. In how many ways can applicants be chosen to fill the vacancies?

This is simply the number of ways in which three candidates can be chosen from five without repeating any group of three or

$$^5C_3 = \frac{5!}{3!\,2!} = \frac{5\times4\times3\times2\times1}{3\times2\times1\times2\times1} = 10$$

Example 2.—Show that $^nC_r = \dfrac{n-r+1}{r}\,{}^nC_{r-1}$ and deduce that $^nC_0 = 1$.

$$^nC_r = \frac{n!}{(n-r)!\,r!} = \frac{n!}{(n-r+1)!\,(r-1)!} \times \frac{n-r+1}{r}$$
$$= {}^nC_{r-1} \times \frac{n-r+1}{r}$$

Put $r = 1$ then $^nC_1 = {}^nC_0 \times n$

But $^nC_1 = \dfrac{n!}{(n-1)!\,1!} = n$ therefore $^nC_0 = 1$.

Example 3.—In how many different ways may n things be divided into groups of p, q, and r where $p + q + r = n$?

The number of combinations of n things taken p at a time is ^nC_p. With each of these combinations the remaining $(n - p)$ things can be taken q at a time in $^{n-p}C_q$ ways. So the total number of ways is

$$^nC_p \times {}^{n-p}C_p = \frac{n!}{p!\,(n-p)!} \times \frac{(n-p)!}{q!\,(n-p-q)!} = \frac{n!}{p!\,q!\,r!}$$

EXERCISES X

1. Using equation (1) calculate $^4C_2$, $^9C_5$, $^6C_4$, $^{10}C_1$, $^{10}C_9$ and $^{10}C_5$.

2. A cricket team is selected from 14 possible players. How many different combinations of players can be chosen?

3. It is considered that the only way to maintain peace between 6 countries is to have non-aggression pacts between every possible pair of countries. How many pacts are necessary?

4. In a rowing eight, 2 men can only row stroke side and 3 can only row bow side. How many different ways are there of arranging the crew?

5. Use Example 3 to find how many ways a tennis party of 10 people can be split up into 2 fours and a pair.

6. A bag contains 6 black balls and 3 white balls.

    (a) In how many ways can 4 balls be drawn from the bag?

    (b) In how many ways can 4 black balls be drawn?

    (c) In how many ways can 3 black balls and 1 white ball be drawn?

7. A customer buying a dozen eggs always examines a sample of 3 to see if they are fresh. In how many ways can she pick the sample? If the dozen includes 3 bad eggs in how many ways can she take a sample which includes at least one bad egg?

8. A coin is tossed 4 times. Show that the number of different sequences of heads and tails is 16. In how many ways can sequences be obtained containing 0, 1, 2, 3 and 4 heads respectively? Verify that the sum of these ways is 16.

9. Generalise the result of question 8 to a sequence of n tosses and show that $2^n = \sum_0^n C_r$.

10. A die is a cube with its sides numbered 1 to 6. Two dice are thrown. In how many ways can an even score be obtained?

11. In Exercise 10 in how many ways can a score of 6 be obtained?

12. A claim to clairvoyancy is tested by asking the professed clairvoyant to choose the 4 red cards from a concealed hand containing 4 red cards and 4 black. The clairvoyant is in fact a charlatan and chooses the cards entirely at random.

(a) In how many ways can he choose any 4 cards?

(b) In how many ways can he choose 3 red and 1 black?

13. Show that $^nC_r = {^nC_{n-r}}$.

14. If $^{2n}C_2 = 5^nC_2$ find n.

15. If $^{16}C_r = {^{16}C_{r+2}}$ find $^rC_3$.

16. In how many ways may n books be given to p persons when there is no restriction on how many books each person may receive?

17. A box contains w white marbles and r red marbles. Show that the total number of selections of some or all of the marbles is $(w+1)(r+1) - 1$. (Hint. The white marbles may be disposed of in $w + 1$ ways since we may take $0, 1, 2 \ldots w$ of them.)

18. In Exercise 17 take $w = 3$ and $r = 2$ and denote by w^sr^t a selection consisting of s white and t red marbles. Write down the total number of possible selections.

19. Of $w + r + c$ marbles w are white, r are red and the rest are different colours. Show that the total number of different selections is $(w + 1)(r + 1) 2^c - 1$.

20. There are m boxes of which the first contains n balls; the second $2n$ balls; the third $3n$ balls and so on. Show that the number of ways of taking n balls out of each box is $\dfrac{(mn)!}{(n!)^m}$.

(Hint. For the first, second and third boxes the number of ways are respectively ^nC_n, $^{2n}C_n$, $^{3n}C_n$.)

4.3   The Definition of Probability

If an action can have any one of n equally likely results and if r of these results produce an event E and the remainder do not produce E then the probability or chance of E occurring as a result of the action is defined to be $p(E) = r/n$.

For example let the action be the rolling of a six-sided die and let the event E be an odd score. The action can have six results all of which are equally likely, namely obtaining a score of $1, 2 \ldots$ or 6. Of these six results three are favourable to the event namely scores of $1, 3$ or 5. From the definition of probability therefore, the probability or chance of obtaining an odd score is $3/6$ or $1/2$.

In an elementary treatment it is not possible to give a completely rigorous definition of probability. The reader is invited to criticise the above definition which, nevertheless, can be accepted as adequate for the purposes of this book.

Example 1.—A bag contains 9 balls, two of which are red, three blue, and four black. Three balls are drawn from the bag at random, that is every ball has an equal chance of being included in the three. What is the chance that

    (i) the three balls are different colours?

    (ii) two balls are the same colour and the third different?

    (iii) the balls are all the same colour?

(i) The number of ways in which three balls can be drawn from 9 is

$$^9C_3 = \frac{9!}{6!\ 3!} = 84,$$ and these are all equally likely results.

A red ball can be drawn in 2 ways, and blue in 3 and a black in 4 so that the total number of ways of drawing three differently coloured balls is $2 \times 3 \times 4 = 24$. Therefore the required chance is 24/84 or 2/7.

(ii) Two red balls can be drawn only in one way and then a blue or black ball in 7 ways so that two red balls and another colour can be drawn in 1×7 or 7 ways.

Two blue balls can be drawn in $^3C_2$ ways and then a red or black ball in 6 ways, so that two blue balls and another colour can be drawn in $6 \times {}^3C_2$ or 18 ways.

Two black balls can be drawn in $^4C_2$ ways and then another colour in 5 ways so that two black and another colour can be drawn in $5 \times {}^4C_2$ or 30 ways.

The total number of ways in which two balls of the same colour and a third of a different colour may be drawn is $7 + 18 + 30 = 55$. Therefore the required chance is 55/84

(iii) Three blue balls can be drawn in 1 way and 3 black in $^4C_3$ or 4 ways so that the total number of ways of drawing three balls of the same colour is 5 and the chance is 5/84.

Example 2.—A hand of five cards is dealt from a well shuffled pack. What is the probability that the hand consists of five cards in sequence but not necessarily of the same suit?

The number of ways in which 5 cards can be drawn from 52 is $^{52}C_5$.

Consider any particular sequence say 8, 9, 10, J and Q. Each card can be any one of 4 suits so the number of sequences starting with 8 is 4^5. Also there are 9 possible sequences from A, 2, 3, 4, and 5 to 9, 10, J, Q and K. Therefore the total number of ways of dealing a sequence of 5 cards is 9×4^5 and the required chance is given by $9 \times 4^5/{}^{52}C_5$ or approximately 1/282.

4.4 Certainty and Impossibility

If an action can have any one of n results and if all of these results produce an event E then the chance that E will happen is, by definition n/n or 1. In these conditions it is absolutely certain that the event E must happen and so certainty is represented by 1 in the numerical measure of probability.

In the same way if none of the results produce an event E it is impossible that E should happen as a consequence of the action. The chance that E should happen is $0/n$ or 0. Thus impossibility is represented by 0 in the numerical measure of probability. Any probability p, therefore, is a number such that $0 \leqslant p \leqslant 1$.

The words certainty and impossibility are sometimes used loosely and it is interesting to consider their implications a little further. The colloquial use of "certain" and "impossible" very often denote no more than a reasonable degree of belief or disbelief. The journalist who wrote "This cut [in tobacco imports] is certain to lead to grave industrial unrest" was merely stating an opinion which, however probable, could not in the mathematical sense be called a certainty. Then again the words an "impossible task" are sometimes used to describe, not a failure, but some unusually praiseworthy achievement. It would be pedantic to insist on the exact use of these words in every case, but it is important to remember that in probability theory "certain" and "impossible" have a precise meaning.

EXERCISES XI

1. Five cards are drawn at random from a pack. Find the chance that they are all from the same suit.

2. Two dice are thrown. What are the probabilities that the total score is 5; 1; 10; 14; and that the total score is less than 13?

3. If a letter be taken at random from the word "polyanthus" what is the chance that it is a vowel?

4. What is the chance that a card drawn at random from a pack is (a) an ace, (b) the ace of spades?

5. What is the chance of throwing a number greater than 4 with a die?

6. What is the chance of throwing at least one 6 in a throw of 3 dice?

7. In drawing 4 cards from a pack what is the chance that one should be from each suit?

8. A black card has been removed from a pack. Two cards are drawn at random. What is the probability that they will be (a) both red, (b) both black?

9. What is the chance of throwing a number higher than 9 with 2 dice?

10. Out of 10 steel valve springs 3 are defective. Two springs are chosen at random for testing. What is the probability that both test specimens are (a) not defective, (b) defective?

11. In Exercise 10, what is the chance of not getting a defective spring if 3 springs are tested. Draw a graph showing P against n where $P =$ chance of getting no defective springs in the sample and $n =$ sample size ($n = 1, 2 \ldots 5$).

12. A box contains $2N$ balls of which $2M$ are white. A second box contains $3N$ balls of which $3M$ are white. Two balls are drawn from each box. Which box is more likely to give both white balls as a result?

4.5 Total Probability or the Probability of "Either—or"

In tossing a coin either a head or a tail may turn up but both events cannot happen in one throw. The events are then said to be "mutually exclusive". In a single throw of a die scores of $1, 2 \ldots 6$ are mutually exclusive events. The occurrence of any score necessarily excludes all the others.

THEOREM. If E_1 and E_2 are two mutually exclusive events with probabilities p_1 and p_2 then the probability, p, that either E_1 or E_2 will happen is given by $p = p_1 + p_2$.

PROOF. An action has any one of n equally likely results of which r_1 produce E_1, and r_2 produce E_2, and no r_1 belongs to r_2. Then $r_1 + r_2$ results will produce either E_1 or E_2, so that by definition p, the probability of either E_1 or E_2 occurring is given by

$$p = \frac{r_1 + r_2}{n}$$

But p_1, the probability of E_1 occurring is given by $p_1 = r_1/n$ and similarly $p_2 = r_2/n$, so that $p = p_1 + p_2$.

This result can readily be extended to N mutually exclusive events $E_1, E_2 \ldots E_N$ with probabilities $p_1, p_2, \ldots p_N$, so that the total probability p (the probability of either E_1 or $E_2 \ldots$ or E_N) is given by

$$p = p_1 + p_2 + \ldots + p_N$$

Corollary. If p is the probability that an event E will happen then the probability q that the event will not happen is given by $q = 1 - p$. For it is certain that the event must either happen or not happen and therefore $p + q = 1$ or $q = 1 - p$.

4.6 Compound Probability or the Probability of "Both—and"

If a coin is tossed and a die is thrown there is a probability of $\frac{1}{2}$ that the coin will come down heads and a probability of $1/6$ that the die will give a score of 6. These events are called "independent" since the result of the coin could have no effect on the die nor can the result of the die have any effect on the coin.

THEOREM. If E_1 and E_2 are two independent events with probabilities p_1 and p_2, then the chance p that both E_1 and E_2 occur is given by $p = p_1 \times p_2$.

PROOF. Suppose that out of n_1 results r_1 entail E_1 and out of n_2 results r_2 entail E_2 so that $p_1 = r_1/n_1$ and $p_2 = r_2/n_2$.

There are $n_1 \times n_2$ combinations of all the different results and out of these there are $r_1 \times r_2$ combinations of results which entail both E_1 and E_2 so that by definition p, the probability of both E_1 and E_2 occurring is given by

$$p = \frac{r_1 \times r_2}{n_1 \times n_2}$$

so that $p = p_1 \times p_2$

This result can be extended to N independent events $E_1, E_2 \ldots ,$ E_N with probabilities $p_1, p_2 \ldots p_N$ so that the compound probability p (the probability of $E_1, E_2 \ldots E_N$ together) is given by $p = p_1 \times p_2 \times \ldots p_N$.

This theorem can be extended to events which are not independent by considering them in a specified order of occurrence. If p_1 is the probability of E_1 and if, when E_1 has happened p_2 is the probability of E_2, then the probability p of E_1 and then E_2 is given by

$$p = p_1 \times p_2.$$

Example 1.—A bag contains 4 red balls and 3 blue balls. Two drawings of 2 balls are made. Find the chance that the first drawing gives 2 red balls and the second drawing 2 blue balls,

(a) if the balls are returned to the bag after the first draw

(b) if the balls are not returned.

(a) The number of ways in which any two balls may be drawn is $^7C_2$. The number of ways in which two red balls may be drawn is $^4C_2$. Therefore the probability of drawing two red balls is $^4C_2/^7C_2 =$
$$\frac{4 \times 3}{7 \times 6} = \frac{2}{7}$$
Similarly the probability of drawing two blue balls is $^3C_2/^7C_2 =$
$$\frac{3 \times 2}{7 \times 6} = \frac{1}{7}$$

Therefore the chance of the compound event is $\dfrac{2}{7} \times \dfrac{1}{7} = \dfrac{2}{49}$

(b) As before the chance of drawing two red balls is $\frac{2}{7}$. The balls are not returned to the bag and the number of ways in which a further two balls may be drawn is $^5C_2$, so that the chance of drawing two blue balls is given by $^3C_2/^5C_2 = \dfrac{3 \times 2}{5 \times 4} \quad \dfrac{3}{10}$ and the chance of the compound

event is $\dfrac{3}{35}$.

In (a) of this example the two events are independent, but in (b) they are clearly not independent since the chance of drawing two blue is affected by the first draw.

Example 2.—A biased coin is tossed a large number of times and it is observed that 3 out of 5 times it comes down heads. What is the chance in 4 throws of getting 2 heads and 2 tails?

The probability of getting a head is $\frac{3}{5}$ and that of a tail is $\frac{2}{5}$. The chance therefore of getting any particular arrangement of 2 heads and 2 tails is $(\frac{3}{5})^2 \times (\frac{2}{5})^2$. The number of possible arrangements of two heads and two tails is $^4C_2$ and the required chance is therefore

$$^4C_2 \, (\tfrac{3}{5})^2 \times (\tfrac{2}{5})^2 = \tfrac{216}{625}$$

Example 3.—The probabilities of N independent events are p_1, $p_2 \ldots p_N$. Find an expression for the probability that at least one of the events will happen. Use the result to find the chance of obtaining at least one 6 in a throw of four dice.

For each event the chance that it will not happen is given by $(1 - p_1), (1 - p_2) \ldots (1 - p_N)$. The chance therefore that none of the events happens is given by $(1 - p_1) (1 - p_2) \ldots (1 - p_N)$, and since it is certain either that no event will happen or that at least one event will happen the probability that at least one event will happen is given by $1 - (1 - p_1) (1 - p_2) \ldots (1 - p_N)$.

The probability of obtaining a 6 in a throw of a die is 1/6 so that, using the above result the chance of at least one 6 in a throw of four dice is given by

$$1 - (\tfrac{5}{6})^4 = \tfrac{625}{1296}.$$

The method used in this example should be noted. The calculation of the probability that an event will happen is often simplified by first finding the probability that the event will not happen.

Example 4.—A and B alternately cut a pack of cards and the pack is shuffled after each cut. If A starts and the game is continued until one cuts a diamond, what are the respective chances of A and B first cutting a diamond?

The chance that A will win at his first cut is $\frac{1}{4}$; the chance of his winning at his second cut is the product of the probability that neither A nor B cut a diamond and the probability that A cuts a diamond at his second cut or $(\frac{3}{4})^2\frac{1}{4}$. Therefore A's total chance of winning is given by

$$p_A = \tfrac{1}{4} + (\tfrac{3}{4})^2 \tfrac{1}{4} + (\tfrac{3}{4})^4 \tfrac{1}{4} + \cdots$$

$$= \frac{1}{4} \cdot \frac{1}{1 - (\tfrac{3}{4})^2} = \frac{4}{7}$$

Similarly B's total chance of winning is given by

$$p_B = \tfrac{3}{4} \cdot \tfrac{1}{4} + (\tfrac{3}{4})^3 \cdot \tfrac{1}{4} + (\tfrac{3}{4})^5 \tfrac{1}{4} \cdot$$

$$= \frac{3}{16} \cdot \frac{1}{1 - (\tfrac{3}{4})^2} = \frac{3}{7}$$

It will be observed that p_B could have been written down immediately from the relation

$$p_B = 1 - p_A.$$

EXERCISES XII

1. A coin and a die are thrown together. What is the chance of a head and a 3 or a tail and a 4 turning up?

2. The chances of four competitors in a race breaking the record are $\tfrac{1}{4}$, $\tfrac{1}{3}$, $\tfrac{2}{3}$, and $\tfrac{1}{2}$ respectively. What is the probability that the record will be broken?

3. A Gallup Poll establishes that 3 out of 5 people are in favour of a certain proposal. What is the chance that if three people are taken at random there will be a majority against the proposal?

4. A, B and C throw a die in that order and the first to throw a six is to win a prize. What are their respective chances?

5. In a certain town the proportion of rainy to fine days in the month of September is 1 to 3. Assuming that each day is independent of the others what is the chance that a week in September in that town will have (a) no wet days, (b) two wet days?

6. In a bag are 8 balls, 7 black and 1 white. Six black balls are in a second bag. Five balls are taken from the first bag and placed in the second and then five balls are taken from the second bag and placed in the first. What is the probability that the white ball is now in the first bag?

7. A and B draw in that order from a hand of 8 cards containing two aces and the cards are not replaced. What are their respective chances of first drawing an ace?

8. At a round table conference of 10 members the seats are allocated at random. What is the chance that two particular members will sit together?

9. In a large batch of screws 5% are defective. The batch is so large that the chance of obtaining a defective screw is unaltered by sampling. What is the chance of getting at least one defective in samples of 5, 10, 15 and 20 respectively?

10. The respective probabilities that two independent events A and B will occur are p_1 and p_2. Denote by A and $\bar{B}$ the non-occurrence of A and B. Write down the probabilities of AB, $\bar{A}B$, $A\bar{B}$ and $\bar{A}\bar{B}$ and show that their sum is unity.

11. A bag contains r red balls and w white balls where r is greater than w. If they are drawn one by one, show that the chance of drawing first a red, then a white, and so on alternately until only red balls are left is $r!\,w!/(r+w)!$

12. What is the chance that of 24 people selected at random the birthdays of two or more will fall on the same day?

(Hint. Write down the total number of ways in which the birthdays can occur and also the number of ways in which they can occur with the restriction that no two birthdays fall on the same day. Use the approximation $365 \times 364 \times \ldots \times 342 = (353 \cdot 5)^{24}$.)

13. Assuming that the chance of a child being male or female is $\frac{1}{2}$, what is the probability that in a family of 8 there will not be fewer than 3 or more than 5 girls? What is the chance that there will be four girls?

14. A set of 8 cards contains one joker. A and B divide the hand at random, A taking 5 cards and B taking 3. What is the probability that A has the joker? A now throws away 4 cards and B 2, so that each has only one card left. Assuming that the joker has not been discarded what is now the probability that A has the joker?

15. A coin is tossed $2n$ times. What is the probability, $p(2n)$, that there will be the same number of heads as tails? By considering the expressions for $p(2n)$ and $p(2n+2)$ show that this probability decreases as n increases. Illustrate this by calculating $p(2)$, $p(4)$, $p(6)$ and $p(8)$.

4.7 Random Sampling

A sample is a number of objects, one or more, selected from a population or aggregate of similar objects. Thus a dealer buying apples will examine one or two in each barrel. This is his sample which he uses to give him some indication of the quality of the stock. Again in a fuel economy survey the investigators may visit 1,000 families in a town to find out how much electricity is used in the town for domestic purposes. These families are a sample from all the possible families which might be visited. A metallurgist determining the hardness of a steel plate will make a number of separate determinations at different points. These constitute a sample of the very large number of points at which he could take his readings.

So far we have used the word "random" without any explanation or definition since most readers will have some idea of what "randomness" means, although they might find it difficult to express in precise terms. We shall define the expression "random sample" as follows:

DEFINITION. The words "random sample" are a convenient abbreviation of the longer but more accurate phrase "a sample chosen in a random way". A sample is chosen in a random way when every possible sample has an equal chance of being picked.

Suppose a random sample of 3 is to be chosen from a group of 10 men. There are $^{10}C_3$ $=120$ possible selections and the sample will only be random if the selection is made in such a way that every possible sample has an equal chance of being chosen. A bridge hand dealt from a well shuffled pack is a random sample of 13 cards and every possible combination of cards has an equal chance of being dealt, even the sensational "freak" which consists of 13 cards of the same suit.

The object in taking a sample is to learn something about the aggregate and the accuracy of the information will be impaired if the sample is biased so that it is likely to include a large proportion of the exceptional members of the aggregate. If the dealer takes his apples from the top of the barrel he will get fewer bruised apples than if he had taken them from the bottom, and will therefore get a much better impression of the quality of the fruit. If the fuel economist chooses all his families from the lower income group he may underestimate the domestic electricity consumption, since appliances such as electric radiators and cookers are not so common as among the higher income group. The metallurgist will not take all his readings round the edge of the plate where there is a tendency for the metal to be harder, giving an overestimate of the average hardness of the plate.

The problem of bias in sampling can be overcome by ensuring that a random sample is selected, and this often entails a great deal of careful thought. A method which is sometimes adopted is to allot to each member of the aggregate a numbered card and then, having mixed the cards thoroughly, to draw as many cards as equal the sample it is intended to take. For example it was decided to examine medically a sample of workers on a chemical process. A random sample of 10 was chosen from the 78 men involved by giving each man a number from 1 to 78. Seventy-eight cards were then numbered and thoroughly mixed. Ten cards were drawn bearing numbers 52, 8, 11, 43, 39, 72, 19, 61, 12, 50 and the men corresponding to these numbers were examined.

When the number of the aggregate which is being sampled is very large this method becomes impracticable owing to the difficulty of mixing a large number of cards which have a tendency to bind together in small packets. It would be very difficult to choose a random sample of 1,000 families from an aggregate of 20,000 by numbering and shuffling cards. To meet this problem L. H. C. Tippett constructed tables of Random Sampling Numbers which consist of 10,400 four-figure numbers. The digits of these numbers were taken from census reports and their randomness has been confirmed by numerous statistical tests.

TABLE XVI

TWENTY SETS OF TIPPETT'S RANDOM SAMPLING NUMBERS

2952	9792	7979	7002	8126
4167	2762	7203	5911	6111
2370	6107	3563	5356	3170
0560	9025	6008	1089	1300

Random numbers can be constructed by means of a good (unbiased) six-sided die according to the following scheme.

First Throw:	1, 2 or 3					4, 5 or 6				
Second Throw:	6	1	2	3	4	6	1	2	3	4
Random Digit:	0	1	2	3	4	5	6	7	8	9

Divide the digits from 0 to 9 into two equal groups as shown in the third row of the table.

First Throw: Throw the die and determine by the result the group from which the random digit is to come. If 1, 2 or 3 is scored the first group is chosen and 4, 5 or 6 gives the second group.

Second Throw: Throw the die again. Any number except 5 will determine the random digit. If a 5 turns up repeat throwing until another number is obtained.

The reader should easily verify the following sequence of throws.

First Throw	Second Throw	Number Selected
2	4	4
5	4	9
4	5, 1	6
3	5, 5, 1	1
3	6	0

Example 1. Select a random number between 0 and 9,999 using a die First determine the integer in the thousands place say, for example, 7. Repeat this for integers in the hundreds, tens and units place. If the integer in the thousands place is zero it is, of course, not rejected. Numbers such as 0198 (198), 0082 (82) or 0003 (3) are as valid as, say, 3,967.

Example 2. Select a random number between 0 and 1,199. The easiest way to do this is to first find a random number between 0 and 9,999 and then reduce this to the range 0 to 1,199 by multiplying by $\frac{1200}{10000}$ and neglecting any fractional part. For example, 8,327 is obtained by a random process. $8,327 \times \frac{12}{100} = 999 \cdot 24$, and the required random number between 0 and 1,199 is 999. Similarly to pick a random number between 0 and 37 first find a random number between 0 and 99, multiply by $\frac{38}{100}$ and neglect the fractional part.

This process can be applied to numbers of any size.

The applications of probability to the interpretation of statistical data which are described in the next few chapters depend on the data being derived from random samples. Failure to satisfy this condition can render an investigation not only useless but mischievous because of the misleading information it gives. Examples of this are not uncommon. A social survey made some years ago was based on information collected by personal visits to houses in an industrial town. The houses to be visited were chosen in an entirely satisfactory random manner. However the instruction was given that if nobody was at home when a visit was paid then the enquiry should be made at the house next door. It was only realised some time later, after the investigation had been completed, that this instruction had introduced a serious bias in the results. Childless families are much more likely to leave an empty house during the day since the adults may all be out at work. By omitting the unattended houses a sample was obtained which was biased with an unduly high proportion of families with young children. Since one of the objects of the investigation was to determine the average family size this was a serious fault.

Another very well known example of faulty random sampling happened in U.S.A. when Roosevelt stood for his second term of office. A Literary Digest conducted an enormous survey of about 10,000,000 people taking the names from telephone directories and lists of motor car owners. As a result it was predicted that Roosevelt would lose the election by 20% of the votes cast. In fact Roosevelt was returned to office by a 20% majority. Obviously the sample was heavily biased in favour of the wealthier American and therefore in favour of the Republicans who were opposing Roosevelt.

SUMMARY OF CHAPTER IV

1. If r events can happen in $n_1, n_2 \ldots n_r$ ways the total number of ways in which the r events can take place is $n_1 \times n_2 \times \ldots \times n_r$.

2. The number of combinations of n things taken r at a time is ^nC_r where

$$^nC_r = \frac{n!}{(n-r)!\, r!}$$

and $n! = n(n-1)(n-2) \ldots 3 \times 2 \times 1$.

3. If an action can have any one of n equally likely results and if r of these results produce an event E then p, the probability of E, is given by

$$p = \frac{r}{n}$$

4. If p_1, p_2 are the probabilities of two mutually exclusive events then p the probability that either one or other of the events will happen is given by

$$p = p_1 + p_2$$

5. If p is the probability that an event will happen and q is the probability that the event will not happen then

$$p + q = 1$$

6. If p_1, p_2 are the probabilities of two independent events then the probability p that both will happen is given by

$$p = p_1 \times p_2$$

7. A sample is chosen in a random way when all possible samples have an equal chance of being picked.

EXERCISES XIII

These exercises are most suitably carried out by a team. Equipment required is one die.

1. Determine 20 random numbers between 0 and 99 and calculate their mean and standard deviation. They will be approximately $\mu = 50$ and $\sigma = 30$.

2. In a class of 30 or 40 students select a random sample of 10 by giving each student a number and then choosing 10 random numbers. Calculate the average age of the sample and compare it with the average age of the aggregate (the class). The same student may be picked twice. If so, would you include his age twice in the ten ages?

3. Divide a square into 25 square sections and number them. Determine a random set of 5 sections. (This was a method used in determining points at which to take hardness readings on a steel plate.)

4. The following frequency distribution gives the results of elasticity tests made on 424 samples of brass. Only mid cell values are shown.

Elasticity	Frequency	Individual Numbers	Elasticity	Frequency	Individual Numbers
32	2	1–2	40	62	243–304
33	4	3–6	41	53	305–357
34	8	7–14	42	32	358–389
35	19	15–33	43	19	390–408
36	33	34–66	44	10	409–418
37	49	67–115	45	4	419–422
38	61	116–176	46	1	423
39	66	177–242	—	1	424

Numbers are allotted serially to each class and each individual in the class receives a number. For example, numbers 3, 4, 5 and 6 are allotted to the specimens with elasticity 33, 7, 8 . . . 14 to the specimens with elasticity 34 and so on.

Every number from 1 to 424 corresponds to a specimen with a given elasticity. Thus 343 corresponds to a specimen with elasticity 41, numbers 60 and 110 both correspond to specimens with elasticity 37.

 i. Pick a random sample of 20 specimens from the distribution and calculate the average elasticity. Compare it with the average of the whole distribution.

ii. Pick ten random samples of 5, calculate the range for each sample and the average range R. Calculate σ, the standard deviation of the whole distribution, and verify that the ratio $\bar{R}/\sigma$ is approximately 2·3.

CHAPTER V

The Binomial and Poisson Distributions

5.1 A Theoretical Distribution

This chapter will describe how the theory of probability can be used to determine the type of frequency distributions which will be obtained when random samples are drawn from certain types of population. The theoretical results can be verified by practical experiments and it is recommended that this should be done.

Consider a sampling experiment in which random samples of 10 are drawn from a large number of marbles in a bag. 20% of the marbles are red and the rest are blue, so that a marble drawn at random from the bag has a 1/5 chance of being red and a 4/5 chance of being blue. The number of marbles forming the population must be large enough for the chance to be effectively unchanged when a finite sample is drawn. It is a simple exercise in probability to calculate the chance that a random sample of 10 marbles will contain x red marbles where x can be any number from 0 to 10. The probability of drawing x red marbles and $(10 - x)$ blue marbles in any preassigned order is $(0 \cdot 2)^x (0 \cdot 8)^{10-x}$ and there are $^{10}C_x$ possible orders in which the sample may be drawn. Therefore if $P(x)$ is the probability of drawing a sample of 10 containing x red marbles in any order then

$$P(x) = {}^{10}C_x \, (0 \cdot 2)^x \, (0 \cdot 8)^{10-x} \tag{5.1}$$

Another way of describing $P(x)$ is to say that if a large number of samples are drawn from the bag a fraction $P(x)$ of these samples will contain x red marbles. In other words if N is the total number of samples drawn then approximately $N.P(x)$ of them will contain x red marbles. By working out all values of $N.P(x)$ from $x = 0$ to $x = 10$ a theoretical distribution will be obtained which should give approximately the results of the experiment.

The calculations are considerably simplified by the following algebraic relation between $P(x)$ and $P(x + 1)$.

$$P(x) = \frac{10!}{x! \, (10 - x)!} \, (0 \cdot 2)^x (0 \cdot 8)^{10-x}$$

$$\text{also } P(x + 1) = \frac{10!}{(x + 1)! \, (9 - x)!} \, (0 \cdot 2)^{x+1} \, (0 \cdot 8)^{9-x}$$

$$= \frac{10 - x}{x + 1} \cdot \frac{10!}{x! \, (10 - x)!} \cdot \frac{0 \cdot 2}{0 \cdot 8} \, (0 \cdot 2)^x (0 \cdot 8)^{10-x}$$

$$= \frac{1}{4} \cdot \frac{10 - x}{x + 1} \, P(x) \qquad (5.2)$$

Calculate $P(0) = (0 \cdot 8)^{10} = 0 \cdot 1074$

Put $x = 0$ in equation (5.2) to obtain:

$$P(1) = \frac{1}{4} \cdot \frac{10}{1} \, P(0)$$

$$= 2 \cdot 5 \times 0 \cdot 1074 = 0 \cdot 2685.$$

Now put $x = 1$ in equation (5.2)

$$P(2) = \frac{1}{4} \cdot \frac{9}{2} \, P(1)$$

$$= 1 \cdot 125 \times 0 \cdot 2685 = 0 \cdot 3021$$

Continuing in this way all the $P(x)$ can be calculated and are shown in Table XVII together with values of $NP(x)$ for $N = 300$.

The sum of the $P(x)$, $\Sigma_0^{10} \, P(x)$, should of course be unity, but sometimes there is a small discrepancy due to rounding off errors. Any required degree of accuracy can be obtained by increasing the number of significant figures in the calculation of $P(0)$ but generally four-figure accuracy is sufficient.

TABLE XVII

THEORETICAL DISTRIBUTION OF RED MARBLES IN RANDOM SAMPLES
OF TEN

x, number of red marbles in the sample	$P(x)$, chance of obtaining a sample with x red marbles	$300 \, P(x)$, expected number of samples
0	0·1074	32
1	0·2685	81
2	0·3021	91
3	0·2014	60
4	0·0881	26
5	0·0264	8
6	0·0055	2
7	0·0008	0
8	0·0001	0
9	0·0000	0
10	0·0000	0
Totals	1·0003	300

Thus, out of 300 random samples about 32 would be expected to contain no red marbles, 81 would contain 1 red marble, and so on.

5.2 Experimental Verification

The above results were tested by an experiment in which about 500 marbles, 20% of which were red, were well mixed in a bag. An investigator then drew a handful of marbles from the bag and counted out 10. The investigator was blindfolded while he was doing this to prevent any conscious or unconscious colour preference being exercised and thereby making the sample non-random. The number of red marbles in the sample was noted and the sample was returned to the bag which was again well mixed. This was repeated 300 times and the results are shown in Table XVIII along with the theoretical figures from Table XVII.

TABLE XVIII

COMPARISON OF THEORETICAL AND EXPERIMENTAL RESULTS

x, number of red marbles in sample	Number of samples with x red marbles (*theoretical*)	Number of samples with x red marbles (*experimental*)
0	32	29
1	81	82
2	91	88
3	60	64
4	26	25
5	8	8
6	2	3
7	0	1
8	0	0
Totals 300		300

The agreement between experiment and theory is close and it can be shown (Chapter 10) that the small discrepancies can be accounted for by random sampling errors.

EXERCISES XIV

Instead of marbles pieces of marked cardboard can be used. The pieces should be cut fairly small to minimise the risk of binding together in small bundles. This would almost certainly upset the results of the experiment since sampling would then not be random.

1. For a sample size 12 and for a probability of 25% show that

$$P(x + 1) = \frac{1}{3} \cdot \frac{12 - x}{x + 1} P(x)$$

2. Prepare an artificial population of marbles (or cards) of which 25% are of one colour, say red, and the rest have a different colour. At least

100 marbles should be used. Draw N samples of 12 at random and construct a frequency table showing the results. The samples must be returned to the bag and well mixed after each draw. The size of N will depend on the number of persons assisting and also on their patience, but it should not be less than 200. Use the results of Ex. 1, and compare values of $NP(x)$ with the experimental results.

3. Calculate the average and standard deviation of the data obtained in the previous exercise. They should be approximately 3·0 and 1·5.

4. Four dice are thrown and the number of sixes in each throw are recorded. This is repeated 108 times. Write down the theoretical frequencies of 0, 1, 2, 3 and 4 sixes. Calculate the mean number of sixes in a single throw.

5. Carry out the experiment described in Ex. 4, either by throwing 4 dice or by throwing a single die 4 times, and record the frequencies. From the observed results calculate the mean number of sixes in a throw.

6. A coin is tossed six times and the number of heads is noted. This is repeated 128 times. Write down the theoretical frequencies and calculate the average number of heads.

7. Carry out the experiment described in Ex. 6 and compare the experimental frequencies with the theoretical frequencies.

8. Draw a card at random from a well shuffled pack, return the card and repeat 4 times. Note the number of spades. Repeat this 100 times. Calculate the theoretical frequency distribution and compare it with the experimental distribution (some discrepancy may be expected here owing to the difficulty of thoroughly mixing a pack of cards).

9. Consider a "population" of 12 marbles, $\frac{1}{4}$ of which are red. Use equation 5.1 to calculate the probability of drawing 1 red marble in a sample of 3. Calculate the exact probability by considering the number of ways in which the desired sample can be drawn. Explain the discrepancy. Justify your explanation by calculating the exact probability for a population of 120 marbles.

10. A population N contains a fraction p of things of one kind. Calculate the exact probability that a random sample of n consists entirely of the things of one kind. Show that as N tends to infinity this probability becomes p^n.

5.3   The Binomial Distribution

The Binomial distribution was first discovered early in the eighteenth century by the mathematician, Jacob Bernoulli. The ideas involved have been introduced in the preceding paragraphs.

Call the occurrence of an event a "success" and its non-occurrence a "failure". Let p be the probability of a "success" and let q be the probability of a "failure", so that $q = 1 - p$. Then in m independent trials the probability that there will be x successes and $(m - x)$ failures is given by

$$P(x) = {}^{m}C_{x} \cdot p^{x} \cdot q^{m-x} \tag{5.3}$$

Theoretically the Binomial distribution only applies when the population being sampled is infinite so that p remains unaltered by sampling. In practice the distribution can be applied to finite populations so long as they are not too small. See Exercises XIV, 9, 10.

For example in Section 5.1 the trial was drawing a marble and the "success" was obtaining a red marble for which $p = 0\cdot2$ and $q = 0\cdot8$. Also since 10 marbles were drawn, in that experiment $m = 10$.

Now the Binomial Theorem states that the expansion of $(q + p)^m$ where m is a positive integer is given by

$$(q + p)^m = q^m + {}^mC_1 q^{m-1}p + {}^mC_2 q^{m-2}p^2 + \ldots + {}^mC_x q^{m-x}p^x + \ldots + p^m \tag{5.4}$$

and the probability denoted by $P(x)$ is given by the $(x + 1)$st term of the expansion of $(q + p)^m$.

Using the notation $P(x)$, equation 5.4 can be written as

$$(q + p)^m = P(0) + P(1) + P(2) + \ldots + P(x) + \ldots + P(m).$$

The right-hand side of this equation represents the sum of $(m + 1)$ mutually exclusive events of which one must occur and so

$$P(0) + P(1) + \ldots + P(x) + \ldots + P(m) = 1.$$

This could also be shown by observing that $(q + p) = 1$ and so $(q + p)^m$ must also be 1. Fig. 28 shows a number of histograms for different values of p and m.

Example 1. Five coins are tossed and the number of heads is noted. What are the chances of getting 0, 1 . . . 5 heads? If this is repeated 128 times, on approximately how many occasions could 0, 1 . . . 5 heads be expected?

The chance of obtaining a head is $\frac{1}{2}$ so that the required probabilities are given by the expansion of $(\frac{1}{2} + \frac{1}{2})^5$.

$$(\tfrac{1}{2} + \tfrac{1}{2})^5 = (\tfrac{1}{2})^5 (1 + 5 + 10 + 10 + 5 + 1)$$

and the probabilities are $\frac{1}{32}, \frac{5}{32}, \frac{10}{32}, \frac{10}{32}, \frac{5}{32}, \frac{1}{32}$.

The number of occasions on which 0, 1 . . . 5 heads will appear on the average in 128 trials are given by $128(\frac{1}{2} + \frac{1}{2})^5 = 4(1 + 5 + 10 + 10 + 5 + 1)$ and so are 4, 20, 40, 40, 20 and 4.

Example 2. A marksman can hit a target 2 out of 3 times. In 4 shots what are his chances of hitting it 0, 1, 2, 3 or 4 times?

The probability that he will miss the target is $\frac{1}{3}$ so the required chances are given by the expansion of

$$(\tfrac{1}{3} + \tfrac{2}{3})^4 = (\tfrac{1}{3})^4 + 4(\tfrac{1}{3})^3 (\tfrac{2}{3}) + 6(\tfrac{1}{3})^2 (\tfrac{2}{3})^2 + 4(\tfrac{1}{3}) (\tfrac{2}{3})^3 + (\tfrac{2}{3})^4 \text{ and are } \tfrac{1}{81},$$
$\frac{8}{81}, \frac{24}{81}, \frac{32}{81}$ and $\frac{16}{81}$.

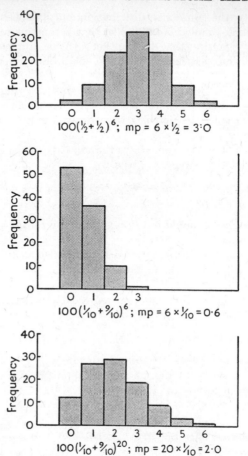

FIG. 28. Histograms of binomial distributions for different values of m and p.

5.4 The Mean and Standard Deviation of the Binomial Distribution

This section may be omitted by non-mathematical readers but the results are important and should be remembered. It will be shown that the mean, μ, and standard deviation, σ, of the Binomial distribution $P(r) = {}^mC_r q^{m-r} p^r$ are given by

$$\mu = mp$$
$$\sigma = \sqrt{mpq}$$

Consider a Binomial distribution in which the frequencies of occurrence of an event, given by the expansion of $N(q + p)^m$, are $N.q^m$, $N \cdot {}^mC_1 \cdot p \cdot q^{m-1}$, $N \cdot {}^mC_2 \cdot p^2 \cdot q^{m-2}$, $\ldots N \cdot {}^mC_{m-1} \cdot p^{m-1}q$, and $N.p^m$. Proceed to calculate the mean and standard deviation by constructing Table XIX.

TABLE XIX

CONSTANTS OF THE BINOMIAL DISTRIBUTION

Number of occurrences (x)	Number of samples (n)	nx	nx^2
0	$N . q^m$	0	0
1	$N . {}^mC_1 . p . q^{m-1}$	$N . 1 . {}^mC_1 . p . q^{m-1}$	$N . 1^2 . {}^mC_1 . p . q^{m-1}$
2	$N . {}^mC_2 . p^2 . q^{m-2}$	$N . 2 . {}^mC_2 . p^2 . q^{m-2}$	$N . 2^2 . {}^mC_2 . p^2 . q^{m-2}$
3	$N . {}^mC_3 . p^3 . q^{m-3}$	$N . 3 . {}^mC_3 . p^3 . q^{m-3}$	$N . 3^2 . {}^mC_3 . p^3 . q^{m-3}$
$\cdot$	$\cdot$	$\cdot$	$\cdot$
$\cdot$	$\cdot$	$\cdot$	$\cdot$
$\cdot$	$\cdot$	$\cdot$	$\cdot$
$m-1$	$N . {}^mC_{m-1} . p^{m-1} . q$	$N(m-1) . {}^mC_{m-1} . p^{m-1} . q$	$N . (m-1)^2 . {}^mC_{m-1} . p^{m-1} . q$
m	$N . p^m$	$N . m . p^m$	$N . m^2 . p^m$

The sum of the terms in the column headed (n) is given by

$$\Sigma(n) = N(q^m + {}^mC_1 . q^{m-1} . p + {}^mC_2 . q^{m-2} . p^2 + \ldots + p^m)$$
$$= N(q + p)^m = N.$$

For the column headed (nx)

$$\Sigma(nx) = N\left[mpq^{m-1} + \frac{2m(m-1)}{2 . 1} . p^2 . q^{m-2} + \frac{3m(m-1)(m-2)}{3 . 2 . 1} . p^3 . q^{m-3} \right.$$
$$\left. + \ldots + (m-1) . mp^{m-1} . q + mp^m \right]$$

Take the common factor mp outside the bracket

$$\Sigma(nx) = Nmp\left[q^{m-1} + (m-1) . pq^{m-2} + \frac{(m-1)(m-2)}{2 . 1} . p . {}^2q^{m-3} + \right.$$
$$\left. \ldots + (m-1) . p^{m-2} . q + p^{m-1} \right]$$
$$= Nmp (q + p)^{m-1} = Nmp$$

For the column headed (nx^2)

$$\Sigma(nx^2) = N[{}^mC_1 . pq^{m-1} + 2^2 . {}^mC_2 . p^2 . q^{m-2} + 3^2 . {}^mC_3 . p^3 . q^{m-3} +$$
$$\ldots + m^2 . p^m]$$
$$= N\left[mpq^{m-1} + 2m(m-1)p^2 . q^{m-2} + \frac{3m(m-1)(m-2)}{2 . 1} p^3 . q^{m-3} \right.$$
$$\left. + \ldots + m^2 . p^m \right]$$

Take mp outside the bracket and write the result in two separate sums

$$\Sigma \, nx^2 = Nmp\left\{ q^{m-1} + (m-1)pq^{m-2} + \frac{(m-1)(m-2)}{2 \cdot 1}\, p^2 \cdot q^{m-3} + \right.$$
$$\left. \cdots + p^{m-1} \right\} + Nmp\left\{ 0 + (m-1)\, p \cdot q^{m-2} + \right.$$
$$\left. (m-1)(m-2)p^2 \cdot q^{m-3} + \cdots + (m-1)p^{m-1} \right\}$$

The expression inside the first bracket is equal to $(q + p)^{m-1}$ and is therefore 1. Take $(m - 1)\,p$ outside the second bracket.

$$\Sigma \, nx^2 =$$
$$Nmp + Nm(m-1)p^2 \left\{ q^{m-2} + (m-2)p \cdot q^{m-3} + \cdots + p^{m-2} \right\}$$

The expression in the second bracket is equal to $(q + p)^{m-2}$ and so is 1, and finally

$$\Sigma \, nx^2 = Nmp + Nm\,(m - 1)\, p^2$$
$$= Nmp \left\{ 1 + (m - 1)\, p \right\}$$

The average, μ, is given by

$$\mu = \frac{\Sigma\,(nx)}{\Sigma\,(n)} = \frac{Nmp}{N}$$

Therefore $\mu = mp$ \hfill (5.5)

The sum of the squared deviations from the mean is given by

$$\Sigma\,(nx^2) - N\mu^2 = Nmp \left\{ 1 + (m - 1)\, p \right\} - Nm^2p^2$$
$$= Nmp \left\{ 1 + mp - p - mp \right\}$$
$$= Nmp\,(1 - p) = Nmpq$$

Therefore $\sigma = \sqrt{\dfrac{Nmpq}{N}} = \sqrt{mpq}$ \hfill (5.6)

Example 1.   Calculate the theoretical values for μ and σ in the experiment in paragraph 5.1 and compare with the experimental values.

Here $m = 10$ and $p = \frac{1}{5}$, $q = \frac{4}{5}$.

Therefore $\mu = mp = 10 \times \frac{1}{5} = 2$

$$\sigma = \sqrt{mpq} = \sqrt{10 \times \tfrac{1}{5} \times \tfrac{4}{5}}$$

$$= \frac{2}{5}\sqrt{10} = 1\cdot26.$$

The values of $\bar{x}$ and s calculated from the experimental data are $= 2\cdot05$ and $s = 1\cdot30$.

Example 2.   Verify equations 5.5 and 5.6 for $m = 2$. In this case Table XIX becomes

x	n	nx	nx^2
0	Nq^2	0	0
1	$2Npq$	$2Npq$	$2Npq$
2	Np^2	$2Np^2$	$4Np^2$

$$\Sigma(n) = N(q + p)^2 = N$$
$$\Sigma(nx) = 2Np(q + p) = 2Np$$
$$\Sigma(nx^2) = 2Np(q + 2p) = 2Np(1 + p)$$
$$\mu = \Sigma(nx)/\Sigma(n) = 2p$$
$$\Sigma(nx^2) - N\mu^2 = 2Np(1 + p) - 4Np^2$$
$$= 2Np(1 + p - 2p) = 2Npq$$
$$\sigma = \sqrt{2pq}$$

Example 3. A and B play a game in which A's chance of winning is $\frac{2}{3}$. In a series of 8 games what is the probability that A will win 6 or more games?

Let $P(x)$ be the probability that A wins x games so that

$$P(x) = {}^8C_x \left(\tfrac{2}{3}\right)^x \left(\tfrac{1}{3}\right)^{8-x}$$

The required chance is given by

$$P(6) + P(7) + P(8)$$
$$= {}^8C_6 \left(\tfrac{2}{3}\right)^6 \left(\tfrac{1}{3}\right)^2 + {}^8C_7 \left(\tfrac{2}{3}\right)^7 \left(\tfrac{1}{3}\right) + {}^8C_8 \left(\tfrac{2}{3}\right)^8$$
$$= \frac{2^6}{3^8} \left[{}^8C_6 + 2 \cdot {}^8C_7 + 2^2 \right]$$
$$= \frac{2^6}{3^8} \left[28 + 16 + 4 \right] = \frac{64 \times 48}{81 \times 81} = \frac{1,024}{2,187}$$

Therefore A has an approximately 50% chance of winning 6 or more games.

EXERCISES XV

1. In a packet of flower seeds $\frac{2}{5}$ are known to be pink flowering and the remainder are yellow. Calculate the probabilities of getting 0, 1 . . . 6 pink flowers in a row of six plants. If 250 rows each of 6 plants are planted, approximately how many will contain (a) all pink flowers, (b) all yellow flowers?

2. The production of a radar component is checked by examining samples of 4. The following table shows the number of defective components found in 200 samples. Calculate the proportion of defective

components. Assuming the Binomial law holds, use this value to calculate the theoretical distribution of defectives and compare with the original figures.

Number of defectives	0	1	2	3	4
Number of samples	62	85	40	11	2

3. The values of μ and σ for a Binomial distribution are $\mu = 6$, $\sigma = 2$. Find m, p and q.

4. Verify equations 5.5 and 5.6 for $m = 3$.

5. Calculate the theoretical values of μ and σ in Ex. XIV, 2 and compare with the experimental values.

6. Calculate the theoretical values for μ and σ in Ex. 1 and Ex. 2 above.

7. In ten throws of a coin what is the chance of obtaining 7 or more heads or tails?

8. The incidence of occupational disease in an industry is such that the workmen have a 20% chance of suffering from it. What is the probability that out of six workmen 4 or more will contract the disease?

9. Two chess players observe that 3 out of 5 of their games end in a draw. In a series of 8 games what is the chance that there are not more than 2 undrawn games?

10. In a precision bombing attack there is a 50% chance that any one bomb will strike the target. Two direct hits are required to destroy the target completely. How many bombs must be dropped to give a 99% chance or better of completely destroying the target?

5.5 The Poisson Distribution

The Binomial distribution assumes a very convenient form when p is very small and m is large. Let the average number of successes $mp = a$.

We shall show that when these conditions are satisfied $P(x)$, the probability of x successes is given by

$$P(x) = e^{-a}\,\frac{a^x}{x!}$$

and the mean μ, and standard deviation σ, of the distribution are given by

$$\mu = a$$
$$\sigma = \sqrt{a}$$

The proof which follows may be omitted by non-mathematical readers but the results should be remembered.

Consider the general term in the Binomial distribution

$$P(x) = {}^mC_x \cdot p^x \cdot q^{m-x}$$

Write this as

$$P(x) = \frac{m!}{x!\,(m-x)!} \cdot p^x \cdot (1-p)^{m-x}$$

$$= \frac{m\,(m-1)\,(m-2)\,\ldots\,(m-x+1)}{x!\,(1-p)^x} \cdot p^x \cdot (1-p)^m$$

$$= \frac{mp\,(mp-p)\,(mp-2p)\,\ldots\,(mp-\overline{x-1}p)}{x!\,(1-p)^x}\,(1-p)^m$$

Now write $mp = a$ so that $p = \dfrac{a}{m}$

Then $P(x) = \dfrac{a\,(a-p)\,(a-2p)\,\ldots\,(a-\overline{x-1}p)}{x!\,(1-p)^x} \cdot \left(1-\dfrac{a}{m}\right)^m$ (5.7)

This expression can now be simplified.

Since p is very small it is approximately true that

$$(1-p)^x = 1$$

and $a\,(a-p)\,(a-2p)\,\ldots\,(a-\overline{x-1}p) = a^x$

Also, since m is large, it is approximately true that $\left(1-\dfrac{a}{m}\right)^m = e^{-a}$

Therefore equation (5.7) becomes

$$P(x) = e^{-a} \cdot \frac{a^x}{x!} \tag{5.8}$$

This expression was first derived by Poisson in 1837 and is known by his name. Since it involves only one constant, a, it is easier to tabulate than the Binomial distribution which involves two independent constants, m and p. Fig. 29 shows the Poisson distribution histograms for a number of values of a.

By using the fact that for the Binomial distribution $\mu = mp$ and $\sigma = \sqrt{mpq}$ it is easy to deduce corresponding expressions for the Poisson where $p = \dfrac{a}{m}$ and q is very nearly equal to 1. In fact for the Poisson distribution

$$\mu = a \tag{5.9}$$

$$\sigma = \sqrt{a} \tag{5.10}$$

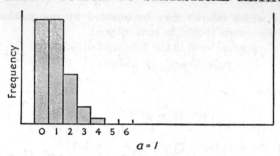

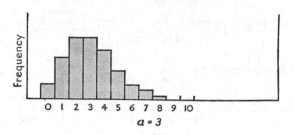

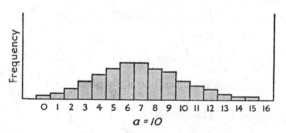

FIG. 29.   Poisson distribution for different values of a.

Example 1.   During the final checking of 325 pages of gunnery tables a number of printers' errors were discovered and the following table gives the frequency distribution.

Number of errors per page (x)	Frequency of occurrence (n)	nx
0	211	0
1	90	90
2	19	38
3	5	15
4	0	0
Totals	325	143

The average number of printers' errors per page is given by:

$$\bar{x} = \frac{143}{325} = 0{\cdot}44$$

In this example, although the chance of any particular figure in a page being wrong is small, there are a large number of figures in each page so that $\bar{x}$, the average or expected number of errors per page, is finite. These are conditions where the Poisson distribution might be expected to apply and this was tested by calculating

$$NP(x) = Ne^{-a}\frac{a^x}{x!}$$

$\bar{x}$ is an estimate of a so we take

$$a = 0\cdot44 \qquad\qquad N = 325$$

The calculation is simplified by using the relation

$$NP(x+1) = \frac{a}{x+1}NP(x)$$

and the fact that

$$NP(0) = 325\,e^{-0\cdot44} = 209\cdot3$$

The results are shown in Table XX

TABLE XX

DISTRIBUTION OF ERRORS IN GUNNERY TABLES

Number of errors per page (x)	Frequency (obtained from Poisson law)	Observed frequency
0	209·3	211
1	92·1	90
2	20·3	19
3	3·0	5
4	0·3	0
Totals	325·0	325

The experimental results show very good agreement with the theoretical Poisson distribution.

5.6 The Poisson Distribution Chart

The Poisson distribution has played a large part in many industrial sampling problems particularly in those dealing with large scale mass production. For example a manufacturer of torch batteries knows that in spite of every precaution there is a small unavoidable percentage of defective batteries which are not up to specification. This has been established at 0·8% or about 8 defective batteries in every thousand. The batteries are packed for retail in cartons each containing 200 and the manufacturer wants to know the chance of a carton containing x defective batteries where x may be 0, 1, 2 . . . Manufacturing conditions are such that each carton can be assumed to contain a random sample of the production.

This is a case where the Poisson distribution holds. The average number of defectives per carton, a, is given by

$$a = 200 \times 0.008 = 1.6$$

and the chance of a carton containing x defectives is

$$P(x) = e^{-a} \frac{a^x}{x!}$$

The results for different values of x are shown in Table XXI.

TABLE XXI

Number of defectives in a carton, x	Probability, $P(x)$, that a carton contains x defectives
0	0.202
1	0.323
2	0.258
3	0.138
4	0.055
5	0.018
6	0.005
7	0.001
Total	1.000

Usually in a situation like this the manufacturer is interested, not so much in the individual probabilities of getting different numbers of defectives in a carton, but rather in the chance of getting x *or more* defectives in a carton. Thus from the above table the chance of getting 5 or more defectives is $0.018 + 0.005 + 0.001 = 0.024$ or nearly $2\frac{1}{2}\%$. Another way of expressing this is to say that about $2\frac{1}{2}\%$ of the cartons will contain 5 or more defective batteries.

It will be convenient to have a short notation for the probability that a variable x will be greater than or equal to an arbitrary value X and this will be denoted by $P(x \geqslant X)$. The symbol $\geqslant$ is a shorthand notation for the words "greater than or equal to". Thus, in the above example, $P(x \geqslant 5) = 0.024$.

For the Poisson distribution a general expression for $P(x \geqslant X)$ is given by

$$P(x \geqslant X) = P(X) + P(X+1) + P(X+2) + \ldots$$

$$= e^{-a} \left[\frac{a^X}{X!} + \frac{a^{X+1}}{(X+1)!} + \frac{a^{X+2}}{(X+2)!} + \ldots \right]$$

The Poisson distribution chart in Fig. 30 is arranged so as to give $P(x \geqslant X)$ for different values of a and X. The chart is used to find $P(x \geqslant X)$ as follows:

(1) Find the position corresponding to a on the horizontal scale and find where the vertical at this point intersects the curve marked X.

(2) On the vertical scale read the co-ordinate of the point of intersection. This gives the value of $P(x \geqslant X)$.

(*Note.*—To enable small and large values of $P(x \geqslant X)$ to be read accurately, the scale is not linear.)

Example 1.   Verify the calculated value of $P(x \geqslant 5)$ in the example dealing with torch batteries. Here $a = 1 \cdot 6$, $X = 5$.
The vertical at $a = 1 \cdot 6$ intersects the curve $X = 5$ at a point whose vertical co-ordinate is about $0 \cdot 023$. Therefore from the chart
$$P(x \geqslant X) = 0 \cdot 023.$$

Example 2.   A firm making an electrical switch produce about 1% defective. What is the chance of getting at least 6 defectives in a box of 200 switches.
$$\text{Here } p = 0 \cdot 01, m = 200$$
$$\text{Therefore } a = mp = 2.$$
On the Poisson chart the intersection of the line $a = 2$ with the curve $X = 6$ has a vertical co-ordinate $P(x \geqslant X) = 0 \cdot 015$. Therefore the chance of finding at least 6 defectives is $0 \cdot 015$ or $1 \cdot 5\%$.

Example 3.   A manufacturer packs automobile sparking plugs in boxes of 60. In the interest of his manufacturing reputation not more than 5% of these boxes should have 4 or more defective sparking plugs. At what level should his average rate of defectives be kept to ensure this? Assume that a box is a random sample of 60 plugs.
This is an example in which the Poisson chart is used in reverse.
In a random sample of 60 the chance of obtaining 4 or more defective plugs must not be greater than $0 \cdot 05$. That is
$$P(x \geqslant 4) = 0 \cdot 05$$
The first step is to find from this the value of a, the expected or average number of defectives in a box.
On the Poisson chart read $P = 0 \cdot 05$ on the vertical scale. Draw a horizontal line at that point and find its intersection with the curve $x = 4$. The horizontal co-ordinate of that point is given by $a = 1 \cdot 35$. (Interpolate by eye between $a = 1 \cdot 3$ and $a = 1 \cdot 4$.) Then if p is the required value of the rate of defectives
$$a = mp, \text{ and since } m = 60$$
$$p = \frac{a}{60} = \frac{1 \cdot 35}{60} = 0 \cdot 0225 \text{ or } 2\tfrac{1}{4}\%$$

5.7 Matching Theoretical and Experimental Distributions

The only way to determine whether any specified theoretical distribution, such as the Binomial or Poisson, will adequately

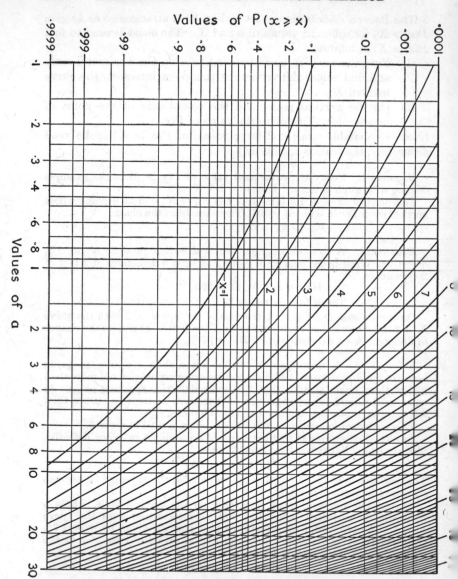

Fig. 30. The Poisson summation chart.

represent experimental data is to calculate the theoretical frequencies using the constants of the distributions, n and p for the Binomial and a for the Poisson, which are obtained from the experimental results. The theoretical frequencies can then be compared with the observed frequencies. At this stage we have no criterion for deciding when a theoretical distribution gives a good fit to experimental results but a method for doing this will be described later in Chapter X. (The χ^2 distribution.)

The experiment of drawing marbles from a bag in random samples of 10 was designed to satisfy the requirements which would give a Binomial distribution and if the experimental results had not been distributed according to the Binomial law there would have been good reason to suspect that the sampling was not random. The figures giving the distribution of printer's errors in gunnery tables might be expected to conform to the Poisson law but this could only be demonstrated by calculating the theoretical Poisson frequencies and comparing them with the observed data. Consider now an experiment in which the Poisson distribution did not hold.

The Concise Oxford Dictionary uses *italic* type to print words which are either incompletely naturalised or completely foreign such as *couloir* and *soi-disant*. One hundred pages selected at random gave the following distribution of foreign words. The corresponding Poisson frequencies clearly do not give a good fit.

TABLE XXII

A DISTRIBUTION OF FOREIGN WORDS IN THE CONCISE
OXFORD DICTIONARY

Number of foreign words per page	Observed frequency	Poisson frequency
0	48	37
1	27	37
2	12	18
3	7	6
4	4	2
5	1	0
6	1	0
	Totals 100	100

The discrepancy may be due to a tendency for foreign words to occur in groups of words associated by a common language. Thus on one page there are found three words of German origin, "kriegspiel", "kultur" and "kulturkampf". This conflicts with a condition for the Poisson distribution which assumes that the events are independent.

SUMMARY OF CHAPTER V

1. The frequencies of the Binomial distribution are given by
$$P(x) = {}^mC_x \, p^x q^{m-x}$$
where p denotes the probability of a "success" and m is the sample size.

2. The mean μ and standard deviation σ of the Binomial distribution are given by the equations
$$\mu = mp$$
$$\sigma = \sqrt{mpq}$$

3. The frequencies of the Poisson distribution are given by
$$P(x) = e^{-a} \frac{a^x}{x!}$$
where a is the average number of successes.

4. The mean and standard deviation of the Poisson distribution are
$$\mu = a$$
$$\sigma = \sqrt{a}$$

5. The Poisson distribution chart gives $P(x \geqslant X)$ when a and X are known. $P(x \geqslant X)$ denotes the probability of obtaining X or more "successes".

EXERCISES XVI

1. Show that an alternative expression for $P(x \geqslant X)$ is
$$P(x \geqslant X) = 1 - e^{-a} \left[1 + a + \frac{a^2}{2!} + \dots + \frac{a^{X-1}}{(X-1)!} \right]$$

2. Use the result of Ex. 1 to calculate values for $P(x \geqslant X)$ when $a = 0.5, X = 2$ and also when $a = 2, X = 3$. Verify these results on the Poisson chart.

3. Use the Poisson chart to find $P(x \geqslant X)$ when $a = 3, X = 6$; $a = 2.5$, $X = 2$ and find a when $P(x \geqslant 7) = 0.08$; $P(x \geqslant 1) = 0.50$.

4. If $P(X)$ is the probability of obtaining exactly X defectives in a trial show that
$$P(x \geqslant X) = P(X) + P(x \geqslant X + 1)$$
    (a) by argument,
    (b) by algebra.
Use this result to find $P(4)$ from the Poisson chart when $a = 2$. Verify the result from the relation
$$P(X) = e^{-a} \frac{a^x}{X!}$$

5. From records of 10 Prussian army corps kept over 20 years the following data was obtained showing the number of deaths caused by the kick of a horse. Determine a, the average number of deaths per army corps per annum, and calculate the theoretical Poisson frequencies. (Data of L. von Bortkiewicz.)

Number of deaths per army corps per annum	Frequency of occurrence
0	109
1	65
2	22
3	3
4	1
	Total 200

6. Two manufacturers A and B make the same type of component. A sells them in boxes of 100 and B in boxes of 50. A customer has noticed that the chance of getting 5 or more defects in a box is the same in each case, namely, 0·045. Calculate the per cent defective for both A and B. If A now started to sell components in boxes of 50 what is the chance that the customer will get a box from A containing 5 or more defects?

7. Fit a Poisson distribution to the data provided in Table XVII taking $a = 2$. Compare with the frequencies given by the Binomial distribution.

8. A card was drawn from a pack of playing cards and then replaced and the pack shuffled. This was repeated 10 times and the number of black suit cards was noted. A thousand results were obtained in this way and are given here. The number of black cards is denoted by x.

$x =$	0	1	2	3	4	5	6	7	8	9	10	Total
$n =$	2	8	46	116	211	243	208	119	40	7	0	1,000

(a) What are the values of m, and N and the theoretical value of p?

(b) What distribution would be expected to apply?

(c) Calculate the theoretical frequencies and compare with the experimental frequencies.

9. From the experimental data in Ex. 8 calculate the mean and standard deviation and compare with the theoretical values.

10. In an industrial area the deposition of grit particles from the atmosphere was measured by counting the number of particles greater than 1 mm, deposited on 200 prepared cards exposed at various sites in the area. The counts recorded were:

Number of particles	0	1	2	3	4	5	6	Total
Number of cards	46	71	48	23	9	3	0	200

Calculate the theoretical frequencies given by the theoretical frequencies given by the Poisson distribution with the same mean as the experimental data.

11. From the data of Ex. 10 calculate the standard deviation and verify that for the Poisson distribution it is approximately true that $\sigma = \sqrt{a}$.

12. Articles are produced in large quantities and about 2% of them are defective. They are despatched in batches of equal numbers. How large should a batch be to ensure that not more than 1 in 5 contain more than 2 defective articles?

13. Assume that the chance of being killed in an accident in a coal mine during a year is 1/1,400. Use the Poisson distribution to calculate the probability that in a mine employing 350 miners there will be at least one fatal accident in a year.

14. A bombing technique secures 1 out of 10 hits in the target area. Use the Poisson curves to determine how many bombs should be launched in order to have a 90% chance of securing at least 8 hits.

CHAPTER VI

The Normal Distribution

6.1 A Continuous Distribution

In 1883 a group of investigators published the results of measuring the heights of 8,585 adult males born in the British Isles. This branch of study which deals with the measurements of human beings is known as anthropometry. (From the Greek: *anthropos*, man; *metron*, measure.) The 8,585 heights, recorded in inches, are given in Table XXIII.

TABLE XXIII

HEIGHTS OF BRITISH ADULT MALES

Height without shoes (*inches*)	Number of men	Height without shoes (*inches*)	Number of men
57–	2	68–	1,230
58–	4	69–	1,063
59–	14	70–	646
60–	41	71–	392
61–	83	72–	202
62–	169	73–	79
63–	394	74–	32
64–	669	75–	16
65–	990	76–	5
66–	1,223	77–	2
67–	1,329		
		Total	8,585

In the report on this investigation it was stated that measurements were taken to the nearest $\frac{1}{8}$-in. so that the class limits are $56\frac{15}{16}$ ins.–$57\frac{15}{16}$ ins., $57\frac{15}{16}$ ins.–$58\frac{15}{16}$ ins., etc., and the class mid-points are $57\frac{7}{16}$ ins., $58\frac{7}{16}$ ins., etc. For the purpose of illustration it is sufficient to assume that the mid-points are at $57\frac{1}{2}$ ins., $58\frac{1}{2}$ ins., etc., and the histogram constructed from this data is shown in Fig. 31.

There is an important distinction between this example and those which were discussed in Chapter V. If the height of a man falls in the class 61 ins.–62 ins. it is possible for the height to take any value between these limits and similarly for all the other classes between

115

57 ins. and 78 ins. In this sense the height is called a "continuous variable". In all the examples of Chapter V the variable was only capable of taking integral values such as 0, 1, 2 and so on. For instance, in paragraph 5.2, 10 marbles were drawn from a bag and the variable here was the number of red marbles. This variable was restricted to values such as 0, 1, 2 . . . 10 for it is impossible to imagine drawing a sample containing $1\frac{1}{2}$ or 4·679 red marbles.

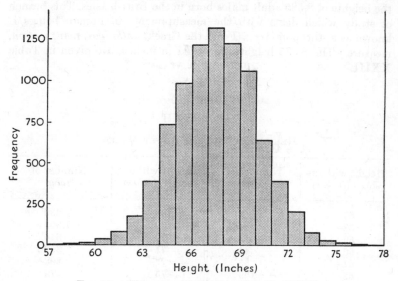

FIG. 31.   Histogram of the data of Table XXIII.

In the present example let x ins. denote the height and let y denote the number of men of height x ins. The question which is to be considered in this chapter may be expressed in this way. Can a relation be found between y and x such as

$$y = f(x) \tag{6.1}$$

which has the property of describing the data? If such a relation does exist it would be expected to have the following features.

(a) Since x is a continuous variable the graph $y = f(x)$ should be a continuous curve.

(b) If the graph is drawn on the same scale as the histogram in Fig. 31 it will resemble the histogram in shape.

6.2.   The Normal Distribution Curve

In 1753 De Moivre obtained an expression for $f(x)$ based on the theory of probability. His work was apparently overlooked and the same result was obtained independently later in the eighteenth century by other workers in the field of probability. Notable among these was Gauss and the curve is sometimes called the Gaussian curve or the Gaussian distribution. It is more usual however to refer to the Normal curve or the Normal distribution.

The theoretical derivation of the Normal curve is mathematically beyond the scope of this book and only the result will be given. The relation is

$$y = \frac{N}{\sigma \sqrt{2\pi}} \, e^{-\frac{(x - \mu)^2}{2\sigma^2}} \tag{6.2}$$

where N = the total number of observations

μ = the mean of the distribution

σ = the standard deviation of the distribution.

This is the curve which has been found to give an adequate fit to statistical data drawn from a great variety of sources. At one time it was held by some that the Normal curve should describe the frequencies of continuous variables occurring in all fields of natural sciences. Exceptions were felt to be abnormal in the sense that they required explanation. These ideas have long been abandoned (See 6.8) although the Normal Distribution remains fundamentally important as the basis of much statistical work.

Example 1.—Find the equation of the Normal curve from the data in section 6.1 and draw the curve on the same scale as the histogram.

From the data we know that $N = 8,585$

Calculation gives the values of the mean and standard deviation as

$$\mu = 67 \cdot 52 \text{ ins.}$$
$$\sigma = 2 \cdot 57 \text{ ins.}$$

Therefore from equation 6.2

$$y = \frac{8,585}{\sqrt{2\pi} \times 2 \cdot 57} \, e^{-\frac{(x - 67 \cdot 52)^2}{2 \times (2 \cdot 57)^2}}$$

or $y = 1,333 \, . \, e^{-\cdot 07728 \, (x - 67 \cdot 52)^2}$

This is the equation of the Normal curve. To draw the curve it is necessary to calculate y for selected values of x. Take logarithms on both sides

$\log_{10} y = 3 \cdot 1249 - 0 \cdot 07728 \, (x - 67 \cdot 52)^2 \, \log_{10} e$ or, since $\log_{10} e = 0 \cdot 4343$,

$\log_{10} y = 3 \cdot 1249 - 0 \cdot 0329 \, (x - 67 \cdot 52)^2$

Now x may be given any values whatsoever but it will obviously simplify the working if x is given values which makes $(x - 67 \cdot 52)$ an integer, say $x = 57 \cdot 52, 58 \cdot 52$, etc. It is most convenient to set out the working in tabular form.

x	$x - 67.52$	$(x - 67.52)^2$	$0.0329 \times$ $(x - 67.52)^2$	$\log_{10} y$	y
57·52	−10	100	3·290	−0·165	1
58·52	− 9	81	2·765	0·360	2
59·52	− 8	64	2·106	1·019	10
60·52	− 7	49	1·612	1·513	33
61·52	− 6	36	1·184	1·941	87
62·52	− 5	25	0·822	2·303	201
63·52	− 4	16	0·526	2·599	397
64·52	− 3	9	0·296	2·829	675
65·52	− 2	4	0·132	2·993	984
66·52	− 1	1	0·033	3·092	1,236
67·52	0	0	0	3·125	1,334
68·52	1	1	0·033	3·092	1,236

It is not necessary to continue the table because just as the value of y is the same for $x = 66.52$ and $x = 68.52$ ($= 67.52 \pm 1$) so the values of y are the same for $x = 67.52 \pm 2$, 67.52 ± 3, etc. If now the points (x, y) are plotted on the same scale as the histogram and joined by a smooth curve, we get the result shown in Fig. 32. The resemblance in shape between the curve and the histogram is apparent.

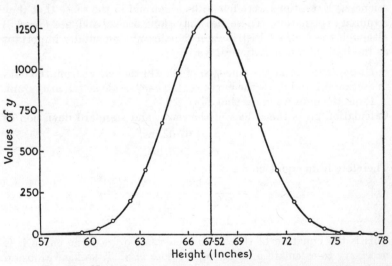

Fig. 32.   Normal curve derived from the data of Table XXIII.

EXERCISES XVII

1. Taking $N = 1,000$ plot the two curves for which $\mu = 0$ and $\sigma = 1$ and 2 respectively.   (In this case the equations are $y = \dfrac{1,000}{\sqrt{2\pi}} \cdot e^{-\frac{1}{2}x^2}$ and $y = \dfrac{1,000}{2\sqrt{2\pi}} \cdot e^{-\frac{1}{8}x^2}$).

2. A ruler is marked in inches only. Fifty people estimate the length of a line to the nearest tenth of an inch with the following results:

Estimate of length	6·2″	6·3″	6·4″	6·5″	6·6″	6·7″	6·8″	6·9″	7·0″
Number of people	1	2	5	11	12	10	7	1	1

Fit a Normal frequency curve to the data. Draw the curve and the histogram.

3. Obtain the chest measurements of 100 students. Draw the histogram and the Normal curve calculated from the data.

4. The diameters of circular shafts are measured over a period of manufacture and the average and standard deviation are given by $\mu = 1·79$ in., $\sigma = 0·04$ in. Taking any convenient value of N (100 or 1,000 say) draw the Normal frequency curve. If the specification limits on diameter are 1·80 in. $\pm$ 0·09 in. shade the areas on the curve which lie outside the specification limits.

5. The ranging error of a field-gun is given by $\sigma = 15$ ft. Taking the mean point of impact as zero (i.e., $\mu = 0$) draw the Normal frequency distribution describing the fall of shot.

6. The following table gives the frequency distribution of weights of adult males born in the United Kingdom (*Report of Anthropometric Committee to the British Association*, 1883).

Weight in lb.	Frequency	Weight in lb.	Frequency
90 –	2	190 –	263
100 –	34	200 –	107
110 –	152	210 –	85
120 –	390	220 –	41
130 –	867	230 –	16
140 –	1,623	240 –	11
150 –	1,559	250 –	8
160 –	1,326	260 –	1
170 –	787	270 –	—
180 –	476	280 –	1

Assuming that the mid-class values are 95, 105, etc., construct the histogram. Calculate N, μ and σ and draw the Normal frequency distribution on the same scale as the histogram. Does the theoretical distribution appear to fit the histogram?

7. Draw on the same scale the two Normal frequency distributions which have $\mu = 8$; $\sigma = 2$ and $\mu = 10$; $\sigma = 2$. Shade the overlapping area. Compare the size of this area with that of the two Normal frequency distributions which have $\mu = 8$; $\sigma = 1$ and $\mu = 10$; $\sigma = 1$.

8. The following table gives the electrical resistances of 138 carbon rods tested at the same temperature.

Resistance in ohms.

(Mid-class value)	310	311	312	313	314	315	316	317	318	319	320
Frequency	1	2	6	21	25	32	24	18	5	3	1

Calculate the mean resistance and standard deviation and draw the Normal frequency distribution. Compare it with the histogram representing the data.

6.3 Some Properties of the Normal Distribution Curve

THE MODIFIED EQUATION OF THE NORMAL CURVE

A simplification of equation 6.2 can be made if the origin of the x-scale is moved to $x = \mu$. Equation 6.2 now becomes

$$y = \frac{N}{\sigma\sqrt{2\pi}} \cdot e^{\frac{-x^2}{2\sigma^2}}. \tag{6.3}$$

where x represents not the actual measurement but the deviation of a measurement from the mean, μ.

THE AREA UNDER THE NORMAL CURVE. N occurs in equation 6.3 merely as a constant proportional factor and if it is omitted the equation becomes

$$y = \frac{1}{\sigma\sqrt{2\pi}} \cdot e^{\frac{-x^2}{2\sigma^2}} \tag{6.4}$$

The area under the curve is given by the expression

$$\frac{1}{\sigma\sqrt{2\pi}} \int_{-\infty}^{\infty} e^{-x^2/2\sigma^2} \, dx$$

and it can be shown mathematically that the area under the curve is unity. Therefore if the factor N is re-introduced the area under the corresponding curve becomes N units.

THE SYMMETRY OF THE NORMAL CURVE. Since both $(+ x)^2$ and $(- x)^2$ are positive and have the same value, it can be seen from equation 6.4 that the value of y is the same for $+ x$ and for $- x$. In other words the height of the curve at equal distances on either side of the origin is the same. Therefore the Normal curve is symmetrical about the ordinate at $x = 0$.

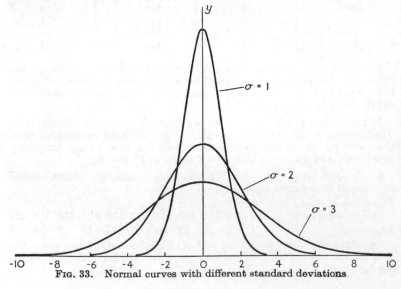

FIG. 33.   Normal curves with different standard deviations.

THE SPREAD OF THE NORMAL CURVE. In Fig. 33 are shown three Normal curves referred to the mean as origin and with standard deviations $\sigma = 1$, 2 and 3. As σ increases the curves become flatter and more extended although it should be observed that they retain the characteristic bell shape. In each case when $x > 3\sigma$ the tails of the curve become flat and nearly touch the x-axis.

THE MODE OF THE NORMAL CURVE. In equation 6.4 for $x = 0$, $e^{\frac{-x^2}{2\sigma^2}} = e^0 = 1$. For all other values of x, positive or negative, $e^{\frac{-x^2}{2\sigma^2}}$ is less than 1. Therefore the maximum value of y occurs at $x = 0$, and is given by $y_{max} = \dfrac{1}{\sigma\sqrt{2\pi}}$ (6.5)

This can be expressed by saying that the mode of the Normal curve is the same as the mean.

THE MEDIAN OF THE NORMAL CURVE. It has been shown that the Normal curve is symmetrical about the origin. Therefore the ordinate at $x = 0$ divides the curve into two equal areas, and so the median of the Normal curve coincides with the mode.

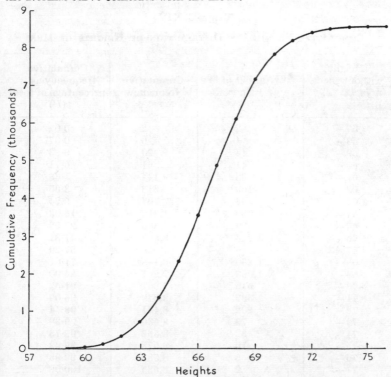

FIG. 34. Cumulative frequency distribution of the data of Table XXIV.

EXERCISES XVIII

1. Use equation 6.4 to show that the values of y_{max} for three Normal curves with standard deviations $= 1, 2$ and 3 are in the ratio $3 : 2 : 1$.

2. Show that the areas on either side of the ordinate $x = \mu$ are each equal to $\frac{1}{2}$.

3. In equation 6.4 take $\sigma = 1$. If $y(x)$ denotes the value of y at x calculate $y(0)$, $y(1)$, $y(2)$ and $y(3)$ and show that $y(3)/y(0) = 0.01$ approximately.

4. In the example of Section 6.1 verify by counting squares, or otherwise, that the area under the curve is approximately equal to N, i.e., 8,585.

6.4   Arithmetic Probability Graph Paper

Chapter II, paragraph 3 showed how the cumulative frequency could be plotted against the variable to give the cumulative frequency curve or ogive. Table XXIV and Fig. 34 show how this is done for the data in Table XXIII when the cumulative frequencies are expressed as percentages of the total frequencies.

TABLE XXIV

CUMULATIVE FREQUENCY DISTRIBUTION OF HEIGHTS OF MEN

Height without shoes, *inches* (x)	Number of men	Cumulative frequency	Cumulative frequency as percentage of total (P)
57 —	2	2	0·02
58 —	4	6	0·07
59 —	14	20	0·23
60 —	41	61	0·71
61 —	83	144	1·68
62 —	169	313	3·65
63 —	394	707	8·24
64 —	669	1,376	16·03
65 —	990	2,366	27·56
66 —	1,223	3,589	41·81
67 —	1,329	4,918	57·29
68 —	1,230	6,148	71·61
69 —	1,063	7,211	84·00
70 —	646	7,857	91·52
71 —	392	8,249	96·09
72 —	202	8,451	98·44
73 —	79	8,530	99·36
74 —	32	8,562	99·73
75 —	16	8,578	99·92
76 —	5	8,583	99·98
77 —	2	8,585	100·00

In Fig. 34 the % cumulative frequencies are plotted against the upper class boundary value, that is 0·02 against 58, 0·07 against 59, so that at any point on the curve the ordinate represents a height and

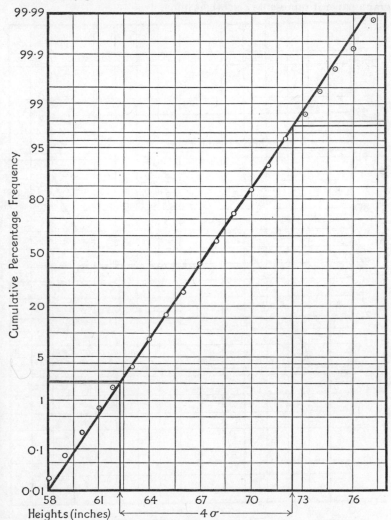

Fig. 35. Data of Table XXIV plotted on arithmetic probability paper.

the abscissa represents the percentage of results which do not exceed that height. The total % cumulative frequency, 100·00, is not plotted since there is no upper limit to the last class.

The scale of % cumulative frequencies on arithmetic probability graph paper is not at a uniform interval as in Fig. 34, but is compressed at each end (near 0% and 100%) in such a way that when the ogive of the Normal distribution is plotted on arithmetic probability graph paper it represents a straight line.

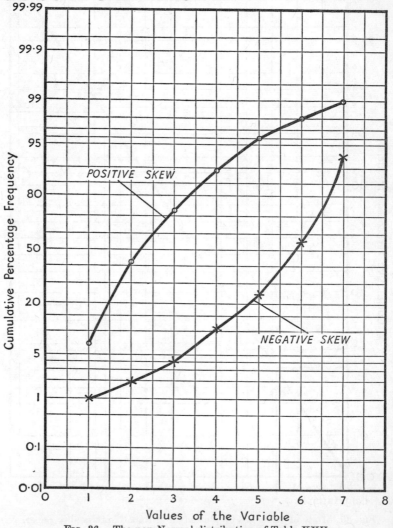

FIG. 36.   The non-Normal distribution of Table XXV.

Fig. 35 shows the data of Table XXIV plotted on arithmetic probability graph paper. A line has been drawn with a ruler which passes through or near to most of the points.

It should be noted that only data which represents a Normal distribution will give a straight line on arithmetic probability graph paper and this provides a useful test as to whether frequency data are Normally distributed. Table XXV shows two artificial frequency distributions both of which are skew, one in the positive sense and the other in a negative sense. When these distributions are plotted on probability graph paper in Fig. 36 the points do not lie on straight lines but on a curve which is concave to the horizontal axis in the case of the positive skew distribution and convex in the case of the negative skew distribution.

TABLE XXV

SKEW DISTRIBUTIONS

Variable (Upper class limit)	Frequency (− ve skew)	% cumulative frequency	Frequency (+ ve skew)	% cumulative frequency
1	1	1	7	7
2	1	2	36	43
3	2	4	30	73
4	7	11	16	89
5	16	27	7	96
6	30	57	2	98
7	31	93	1	99
8	7	100	1	100
Totals 100			100	

When Normally distributed data are plotted on arithmetic probability graph paper the result can be used to obtain estimates for the mean and standard deviation with very little effort.

(1) *Mean.* It has been shown that for the Normal distribution the mean coincides with the median. Therefore the ordinate x (50) at $P = 50\%$ gives the mean of the distribution. For the data plotted in Fig. 35 the mean is 67·5. This compares very well with the calculated value of 67·52.

(2) *Standard deviation.* The standard deviation is given by the relation

$$4\sigma = x\,(97\text{·}72) - x\,(2\text{·}28)$$

where x (97·72) means the value of the ordinate at $P = 97\text{·}72\%$ and x (2·28) means the value at $P = 2\text{·}28\%$. The reason for this relation will appear in section 6.6.

From Fig. 35

$$4 \sigma = 72 \cdot 30 - 62 \cdot 25$$
$$= 10 \cdot 05$$
$$\sigma = 2 \cdot 51$$

This is very close to the calculated value of $\sigma = 2 \cdot 52$.

EXERCISES XIX

1. Plot the data of Ex. XVII, 2 on arithmetic probability graph paper and hence determine the mean and standard deviation.

2. Plot the data of Ex. XVII, 6 on arithmetic probability graph paper. Do the results appear to be Normally distributed?

3. Use probability paper to obtain the mean and standard deviation of the distribution given in Ex. XVII, 8.

4. The following data represent a rectangular distribution in which all the frequencies for equal class intervals are the same. Draw the ogive on ordinary graph paper and compare with the result when plotted on arithmetic probability graph paper.

Variable (upper limit)	1	2	3	4	5	6	7	8	
Frequency	125	125	125	125	125	125	125	125	Total 1,000

5. Number the x-axis of a probability graph paper with any convenient scale such as 1, 2, 3 . . . Draw any straight line slanting upwards from left to right. Calculate the mean, μ, and standard deviation, σ. Read from the graph the percentage of results which are less than $\mu - 3\sigma$, $\mu - 2\sigma, \mu - \sigma, \mu + \sigma, \mu + 2\sigma, \mu + 3\sigma$. These results are perfectly general and true for all Normal distributions since both the scale and the line were chosen arbitrarily.

6. Plot the following results on arithmetic probability graph paper and hence calculate the mean and standard deviation.

Length of Telephone Calls

Time (secs.)	Number of calls
0–100	1
100–200	22
200–300	71
300–400	144
400–500	198
500–600	207
600–700	106
700–800	34
800–900	9
300–1,000	4

Total 796

7. In a certain trade wages are distributed according to the Normal distribution law. The mean wage is £20. The proportion of men receiving less than £17 is 15%. Draw on probability paper the line representing the distribution. What is the standard deviation?

8. The detailed records of an experiment have been lost and the only information that is left is that $\frac{1}{10}$ of the results were less than 4·0, and $\frac{1}{3}$ of the results were less than 2·0. It can be assumed that the results were Normally distributed. Use probability graph paper to find the mean and standard deviation of the results. What percentage of the results were less than 5·0?

6.5   Further Properties of the Normal Distribution Curve

Many properties of the Normal curve can be derived only by using the differential and integral calculus. The use and application of the curve can be understood, however, without reference to the calculus so that non-mathematical readers will be under no disadvantage in omitting this section and the Exercises which follow it. It will be shown that the constants μ and σ of the equation 6.2 do in fact represent the mean and standard deviation of the *frequency curve*.

AN IMPORTANT INTEGRAL.—A well-known result of the integral calculus which will only be stated here is that

$$\int_{-\infty}^{+\infty} e^{-t^2}\, dt = \sqrt{\pi} \tag{6.6}$$

THE AREA UNDER THE CURVE.—The equation of the Normal curve referred to the mean as origin is

$$y = \frac{1}{\sigma\sqrt{2\pi}} \cdot e^{-\frac{x^2}{2\sigma^2}} \tag{6.7}$$

so that the area under the curve, denoted by A, is

$$A = \int_{-\infty}^{+\infty} y\, dx = \frac{1}{\sigma\sqrt{2\pi}} \int_{-\infty}^{+\infty} e^{-\frac{x^2}{2\sigma^2}} \cdot dx$$

Let $t = \dfrac{x}{\sigma\sqrt{2}}$, so that $dt = \dfrac{dx}{\sigma\sqrt{2}}$,

and $A = \dfrac{1}{\sqrt{\pi}} \displaystyle\int_{-\infty}^{+\infty} e^{-t^2} \cdot dt = 1$ using equation 6.6.

The right-hand side of equation 6.7 is therefore the relative frequency density, $f(x)$, of the Normal frequency curve. (See section 1.7.)

Note that x takes all values from $+\infty$ to $-\infty$. Theoretically this is convenient and practically it is unimportant because y becomes very small for values of $|x|$ greater than 3σ.

THE MEAN.—The mean is given by

$$\bar{x} = \int_{-\infty}^{+\infty} x \cdot f(x).dx \text{ where } f(x) \text{ is the relative frequency density,}$$

so that $\bar{x} = \dfrac{1}{\sigma\sqrt{2\pi}} \displaystyle\int_{-\infty}^{+\infty} x \cdot e^{-\frac{x^2}{2\sigma^2}} \cdot dx$

Let $\quad t = \dfrac{x}{\sigma\sqrt{2}}$ as before, then

$$\bar{x} = \frac{\sigma}{\sqrt{2\pi}} \int_{-\infty}^{+\infty} 2t \cdot e^{-t^2} \cdot dt$$

$$= \frac{\sigma}{\sqrt{2\pi}} \left[-e^{-t^2} \right]_{-\infty}^{+\infty} = 0$$

This result can be obtained more directly by observing that $x.f(x)$ is an odd function of x so that

$$\int_{0}^{+\infty} x \cdot f(x) \cdot dx = -\int_{-\infty}^{0} x \cdot f(x) \cdot dx$$

Remembering that the equation of the Normal curve is referred to the mean, μ, as origin, we now have the result that the mean of the curve has the same value as the mean of the data to which it is fitted.

THE STANDARD DEVIATION.—Let the mean square deviation from the mean for the frequency curve be denoted by $\overline{x^2}$. Then, since the mean is at the origin, we have

$$\overline{x^2} = \int x^2 \cdot f(x) \cdot dx = \frac{1}{\sigma\sqrt{2\pi}} \int_{-\infty}^{+\infty} x^2 \cdot e^{-\frac{x^2}{2\sigma^2}} \cdot dx.$$

Substituting $t = \dfrac{x}{\sigma\sqrt{2}}$ as before,

$$\overline{x^2} = \frac{\sigma^2}{\sqrt{\pi}} \int_{-\infty}^{+\infty} t \cdot (2t \cdot e^{-t^2})\, dt$$

$$= \frac{\sigma^2}{\sqrt{\pi}} \cdot t \int_{-\infty}^{+\infty} 2t \cdot e^{-t^2} \cdot dt + \frac{\sigma^2}{\sqrt{\pi}} \int_{-\infty}^{+\infty} 1 \cdot e^{-t^2} \cdot dt$$

$$= 0 + \frac{\sigma^2}{\sqrt{\pi}} \cdot \sqrt{\pi} = \sigma^2$$

The mean and standard deviation of the Normal frequency curve are therefore μ and σ. It has been shown in section 6.2 how the Normal frequency curve is fitted to a numerical distribution by giving μ and σ the numerical values of the mean and standard deviation of the distribution.

EXERCISES XX

1. Show that the Normal curve has a stationary value at the mean and prove that it is a maximum.

2. When the Normal curve is not referred to the mean as origin, i.e.

if $y = \dfrac{1}{\sigma\sqrt{2\pi}} \cdot e^{-\frac{(x-\mu)^2}{2\sigma^2}}$ show that $\displaystyle\int_{-\infty}^{+\infty} xy \cdot dx = \mu$. Interpret this result.

3. Show that the points of inflexion of the Normal curve occur at $x = \mu \pm \sigma$.

4. Show that the slopes of the Normal curve at its points of inflexion are given by $\pm \dfrac{1}{\sigma^2\sqrt{2\pi e}}$.

5. If $\overline{x^4}$ denotes the mean value of the fourth power of the deviations show that $\overline{x^4} = 3\,\sigma^4$.

6. Prove that the mean deviation of the Normal curve is $\sqrt{\dfrac{2}{\pi}} \cdot \sigma$.

6.6   The Normal Probability Tables

It has been shown that if a frequency distribution is adequately fitted by the Normal curve then, given the values of μ and σ, it is possible to represent the distribution by drawing this curve. All the information from the numerical data is summarised in the curve. For example if $\mu = 10$ and $\sigma = 0.5$ the curve corresponding to these values is shown in Fig. 37.

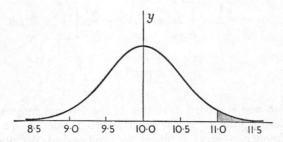

FIG. 37.   The Normal curve for $\mu = 10$, $\sigma = \frac{1}{2}$. The shaded area represents the proportion of results greater than 11.

If now the source of the original data is still available for investigation and one additional measurement is taken what is the probability that this measurement will not be less than a certain value, say 11? This question can be put in another form. If we consider our original data as a sample of finite size from a very large population of measurements what proportion of these measurements consists of values not less than 11?

In Fig. 37 the area to the right of the ordinate at $x = 11$ has been shaded. This shaded area represents the proportion of readings which are not less than 11; the required probability is given by the ratio of the shaded area to the whole area under the curve. But since the whole area under the curve is equal to 1 the probability or proportion is given simply by the shaded area.

The calculation of this area is greatly facilitated by the use of the "Normal Probability Table"—Table XXVI (p. 132). In this table a function $P(d \geqslant D)$ is tabulated against D. Here D is a selected deviation from the mean divided by the standard deviation and corresponding to some selected value of the variable, X, so that

$$D = (X - \mu)/\sigma$$

In the same way d is any observed deviation from the mean divided by the standard deviation and corresponding to an observation x so that

$$d = (x - \mu)/\sigma$$

The function $P\,(d \geqslant D)$ can be interpreted as:

(a) the area under the Normal curve to the right of the ordinate at $X = \sigma D + \mu$,

(b) the probability of obtaining in one trial a measurement x greater than or equal to X (a deviation d greater than or equal to D),

(c) the proportion of the population of measurements which are greater than or equal to $X = \sigma D + \mu$.

For $D = 0$, $P\,(d \geqslant D) = 0.5000$. This expresses the fact that the Normal curve is bisected at the mean.

Referring to Fig. 37, since $\mu = 10$, we have

$$D = (X - \mu)/\sigma$$
$$= (11 - 10) \div \tfrac{1}{2}$$
$$= 2$$

Enter the table at $D = 2$ and read $P\,(d \geqslant D) = 0.0228$. Therefore the chance that a further result would be greater or equal to 11 is 0.0228 or 2.3%.

It should be noted that, since the curve is symmetrical, the area beyond D in the positive direction is the same as the area beyond $-D$ in the negative direction. This is illustrated in Fig. 38. Therefore the probability of getting a result smaller than 9 is also 0.0228 and so the total probability of getting a result outside the limits 10 ± 1 is 2×0.0228 or $= 0.0456$.

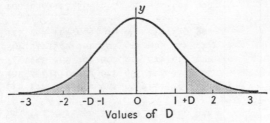

FIG. 38. The symmetry of the Normal curve.

Example 1. From the data given in section 6.1 find the probability that in 1883 a man taken at random would have been (a) over 5 ft. 11 ins. in height, (b) less than 5 ft. 1 in.

In this example $\mu = 67.52$; $\sigma = 2.57$

(a) 5 ft. 11 ins. = 71 ins. and therefore the deviation from the mean is $71 - 67.52 = 3.48$ and $D = \dfrac{3.48}{2.57} = 1.35$

TABLE XXVI

NORMAL DISTRIBUTION

THE FRACTION $P(d \geqslant D)$, WHERE $D = (X - \mu)/\sigma$

Deviate D	Prefix	0·00	0·01	0·02	0·03	0·04	0·05	0·06	0·07	0·08	0·09
0·0	0·5	000	960	920	880	840	801	761	721	681	641
0·1	0·4	602	562	522	483	443	404	364	325	286	247
0·2	0·4	207	168	129	090	052	013	974	936	897	859
0·3	0·3	821	783	745	707	669	632	594	557	520	483
0·4		446	409	372	336	300	264	228	192	156	121
0·5	0·3	085	050	015	981	946	912	877	843	810	776
0·6	0·2	743	709	676	643	611	578	546	514	483	451
0·7		420	389	358	327	296	266	236	206	177	148
0·8	0·2	119	090	061	033	005	977	949	922	894	867
0·9	0·1	841	814	788	762	736	711	685	660	635	611
1·0		587	563	539	515	492	469	446	423	401	379
1·1		357	335	314	292	271	251	230	210	190	170
1·2	0·1	151	131	112	093	075	056	038	020	003	985
1·3	0·0	968	951	934	918	901	885	869	853	838	823
1·4		808	793	778	764	749	735	721	708	694	681
1·5		668	655	643	630	618	606	594	582	571	559
1·6		548	537	526	516	505	495	485	475	465	455
1·7		446	436	427	418	409	401	392	384	375	367
1·8		359	351	344	336	329	322	314	307	301	294
1·9		287	281	274	268	262	256	250	244	239	233
2·0		228	222	217	212	207	202	197	192	188	183
2·1		179	174	170	166	162	158	154	150	146	143
2·2		139	136	132	129	125	122	119	116	113	110
2·3	0·0	107	104	102	990	964	939	914	889	866	842
2·4	0·00	820	798	776	755	734	714	695	676	657	639
2·5		621	604	587	570	554	539	523	508	494	480
2·6		466	453	440	427	414	402	391	379	368	357
2·7		347	336	326	317	307	298	289	280	272	264
2·8		256	248	240	233	226	219	212	205	199	193
2·9	0·00	187	181	175	169	164	159	154	149	144	140

TABLE XXVI—*continued.*

Deviate (D)	Proportion of Whole Area (P)	Deviate (D)	Proportion of Whole Area (P)	Deviate (D)	Proportion of Whole Area (P)	Deviate (D)	Proportion of Whole Area (P)
3·0	·00 135	3·5	·000 233	4·0	·0^4 317	4·5	·0^5 340
3·1	·000 968	3·6	·000 159	4·1	·0^4 207	4·6	·0^5 211
3·2	·000 687	3·7	·000 108	4·2	·0^4 133	4·7	·0^5 130
3·3	·000 483	3·8	·0^4 723	4·3	·0^4 085	4·8	·0^6 793
3·4	·000 337	3·9	·0^4 481	4·4	·0^4 054	4·9	·0^6 479
						5·0	·0^6 287

From the table for this value of D P $(d \geqslant D) = 0.0885$ and so the required probability is 0.0885 or 8.85%.

(b) 5 ft. 1 in. = 61 ins., and the deviation for this value
$$= 61 - 67.52 = -6.52, \text{ and } D = -\frac{6.52}{2.57} = -2.54$$

Remembering that the area below -2.54 is the same as that above $+2.54$ enter the table at $D = 2.54$ and read P $(d \geqslant D) = 0.0055$. Therefore the required probability is 0.0055 or about 0.6%.

The combined chance of selecting a man who was either taller than 5 ft. 11 ins. or shorter than 5 ft. 1 in. would be $0.0885 + 0.0055$ or 0.094 approximately. The proportion of the adult male population between these heights would be $(1 - 0.094)$ or about 0.906.

Example 2. As a result of tests on electric light bulbs it was found that the lifetime of a particular make was distributed normally with an average life of 2,040 hours and a standard deviation of 60 hours. What proportion of bulbs can be expected to have a life (a) of more than 2,150 hours, (b) of more than 1,960 hours?

Here $\mu = 2,040$ and $\sigma = 60$.

(a) As $2,150 - 2,040 = 110$, $D = \dfrac{110}{60} = 1.833$

From the table P $(d \geqslant D) = 0.0336$ for $D = 1.83$

P $(d \geqslant D) = 0.0329$ for $D = 1.84$

By interpolating for $D = 1.833$ we find that the required proportion is 0.0334 or 3.34%.

(*b*) Here we have to find the shaded area shown in Fig. 39. The simplest method is first to find the unshaded area and then subtract from 1. The deviation from the mean is $(1,960 - 2,040) = -80$, so $D = \dfrac{-80}{60} = -1\cdot333$ and $P(d \geqslant D) = 0\cdot0918$ for $D = +1\cdot33$; $P(d \geqslant D) = 0\cdot0901$ for $D = +1\cdot34$. Therefore by interpolation the unshaded area is $0\cdot0912$ and so the required proportion which will have longer life than 1,960 hours is $1 - 0\cdot0912 = 0\cdot9088$ or $90\cdot88\%$.

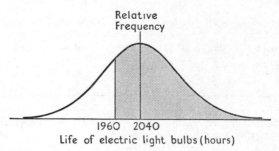

Relative
Frequency

1960   2040
Life of electric light bulbs (hours)

FIG. 39.   The shaded area shows the proportion of bulbs burning for more than 1960 hours.

Example 3.   Steel rods are manufactured to be 3 ins. in diameter but they are acceptable if they are inside the limits 2·99 ins. and 3·01 ins. It is observed that about 5% are rejected oversize and 5% are rejected undersize. Assuming that the diameters are Normally distributed find the standard deviation of the distribution. Hence calculate what the proportion of rejects would be if the permissible limits were widened to 2·985 ins. and 3·015 ins.

The high and low rejects are approximately the same and therefore it can be assumed that the average diameter is 3·00 ins. Since 5% are over the limit 3·01 ins., or, in other words, 5% have deviations greater than the mean by 0·01 ins. or more we have $P(d \geqslant D) = 0\cdot05$. It is now necessary to read from the table a value of D corresponding to this value of $P(d \geqslant D)$.

This is given by $D = 1\cdot65$, and as we know that $X = 0\cdot01$, therefore $\sigma = 0\cdot01/1\cdot65$.

If the limits are now widened the deviation of the upper limit from the mean is given by

$$X = 3\cdot015 - 3\cdot000 = 0\cdot015 \text{ ins.}$$

and $D = 0\cdot015 \times 1\cdot65/0\cdot01 = 2\cdot475$.

For this value of D, $P(d \geqslant D) = 0\cdot0067$ and therefore the proportion of rejects outside the new limits would be $2 \times 0\cdot0067 = 0\cdot0134$ or $1\cdot34\%$.

Example 4.   Derive the relation $4\sigma = x\,(97 \cdot 72) - x\,(2 \cdot 28)$ used in connection with arithmetic probability graph paper.

From the table of the Normal probability integral the proportion of results greater than $\mu + 2\sigma$ is $2 \cdot 28\%$ and so the proportion of results less than $\mu + 2\sigma$ is $97 \cdot 72\%$.

Therefore $\qquad\qquad x\,(97 \cdot 72) = \mu + 2\sigma$

Similarly $\qquad\qquad x\,(2 \cdot 28) = \mu - 2\sigma$

and $\qquad x\,(97 \cdot 72) - x\,(2 \cdot 28) = 4\sigma$

The result is illustrated in Fig. 40.

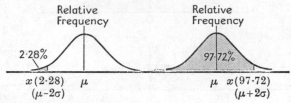

Fig. 40.   Illustration of the relation $4\sigma = x(97.72) - x(2.28)$.

6.7   The Problem of Curve Fitting

In Chapter V when discussing the Binomial and Poisson distributions the actual frequencies which occurred were compared with those predicted by the appropriate theoretical distribution. This can be done for the Normal distribution curve in the following way. When a comparison is to be made the first step is to construct the histogram. The appropriate Normal curve is found by calculating the mean and standard deviation. The Normal Probability Table is then used to calculate the areas of the portions of the Normal curve which lie between ordinates at the class limits of the histograms. If there is a good fit these areas should correspond approximately to the frequencies represented by the columns of the histogram. An example of this procedure will be given in Chapter X.

6.8   Non-Normal Distributions

The Normal distribution is by no means the only continuous variable distribution in the theory of statistics. In section 6.2 it was remarked that early workers had thought that the Normal distribution would fit all sets of measurements occurring in Nature. The occurrence of distributions which were patently non-Normal dispelled this theory. As a consequence statisticians examined other types of theoretical distribution. These will not be discussed here but four well-known theoretical distributions are given in equations 6.8 to 6.11 and are illustrated in Fig. 41.

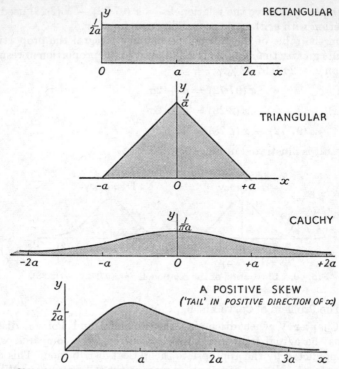

RECTANGULAR

TRIANGULAR

CAUCHY

A POSITIVE SKEW
('TAIL' IN POSITIVE DIRECTION OF x)

FIG. 41.   Some well-known distributions drawn to the same scale.

RECTANGULAR DISTRIBUTION

$$y = \frac{1}{2a} \quad (0 \leqslant x \leqslant 2a) \tag{6.8}$$

TRIANGULAR DISTRIBUTION

$$y = \frac{1}{a^2}(x + a) \quad (-a \leqslant x \leqslant 0)$$
$$y = \frac{1}{a^2}(-x + a) \quad (0 \leqslant x \leqslant a) \tag{6.9}$$

CAUCHY DISTRIBUTION

$$y = \frac{1}{\pi}\frac{a}{a^2 + x^2} \quad (-\infty < x < \infty) \tag{6.10}$$

A "POSITIVE SKEW" DISTRIBUTION

$$y = \frac{x}{a^2} \cdot e^{-\frac{x^2}{2a^2}} \quad (0 \leqslant x < \infty) \tag{6.11}$$

SUMMARY OF CHAPTER VI

1. The equation of the Normal distribution curve is given by

$$y = \frac{N}{\sigma\sqrt{2\pi}} \cdot e^{-\frac{(x-\mu)^2}{2\sigma^2}}$$

where x = variable,

y = frequency corresponding to x,

N = total number of observations,

μ = the mean of the distribution curve,

σ = the standard deviation of the distribution curve.

2. If a new origin for x is taken at the mean the equation of the Normal distribution curve becomes

$$y = \frac{N}{\sigma\sqrt{2\pi}} \cdot e^{-\frac{x^2}{2\sigma^2}}$$

3. The area under the Normal distribution curve is N (analogous to the area of the histogram). It is customary to omit N from the equation and write

$$y = \frac{1}{\sigma\sqrt{2\pi}} \cdot e^{-\frac{x^2}{2\sigma^2}}$$

and y now represents the relative frequency density.

4. The curve is symmetrical about the ordinate at $x = 0$ and the mode occurs at $x = 0$.

5. When the cumulative frequencies of data which are Normally distributed is plotted on probability graph paper the result is a straight line. The mean is given by $x(50)$, the value of x corresponding to $P = 50\%$. The standard deviation is given by

$$4\sigma = x(97 \cdot 72) - x(2 \cdot 28)$$

6. If a Normal curve has a mean μ and standard deviation σ and if D denotes $(X - \mu)/\sigma$ then $P(d \geqslant D)$ can be read from D in Table XXVI.

$P(d \geqslant D)$ can be interpreted as:

(a) the area under the Normal curve to the right of the ordinate at $\sigma D + \mu$,

(b) the chance of obtaining in a trial a measurement whose deviation from the mean is d such that d is greater than or equal to D,

(c) the proportion of the population of measurements which are greater than or equal to $\sigma D + \mu$.

7. The area under the Normal curve outside the ordinates at $\pm D$ is given by $2P (d \geqslant D)$.

8. The area to the left of the ordinate at $+ D$ is given by $1 - P (d \geqslant D)$.

EXERCISES XXI

Unless it is stated otherwise assume in the following questions that the Normal law applies. In answering these questions it is useful to sketch rough diagrams.

1. Find the proportion of the Normal curve included between the limits $\mu \pm \sigma; \mu \pm 2\sigma; \mu \pm 3\sigma$.

2. Exactly 0.5 of the Normal curve is included between the limits $\mu \pm t\sigma$. Find t.

3. A Normal distribution has mean $\mu = 12$ and standard deviation $\sigma = 2$. Find the following areas under the curve.

    (a) From $x = 10$ to $x = 13.5$
    (b) From $x = 11.4$ to $x = 14.2$
    (c) From $x = 9.6$ to $x = 13.8$
    (d) From $x = 6$ to $x = 18$

4. A distribution has $\mu = 0$ and $\sigma = 1$.
Find the values of D such that $P(d \geqslant D)$ is (a) 0.25, (b) 0.80, (c) 0.99, (d) 0.025.

5. A distribution has mean $\mu = 11$ and $\sigma = 1.5$.
What is the value of D such that $P(d \geqslant D)$ is (a) 0.3, (b) 0.9?

6. Express in words the meaning of $P(d \geqslant D_1) - P(d \geqslant D_2)$.
Calculate this expression when $\mu = 6, \sigma = 0.25$ for

    (a) $D_1 = 5.5$, $D_2 = 6.5$
    (b) $D_1 = 5.95$, $D_2 = 6.0$
    (c) $D_1 = 5.6$, $D_2 = 6.8$

7. A hundred standard squash balls are tested by dropping from a height of 100 ins. and measuring the height of bounce. A ball is "fast" if it rises above 32 ins. The average height of bounce was 30 ins. and the standard deviation was $\frac{3}{4}$ ins. What is the chance of getting a "fast" standard ball?

8. Sacks of grain packed by an automatic machine loader have an average weight of 114 lbs. It is found that 10% of the bags are over 116 lbs. Find the standard deviation.

9. In Exercise 8 the machine is adjusted and the average weight per bag is now 113 lbs. Assume that the standard deviation is unaltered and calculate the probability that a bag is now over 116 lbs.

10. Show that the ordinates $y(0)$, $y(\sigma)$, $y(2\sigma)$, $y(3\sigma)$ at $x = 0$, σ, 2σ, 3σ are $\dfrac{1}{\sigma\sqrt{2\pi}}\left(1, \dfrac{1}{\sqrt{e}}, \dfrac{1}{e^2}, \dfrac{1}{e^4\sqrt{e}}\right)$.

Find the areas of the three polygons formed by these ordinates and show that their sum is approximately $\frac{1}{2}$.

11. Two brands of torch batteries have the same average life, 60 hours, but different standard deviations, of $1\frac{1}{2}$ and $2\frac{1}{4}$ hours. In each case what is the chance that a battery will not have a life of longer than 56 hours?

12. In a population of adult men 14% are 5 ft. 11 ins. or over in height and 10% are less than 5 ft. 1 in. Find the mean and standard deviation of the population using probability tables. Verify your result by using probability graph paper.

13. Construct a sheet of arithmetic probability paper using the Normal probability tables. (Suggestion. On a sheet of ordinary graph paper draw a slanting line. For convenience take $\mu = 0$, $\sigma = 1$ and scale the y-axis from -3 to $+3$).

MATHEMATICAL

14. Find the mean of the rectangular distribution given in equation 6.8. Refer the distribution to the mean as origin and find the standard deviation.

15. Find the mean of the Cauchy distribution (equation 6.10) and show that the standard deviation is infinite.

16. Show that the area under the distribution curve

$$y = \frac{x}{a^2} \cdot e^{-\frac{x^2}{2a^2}} \quad (0 \leqslant x \leqslant \infty)$$

between the ordinates at $x = 0$, $x = a\sqrt{2}$ is $(1 - 1/e)$.

END OF PART ONE

Answers to Exercises in Part One

Exercises I (p. 20)

2. With so great a frequency range it is worth considering whether to use *log* (*frequency*) rather than *frequency*, i.e., arithmetic-logarithmic paper. **3.** See comment on Example 2.

Exercises II (p. 30)

2. The three histograms should be drawn with class intervals of 4 marks. **3.** A class-interval of 0·1 in. is appropriate. **4.** (*a*) 0·5 hours from 0·0 hours; (*b*) 25 marks from 250 marks; (*c*) 100 or 150 hours from 0 hours; (*d*) 1·0 or 1·5 mins. from 0 min.; (*e*) 0·01 lb. from 0·9800 lb.; (*f*) 5,000 from 765,000. **6.** There is little indication of any relation (or "association") between humidity and barometric height for August. Is it safe to generalise this conclusion? Would you expect a similar result for one of the winter months? **7.** (*a*) Bar-chart or straight-line graph; (*b*) bar-chart or pie-chart; (*c*) straight-line graph; (*d*) histogram; (*e*) pie-chart. **8.** (*a*) Bar-chart; (*b*) the last class-intervals could be 75–84 for men, 75–89 for women; but these are only guesses; (*c*) pie-chart; (*d*) pie-chart; (*e*) histogram. The last class-intervals are important, but there is no way of deciding them; intervals of 12 or 15 years for both are suggested. Note the improved figures for the younger ages; (*f*) the effect of the war-time "black-out" is clearly marked; (*g*) straight-line graph or bar-chart; (*h*) class-intervals of 75–84 for males, 75–89 for females; (*j*) histogram. Note that the intervals 0–50 and 51–100 are unequal; suggest that 0–50 be taken as 1–50. The last interval has to be guessed; 200 pupils is suggested, giving 501–700 for the last class; (*k*) straight-line graph.

Exercises III (p. 40)

1. (*a*) 13 stigmata; (*b*) 6 tentacles; **2.** Modes are both in the 35–39 year group; medians are 33 and 36 years. **4.** 21 years (male); 23 years (female). **5.** 149 pupils. **7.** $y = (\sin x - x \cos x)/\pi; x = 1·92$.

Exercises IV (p. 42)

1. 15, 55, 225, 62.

Exercises V (p. 46)

1. 5·63 petals. **2.** (*a*) 12·72 stigmata; (*b*) 6·15 tentacles. **3.** 34·3 years and 36·6 years. It is assumed in this and all other statistics involving ages that, for example, 4 years 5 months and 4 years 7 months are both included in the age group 0–4 years, i.e., that ages are not stated correct to the nearest year. The class mid-points are then 2·5, 7·5, etc. The class mid-points of the last groups are 80 and 82·5 years. **5.** 177 pupils. The first group is taken as 1–50, the last group as 501–700. **6.** (*a*) 69·25%; (*b*) 52·75%. **7.** 118·8 A.W.

Exercises VI (p. 55)

1. January 13th—104; June 15th—110. **2.** (a) 89; (b) 105; (c) 119.
3. 134, 156, 163, 173. **19.** In distribution B take 1, 2, 3 . . . as the mid-class values.

	Mode	Median	Mean	
A	6	6	6·0	marks
B	2	3	3·7	× 0·1 oz.
C	3	3	3·7	

20. 14·5 years; 13·6 years. **21.** 16·8 runs. **23.** 9·0 and 10·9 bracts/cluster.
24.

	Median	Mean
Old	1,175	1,178
Young	1,225	1,233

The answer appears to be "Yes", but it needs further examination
(Ch. 7—Tests of Significance). **25.** 34·1 years; 36·2 years. **26.** £5,090 p.a.;
£4,660 p.a. The mid-class values were taken as $2\frac{1}{4}$, $2\frac{3}{4}$, $3\frac{1}{2}$, etc. **27.** 34·2
years (1940); 41·2 years (1970). The mid-class values were taken as
$2\frac{1}{2}$, $7\frac{1}{2}$, $12\frac{1}{2}$, etc.

Exercises VII (p. 68)

1. V.g. —100% to 74%; credit—73% to 55%; pass—54% to 34%
fail—33% to 0%. **5.** X, 1·8%; Y, 2·2%.

Exercises VIII (p. 73)

1. P, 2·68 × $\frac{1}{4}$ ins. = 0·67 ins.; Q, 2·80 × $\frac{1}{4}$ ins. = 0·70 ins. **2.** 16·1
units. **4.** (a) With intervals 28·80 ins.—29·00 ins., etc., s = 0·311 ins.
(b) with intervals 100–96, 95–90, etc., s = 11·92.

5.

	5	10	15
$\bar{x}$ =	51·97	52·01	51·90
s =	20·0	20·1	20·4

Increase of class-interval does not systematically affect $\bar{x}$, but may
systematically increase s. An adjustment for the grouping error in s can
be made by "Sheppard's correction" for some types of distribution.
6. C.V.(A) = 0·117; C.V.(B) = 0·122. **7.** $\bar{x}$ = 14·4 mm.; s_x = 0·911 mm.
$\bar{y}$ = 7·97 mm.; s_y = 0·348 mm.; C.V.(x) = 0·063; C.V.(y) = 0·044.;
8. S.D.(A + B) = 19·2; S.D.(A) = 20·0; S.D.(B) = 18·3 **9.** S.D. =
$d\left\{n(n + 1)/3\right\}^{\frac{1}{2}}$; M.D. = $d . n(n + 1)/(2n + 1)$. **13.** Ranges 3 and 5;
M.D.'s from median 0·79 and 0·88; S.I.Q. not applicable. **14.** S.D. (M) =
1·54 bracts/cluster; S.D.(I) = 1·63 bracts/cluster. **15.** S.D.(H) = 1·714
feet; S.D.(V) = 1·885 feet. **16.** M.D.'s from 34·5 are 11·1 (women) and
10·3 (men); S.I.Q.'s are 10·6 (women) and 10·0 (men). **17.** S.D.(x) =
2·51; S.D.(y) = 2·48. **18.** S.D.(A) = 2·93 sec.; S.D.(B) = 2·41 sec.
19. S.D. 6 are: $\frac{1}{2}\sqrt{139}$, (A); $\frac{1}{2}\sqrt{198}$, (B); $\frac{1}{2}\sqrt{59}$, (C). **20.** 6·077 units.
26. (a) $2(\pi^2 - 8)/\pi^2$; (b) $(\pi^2 - 6)/12$. **27.** 12; 6 $\log_e$ 2; 14·9.

Exercises IX (p. 78)

1. 360. **3.** 96. **4.** 5,040. **5.** 20. **6.** 36. **7.** 729. **8.** 81. **9.** 10,000.
10. $20^4 × 8^3$. **11.** 1,296. **12.** 15,120,

Exercises X (p. 81)

1. 6; 126; 15; 10; 10; 252. **2.** 364. **3.** 15. **4.** 1,728. **5.** 3,150. **6.** (a)
126; (b) 15; (c) 60. **7.** 220; 136. **8.** 1; 4; 6; 4; 1. Sum = 2^4. **10.** 18. **11.** 5.
12. (a) 70; (b) 16. **14.** 3. **15.** 35. **16.** p^n. **18.** 11.

EXERCISES XI (p. 84)

1. 33/16,660 or approx. 1/505. **2.** 1/9; 0; 1/12; 0; 1. **3.** 3/10. **4.** 1/13; 1/52. **5.** 1/3. **6.** 91/216. **7.** 2197/20825. **8.** (a) 13/51; (b) 12/51. **9.** 1/6. **10.** (a) 7/15; (b) 1/15. **12.** The second.

EXERCISES XII (p. 88)

1. 1/6. **2.** 17/20. **3.** 44/125. **4.** 36/91; 30/91; 25/91. **5.** 2,187/16,384; 5,103/16,384. **6.** 29/44. **7.** 4/7; 3/7. **8.** 2/9. **9.** 0·23; 0·40; 0·54; 0·64. **10.** $p_1 p_2$; $(1 - p_1)p_2$; $(1 - p_2)p_1$; $(1 - p_1)(1 - p_2)$. **12.** 0·46. **13.** 91/128; 35/128. **14.** 5/8; 5/8. **15.** $p(2n) = {}^{2n}C_n/2^{2n}$.

EXERCISES XIV (p. 97)

4. $52\frac{1}{12}$; $41\frac{2}{3}$; $12\frac{1}{2}$; $1\frac{2}{3}$; $\frac{1}{12}$; $\frac{2}{3}$. **6.** 2, 12, 30, 40, 30, 12, 2; 3. **8.** 25/64; $4\frac{11}{16}$; $21\frac{3}{32}$; $42\frac{3}{16}$; $31\frac{41}{64}$. **9.** 27/64; 27/55; very nearly 27/64.

EXERCISES XV (p. 103)

1. $\frac{1}{5^6}$ × (64, 576, 2,160, 4,320, 4,860, 2,916, 729); (a)1; (b) 12. **2.** $p = 0\cdot2575$; 61, 84, 44, 10, 1. **3.** 18, $\frac{1}{3}$, $\frac{2}{3}$. **5.** 3; 1·5. **6.** 2·4 and 1·2; 1·03 and 0·87. **7.** 11/32. **8.** 53/3,125. **9.** 0·3154. **10.** 11.

EXERCISES XVI (p. 112)

2. 0·09; 0·32. **3.** 0·03, 0·71; 3·75, 0·7. **4.** 0·09. **5.** $a = 0\cdot61$; 109; 66, 20, 4, 1. **6.** A, 1·9%; B, 3·8%; 0·003. **7.** 41, 81, 81, 54, 27, 11, 4, 1. **8.** (a) $m = 10$, $N = 1,000$, $p = 0\cdot5$; (b) Binomial; (c) 1, 10, 44, 117, 205, 246, 205. 117, 44, 10, 1. **9.** $m = 4\cdot971$, $s = 1\cdot56$; $\mu = 5\cdot00$, $\sigma = 1\cdot58$. **10.** 48, 68, 49, 24, 8, 2, 1. **11.** $a = 1\cdot435$, $\sigma^2 = 1\cdot39$. **12.** 75. **13.** 0·22. **14.** 120.

EXERCISES XVII (p. 118)

2. $y = 124\cdot7\ exp\left\{ - 19\cdot1(x - 6\cdot6)^2 \right\}$. **6.** $N = 7,749$, $m = 157\cdot23$ lbs., $s = 21\cdot34$. **8.** $m = 314\cdot96$ ohms, $s = 1\cdot77$ ohms.

EXERCISES XVIII (p. 122)

3. 0·399; 0·242; 0·0540; 0·00443.

EXERCISES XIX (p. 126)

1. $m = 6\cdot545$ ins., $s = 0\cdot154$ ins. (from graph). **2.** $m = 157$ lbs., $s = 21\cdot25$ lbs. (distribution is only approx normal). **3.** $m = 31\cdot44$ ohms. $s = 1\cdot86$ ohms (from graph). **6.** $m = 431$ secs.; $s = 144$ secs. (from graph). **7.** £2·9. **8.** $m = 2\cdot5$, $s = 1\cdot2$; 98·4%.

EXERCISES XXI (p. 138

1. 68·27%, 95·45%, 99·73%. **2.** $t = 0\cdot67$. **3.** (a) 0·6147; (b) 0·4822; (c) 0·7008; (d) 0·9973. **4.** (a) 0·675; (b) − 0·84; (c) − 2·33; (d) 1·96. **5.** (a) 10·21; (b) 9·08. **6.** The area of the Normal curve between the ordinates at D_1 and D_2. (a) 0·9545; (b) 0·0793; (c) 0·9451. **7.** 0·0038. **8.** $\sigma = 1\cdot56$. **9.** 2·74%. **10.** Area is 0·4976 approx. **11.** 0·0038; 0·0375. **12.** 66·4 ins.; 4·24 ins. **14.** $\mu = a$; $\sigma = a/\sqrt{3}$. **15.** $\mu = 0$. **16.** $1 - 1/e$.

Part Two

CHAPTER VII
Tests of Significance

7.1 Significance Testing

In this section a number of ideas are introduced which will be unfamiliar to most readers. The easiest approach is to consider a simple example which will illustrate the application of these ideas and then to discuss them in more detail.

A coin may be biased. To test whether this is so it is necessary to formulate some hypothesis about the behaviour of the coin and then carry out an experiment to discover whether in fact the hypothesis can account for the results of the experiment. This hypothesis is to be tested on the assumption that it is true and is called the *null hypothesis*. Consider for example the null hypothesis that the coin is not biased; in other words, that the chance of getting a head (or a tail) in any single throw is a half. It is decided to test this by tossing the coin ten times and observing whether the results can be reasonably explained by the null hypothesis. First a table is calculated showing the chance, on the null hypothesis, of any observed set of ten throws. This is given by the binomial expansion of $(\frac{1}{2} + \frac{1}{2})^{10}$ and the results are set out in Table XXVII.

TABLE XXVII

No. of heads	Probability	No. of heads	Probability
0	0·001	6	0·205
1	0·010	7	0·117
2	0·044	8	0·044
3	0·117	9	0·010
4	0·205	10	0·001
5	0·246		

The chance of getting 10 heads or tails is $0·001 + 0·001 = 0·002$.

The chance of getting 9 or 10 heads or tails is $0·011 + 0·011 = 0·022$.

The chance of getting 8, 9 or 10 heads or tails is $0·055 + 0·055 = 0·110$ and so on.

All this preliminary skirmishing is necessary in order to interpret correctly any possible result of the experiment. Thus if the experiment results in 10 heads or 10 tails the chance of this happening, if the null hypothesis is true, is only 0·002 and would only occur twice in 1,000 experiments. This is a rare event. Rather than accept such an unusual event it is logical to reject the null hypothesis and say that there is evidence that the coin is biased.

If the experiment gives 9 heads or 9 tails, the chance of getting a result as uneven as this or more uneven, i.e., 9 or 10 heads or 9 or 10 tails, is 0·022. This again is a moderately rare event if the null hypothesis is true and would therefore lead to the rejection of the null hypothesis.

The chance of getting 8 or more heads or tails on the null hypothesis is 0·110. This is not a very improbable event and would happen in about 1 out of 10 experiments. There is therefore no very good reason for rejecting the hypothesis.

It is customary before starting any experiment to select some critical probability, for example 5%, which is called the 5% *significance level*. If the observed set of results has a probability greater than 5%, the null hypothesis is not rejected and the result of the experiment is said to be *not significant at the 5% level*. If on the other hand the probability is less than 5%, the null hypothesis is rejected and the result is *significant at the 5% level*.

The experiment which was carried out actually gave 7 heads and 3 tails. The chance of getting a result as uneven as this with an unbiased coin is the chance of getting 7 or more heads or tails or (from Table XXVII) 0·344. This is certainly not a rare event and the null hypothesis is not rejected or in other words the result is not significant at the 5% level.

THE TWO-TAIL NATURE OF THE TEST. It may be argued that the calculation of the significance of the result could have been done as follows. When the experiment gave 7 heads and 3 tails reference to Table XXVII would show that the chance of obtaining 7 or more heads is $0·117 + 0·044 + 0·010 + 0·001 = 0·172$ and the decision whether to reject the hypothesis could be made on this figure rather than on 0·344 which arose from considering also the chance of getting 7 or more tails. This, however, would be wrong since a result which gave 7 tails and 3 heads would be considered equally as evidence of bias and therefore the chance of its happening must be included. The test is called a "two-tail test" since it takes into account both "tails" of the frequency distribution as shown in Fig. 42. Most statistical tests are of this two-tail type. An example will be given later (section 7.2) of a single-tail test.

It should be noticed that the whole area of the tails is taken into account and not merely the areas (i.e., probabilities) corresponding to exactly 7 heads or 7 tails. This is the invariable procedure in all significance testing.

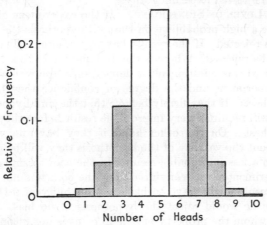

FIG. 42. The shaded area shows the chance of getting 7 or more heads or tails.

7.2 How to Conduct a Statistical Experiment

A clear appreciation of the problem and how to investigate it is necessary if useful results are to be obtained. The main steps may be summarised as

(a) The statement of the problem and the formulation of the null hypothesis.

(b) The selection of a level of significance.

(c) The experimental testing of the hypothesis and the interpretation of the experimental results.

(a) THE STATEMENT OF THE PROBLEM AND THE NULL HYPOTHESIS. The statement of the problem should suggest the most appropriate choice of null hypothesis. In the coin tossing example the problem was whether the coin was biased. In other words does $p = \frac{1}{2}$ where p is the probability of a head (or tail)? The null hypothesis was chosen to be $p = \frac{1}{2}$. Consider a slightly different problem, namely whether the coin is biased in such a way that p, the chance of throwing a head, is $\frac{1}{4}$. For this problem the appropriate null hypothesis would be $p = \frac{1}{4}$.

Two more examples will be given. In accepting a consignment of jute bags the user wants to know whether the average warp strength of the batch is 100 lbs. The appropriate null hypothesis is that the mean batch warp strength is 100 lbs. and a sampling experiment will decide whether the hypothesis should be rejected. Another problem may be to decide whether the average warp strength of two consignments is the same. Here the appropriate null hypothesis is that the difference between the two batch averages is zero and again the hypothesis can be tested experimentally.

(b) THE LEVEL OF SIGNIFICANCE. If the experiment gives results which have a high probability on the null hypothesis the hypothesis will not be rejected. If the results have a low probability the hypothesis will be rejected. Where is the dividing line? To a large extent the answer to this question must depend on those who are carrying out the experiment and the degree of confidence they have in the null hypothesis. If they firmly believe that the null hypothesis must be true it will require a very improbable result before they will reject the hypothesis. On the other hand if they have no very strong feelings about the validity of the hypothesis they will be prepared to reject it on a less improbable result. In the coin tossing experiment if the experimenter was convinced that the coin was not biased the observed result might have to have a probability of $0 \cdot 1\%$, or even less, before he would reject the hypothesis of no bias. An experimenter to whom the property of bias in coins is not inconceivable or even unlikely would reject the hypothesis if the result only had a probability of 5% or even 10%.

While remembering that the attitude of mind must always have some bearing on the level of significance which is chosen the following values are suggested as a working guide.

P, the probability of the experimental result on the null hypothesis, more than 5%:   Do not reject the hypothesis.

P between 5% and 1%:   Reject the hypothesis with reasonable confidence.

P less than 1%:   The hypothesis may be confidently rejected.

(c) THE INTERPRETATION OF THE EXPERIMENTAL RESULTS. In the coin tossing experiment the interpretation of the results depended on a table of probabilities (Table XXVII) which was calculated from the Binomial distribution. Some assumption about the nature of the distribution of the results is always made. This will be referred to again in other sections of this chapter.

Example. A professor claimed that he could often tell, while they were still in their first year, whether his students would obtain 1st, 2nd, 3rd or 4th classes in their final examinations. To substantiate his claim he forecast the fates of 8 students and was right in 5 cases. Does this confirm his claim?

The null hypothesis is that he has not in fact any special gift and that his chance of naming a student's class is therefore $\frac{1}{4}$. A 5% significance level is chosen.

The chance of his placing correctly 5 or more is

$$^8C_5(\tfrac{1}{4})^5 (\tfrac{3}{4})^3 + {}^8C_6(\tfrac{1}{4})^6 (\tfrac{3}{4})^2 + {}^8C_7(\tfrac{1}{4})^7 (\tfrac{3}{4}) + {}^8C_8(\tfrac{1}{4})^8$$
$$= (\tfrac{1}{4})^8 [1{,}512 + 252 + 24 + 1]$$
$$= 1{,}789/65{,}536 = 0{\cdot}027.$$

This is an example of a one-tail test. The professor's claim is that he has some ability in forecasting the results correctly, that is he can do it more often than would be expected on the average. It is not therefore necessary to include the cases when his guesses are in fact wrong more often than would be expected on the average. The significance level of the result is therefore $0{\cdot}027$ or $2{\cdot}7\%$ and the hypothesis is rejected. The professor has established his claim.

EXERCISES XXII

1. You are asked to carry out an investigation to discover whether there is any difference between weights at birth of boys and girls.

    (a) What is the appropriate null hypothesis?

    (b) Invent two other possible hypotheses.

2. A marksman says he can hit the bull's-eye on the average 3 times out of 4. A shoot is arranged to test this. Consider the following hypotheses, namely, that on the average the proportion of times he hits the bull's-eye is (a) $\frac{1}{2}$; (b) not at all; (c) either $\frac{1}{2}$ or $\frac{1}{3}$; (d) between $\frac{1}{2}$ and $\frac{3}{4}$; (e) $\frac{3}{4}$; (f) between $\frac{3}{4}$ and 1; (g) $\frac{1}{4}$.
Which is the null hypothesis?

3. The average age of workers in a factory is said to be 38. A sample is taken to test this.
State two possible hypotheses, one of which is the appropriate null hypothesis.

4. Even if the null hypothesis is true it may be rejected by a remote chance coming off as is bound to happen from time to time. Describe a way in which a wrong decision may be made if the null hypothesis is in fact not true.

5. A hypothesis might seem to you to be either very plausible or very far fetched. For which would you require a higher level of significance before rejecting the hypothesis?

6. This should be carried out as a class experiment. You want to discover whether individual members of the class tend to overestimate or underestimate lengths. A person who is not undergoing the test draws 12 lines on the blackboard or on a sheet of paper. The lines should be of varying length between, say, 2 ins. and 24 ins., and should not be arranged in any particular order of magnitude. The length of each line must be accurately known only to the person who draws the lines. A member of the class writes down his estimates of the lengths. These are then checked with the true values and marked $+$ if an overestimate and $-$ if an underestimate. The result will be in the form $n_1(+)$ and $n_2(-)$, $n_1 + n_2 = 12$. Estimate the significance of this result on the null hypothesis that no tendency to over or underestimate exists, and using the binomial expansion of $(\frac{1}{2} + \frac{1}{2})^{12}$.

7. A buyer for a firm wants to know whether there is any difference in quality between the material supplied by two manufacturers. He asks his firm for a report on the comparative quality of the next 8 deliveries and finds that in 7 cases manufacturer A's material has been more satisfactory than B's, and in only 1 case has B's material been better than A's. Formulate the appropriate null hypothesis and test it using the 5% significance level as a criterion for rejection.

8. A coin is suspected of bias so that the chance of a head is given by $p = \frac{3}{4}$. The appropriate null hypothesis is tested by tossing the coin 6 times. Two heads are observed in 6 throws. Is this significant at the 5% level?

(*Note.*—When the frequency table is calculated and the histogram is drawn it will be seen that the distribution is so skew that all results in one tail of the distribution have a probability greater than 5%. For this reason evidence for the rejection of the hypothesis must depend only on extreme results in the other tail. Strictly speaking, this is not a true one-tail test since extreme results in both tails would be accepted as evidence on which to reject the hypothesis if their probabilities were small enough.)

9. An investigation is carried out to find whether modifications to a manufacturing process

(a)   have improved the quality of the product,

(b)   have altered the quality of the product.

In which case would you use a one-tail test?

10. Give two examples of problems for which a one-tail test would be appropriate.

7.3   Significance Tests.   Binomial Distribution

Suppose that the coin tossing experiment was extended to 100 throws and gave 62 heads and 38 tails. It would be very tedious to calculate a table like Table XXVII for such large numbers, but this can be avoided by making use of a very important fact. When n is large the Binomial distribution is closely approximate to the Normal distribution with the same mean and standard deviation. In this example the mean and standard deviation are given by

$$np = 100 \times \tfrac{1}{2} = 50$$

$$\sqrt{npq} = \sqrt{100 \times \tfrac{1}{4}} = 5$$

Fig. 43 shows the histogram of the Binomial expansion $(\frac{1}{2} + \frac{1}{2})^{100}$ and the Normal curve with mean 50 and standard deviation 5.

If n is large the agreement remains good even if p is not equal to $\frac{1}{2}$. The area of the tail of the histogram above and including 62 is given

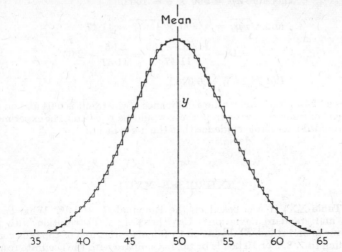

FIG. 43. Histogram of the binomial distribution $(\frac{1}{2} + \frac{1}{2})^{100}$ and the Normal curve with mean 50 and s.d. 5.

very closely by the area of the Normal curve above 61·5. The reason that the limit is 61·5 and not 62 is that the rectangle corresponding to 62 stands on the base 61·5 to 62·5. To find the area of the tail of the Normal curve calculate D where

$$D = \frac{61 \cdot 5 - 50}{5} \left(c.f.\ D = \frac{X - \mu}{\sigma} \right)$$

$$= 2 \cdot 3$$

From Table XXVI $P(d \geqslant 2 \cdot 3) = 0 \cdot 01$ and therefore for the two tails the area is 0·02. In other words the chance of getting 62 or more heads or tails in 100 throws is about 0·02. This result is significant at the 5% level and the null hypothesis should be rejected.

Some readers may suspect a paradox here. The first experiment of 10 throws gave 70% heads and the result was said to be not significant while the second experiment giving only 62% heads is significant. The reason for this is that the much larger number of throws in the second experiment allows more discrimination in assessing the significance of the result.

Example. The possible bias of a die is investigated. The null hypothesis is formulated namely that there is no bias. In 960 throws 184 fours were counted. Is this result significant?

On the null hypothesis the chance of getting a four is $\frac{1}{6}$.

Therefore $np = 960 \times \frac{1}{6} = 160$

and $\sqrt{npq} = \sqrt{960 \times \frac{1}{6} \times \frac{5}{6}} = 11.47$

$$D = \frac{183.5 - 160}{11.47} = \frac{23.5}{11.47} = 2.05$$

$$P(d \geqslant 2.05) = 0.0202.$$

This is a "2-tail test" and so the significance of the result is 0.04 and on the 5% level of significance the hypothesis would be rejected. The experiment has provided reasonable evidence that the die is biased.

EXERCISES XXIII

1. Table XXVII was based on the Binomial $(\frac{1}{2} + \frac{1}{2})^{10}$. What is the mean and standard deviation? Use the Normal distribution with the same mean and standard deviation to calculate the area of the tails corresponding to 7, 8, 9 or 10 heads or tails. Compare with the accurate results given by the Binomial distribution. (The agreement is poor since n is too small for the approximation to apply.)

2. In a sample survey in Great Britain 4,367 individuals were selected at random. Of these 2,361 were female. Does this result lead to the rejection of the hypothesis that 53% of the population are female?

3. (Weldon's data.) In 315,672 throws of a die a 5 or 6 turned up 106,602 times. Is this sufficient evidence that the die is biased?

4. From a sample of pea plants the number of round peas is 336 and the number of angular peas is 101. Is this in agreement with the Mendelian theory which says that on the average the ratio of round to angular peas is 3 : 1? State the null hypothesis and give the level of significance of the observed result.

5. In a table of 4 figures logarithms count the number of nines appearing in the fourth decimal place of the logarithms of 1.0, 1.1, 1.2 . . . 9.9. Does this result reject the hypothesis that a 9 has a chance of $\frac{1}{10}$ of appearing? Repeat the experiment for the third, second and first place of decimals.

6. Most cheap dice have some bias although it may only be slight. As a co-operative experiment test a die for bias by making 10,000 throws and noting the number of sixes. Calculate the significance level of your result.

7. A test for telepathic communication. Two investigators investigated the possibility of "thought reading". One unseen to the other threw a die and, having recorded it, thought of the number turned up for 30 seconds. The second investigator wrote down what number he thought it was. On

checking their figures there was agreement 118 times in 600 throws. Is this result significant

(a) on the 1% level?

(b) on the 5% level?

(The one-tail test should be used since the investigators are only interested in the ability to transfer the actual number thought about. For what enquiry would the two-tail test be appropriate?)

If there are facilities and time, this exercise should be carried out as an experiment. It is an interesting subject for investigation.

8. What is the *least* number of throws of a coin which would be necessary to establish evidence of bias on

(a) 5% level of significance?

(b) 1% level of significance?

(c) 0·1% level of significance?

7.4 Sample Estimate of Population Values

When a sample is taken from a population it is usually the case that the population mean and standard deviation are unknown and the sample is used to provide estimates of them. From this point onwards it will be important to distinguish carefully between the (unknown) population mean and standard deviation and the sample estimates. In later chapters this same distinction will be observed for other statistics.

In order to preserve this distinction clearly, the following rule will be observed. Greek letters will be used to denote population values and the corresponding Roman letters will be used for the sample estimates. Thus μ and σ are used to denote the unknown mean and standard deviation of a population; m and s are used to denote the sample estimates of μ and σ. This can be written briefly as

$$m = \text{Est} (\mu)$$

$$s = \text{Est} (\sigma)$$

So far m and s have been calculated from the equations

$$m = \Sigma_1^n \, x_i/n \tag{7.1}$$

$$\text{and } s^2 = \Sigma_1^n \, (x_i - m)^2/n \tag{7.2}$$

where x_i ($i = 1, 2 \ldots n$) are the n sample values.

Now, while it is usually true that m calculated from equation (7.1) gives the best estimate of μ, the best estimate of σ is given, not by equation (7.2) but by $s^2 = \Sigma_1^n \, (x_i - m)^2/(n - 1)$ (7.3)

where the divisor is not n but $(n - 1)$. No proof of equation (7.3) will be given but the equation is important and should be remembered.

Example. Calculate the sample estimates of the population mean and standard deviation from the following four sample measurements, 2, 1, 4, 5.

$$\Sigma x = 2 + 1 + 4 + 5 = 12$$

$$\Sigma x^2 = 4 + 1 + 16 + 25 = 46$$

$$m = \frac{\Sigma x}{n} = \frac{12}{4} = 3$$

$$\Sigma(x - m)^2 = \Sigma x^2 - nm^2$$

$$= 46 - 36 = 10$$

$$s^2 = \frac{\Sigma(x - m)^2}{n - 1} = \frac{10}{4 - 1} = \frac{10}{3} = 3{\cdot}33$$

$$s = 1{\cdot}83$$

Therefore, Est. $(\mu) = 3$

Est. $(\sigma) = 1{\cdot}83$

It is obvious that the use of the correct divisor $(n - 1)$ instead of n will only be important when n is small. If s is calculated using the divisor n then the best estimate of σ is given by multiplying s by the factor $\sqrt{\dfrac{n}{n - 1}}$. Table XXVIII shows values of this factor for different values of n.

TABLE XXVIII

VALUES OF $\sqrt{\dfrac{n}{n - 1}}$

n	2	3	4	5	10	20	50	100	1,000
$\sqrt{\dfrac{n}{n-1}}$	1·414	1·224	1·155	1·118	1·054	1·026	1·010	1·005	1·001

The divisor $n - 1$ represents the numbers of *degrees of freedom* of the estimate of σ. This name is explained by observing that although s is calculated from the n deviations $(x_i - m)$ these deviations are not independent since they must satisfy the relation

$$\Sigma_1^n (x_i - m) = \Sigma_1^n (x_i) - nm = 0 \quad \text{(from equation 7.1)}$$

Therefore the calculation of s is based on $n - 1$ *independent* values of $(x_i - m)$ or in statistical language the best estimate of σ is based on $n - 1$ degrees of freedom.

7.5 The Frequency Distribution of Means

If observations are collected, not individually, but as random samples of n, a frequency distribution can be constructed for the means of the samples in the same way as is done for individual results. These two distributions represent two distinct populations, namely the population of sample means and the population of the individuals. The means and standard deviations of the two distributions bear a simple relation to each other which will first be stated and will then be illustrated by an example.

If μ and σ are the mean and standard deviation of the population of individuals and μ_n and σ_n are the mean and standard deviation of the means of samples of size n then it can be shown theoretically that

$$\mu_n = \mu \tag{7.4}$$
$$\sigma_n = \sigma/\sqrt{n} \tag{7.5}$$

The first equation expresses the fairly obvious fact that the mean of sample means is the same as the mean of the individual observations. The second equation shows that the population of means is more closely packed round the mean than the individual observations. This is the mathematical statement of the reason that most people place more reliance in the average of a number of measurements rather than in a single observation. Fig. 44 shows the Normal distribution for individual measurements and also for means of samples of 2 and 10.

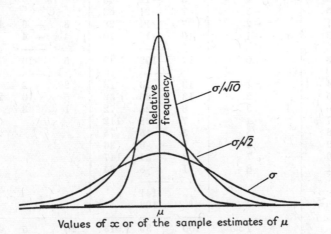

Values of x or of the sample estimates of μ

FIG. 44. The effect of sample size on the distribution of means.

Example. Heights of 100 tomato plants were measured six months after sowing. The plants were taken in groups of five selected at random so that the 100 observations were grouped in 20 samples of 5. Table XXIX shows the results, the recorded height referring to the mid-cell value.

TABLE XXIX

DATA ON TOMATO PLANTS

Height of plant (*inches*)	6	7	8	9	10	11	12	13	14	15	16	17	18	19	20	21	Total
No. of individual observations	4	2	1	3	7	7	10	17	13	13	8	7	3	1	3	1	100
No. of averages	–	–	–	–	–	3	4	5	2	5	1	–	–	–	–	–	20

The work of calculating the means and standard deviations can be combined in a single table.

Height of plant	Deviations from working mean (13 ins.)	Individuals *No. of results*			Averages *No. of results*		
	x	n	nx	nx^2	n	nx	nx^2
6	−7	4	−28	196			
7	−6	2	−12	72			
8	−5	1	− 5	25			
9	−4	3	−12	48			
10	−3	7	−21	63			
11	−2	7	−14	28	3	− 6	12
12	−1	10	−10	10	4	− 4	4
13	0	17	−102	0	5	−10	0
14	1	13	13	13	2	2	2
15	2	13	26	52	5	10	20
16	3	8	24	72	1	3	9
17	4	7	28	112			
18	5	3	15	75			
19	6	1	6	36			
20	7	3	21	147			
21	8	1	8	64			
			141				
			−102				
Totals		100	39	1,013	20	5	47

For individual observations

$$m = 13 + \frac{39}{100} = 13 \cdot 39$$

$$s^2 = \frac{\Sigma(x - m)^2}{n - 1} = \frac{1{,}013 - 100\,(0 \cdot 39)^2}{99} = \frac{997 \cdot 79}{99}$$

$$= 10 \cdot 08$$

$$s = \sqrt{10 \cdot 08} = 3 \cdot 17$$

For the distribution of averages

$$m_n = 13 + \frac{5}{20} = 13 \cdot 25$$

$$s_n{}^2 = \frac{47 - 20\,(0 \cdot 25)^2}{19} = 2 \cdot 408$$

$$s_n = \sqrt{2 \cdot 407} = 1 \cdot 55$$

Comparing these experimental values with the theoretical values given by equations 7.4 and 7.5

$$m_n = m = 13 \cdot 39 \ (\text{instead of } 13 \cdot 25)$$

$$s_n = \frac{s}{\sqrt{n}} = \frac{3 \cdot 17}{\sqrt{5}} = 1 \cdot 42 \ (\text{instead of } 1 \cdot 55)$$

The slight discrepancies are due to the fact that a finite number of grouped observations are being used to demonstrate a relation which strictly applies only to theoretically infinite populations. The agreement is nevertheless quite good.

EXERCISES XXIV

1. The following data gives the thickness in mm. of 200 steel washers collected in 50 random samples of 4. Calculate the mean, m, and standard deviations, s, of the 200 individual measurements. Calculate the 50 averages and work out the mean and standard deviation of the averages. Compare with m and $\dfrac{s}{\sqrt{n}}$.

Sample	1	2	3	4	5	6	7	8	9	10
	7·69	7·76	7·76	7·74	7·64	7·65	7·70	7·64	7·65	7.60
	7·62	7·74	7·54	7·58	7·71	7·71	7·65	7·75	7·65	7·66
	7·65	7·75	7·61	7·70	7·63	7·68	7·64	7·50	7·66	7·56
	7·73	7·54	7·74	7·76	7·74	7·64	7·69	7·82	7·80	7·64

Sample	11	12	13	14	15	16	17	18	19	20
	7·79	7·64	7·64	7·58	7·71	7·71	7·74	7·73	7·65	7·59
	7·76	7·81	7·74	7·73	7·58	7·61	7·69	7·75	7·66	7·76
	7·64	7·73	7·60	7·77	7·69	7·60	7·71	7·61	7·76	7·66
	7·69	7·74	7·66	7·64	7·70	7·68	7·74	7·71	7·63	7·65

Sample	21	22	23	24	25	26	27	28	29	30
	7·68	7·55	7·68	7·64	7·78	7·77	7·74	7·66	7·76	7·63
	7·55	7·61	7·70	7·74	7·64	7·64	7·65	7·71	7·74	7·64
	7·71	7·69	7·69	7·71	7·70	7·71	7·75	7·65	7·65	7·66
	7·69	7·75	7·56	7·67	7·65	7·71	7·69	7·65	7·61	7·64

Sample	31	32	33	34	35	36	37	38	39	40
	7·60	7·55	7·74	7·66	7·71	7·62	7·58	7·56	7·75	7·61
	7·69	7·70	7·69	7·70	7·69	7·65	7·71	7·74	7·66	7·71
	7·71	7·73	7·80	7·68	7·76	7·61	7·63	7·70	7·81	7·55
	7·66	7·74	7·69	7·76	7·78	7·64	7·69	7·71	7·73	7·66

Sample	41	42	43	44	45	46	47	48	49	50
	7·75	7·56	7·76	7·76	7·74	7·70	7·61	7·81	7·75	7·63
	7·70	7·73	7·61	7·64	7·64	7·71	7·69	7·73	7·75	7·69
	7·68	7·77	7·74	7·82	7·68	7·66	7·73	7·56	7·66	7·63
	7·50	7·60	7·54	7·64	7·61	7·76	7·73	7·74	7·50	7·58

2. A man keeps a daily record of the times it takes him to walk to work in the morning. Over a period of some months his average time is 15·2 minutes with a standard deviation of 1·37 minutes. He now changes his method and records only a weekly average for a six-day working week. Assuming that conditions are unchanged what should he expect the new average and standard deviation to be when based on weekly records.

3. A wage survey in a manufacturing industry gives a value for σ of 10s. 3d. and for σ_n of 2s. 8d. but omitted to state the sample size. Estimate a probable value for n.

4. Tests are carried out on the breaking strength of a synthetic fibre and results are recorded as averages of samples of 25. The standard deviation of the sample averages is 2·7 lb. What is the probable standard deviation of individual tests?

7.6 Mathematical Note

A variable z is related to two other variables x and y by the relation

$$z = ax + by \qquad (7.6)$$

where a and b are constants. The variables x and y are subject to small random errors and therefore z is also subject to error. For example, x could be the measured weight of a beaker and y the estimated volume of the liquid it contains. Then if $a = 1$ and $b =$ known density of liquid, z gives the weight of beaker and liquid, and errors in x and y will affect z.

Suppose n measurements are made of x and y then for each pair of measurements

$$z_r = ax_r + by_r \ (r = 1, 2 \ \ldots \ n)$$

$$\text{and } \bar{x} = \frac{1}{n}\Sigma x_r : \bar{y} = \frac{1}{n}\Sigma y_r$$

$$\text{but } \bar{z} = \frac{1}{n}\Sigma z_r = \frac{1}{n}\Sigma\,(ax_r + by_r)$$

$$= a\,.\frac{1}{n}\,.\Sigma x_r + b\,.\frac{1}{n}\,.\Sigma y_r$$

$$= a\bar{x} + b\bar{y} \qquad (7.7)$$

Equation 7.7 gives the relation between the mean of x and y and the mean of z. It simplifies the algebra and does not affect the conclusions if, in what follows, it is assumed that x and y are deviations from the mean so that

$$\bar{x} = 0 \qquad\qquad \bar{y} = 0$$

and therefore from equation 7.7, $\bar{z} = 0$

It is now true that

$$
\left.
\begin{aligned}
\Sigma_1^n x_r^2 &= (n - 1)s_x^2 \\
\Sigma_1^n y_r^2 &= (n - 1)s_y^2 \\
\Sigma_1^n z_r^2 &= (n - 1)s_z^2
\end{aligned}
\right\}
\tag{7.8}
$$

A relation will now be established giving s_z in terms of s_x and s_y just as equation 7.7 gives $\bar{z}$ in terms of $\bar{x}$ and $\bar{y}$.

For

$$
\begin{aligned}
\Sigma_1^n z_r^2 &= \Sigma_1^n (ax_r + by_r)^2 \\
&= \Sigma_1^n (a^2 x_r^2 + b^2 y_r^2 + 2ab x_r y_r) \\
&= a^2 \Sigma_1^n x_r^2 + b^2 \Sigma_1^n y_r^2 + 2ab \Sigma_1^n x_r y_r
\end{aligned}
\tag{7.9}
$$

The last term on the right-hand side of this equation contains the sum $\Sigma_1^n x_r y_r$ that is the sum of n products of two variables which can take both positive and negative values. If the two variables are *statistically independent* (an explanation of this will be given later) the sum will contain roughly the same number of positive and negative products and its value will be approximately zero.

Equation 7.9 therefore becomes

$$\Sigma z_r^2 = a^2 \Sigma_1^n x_r^2 + b^2 \Sigma_1^n y_r^2$$

and dividing by $(n - 1)$ and using equation 7.8 this can be written

$$s_z^2 = a^2 s_x^2 + b^2 s_y^2 \tag{7.10}$$

Statistical independence between x and y implies that there is no association between x and y whereby the value of one variable influences the value of the other. This is analogous to the description of independent events given in Chapter IV on page 86. If an association did exist it might happen that negative values of x were associated with negative values of y and similarly for positive values, so that the sum $\Sigma_1^n x_r y_r$ would consist of approximately n positive quantities and would therefore not be nearly zero. Methods of dealing with associated variables are discussed in Chapter IX.

Equation 7.10 can be extended to any number of variables.

For example, if $z = ax + by + cu$

then $s_z^2 = a^2 s_x^2 + b^2 s_y^2 + c^2 s_u^2$

and generally, if $\quad z = a_1 x_1 + a_2 x_2 + \ldots + a_n x_n$

and if the sample estimate of the standard deviation, i.e. the standard error, of x_r is s_r ($r = 1, 2, \ldots n$) then

$$\sigma_z^2 = a_1^2 \cdot s_1^2 + a_2^2 \cdot s_2^2 \ldots + a_n^2 \cdot s_n^2$$

$$= \Sigma_1^n \, a_r^2 \cdot s_r^2 \tag{7.11}$$

If the sample size is now made indefinitely large, equations 7.10 and 7.11 become

$$\sigma_z^2 = a^2 \cdot \sigma_x^2 + b^2 \cdot \sigma_y^2 \tag{7.12}$$

and $\qquad \sigma_z^2 = \Sigma_1^n \, a_r^2 \cdot \sigma_r^2 \tag{7.13}$

where the σ's are population standard deviations.

Corollary 1.   If the x_r are all variables from the same population with standard deviation σ then $\sigma_r = \sigma$ ($r = 1, 2 \ldots n$). To find the standard deviation of the average of n results write $\bar{x} = \dfrac{1}{n} \cdot x_1 +$

$\dfrac{1}{n} \cdot x_2 \ldots + \dfrac{1}{n} \cdot x_n$. Then from equation 7.13

$$\sigma_{\bar{x}}^2 = \frac{1}{n^2} \cdot \Sigma \sigma^2 = \frac{\sigma^2}{n}$$

or $\sigma_{\bar{x}} = \sigma / \sqrt{n}$

This is the result described in section 7.3.

Corollary 2.   In equation 7.6 put $a = b = 1$, so that

$$z = x + y$$

and $\qquad \sigma_z^2 = \sigma_x^2 + \sigma_y^2$

i.e., the variance of the sum of two independent variables is the sum of their variances.

Similarly, if $a = 1, b = -1$, so that

$$z = x - y$$

then again $\qquad \sigma_z^2 = \sigma_x^2 + \sigma_y^2$

or the variance of the difference between two independent variables is the sum of their variances. This result is perhaps a little unexpected and it should be remembered. It shows that the standard errors of the sum and difference of two independent variables are the same.

It may happen that z is not a linear function of x and y but is given by a more complicated functional relation.

$$\text{Let } z = f(x, y)$$

Then if δx and δy are small errors made in measuring x and y the resultant error in z is approximately

$$\delta z = \frac{\partial f}{\partial x} \cdot \delta x + \frac{\partial f}{\partial y} \cdot \delta y \qquad (7.14)$$

Here $\dfrac{\partial f}{\partial x}$ and $\dfrac{\partial f}{\partial y}$ are the partial differential coefficients of $f(x, y)$ with

respect to x and y and are approximately constant for small errors in x and y. Equation 7.14 is thus equivalent to 7.6 and so from equation 7.10

$$\sigma_z^2 = \left(\frac{\partial f}{\partial x}\right)^2 \cdot \sigma_x^2 + \left(\frac{\partial f}{\partial y}\right)^2 \cdot \sigma_y^2 \qquad (7.15)$$

Example. A number of estimates are made of the density p of a solid by repeating measurements of the mass and volume, m and v, and calculating $p = m/v$. If σ_m and σ_v are the standard deviations of m and v find an expression for σ_p.

$$p = f(m, v) = m/v$$

$$\frac{\partial f}{\partial m} = \frac{1}{v}$$

$$\frac{\partial f}{\partial v} = \frac{-m}{v^2}$$

Therefore, from equation 7.15

$$\sigma_p^2 = \frac{1}{v^2} \cdot \sigma_m^2 + \frac{m^2}{v^4} \cdot \sigma_v^2$$

In practice, m and v are not known and it is necessary to take the mean values $\overline{m}$ and $\overline{v}$ in place of m and v.

This method is useful in directing attention towards the variable which requires the most precise determination.

For example, if $\overline{v} = 2$ c.c. and $\overline{m} = 10$ gms. approximately, then

$$\sigma_p^2 = 0 \cdot 25\, \sigma_m^2 + 6 \cdot 25\, \sigma_v^2$$

from which it is clear that errors in measuring v are more important than errors of comparable magnitude in m.

EXERCISES XXV

1. The voltage V of a cell can be calculated by measuring I and R, the current and the resistance, and using the relation $V = IR$. Show that

$$\sigma_V^2 = I^2\, \sigma_R^2 + R^2\, \sigma_I^2$$

2. A pendulum is used to calculate g, the gravitational acceleration from the equation $g = 4\pi^2 l/T^2$ when l is the length of the pendulum and T is the time of one complete oscillation. Find σ_g in terms of σ_l and σ_T. If l is approximately $1 \cdot 5$ ft. and $T = 1 \cdot 36$ seconds, which variable has most effect on σ_g?

3. The "coefficient of variation", c, of a sample is defined as the ratio of the standard deviation to the mean, expressed as a percentage, so that $c = 100 \, \sigma/\bar{x}$.

Given that $\sigma_{\bar{x}} = \sigma/\sqrt{n}$

$$\sigma_{\sigma} = \sigma/\sqrt{2n}$$

Show that $\sigma_c = c \sqrt{\dfrac{1 + 2(c/100)^2}{2n}}$

7.7 Significance Tests. Means and Standard Deviations

A certain colliery is supposed to supply coal of ash content about 15 (expressed as a percentage by weight). To test this, twenty random samples of the colliery's coal are selected and tested, the null hypothesis being that the ash content is in fact 15. The results of the twenty tests gave an average ash content of 16·8 with a standard deviation based on 19 degrees of freedom of 3·6. Is this sufficient evidence on which to reject the hypothesis?

Since 3·6 is the individual standard deviation it follows that the standard deviation of average of samples of 20 is given by s where

$$s = 3 \cdot 6/\sqrt{20} = 0 \cdot 805$$

This means that if a large number of samples of 20 had been taken the sample averages would have been distributed about the population average with standard deviation $s = 0 \cdot 805$. If the sample averages are Normally distributed about 15 as mean it is easy to estimate the chance of a deviation as big as or bigger than 1·8 by calculating D where

$$D = \frac{m - \mu}{s} = \frac{16 \cdot 8 - 15}{0 \cdot 805} = \frac{1 \cdot 8}{0 \cdot 805} = 2 \cdot 2$$

From Table XXVI $P(d \geqslant 2 \cdot 2) = 0 \cdot 014$ and, therefore, remembering that it is a two-tail test, the significance of the result is $2 \times 0 \cdot 014 = 0 \cdot 028$. This is sufficient to reject the null hypothesis and the samples therefore provide evidence that the ash content of the coal is higher than 15.

It should be observed that D is calculated, using $s = 3 \cdot 6/\sqrt{20}$. This is because the distribution being considered is the distribution of averages and not of individuals. The formal steps of this example are

(1) The problem. Is this colliery's coal what it purports to be?

(2) The hypothesis. There is in fact no deviation from the specification value 15.

(3) The experiment. Twenty random samples were tested for ash content.

(4) The interpretation of the results. The experimental result was proved significant and the null hypothesis rejected.

There is a very important assumption made in carrying out the interpretation of the results. The table of the Normal distribution was used to determine the significance of the results thereby implying that the sample averages are distributed normally. The reason for this lies in the following statement:

"Even when the distribution of individuals is not Normal it is nearly always true that averages and, to a lesser extent, standard deviations of random samples from the population of individuals are approximately normally distributed if the sample size is not too small." This important statement must be made without proof as this requires rather advanced mathematics, but its truth is the foundation of many statistical tests and it should be remembered.

THE t-TEST. A sample of n is drawn from a Normal population whose standard deviation is known to be σ. Since σ is known the standard deviation of the sample mean is also known and is $\sigma/\sqrt{n}$. It is therefore possible to test the hypothesis that the population mean is μ by calculating $D = \dfrac{m - \mu}{\sigma/\sqrt{n}}$ and using the table of the Normal probability integral (Table XXVI, p. 132).

However, in most practical examples σ is not known, so we have to estimate σ from the sample and base our test on $t = \dfrac{m - \mu}{s/\sqrt{n}}$ where $s =$ Est (σ) calculated on $n - 1$ degrees of freedom. This was done in the example on the ash content of coal.

Now if n, the sample size, is small s, the sample estimate of σ based on $n - 1$ degrees of freedom, may not be very accurate and can differ from σ quite appreciably. When this happens it is no longer correct to assume that $t = \dfrac{m - \mu}{s/\sqrt{n}}$ is normally distributed and if the Normal probability table is used there will be some error in the calculation of the significance of the result.

This difficulty was overcome in 1908 by "Student" (pen name of W. S. Gosset) who established the theoretical distribution of t. A rigorous proof of Student's t-distribution was provided some years later by R. A. Fisher. The discovery of the t-distribution made it possible to calculate tables giving the significance levels of observed values of t. Table XXX shows values of t corresponding to different degrees of freedom and different significance levels. These significance levels correspond to the two-tail test and therefore give the probability that t will exceed the tabular entry in absolute value. If the one-tail test is used the tabular significance level must be halved.

Example 1. In the example on ash content of coal we found that $t = 2 \cdot 2$ based on 19 degrees of freedom. From the table the value of t at the 5% level for 19 degrees of freedom is $2 \cdot 09$ and therefore, since the calculated value of t exceeds this, the result is significant at the 5% level and the hypothesis is rejected.

TABLE XXX

PERCENTAGE POINTS OF THE t-DISTRIBUTION

f	\multicolumn{8}{c}{$P(\%)$}
	50	25	10	5	2·5	1	0·5	0·1
1	1·00	2·41	6·31	12·7	25·5	63·7	127	637
2	·816	1·60	2·92	4·30	6·21	9·92	14·1	31·6
3	·765	1·42	2·35	3·18	4·18	5·84	7·45	12·9
4	·741	1·34	2·13	2·78	3·50	4·60	5·60	8·61
5	·727	1·30	2·01	2·57	3·16	4·03	4·77	6·86
6	·718	1·27	1·94	2·45	2·97	3·71	4·32	5·96
7	·711	1·25	1·89	2·36	2·84	3·50	4·03	5·40
8	·706	1·24	1·86	2·31	2·75	3·36	3·83	5·04
9	·703	1·23	1·83	2·26	2·68	3·25	3·69	4·78
10	·700	1·22	1·81	2·23	2·63	3·17	3·58	4·59
11	·698	1·21	1·80	2·20	2·59	3·11	3·50	4·44
12	·695	1·21	1·78	2·18	2·56	3·05	3·43	4·32
13	·694	1·20	1·77	2·16	2·53	3·01	3·37	4·22
14	·692	1·20	1·76	2·14	2·51	2·98	3·33	4·14
15	·691	1·20	1·75	2·13	2·49	2·95	3·29	4·07
16	·690	1·19	1·75	2·12	2·47	2·92	3·25	4·01
17	·689	1·19	1·74	2·11	2·46	2·90	3·22	3·96
18	·688	1·19	1·73	2·10	2·44	2·88	3·20	3·92
19	·688	1·19	1·73	2·09	2·43	2·86	3·17	3·88
20	·687	1·18	1·72	2·09	2·42	2·85	3·15	3·85
21	·686	1·18	1·72	2·08	2·41	2·83	3·14	3·82
22	·686	1·18	1·72	2·07	2·41	2·82	3·12	3·79
23	·685	1·18	1·71	2·07	2·40	2·81	3·10	3·77
24	·685	1·18	1·71	2·06	2·39	2·80	3·09	3·74
25	·684	1·18	1·71	2·06	2·38	2·79	3·08	3·72
26	·684	1·18	1·71	2·06	2·38	2·78	3·07	3·71
27	·684	1·18	1·70	2·05	2·37	2·77	3·06	3·69
28	·683	1·17	1·70	2·05	2·37	2·76	3·05	3·67
29	·683	1·17	1·70	2·05	2·36	2·76	3·04	3·66
30	·683	1·17	1·70	2·04	2·36	2·75	3·03	3·65
40	·681	1·17	1·68	2·02	2·33	2·70	2·97	3·55
60	·679	1·16	1·67	2·00	2·30	2·66	2·91	3·46
120	·677	1·16	1·66	1·98	2·27	2·62	2·86	3·37
∞	·674	1·15	1·64	1·96	2·24	2·58	2·81	3·29

Example 2. The following value of t is based on 3 degrees of freedom. Is it significant at the 5% level? $t = 2·4$.

From Table XXX the 5% significance level of t corresponding to 3 degrees of freedom is 3·18 and therefore the observed result is not significant. If the Normal probability table had been used the probability of the observed result would have been given as 0·016 and the result would have been wrongly judged significant.

The difference between the t-table and the Normal probability table is small when the number of degrees of freedom is greater than 20. This is because, for a sample of this size, the sample estimate of σ is fairly accurate and therefore the assumption that t is normally distributed is not far out. The entry in the t-table corresponding to an infinite number of degrees of freedom is in fact calculated from the Normal probability curve.

The following relation due to R. A. Fisher is of interest.

If D is the Normal probability deviate such that the chance of getting a deviation greater in absolute value than D is P and if t is calculated on f degrees of freedom then t_p, the $P\%$ point, or $P\%$ significance level of t is given by

$$t_p = D \left[1 + \frac{1 + D^2}{4f} + \frac{(3 + 16D^2 + 5D^4)}{96f^2} + \text{etc.} \right]$$

Suppose we want to calculate t_p for 10 degrees of freedom at $P = 5\%$.

Then from Table XXVI, $D = 1.96$.

(Table XXVI is entered at $P = 2\frac{1}{2}\%$ since the total area of the tails must be 5%.)

$$D^2 = 3.842 \qquad\qquad D^4 = 14.76$$
$$1 + D^2 = 4.842 \qquad 3 + 16D^2 + 5D^4 = 138.3$$
$$f = 10$$
$$\therefore \quad t_p = 1.96 \left[1 + \frac{4.842}{40} + \frac{138.3}{9600} \right] \text{approx.}$$
$$= 1.96 \times 1.135 = 2.22$$

The value given in Table XXX is 2.23.

Fisher's equation for t_p illustrates how when f is large $t_p = D$ very nearly.

Example 3. The average breaking strength of steel rods is specified to be 18·5 thousand pounds. To test this a sample of 14 rods was tested and gave the following results (in units of 1,000 lbs.): 15, 18, 16, 21, 19, 21, 17, 17, 15, 17, 20, 19, 17, 18. What is the appropriate hypothesis and is the result of the experiment significant?

The appropriate hypothesis is that the mean breaking strength is 18·5 units.

To test this calculate m and s.

$$\Sigma x = 250$$
$$\Sigma x^2 = 4{,}514$$
$$m = 250/14 = 17.86$$
$$\Sigma(x - m)^2 = 4{,}514 - \frac{250 \times 250}{14} = 4{,}514 - 4{,}464.3 = 49.7$$

$$s^2 = \frac{1}{13}\,\Sigma(x - \bar{x})^2 = 3{\cdot}823$$

$$\text{and } s = \sqrt{3{\cdot}823} = 1{\cdot}955$$

$$\frac{s}{\sqrt{14}} = \frac{1{\cdot}955}{\sqrt{14}} = 0{\cdot}5224$$

$$t = (\mu - m)/s/\sqrt{14} = \frac{0{\cdot}64}{0{\cdot}5224} = 1{\cdot}23$$

From Table XXX of the t-distribution with $f = 13$ the 10% value of t is 1·77. Since the calculated value is less than this the result is not significant at the 10% level and the hypothesis is not rejected.

Example 4.   To test if a small electric current affected the growth of maize seedlings 10 pairs of plants were grown in parallel boxes, and one member of each pair was "treated" by receiving a small electric current. The differences in height between the treated and untreated in mm. were (treated) — (untreated), 6·0, 1·3, 10·2, 23·9, 3·1, 6·8, — 1·5, — 14·7, — 3·3 and 11·1.

Here the null hypothesis is that the electric current does not affect the growth so that the observed differences are random observations from a population with zero mean. To test this, calculate

$$\Sigma x = 42{\cdot}9$$
$$\Sigma x^2 = 1{,}121{\cdot}23, n = 10, \qquad\qquad f = n - 1 = 9$$
$$m = 4{\cdot}29$$

$$\Sigma(x - m)^2 = 1{,}121{\cdot}23 - \frac{42{\cdot}9 \times 42{\cdot}9}{10} = 1{,}121{\cdot}23 - 184{\cdot}04 = 937{\cdot}19$$

$$s^2 = \frac{937{\cdot}19}{9} = 104{\cdot}13$$

$$s^2/10 = 10{\cdot}413 \text{ and } s/\sqrt{10} = 3{\cdot}227$$

$$t = (m - \mu)/s/\sqrt{10} \text{ and here } \mu = 0 \text{ by hypothesis}$$

$$\text{so } t = 4{\cdot}29/3{\cdot}227 = 1{\cdot}33$$

From Table XXX with $f = 9$, the 10% value of t is 1·83 and this is larger than the observed value. The result is therefore not significant at the 10% level and the hypothesis is not rejected. In other words the sample does not provide satisfactory evidence that the electric treatment has made any difference to the growth of maize seedlings. (Data of this example due to Collins, Flint and McLane.)

DIFFERENCES BETWEEN MEANS. Two samples of n_1 and n_2 observations are drawn from two populations and have means m_1 and m_2. The population standard deviations, σ, are assumed to be the same, and σ can be estimated by s_1 or s_2, the sample standard deviations where

$$s_1^2 = \frac{\Sigma(x_1 - m_1)^2}{n_1 - 1} \tag{7.16}$$

$$s_2^2 = \frac{\Sigma(x_2 - m_2)^2}{n_2 - 1} \tag{7.17}$$

To obtain a combined estimate of σ from both these samples it is necessary to divide the total sum of squared deviations by the number of degrees of freedom. Therefore if s is the combined estimate of σ

$$s^2 = \frac{\Sigma(x_1 - m_1)^2 + \Sigma(x_2 - m_2)^2}{n_1 + n_2 - 2} \qquad (7.18)$$

and this estimate of σ is based on $f = n_1 + n_2 - 2$ degrees of freedom.

Another way of expressing s^2 is to use equations 7.16 and 7.17 and write

$$s^2 = \frac{(n_1 - 1)s_1^2 + (n_2 - 1)s_2^2}{n_1 + n_2 - 2} \qquad (7.19)$$

It follows that the standard deviations of the means m_1 and m_2 are $s/\sqrt{n_1}$ and $s/\sqrt{n_2}$ where s is calculated from 7.18 or 7.19.

It has been shown that the variance of the difference between two independent variables is equal to the sum of the variances of the variables.

$$\text{If } z = x - y$$

$$\text{then } s_z^2 = s_x^2 + s_y^2$$

Therefore variance $(m_1 - m_2) = \dfrac{s^2}{n_1} + \dfrac{s^2}{n_2}$

so that the standard deviation of the difference $(m_1 - m_2)$ is $s\sqrt{\dfrac{1}{n_1} + \dfrac{1}{n_2}}$. To find whether the difference between m_1 and m_2 is significant calculate

$$t = (m_1 - m_2)/s\sqrt{\frac{1}{n_1} + \frac{1}{n_2}}$$

and find the probability of the result from the Normal probability table, Table XXVI if $f = n_1 + n_2 - 2$ is large. If f is not large use the table of the t-distribution, Table XXX, entering it with $n_1 + n_2 - 2$ degrees of freedom.

Example 5. The heights of a random sample of 1,304 Scotsmen had a mean of 68·5456 ins. with standard deviation 2·480 ins. A random sample of 6,194 Englishmen gave an average height of 67·4375 ins. and a standard deviation of 2·548 ins. Is this difference significant?

$$m_1 = 68\cdot5456 \qquad\qquad m_2 = 67\cdot4375$$

$$m_1 - m_2 = 1\cdot1081$$

From equation (4)

$$s^2 = \frac{1{,}303\,(2{\cdot}480)^2 + 6{,}193\,(2{\cdot}548)^2}{7{,}496}$$

$$= 6{\cdot}433$$

$$s^2\left(\frac{1}{n_1} + \frac{1}{n_2}\right) = 6{\cdot}433\left(\frac{1}{1{,}304} + \frac{1}{6{,}194}\right)$$

$$= 6{\cdot}433\,(0{\cdot}0007669 + 0{\cdot}0001614)$$

$$= 0{\cdot}005972$$

$$s\sqrt{\left(\frac{1}{n_1} + \frac{1}{n_2}\right)} = \sqrt{0{\cdot}005972} = 0{\cdot}0773$$

$$t = \frac{m_1 - m_2}{s\sqrt{\dfrac{1}{n_1} + \dfrac{1}{n_2}}} = \frac{1{\cdot}1081}{0{\cdot}0773} = 14{\cdot}3$$

For such a large value of t the probability is very small (less than 10^{-23}) and the result is highly significant.

Example 6.   The densities of sulphuric acid in two containers were measured, four determinations being made on one container and six on the other. Do the results lead to the rejection of the hypothesis that the acids have the same density?

Container *A*.   1·842, 1·846, 1·843, 1·843

Container *B*.   1·848, 1·843, 1·846, 1·847, 1·847, 1·845

The arithmetic will be simplified if 1·840 is subtracted from each figure and the remainder multiplied by 1,000.

Container A	Container B
2	8
6	3
3	6
3	7
	7
	5

$$\Sigma x = \overline{14} \qquad\qquad \Sigma x = \overline{36}$$

$$m_1 = \frac{14}{4} = 3{\cdot}5 \qquad\qquad m_2 = \frac{36}{6} = 6{\cdot}0$$

$$\Sigma(x - m_1)^2 = 58 - \frac{14^2}{4} \qquad\qquad \Sigma(x - m_2)^2 = 232 - \frac{36^2}{6}$$

$$= 9 \qquad\qquad\qquad\qquad\qquad = 16$$

The combined estimate of the population standard deviation is given by s where $s^2 = \dfrac{9 + 16}{8} = 3{\cdot}125$ based on 8 degrees of freedom.

$$s^2\left(\frac{1}{n_1} + \frac{1}{n_2}\right) = 3\cdot125\left(\frac{1}{4} + \frac{1}{6}\right)$$
$$= 1\cdot302$$

$$s\sqrt{\left(\frac{1}{n_1} + \frac{1}{n_2}\right)} = 1\cdot141$$

$$= \frac{m_1 - m_2}{s\sqrt{\dfrac{1}{n_1} + \dfrac{1}{n_2}}} = \frac{2\cdot5}{1\cdot141} = 2\cdot19$$

Entering Table XXX with $f = 8$ degrees of freedom the 5% value of t is $2\cdot31$. Since the observed value is less than this the result is not significant at the 5% level and the hypothesis that the acids have the same density is not rejected. The reader should verify that another conclusion would have been reached if the Normal probability table had been used.

Example 7. In the previous example suppose that there were adequate grounds for saying that if a real difference existed it must be because the acid in container A is less dense than that in B. For example, container A might have been exposed to conditions when it was possible for the acid to be slightly diluted.

This is a problem for which the one-tail test would be used. For such a test the column headed $P\%$ in the table of the t-distribution corresponds to a significance level of $\frac{1}{2}P\%$.

The calculated value of t was $2\cdot19$ based on 8 degrees of freedom.

For the one-tail test the $2\frac{1}{2}\%$ value of t from Table XXX is $2\cdot31$ and the 5% value (from the column headed 10%) is $1\cdot86$. The observed result is therefore significant at the 5% level and the hypothesis is rejected.

DIFFERENCES BETWEEN STANDARD DEVIATIONS. Two populations have unknown standard deviations σ_1 and σ_2. Samples n_1 and n_2 give estimates s_1^2, and s_2^2 of the population variances based on f_1 $(= n_1 - 1)$ and f_2 $(= n_2 - 1)$ degrees of freedom respectively. Calculate $F = s_1^2/s_2^2$ where s_1^2 is always the greater of the two variances so that F is always greater or equal to unity. Denote F by $F(f_1, f_2)$.

Example 8. For estimates of standard deviations, 5 and 2 based on 10 and 4 measurements respectively $F(9, 3) = 6\cdot25$. For estimates of standard deviations 2 and 6 based on 12 and 8 measurements $F(7, 11) = 9$.

If the null hypothesis is that there is no difference between the variabilities of the two populations, that is $\sigma_1 = \sigma_2$ then there are usually two alternatives to the null hypothesis which may be considered:

      (i) The one-sided test $\sigma_1 > \sigma_2$
or (ii) The two-sided test $\sigma_1 \neq \sigma_2$

The nature of the problem will determine which alternative hypothesis is appropriate; situations where the one-sided test is used occur more frequently.

The mathematical expression for the probability distribution of F is known and from it can be calculated tables giving the probabilities of obtaining values of F as big or greater than the calculated value if the null hypothesis is true. If the probability is small the null hypothesis is rejected. Two such tables (Tables XLII and XLIII on pages 329, 330) are given for the 5% and 1% significance levels for the one-sided test. For the two-sided test the significance levels should be doubled.

Example 9. Two candidates for a post in a chemical laboratory are asked to make a number of determinations of arsenic in a homogenous chemical mixture. Candidate A completes 25 analyses with a standard deviation 8. Candidate B has time for only 6 analyses giving a standard deviation of 12. Is this evidence of a difference in precision between the candidates?

$$F(5, 24) = 12^2/8^2 = 2 \cdot 25$$

The question is appropriate to a two-sided test and from Table XLII the 2% level of $F(5, 24)$ is $3 \cdot 90$ so the result is not significant at the 2% level (it is significant at the 10% level).

Example 10. Tests with a gun show a range accuracy expressed by a standard deviation of 60 yards estimated from 10 firings. A modification is made to the gun designed to improve the range accuracy. A further 4 tests give a standard deviation of 20 yards. Has the modification been effective?

$$F(9, 3) = 9$$

This is a single-sided test and the 5% value of F is $8 \cdot 81$. The improvement is just significant at the 5% level.

Where the variance of one population is known or assumed the entry to the table is made in the appropriate row or column with degrees of freedom corresponding to infinity.

Example 11. The normal variability of pin diameter on a mass production process is given by a standard deviation of $0 \cdot 008''$. A sample of 25 pins gives a standard deviation of $0 \cdot 006''$. Is this evidence of a significant change in precision?

$$\sigma_1^2/s_2^2 = 1 \cdot 78$$

This is a two-sided test and at the 10% significance level.

$$F(\infty, 24) = 1 \cdot 73$$

The result is therefore just significant at the 10% level.

Example 12. A metering device gives flow measurements with an accuracy expressed by a standard deviation of $2 \cdot 0\%$. A trial with a less sophisticated device gives a standard deviation of $2 \cdot 5\%$ based on 16 measurements. Is the apparent deterioration significant at the 5% level?

$$s_1^2/\sigma_2^2 = 1 \cdot 56$$
$$F(15, \infty) = 1 \cdot 67 \text{ (one-sided test) at the 5% level}$$

and the deterioration is therefore not significant at the 5% level.

7.8 Confidence limits. Means and Standard Deviations

CONFIDENCE INTERVALS FOR THE MEAN. The mean of a sample of size n drawn from a Normal or approximately Normal, population of individuals with mean μ and standard deviation σ can be regarded as a single random sample from the whole population of similar means. This population of means will also have mean μ, but its standard deviation will be $\sigma/\sqrt{n}$ (Section 7.5). If the values of σ and μ are unknown, the sample mean m provides an estimate of μ and the sample standard deviation s provides an estimate of σ. The magnitude of $s/\sqrt{n}$ provides a measure of the uncertainty in the value of m as an estimate of μ. This uncertainty can be most simply expressed by means of a "confidence interval."

We know that $\dfrac{m - u}{s/\sqrt{n}}$ (or $\dfrac{u - m}{s/\sqrt{n}}$, since the choice of sign does not affect the argument) is distributed as Student's t with $(n - 1)$ degrees of freedom. If $p\%$ is a specified percentage and $t(p)$ the corresponding percentage point (Table XXX), we can write

$$-t(p) \leqslant \frac{\mu - m}{s/\sqrt{n}} \leqslant t(p)$$

which is equivalent to

$$m - t(p)\, s/\sqrt{n} \leqslant \mu \leqslant m + t(p)\, s/\sqrt{n}.$$

We can therefore assert that

$$P[m - t(p)\, s/\sqrt{n} \leqslant \mu \leqslant m + t(p)\, s/\sqrt{n}] = (100 - p)\%$$

This expression states that, with a confidence expressed as a probability of $(100 - p)\%$, the unknown value of μ lies *within* the interval $m \pm t(p)\, s/\sqrt{n}$ or, alternatively, that the risk that the unknown value of μ lies *outside* this interval is $p\%$.

For example, for $s/\sqrt{n} = 1\cdot5$, $n = 12$, $m = 16\cdot8$, the 10% point of the t-distribution for 11 d.f. is $1\cdot80$. Hence the 90% confidence interval for μ is

$$16\cdot8 \pm 1\cdot80 \times 1\cdot5 \text{ or } 16\cdot8 \pm 2\cdot7 \text{ or } 17\cdot7 \text{ to } 19\cdot5$$

The degree of confidence can be increased to 95% by substituting the 5% point for t. For 11 d.f. the 5% point is $2\cdot20$. Hence the 95% confidence interval for μ is

$$16\cdot8 \pm 2\cdot20 \times 1\cdot5 \text{ or } 16\cdot8 \pm 3\cdot3 \text{ or } 13\cdot5 \text{ to } 20\cdot1.$$

Similarly the 99% confidence interval for μ is

$$16\cdot8 \pm 3\cdot11 \times 1\cdot5 \text{ or } 16\cdot8 \pm 4\cdot7 \text{ or } 12\cdot1 \text{ to } 21\cdot5.$$

The confidence intervals thus expressed are not unique. The intervals calculated above, however, are central with respect to m, the sample mean. They need not be. Other $(100 - p)\%$ confidence intervals, in which the $p\%$ risk is unequally shared by the two tails, could be found. But if the distribution is unimodal and symmetrical, as are the Normal and t-distributions, then the confidence interval centred about m is the shortest of all possible intervals for a given value of p.

7.8 Confidence Intervals for Standard Deviation or Variance

In determining confidence intervals for the variance and therefore for the standard deviation it is possible to use the table of the χ^2-distribution (Table XXXIX). The use of χ^2 depends on the fact that $\Sigma (x - \bar{x})^2/\sigma^2$ or $(n - 1)s^2/\sigma^2$ is distributed as χ^2 with $(n - 1)$ degrees of freedom

Example 13.   Let $s^2 = 1 \cdot 00$ for a sample for which $n = 9$ and let it be required to calculate the 90% confidence limits for s^2 and s.

The 95% and 5% points of χ^2 for $9 - 1 = 8$ degrees of freedom are $2 \cdot 7$ and $15 \cdot 5$. We can therefore write

$$P(15 \cdot 5 > 8s^2/\sigma^2 > 2 \cdot 7) = 0 \cdot 9$$

Invert the inequalities

$$1/15 \cdot 5 < \sigma^2/8s^2 < 1/2 \cdot 7$$

to give $$0 \cdot 52s^2 < \sigma^2 < 2 \cdot 93s^2$$

So, for $s^2 = 1 \cdot 00$, $n = 9$ the 90% confidence intervals are $0 \cdot 52 < \sigma^2 < 2 \cdot 93$ for the variance and $0 \cdot 72 < \sigma < 1 \cdot 71$ for the standard deviation.

Example 14.   Calculate the 95% confidence limits for the standard deviation, $0 \cdot 006''$, of pin diameter estimated from 25 samples.
From the χ^2-table (24 degrees of freedom)

$$P(39 \cdot 36 > 24s^2/\sigma^2 > 12 \cdot 40) = 0 \cdot 95$$

leading to $0 \cdot 78s < \sigma < 1 \cdot 39s$ so that the 95% confidence limits of the standard deviation are $0 \cdot 0047''$ and $0 \cdot 0083''$.

SUMMARY OF CHAPTER VII

1. The *null hypothesis* is the hypothesis which is tested on the assumption that it is true. The *level of significance* is a probability.

2. The main steps in a statistical experiment are
   (a) The statement of the problem and the formulation of the null hypothesis.
   (b) The selection of a level of significance.
   (c) The experimental testing of the hypothesis and the interpretation of the experimental results.

3. If the probability of the observed results is less than the level of significance the null hypothesis is rejected. The following values are suggested:

P, the probability of the experimental result on the null hypothesis, more than 5%	Do not reject the hypothesis.
P, between 5% and 1%	Reject the hypothesis with reasonable confidence.

P less than 1%   The hypothesis may be confidently rejected.

4. When n is large the Binomial distribution is closely approximate to the Normal distribution with mean and standard deviation given by

$$\mu = np$$
$$\sigma = \sqrt{npq}$$

5. The best sample estimate of the population standard deviation is given by s, where

$$s^2 = \Sigma_1^n (x_i - m)^2 / (n - 1).$$

$(n - 1)$ is the number of *degrees of freedom* of the estimate.

6. If μ and σ are the mean and standard deviation of the population of individuals and μ_n and σ_n are the mean and standard deviation of the means of samples of size n then it can be shown theoretically that

$$\mu_n = \mu$$
$$\sigma_n = \sigma / \sqrt{n}$$

7. If $z = x \pm y$ where x and y are independent
then $\sigma_z^2 = \sigma_x^2 + \sigma_y^2$

8. From a sample of n the sample mean and standard deviation are m and s, where s is based on $(n - 1)$ degrees of freedom. To test the hypothesis that the population mean is μ calculate

$$t = \frac{m - \mu}{s / \sqrt{n}}$$

and use the t-table (Table **XXX**, p. 164).

9. Two samples of n_1 and n_2 observations have means m_1 and m_2. To test whether the difference between the means is significant calculate

$$s^2 = \frac{\Sigma(x_1 - m_1)^2 + \Sigma(x_2 - m_2)^2}{n_1 + n_2 - 2}$$

and then calculate

$$t = (m_1 - m_2) / s \sqrt{\frac{1}{n_1} + \frac{1}{n_2}}$$

10. Two samples of n_1 and n_2 observations have standard deviations s_1 and s_2 based on $f_1 = n_1 - 1$ and $f_2 = n_2 - 1$ degrees of freedom, respectively. To test whether the difference between the standard deviations is significant calculate

$$F = s_1^2 / s_2^2 \ (s_1 > s_2)$$

Refer to Tables XL and XLI for the 5%, 1% significance levels of F for a one-sided test. For a two-sided test double the levels of significance.

11. Where sample estimates of the mean and standard deviation are m and s there is a probability of $(100 - p)\%$ that the unknown value of μ, the population mean, will be between the $p\%$ confidence limits

$$m \pm t(p)\, s/\sqrt{n}$$

where $t(p)$ is the $p\%$-age point of the t-distribution (Table XXX).

12. The confidence limits of the variance or standard deviation are obtained by using the χ^2-table (Table XXXIX, p. 234). If $2p\%$ is the required confidence interval and s is the standard deviation estimated from a sample of n then

$$P[\chi^2_{1-p} \geqslant (n-1)s^2/\sigma^2 \geqslant \chi^2_p] = 2p$$

leading to

$$(n-1)s^2/\chi^2_{1-p} \leqslant \sigma^2 \leqslant (n-1)s^2/\chi^2_p$$

EXERCISES XXVI

1. A sample has mean and standard deviation $\bar{x} = 13\cdot42$; $s = 1\cdot36$. The null hypothesis states that $\mu = 13$. What is the significance of this result if the sample size is 10, 25, 50, 100?

2. To test the hypothesis that $\mu = 124$ a sample of 40 observations was collected. What would be the deviation of the sample average from 124 in order to lie on the 5% significance level if s, the sample standard deviation, was 0·5, 1·4, 3·6, 10·2?

3. The following table shows the additional hours of sleep gained by 15 patients taking two soporifics.

Patien	Soporific A	Soporific B	Difference (B–A)
1	+ 1·2	1·5	0·3
2	+ 1·8	1·6	0·2
3	− 0·2	0·4	0·6
4	− 0·7	0·0	0·7
5	+ 0·1	2·5	2·4
6	+ 3·1	4·5	1·4
7	+ 2·2	1·9	− 0·3
8	− 1·5	2·2	3·7
9	0·0	3·0	3·0
10	2·1	1·9	− 0·2
11	1·9	3·4	1·5
12	− 2·0	4·6	6·6
13	1·5	5·1	3·6
14	0·8	3·2	2·4
15	0·6	− 0·8	− 1·4

Calculate the mean and standard deviation of the differences and decide whether the difference between the effect of the soporifics is significant on the 5% level.

4. The size of a contact gap in an electrical component is measured in two samples of 200 taken from the work of two different shifts. The results are given below. Does the work of the two shifts differ significantly on the 1% level in respect of the average spark gap?

Size of gap (0·01 in.)	2	3	4	5	6	7	8	9
No. of comp. Shift 1	1	2	8	12	24	35	42	35
No. of comp. Shift 2.	0	0	2	1	5	21	26	42

Size of gap (0·01 in.)	10	11	12	13	14	15	Total
No. of comp. Shift 1	30	6	4	1	0	0	200
No. of comp. Shift 2	51	31	11	5	3	2	200

5. In an ordnance factory two different methods of shell filling are compared. The average and standard deviation of weights in a sample of 96 shells filled by an old process are 1·26 lbs. and 0·013 lbs. and a sample of 72 shells filled by a new process gave an average of 1·28 lbs. with a standard deviation of 0·011 lbs. Is the difference in average weights significant on the 5% level?

6. Two chemists estimate the strength of a dilute solution of hydrochloric acid. Their results are an average of 10·162 with a standard deviation of 0·23 based on 15 determinations and 10·341 with standard deviation of 0·12 based on 24 determinations. What is the level of significance of the difference between the chemists' estimates of the acidity on the hypothesis that their results are random variations about the same population mean?

7. Two gauge operators are tested for precision in making measurements. One operator completes a set of 26 readings with a standard deviation of 1·34 and the other does 34 readings with a standard deviation of 0·98. Is the difference in standard deviation significant? It is necessary to interpolate in the F-table.

8. The yield of wax extracted from peat depends on the nature of the solvent used to extract the wax. Two solvents were tested on five samples of peat. The table shows yield of crude wax (% dry peat). Is the effect significant?

Sample	1	2	3	4	5
Solvent A	2·3	10·4	2·4	6·8	4·1
Solvent B	3·2	11·8	2·7	8·6	5·2

(Fuel Research D.S.I.R. Tech. Paper 52.)

9. The following figures show the mean breaking strength index of two types of cotton fibre. Taking the figures in pairs determine whether the mean difference is significant.

Index of Breaking Strengths

Fibre A	7·2	7·7	7·8	7·4	7·6	7·3	7·8	7·7	7·6	7·4
Fibre B	7·2	7·2	7·1	7·6	7·3	7·3	7·3	7·6	7·2	7·9

G

10. The data shows observed and calculated values of water viscosity at different temperatures and also the percentage error. Does the % error differ significantly from zero?

$n(obs) \times 10^5$	$n(calc) \times 10^5$	$\dfrac{n(obs) - n(calc)}{n(obs)} \times 100$
2,545	2,539	$+0\cdot2$
2,454	2,456	$-0\cdot1$
2,337	2,338	$-0\cdot05$
2,246	2,246	0
2,118	2,122	$-0\cdot2$
1,927	1,930	$-0\cdot2$
1,795	1,792	$+0\cdot2$
1,523	1,521	$+0\cdot1$
1,306	1,308	$-0\cdot15$
1,140	1,139	$+0\cdot1$

(E. N. de C. Andrade. *Nature*, 1930, p. 585.)

11. The monthly consumption of scrap by the Iron and Steel Industry for two sets of 12 months are shown below. Is there any significant difference in the variability of consumption in the two years?

Consumption of Scrap (1,000 *tons*)

April 1946–*March* 1947
153   158   143   138   134   144   154   160   144   144   123   148

April 1947–*March* 1948
145   150   158   129   139   162   166   164   145   169   174   175

12. For a sample of 4 drawn from a Normal population, $m = 3\cdot65$ and $s = 0\cdot12$. Find the 90%, 95%, 99% and 99·9% confidence intervals for the mean.

13. Find the 90% confidence interval for the mean breaking strengths of the steel rods of Example 3, Section 7.7, and verify that the specification value of 18·5 thousand pounds lies within it.

14. (*a*) Find the 95% confidence interval for the means of heights of Scotsmen and Englishmen given by the data of Example 5, Section 7.7, and verify that they do not overlap.

(*b*) Find the 95% confidence interval for the difference of the means of the means of the same sample populations and verify that zero lies outside this interval.

15. The estimate of a standard deviation based on (*a*) 5 and (*b*) 50 samples is 4. Calculate the 90% confidence limits of the standard deviation for (*a*) and (*b*).

16. In example 9, Section 7.7, calculate the 95% confidence limits of the standard deviations of candidates A and B.

17. From ten samples $\Sigma x = 10$ and $\Sigma x^2 = 35$. Find the 95% confidence limits of the population variance.

CHAPTER VIII

Regression

8.1 Distributions With More Than One Variable

The distributions considered up to this point have been such that there has been only one variable corresponding to each member of the particular universe, e.g., the number of men of a certain height, the number of marks obtained by a candidate in one subject paper of an examination. Such distributions are said to be *univariate*. There are, however, statistical universes in which more than one variable corresponds to each member, e.g., the marks obtained by individual examinees in English, Latin and Mathematics taken separately would form a *trivariate* distribution. We shall here be concerned only with some aspects of *bivariate* distributions, i.e., distributions in which the variables are associated in pairs. A typical example is afforded by the marks obtained by examination candidates in written and oral French, from which data of the following kind would be obtained:

| Candidate | Marks | |
No.	Written	Oral
1	72	64
2	37	48
3	54	52
4	60	54
5	31	10
	etc.	

From such a set of data the question—How does the "oral" mark vary with the "written" mark?—might arise. To answer this and related questions fully, it would be necessary first to tabulate the data in some suitable form, then to represent the data visually in some form analogous to a histogram and finally to assess quantitatively the closeness of the relation between the two variables and the form of that relation.

8.2 Tabulation of Bivariate Distributions

To tabulate the data of bivariate distributions such as that given in the previous paragraph the two variables are divided if necessary by equal and convenient class limits to give not more than about 20 classes of each. A large sheet of paper is divided into squares so that there is one square for each possible combination of classes of the two variables. Each pair of variables is then represented by a point

177

in its appropriate square. The numbers of dots in each square are counted and these numbers are set out in similar tabular form. The results of such a process are shown in Table XXXI where (a) is the dot diagram of the two sets of marks ranging from 1 to 9 and (b) is the completed table.

Each column and row of Table XXXI (b) contains the distribution of one of the variables for a particular value of the second variable; each of these columns and rows, called *arrays*, is thus a frequency distribution of the type we have already considered in earlier chapters.

TABLE XXXI (a)

"DOT DIAGRAM" OF BIVARIATE DISTRIBUTION

Marks in Science (vertical axis)

Marks in Mathematics (horizontal axis)

TABLE XXXI (*b*)

A BIVARIATE DISTRIBUTION

Marks in Science

	1	2	3	4	5	6	7	8	9
9	—	—	—	—	—	—	—	2	3
8	—	—	—	—	1	7	16	14	3
7	—	—	2	3	13	12	14	16	3
6	—	2	3	12	23	19	17	10	—
5	—	1	4	27	26	15	6	2	—
4	3	9	15	26	17	9	4	1	—
3	5	12	17	10	7	7	2	—	—
2	5	8	7	11	8	3	—	—	—
1	4	5	4	2	1	—	—	—	—
	1	2	3	4	5	6	7	8	9

Marks in Mathematics

8.3 Representation of Bivariate Distributions

It was shown in Chapter II how univariate distributions could be represented by histograms. To represent bivariate distributions in an analogous way we should need a series of rectangular solid columns arranged in parallel planes, each plane corresponding to one value or class of the variables. We should thus obtain a solid figure consisting of rectangular columns of various heights; the data of Table XXXI could be represented by standing columns on each square, the height of the column being proportional to the number in the square. Corresponding to a frequency polygon we should have an irregular polyhedron and corresponding to a smooth curve we should obtain a smooth surface. Three-dimensional representations of this kind are called stereograms.

The building up of such a stereogram can be imagined if we consider the errors of aircraft bomb-aimers dropping bombs on a point target. The possible errors are in range, that is, the bomb may fall in front or behind the target, and in "line", that is, to the left or right. If the bombs were made of putty so that they remained exactly where they fell we should expect to see a pile of these putty bombs building up about the target. Such a pile would be a stereogram of the bomb-aimers' two errors if the aircraft made the approach always from the same direction. If the errors in range were on the whole greater than those in line the bombs would form a heap similar to that of which the contours are given, in arbitrary units, in Fig. 45 (*a*). Sections across the contours are shown in Fig. 45 (*b*). They would often be close approximations to Normal curves.

While stereograms provide an excellent means of representing bivariate distributions they are not usually practicable. Some

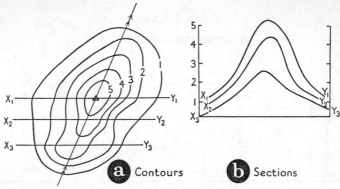

FIG. 45.   (a) Contours.   (b) Sections.   (Stereograms of bombing errors.)

representation in two dimensions is required. This is given to some extent by the table of arrays but a clearer picture is presented by the *scatter diagrams*. In this type of diagram the pairs of variables are represented by a point in a plane, one set of variables being the abscissæ and the other set being the corresponding ordinates, using rectangular axes. The limitation of the scatter diagram is that it is difficult to represent several coincident points in any satisfactory way. With this limitation, however, it clearly indicates the nature of the relation between the two variables and usually suggests what further analytical steps would be most profitable.

The results of physics laboratory experiments usually show very close relation between the two variables measured, and it is comparatively easy to draw one line, straight or smoothly curved, which passes through or near all points when the results are plotted on a scatter diagram. Fig. 46 (a) shows a scatter diagram of this kind of bivariate distribution.

The other extreme is the distribution represented by Fig. 46 (b) in which there is no tendency for the variables to group themselves together in any particular direction. There is no association between variables that give rise to this kind of scatter diagram; the probability of any particular value of one occurring does not depend on the value of the other.

Figs. 46 (c) and (d), illustrating distributions in which the variables show some degree of association, are typical of statistical bivariate distributions. In Fig. 46 (c) the variables tend to group themselves around a straight line or lines; in Fig. 46 (d) the association between the variables could be represented approximately by an equation of the form $y = a + bx + cx^2$. The remainder of this chapter will be concerned with finding the straight lines which best fit some of these distributions.

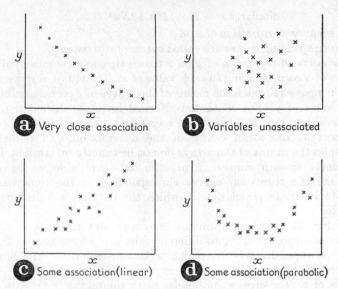

FIG. 46. Types of scatter diagram.

8.4 Curves of Regression

When we are considering the relation between two variables we almost always select one variable as being *independent* and make observations of the other, the *dependent* variable, for various selected values of the first. If this is not explicitly stated then it is usually implied or tacitly assumed. In any formula connecting two variables the subject is the dependent variable; in laboratory experiments the independent variable is that which is the more easily measured or controlled: in graphs the independent variable is usually measured along the "x-axis". In most bivariate distributions there exists this relation, but both variables may take either rôle; it depends on the question we are trying to answer.

In this enquiry into curves of regression we are asking one of the following questions—Given a bivariate distribution (x_1, y_1), (x_2, y_2), etc., what is the curve or the formula which expresses *either* x in terms of y, *or* y in terms of x. It is important to realise that, in general, these two curves or formulae are *not* identical. They are identical only if the relation between x and y is exact for all the pairs of the distribution, i.e., if the curve passes through all the points. If we express y in terms of x, then the equation

$$y = A + Bx + Cx^2 + \ldots$$

is called *the equation of regression of y on x*.

Similarly $x = K + My + Ny^2 + \ldots$

is *the equation of regression of x on y.*

The corresponding curves are called *curves of regression.*

The curve of regression of y on x passes through the means of the arrays of y corresponding to each value of x. The curve of regression of x on y passes through the means of the arrays of x corresponding to each value of y. For continuous Normal bivariate distributions it can be shown that both curves of regression are straight lines which intersect at the mean centre of the distribution. In numerical examples the means of the arrays do not lie exactly on straight lines or simple smooth curves. From the data available we have to estimate the regression curves corresponding to the hypothetical infinite bivariate population of which the data are a finite random sample.

In Fig. 47 (a) the continuous lines represent the ranges of the arrays of x corresponding to different values of y for a sample drawn from an approximately Normal bivariate distribution. The broken lines represent the ranges of the arrays of y corresponding to different values of x. The crosses and circles mark the means of the two sets of arrays and show how the two distinct regression lines arise. In this particular example there is evidently little association between the two variables; in a distribution which had a closer association between the variables the angle between the regression lines would be smaller.

In a similar way Fig. 47 (b) shows the curve of regression of y on x, a parabola, for a different type of distribution.

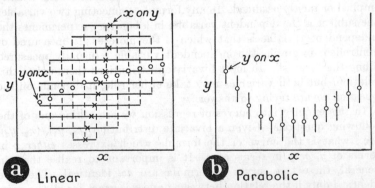

FIG. 47.   Curves of regression as the loci of means of arrays.

8.5   Graphical Determination of Regression Lines

The regression lines of the data of Table XXXI (b) may be obtained fairly quickly, though only approximately, by a method which avoids much of the work of computation. To find the regression of y on x calculate the mean value of y for each individual value of x, e.g., for

$$x = 1, \bar{y} = \frac{1}{17} (3 \times 4 + 5 \times 3 + 5 \times 2 + 4 \times 1) = \frac{41}{17} = 2 \cdot 4.$$

The following pairs of numbers were thus obtained:

x	1	2	3	4	5	6	7	8	9
$\bar{y}$	2·4	3·0	3·5	4·3	4·9	5·4	6·7	7·0	8·0

These points $(x, \bar{y})$ are then plotted on graph paper. In Fig. 48 they are indicated by the small crosses. The position of the mean centre, G, should be estimated and marked. Using a straight edge, preferably of transparent material, the regression line is drawn through G, to fit the row of crosses as well as possible.

The regression equation is of the form

$$y = mx + c \qquad (8.1)$$

where m and c are constants. These can be determined by noting the co-ordinates of two convenient points near the extremes of the lines. The co-ordinates of P and Q (Fig. 48) are seen to be $(1, 2 \cdot 2)$ and $(9, 8 \cdot 6)$ respectively. Substituting in equation 8.1 we have

$$2 \cdot 2 = m + c$$
$$7 \cdot 8 = 9m + c$$

Solving for m and c, $m = 0 \cdot 7$, $c = 1 \cdot 5$, so that the required equation is $y = 0 \cdot 7x + 1 \cdot 5$.

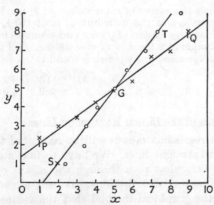

FIG. 48. Graphical determination of regression lines.

The calculated equation will be shown to be $y = 0 \cdot 687x + 1 \cdot 49$ so that the error in this case is negligible.

The regression line of x on y is found similarly, the corresponding values of $\bar{x}$ and y being

| $\bar{x}$ | 2·4 | 3·4 | 3·5 | 4·1 | 5·0 | 5·7 | 6·7 | 7·3 | 8·6 |
| y | 1 | 2 | 3 | 4 | 5 | 6 | 7 | 8 | 9 |

These points are represented by small circles on Fig. 48. The equation of the line is found by substituting the co-ordinates of S and T in the equation $x = ny + d$ where n and d are constants. It is found to be

$$x = 0.75y + 1.25$$

while the calculated equation is

$$x = 0.694y + 1.53$$

EXERCISES XXVII

1. Construct scatter diagrams for bivariate distributions of marks, e.g., for sets of Mathematics and Physics, Mathematics and English, etc., which are available and are of interest. If the data warrant it, group them, find the means of the arrays and draw the regression lines graphically.

2. Plot the barometric height (x) against the humidity (y) for each day for the data (or part of the data) of Tables II and VII. Group the data into convenient classes, find the means of the arrays and draw the regression curves graphically.

3. Draw graphically the regression lines for the data of:

    (a) Ex. XXVIII, 5.
    (b) Ex. XXVIII, 6.
    (c) Ex. XXVIII, 7.

From your graphs find the equations of the regression lines.

4. The table shows the *means* of y for values of x in a bivariate distribution. The mean centre of the distribution is at (10·1, 3·2). Plot the means, draw the line of regression of y on x and estimate from your graph the most probable value of y for $x = 6$, $x = 18$ (i.e., find the ordinates of points lying on the regression line where x is 6 and 18).

| x | 1 | 3 | 5 | 7 | 9 | 11 | 13 | 15 | 17 | 19 |
| y | 1·5 | 1·7 | 2·2 | 2·5 | 3·0 | 3·3 | 3·9 | 4·0 | 4·6 | 5·2 |

8.6 The Equations of the Linear Regression Lines

The analysis of regression curves will be restricted to those of the first degree, i.e., to straight lines. We have to find a method of calculating the two lines that pass through the means of the two sets of arrays for numerical distributions. It will already have been noticed in using the graphical method that the means of the arrays lie only approximately along a line and that some discretion must be used in drawing the line that appears to be the "best fit" of a row of means. How can we select this line of best fit for the rows of means and express it in terms of the data?

Firstly, for a frequency distribution with one variable it is known that the algebraic sum of the deviations from the arithmetic mean is zero. It would be reasonable to choose the line of best fit so that the algebraic sum of the deviations of the points from the line is also zero. This line would then be, in a sense, an "average" of the distribution.

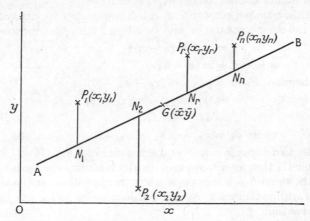

Let P_1, P_2, P_3 . . . P_n be the points of a scatter diagram corresponding to the bivariate distribution (x_1, y_1), (x_2, y_2) . . . (x_n, y_n). Let AB be any straight line drawn so that some of the points P_1, P_2, P_3 . . . P_n lie on one side of it and some on the other. Let the ordinates of P_1, P_2, P_3 . . . P_n meet AB at the points N_1, N_2 . . . N_r . . . N_n (Fig. 49). Then, applying the first criterion, that the sum of the deviations from the arithmetic mean must be zero, we have

$$\Sigma_1^n P_r N_r = 0 \qquad\qquad (8.2)$$

The equation of AB may be represented by

$$y = mx + c \qquad\qquad (8.3)$$

where m and c are constants to be determined.

Since the abscissa of N_r is x_r, the ordinate of N_r must be

$$y = mx_r + c$$

and therefore $P_r N_r = y_r - mx_r - c$.

Substituting in equation 8.2.

$$\Sigma_1^n(y_r - mx_r - c) = 0$$

But $\Sigma_1^n y_r = n\bar{y}$ where $\bar{y}$ is the arithmetic mean of all the y's.

$\Sigma_1^n x_r = n\bar{x}$ where $\bar{x}$ is the arithmetic mean of all the x's

and therefore $n\bar{y} - mn\bar{x} - nc = 0$

or $\bar{y} - m\bar{x} - c = 0$

that is, the line AB must pass through $(\bar{x}, \bar{y})$, the point G which may be called the mean centre of the distribution.

The application of the first criterion does not enable us to determine a unique line, AB, it merely tells us that AB must pass through G and that any line through G would satisfy the condition that the algebraic sum of the deviations $P_r N_r$ is zero.

One of the required constants, c, can however now be expressed in terms of the other constant, m, and equation 8.2 may be rewritten

$$y = mx + (\bar{y} - m\bar{x})$$
$$\text{or } y - \bar{y} = m(x - \bar{x}) \tag{8.4}$$

and therefore
$$\begin{aligned} P_r N_r &= y_r - m(x_r - x) - \bar{y} \\ &= (y_r - \bar{y}) - m(x_r - \bar{x}) \tag{8.5} \\ &= d_y - m \cdot d_x \end{aligned}$$

where $d_y = y_r - \bar{y}$, $d_x = x_r - \bar{x}$.

In order to determine m a second criterion is needed. It was shown in Chapter III that for a frequency distribution with one variable the sum of the squares is a minimum when the deviations are measured from the arithmetic mean. Applying this criterion to the line AB we should have that

$$\Sigma_1^n P_r N_r^2 \text{ is a minimum} \tag{8.6}$$

and, once again, any line satisfying this condition would be, in a sense, an "average" of the distribution.

In algebraic terms and using equation 8.5, equation 8.6 becomes

$$\Sigma_1^n \{d_y - md_x\}^2 \text{ is a minimum}$$

or $\Sigma_1^n \{d_y^2 - 2md_y d_x + m^2 d_x^2\}$ is a minimum

Differentiating with respect to the variable, m, we have

$$-2 \cdot \Sigma_1^n d_y d_x + 2m \cdot \Sigma_1^n d_x^2 = 0$$

$$\text{or} \quad m = \frac{\Sigma_1^n d_y d_x}{\Sigma_1^n d_x^2} \text{ for a minimum.}$$

The *mean* of the products $d_y d_x$ is called the *covariance* of the distribution. If the covariance of a bivariate distribution is known it will be denoted by σ_{xy}; if it is an estimate based on a finite sample from the distribution it will be denoted by s_{xy} which $= \dfrac{1}{n-1} \cdot \Sigma d_y d_x$.

The denominator is $(n-1)$ instead of n because of the loss of one degree of freedom (*see* Section 7.4).

We therefore have here, $m = \dfrac{s_{xy}}{s_x^2} = \dfrac{\Sigma d_y d_x}{\Sigma d_x^2}$ where s_x^2 is the estimated value of the variance of x.

The required equation is then

$$y - \bar{y} = \frac{s_{xy}}{s_x^2} (x - \bar{x})$$

The application of the second criterion therefore enables us to determine a line which may justifiably be called the line of "best fit" for the means of the arrays corresponding to given values of x. It is important to realise that other criteria of best fit are possible and that we have made some very definite assumptions about the distribution. It is possible to obtain other lines of best fit if we postulate different criteria, e.g., that the mean deviation of the y's about the line must be a minimum, or if we make different assumptions about the data, e.g., that some observations should be given more weight than others.

The line represented by the last equation is the line of regression of y on x. In its derivation we have assumed that (a) all the observations have equal weight, (b) that the regression curve required is a straight line for the distribution considered.

The first of these assumptions is usually justified, and, if it is not, some method of weighting the observations can be adopted. An examination of the scatter diagram will show whether the second assumption is acceptable for any given distribution.

As the regression line is defined as the line joining the means of the arrays we found the equation of a line for which the sum of the deviations of the distribution is zero. As it is not possible to find the means of the individual arrays in general terms we are unable to find the line directly. We find only that it must pass through the mean centre of the distribution and we therefore have to look elsewhere for an appropriate and convenient method of selecting a line which meets all our requirements. This was done by postulating that for the required line the mean squared deviations of the y's about the line was a minimum.

The idea of minimising the squared deviations as a criterion of best fit was first suggested by Gauss and is known as the Principle of Least Squares. It has some justification since it can be shown that if both variables are distributed Normally the means of the arrays lie on two straight lines which coincide with the lines found by our method of minimising the variance.

It should be noted that the regression lines are only exceptionally the lines of best fit for the distribution as a whole, they are merely the lines of best fit for the means of the arrays. To find the line of best fit for a distribution we should need to know and allow for the distributions of the errors of both variables. This line coincides with one or other of the lines of regression only in the rare event of all the errors being ascribable to one variable.

The line of regression of y on x is therefore

$$y - \bar{y} = \frac{s_{xy}}{s_x^2} (x - \bar{x}) \tag{8.7}$$

and, similarly, the line of regression of x on y is

$$x - \bar{x} = \frac{s_{xy}}{s_y^2} (y - \bar{y}) \tag{8.8}$$

as the reader can verify.

8.7   The Computation of Regression Equations

The methods of computing $\bar{x}$, $\bar{y}$, s_x^2, s_y^2 have been explained in Chapters II and III. The only new quantity required is $\Sigma d_x d_y$, the sum of the products of the deviations of corresponding values of x and y from their respective means. As in earlier work of this kind the labour of computing $\Sigma d_x d_y$ may be considerably reduced by measuring the deviations from convenient working means and then correcting the sum thus found. Let x_0, y_0 denote the working means, and let $x_0 = \bar{x} + a, y_0 = \bar{y} + b$, where $\bar{x}$, $\bar{y}$ are the true means. The quantity calculated is then $\Sigma(x - x_0) (y - y_0)$, which we will call the "uncorrected value of $\Sigma d_x d_y$" and denote by $\Sigma d_x' d_y'$

We then have $\Sigma d_x' d_y' = \Sigma(x - x_0) (y - y_0)$

$$= \Sigma(x - \bar{x} - a) (y - \bar{y} - b)$$

$$= \Sigma(x - \bar{x}) (y - \bar{y}) - \Sigma a(y - \bar{y}) - \Sigma b(x - \bar{x}) + \Sigma ab$$

$$= \Sigma d_x d_y + \Sigma ab, \text{ since } \Sigma(y - \bar{y}) \text{ and } \Sigma(x - \bar{x}) \text{ are both zero.}$$

Hence $\Sigma d_x d_y = \Sigma d_x' d_y' - nab$ $\tag{8.9}$

where n is the number of pairs of values of x and y.

If $x_0 = y_0 = 0$ are taken as the working means, then

$$\Sigma d_x' d_y' = \Sigma(x - x_0) (y - y_0) = \Sigma xy$$

and $ab = (x_0 - \bar{x}) (y_0 - \bar{y}) = \bar{x}\bar{y}$

and therefore $\Sigma d_x d_y = \Sigma xy - n\bar{x}\bar{y}$

The estimated value of the covariance is therefore given by

$$s_{xy} = \frac{1}{n - 1} \Sigma xy - \frac{n}{n - 1} . \bar{x} . \bar{y} \tag{8.10}$$

Example 1.   The data are set out in the first two columns of Table XXXII. Specimens of a light metal alloy, heat treated in various ways, were subjected to a hardness test and then their ultimate tensile strengths were determined. The column H gives the Brinell hardness number and column U the corresponding ultimate strengths in tons per square inch. When these 20 results are plotted

Table XXXII

Computation of an Empirical Equation

H	U	x	y	xy	x^2
52	12·3	2	3	6	4
54	12·8	4	8	32	16
56	12·5	6	5	30	36
57	13·6	7	16	112	49
60	14·5	10	25	250	100
61	13·5	11	15	165	121
62	15·6	12	36	432	144
64	16·1	14	41	574	196
66	14·7	16	27	432	256
68	16·1	18	41	738	324
69	15·0	19	30	570	361
70	16·0	20	40	800	400
71	16·7	21	47	987	441
71	17·4	21	54	1,134	441
73	15·9	23	39	897	529
76	16·8	26	48	1,248	676
76	17·6	26	56	1,456	676
77	19·0	27	70	1,890	729
80	18·6	30	66	1,980	900
83	18·9	33	69	2,277	1,089
	Totals	346	736	16,010	7,488

on graph paper it is seen that high hardness values are associated
fairly closely with high ultimate strengths, though there is a scatter
of the points about any straight line through them (Fig. 50). It is
required to find an equation from which an estimate of U can be
made for a specimen of known hardness H.

To simplify the working the columns x and y are prepared. The
numbers of column x are such that $x = H - 50$, and those of column y
are given by $y = 10 (U - 12)$, multiplying by 10 to avoid decimal
points. The simpler numbers of columns x and y provide the basis of
the computation. They are simple enough to deal with directly, i.e.,
deviations will be measured from $x = 0$, $y = 0$. Columns xy and x^2
are computed and summed. The crude totals are corrected by means
of the relations 8.9 and 8.10.

$$\bar{x} = 346/20 = 17\cdot3; \quad \bar{y} = 736/20 = 36\cdot8$$
$$\Sigma d_x d_y = \Sigma xy - n\bar{x}\bar{y} = 16{,}010 - 20 \times 17\cdot3 \times 36\cdot8 = 3{,}277\cdot2$$
$$\Sigma d_x^2 = \Sigma x^2 - n\bar{x}^2 = 7{,}488 - 20 \times (17\cdot3)^2 = 1{,}502\cdot2$$

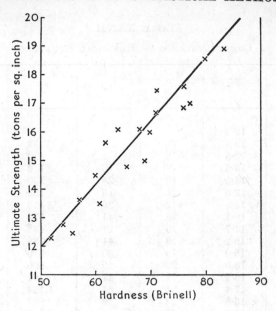

FIG. 50.   Graph of a calculated empirical equation.

Hence the required equation is

$$y - 36\cdot8 = \frac{3,277\cdot2}{1,502\cdot2}(x - 17\cdot3)$$

$$\text{or } y = 2\cdot18x - 0\cdot9$$

Putting $y = 10(U - 12)$ and $x = H - 50$, this becomes

$$10(U - 12) = 2\cdot18(H - 50) - 0\cdot9$$

$$\text{or, finally, } U = 0\cdot22H + 1\cdot0$$

The converted equation of the regression line of y on x gives the required empirical formula for U in terms of H. The line is shown in Fig. 50.

Two variables x and y which, when plotted, show a tendency to group round a curved line, may sometimes show a more near linear association if one of the variables is plotted against a simple function of the other, e.g., if x is plotted against $y^{\frac{1}{2}}$ or y^2 or $\log y$. If a scatter about a straight line can be obtained by such means, then a linear regression line may be computed as in the above example, taking x and the function of y as the variables. Some examples will be found in the exercises at the end of this chapter. The determination of curves of best fit of the second, third, . . . degrees is beyond the scope of this book, although only an extension of the above method is required.

The "trend line" of a time series is sometimes found by this method. The calculation is simplified because the values of x (i.e., time) can be reduced to the series 1, 2, 3. . . .

Example 2. The computation of regression lines for the data of Table XXXI is shown in some detail in Table XXXIII. The calculation of s_x, s_y, the variance of the distributions in x and y have been omitted since these calculations have already been exemplified in Table XV. Apart from the variances, however, it is also necessary to calculate $\Sigma d_x d_y$, for an estimate of the covariance. The arithmetical work of this calculation is lightened, as for earlier computations, if the deviations are first measured from a convenient arbitrary working mean. In the final stage the correction of equation 8.9 is applied.

In Table XXXIII (*a*) the suffix x refers to the marks in mathematics and the suffix y refers to the marks in science. The working mean (x_o, y_o) is taken as (5,5) and the deviations from this mean are denoted by d_x' and d_y'. The data are arranged as a bivariate distribution with the deviations d_x' indicated in the top row and the deviations d in the left-hand column. In the bottom row the data are summed as a distribution in x; in the right-hand column the data are summed as a distribution in y. Both distributions should of course have the same total.

TABLE XXXIII (*a*)

BIVARIATE DISTRIBUTION—DEVIATIONS FROM WORKING MEAN

		d_x'									f_y
		−4	−3	−2	−1	0	1	2	3	4	
	4	—	—	—	—	—	—	—	2	3	5
	3	—	—	—	—	1	7	16	14	3	41
	2	—	—	2	3	13	12	14	16	3	63
	1	—	2	3	12	23	19	17	10	—	86
d_y'	0	—	1	4	27	26	15	6	2	—	81
	−1	3	9	15	26	17	9	4	1	—	84
	−2	5	12	17	10	7	7	2	—	—	60
	−3	5	8	7	11	8	3	—	—	—	42
	−4	4	5	4	2	1	—	—	—	—	16
f_x		17	37	52	91	96	72	59	45	9	478 *Total*

TABLE XXXIII (b)

BIVARIATE DISTRIBUTION—CALCULATION OF THE PRODUCT SUM BY
THE DIRECT METHOD

		d_x'									Sums of rows
		−4	−3	−2	−1	0	1	2	3	4	
	4	—	—	—	—	—	—	—	24	48	72
	3	—	—	—	—	0	21	96	126	36	279
	2	—	—	−8	−6	0	24	56	96	24	186
	1	—	−6	−6	−12	0	19	34	30	—	59
d_y'	0	—	0	0	0	0	0	0	0	—	0
	−1	12	27	30	26	0	−9	−8	−3	—	75
	−2	40	72	68	20	0	−14	−8	—	—	178
	−3	60	72	42	33	0	−9	—	—	—	198
	−4	64	60	32	8	0	—	—	—	—	164
Sums of columns		176	225	158	69	0	32	170	273	108	1,211 Total

The results of the calculations not shown in the Table are:

$$\bar{x} = 5 + (-13)/478 = 5 - 0\cdot027 = 4\cdot973$$
$$\bar{y} = 5 + (-39)/478 = 5 - 0\cdot082 = 4\cdot928$$
$$\Sigma d_x^2 = 1{,}761 - 478 \, (0\cdot027)^2 = 1{,}760\cdot7$$
$$\Sigma d_y^2 = 1{,}745 - 478 \, (0\cdot082)^2 = 1{,}741\cdot8$$

The sum of the products, $\Sigma d_x' d_y'$, may be found directly as shown in Table XXXIII (b). In this table there is an entry corresponding to each entry in Table XXXIII (a), the number entered in (b) being the value of the product $f . d_x' . d_y'$ for the corresponding entry of (a). Thus, the first entry in the top line of (a) is 2, for which d_x' is 3 and d_y' is 4; the corresponding entry in (b) is therefore 2.3.4 = 24. $\Sigma d_x' . d_y'$ is the sum of all the numbers thus obtained. Summing both by rows and columns provides a check on the addition.

A second method of finding $\Sigma d_x' . d_y'$ is shown in Table XXXIII (c). The labour of computing the products $d_x' . d_y'$ can often be reduced by expressing the products in terms of squares, so that tables of squares can be used. This is done by means of the identities:

$$(A + B)^2 = A^2 + B^2 + 2\,AB$$
$$(A - B)^2 = A^2 + B^2 - 2\,AB$$

(8.11)

In our present example it is convenient to use the second of these identities from which we have

$$2\Sigma d_x' . d_y' = \Sigma d_x'^2 + \Sigma d_y'^2 - \Sigma(d_x' - d_y')^2$$

(8.12)

Of the terms on the right-hand side of this identity we already know the first two. To find the third term note that along the diagonals drawn in Table XXXIII (c) the value of $(d'_x - d'_y)$ for any entry is constant. Sum the entries along each diagonal and enter them in a new table against the corresponding value of $(d'_x - d'_y)$. Then $\Sigma(d'_x - d'_y)^2$ can be quickly calculated. In our example it is found to be 1,084. Substituting in equation 8.12 we have

$$\Sigma d'_x \cdot d'_y = \tfrac{1}{2}(1{,}761 + 1{,}745 - 1{,}084) = \tfrac{1}{2} \times 2{,}422 = 1{,}211$$

as was obtained in Table XXXIII (b). Applying now the correction for the mean $\Sigma d_x \cdot d_y = \Sigma d'_x \cdot d'_y - nab = 1{,}211 - 478 \cdot (0 \cdot 027) \cdot (0 \cdot 082)$
$$= 1{,}209 \cdot 4$$

The required equations are therefore:

(a) The regression equation of y on x,

$$y - \bar{y} = \frac{\Sigma d_x d_y}{\Sigma d_x^2} \cdot (x - \bar{x})$$

becomes $$y - 4 \cdot 92 = \frac{1{,}209 \cdot 4}{1{,}760 \cdot 7} (x - 4 \cdot 97)$$

or $$y = 0 \cdot 687 x + 1 \cdot 49.$$

(b) The regression equation of x on y,

$$x - \bar{x} = \frac{\Sigma d_x d_y}{\Sigma d_y^2} (y - \bar{y})$$

becomes $$x - 4 \cdot 97 = \frac{1{,}209 \cdot 4}{1{,}741 \cdot 8} (y - 4 \cdot 92)$$

or $$x = 0 \cdot 694 y + 1 \cdot 53$$

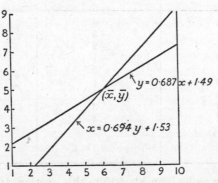

FIG. 51.   Regression lines of the data of Table XXXIII.

The two lines are shown in Fig. 51, intersecting at the point $(4 \cdot 97, 4 \cdot 92)$, the mean centre of the distribution.

TABLE XXXIII (c)

BIVARIATE DISTRIBUTION—CALCULATION OF THE PRODUCT SUM BY THE DIAGONAL METHOD

d'_x									
-4	**-3**	**-2**	**-1**	**0**	**1**	**2**	**3**	**4**	d'_y
						2	3		4
			1	7	16	14	3		3
		2	3	13	12	14	16	3	2
	2	3	12	23	19	17	10		1
0	1	4	27	26	15	6	2		0
	3	9	15	26	17	9	4	1	-1
	5	12	17	10	7	7	2		-2
	5	8	7	11	8	3			-3
	4	5	4	2	1				-4

Left-hand diagonal sums: 4, 11, 50, 112

Bottom diagonal sums: 131 90 50 23 7

f	$d'_x - d'_y$	$f(d'_x - d'_y)^2$
4	-4	64
11	-3	99
50	-2	200
112	-1	112
131	0	0
90	1	90
50	2	200
23	3	207
7	4	112
478		1,084

In the examples considered in this section the choice of the regression line depends on the question asked. A mathematician would probably ask "How do the science marks vary with the pupils' marks in mathematics?" The scientist on the other hand would tend to take the science marks as his independent variable and ask "How do the maths marks vary with the science marks?" It is important to realise that these are different questions and that it is not surprising that different, but equally correct, answers are obtained.

If the data are numerous and cover wide ranges of values they may be grouped into classes by choosing convenient equal class-intervals as in the univariate distributions of Chapters II and III. The number of classes however may be reduced to about 20 for each variable without serious effect upon the accuracy of the results.

EXERCISES XXVIII

1. Using the method of least squares find the linear equations which best express y in terms of x for the data below, assuming that the values of x are exact. From your equations estimate the missing values of y.

(a)	x	1	2	(3)	4	5	6	7	8	(9)	10	11	12
	y	5	6	—	12	11	13	16	16	—	19	23	22
(b)	x	1	2	3	(4)	5	6	7	8	9	10	(11)	12
	y	29	23	20	—	13	12	8	5	4	0	—	−5

2. Find the equation of the line of regression of y on x for the following data:

x	356	337	346	346	351	352	359	353
y	374	354	365	366	369	372	377	374
x		342	339	374	393	425	386	463
y		360	357	397	418	454	410	491

Plot the data and draw the calculated line.

3. Calculate the equation of the linear trend line of the data of Ex. VI, 5 for the last 10 years.

4. Calculate, by the method of least squares, the equation of the trend line of the following data:

Year	1930	1	2	3	4	5	6	7	8	9
y	10	15	13	16	18	18	14	16	20	26
Year	1940	1	2	3	4	5	6	7	8	9
y	31	29	25	20	28	38	37	36	40	43

Plot the data and draw the calculated line.

Compute the regression line equations for each of the following distributions:

5.

	7	—	—	—	—	—	1	2	1
	6	—	—	—	—	1	3	2	1
	5	—	—	—	1	3	5	4	1
y	4	—	—	2	4	4	2	—	—
	3	—	1	4	3	1	—	—	—
	2	1	3	2	1	—	—	—	—
	1	3	2	1	—	—	—	—	—
		1	2	3	4	5	6	7	
					x				

6.

y	1	2	3	4	5	6	7	8	9	10
6	1	1	—	—	—	—	—	—	—	—
5	—	1	3	2	—	—	—	—	—	—
4	—	1	—	3	5	2	1	—	—	—
3	—	—	—	2	3	6	4	3	1	—
2	—	—	—	—	1	3	3	4	2	1
1	—	—	—	—	—	—	2	1	2	2
	1	2	3	4	5	6	7	8	9	10
					x					

7. The values of x and y are the centres of the class intervals.

y	20·7	20·9	21·1	21·3	21·5	21·7	21·9
12·5	—	—	1	3	1	1	—
11·5	—	2	3	3	4	3	1
10·5	1	3	2	3	3	2	—
9·5	2	4	3	1	3	—	—
8·5	3	3	4	3	1	—	—
7·5	—	2	3	2	—	—	—
6·5	1	—	2	—	—	—	—
	20·7	20·9	21·1	21·3	21·5	21·7	21·9
				x			

8. The values of x and y are the centres of the class intervals.

y	17	19	21	23	25	27	29
1·7	—	—	1	—	—	1	2
1·6	—	—	1	—	2	1	—
1·5	—	—	—	3	2	1	1
1·4	—	—	1	4	2	2	2
1·3	—	2	3	3	—	1	—
1·2	—	1	3	3	2	1	—
1·1	1	2	—	2	1	—	—
	17	19	21	23	25	27	29
				x			

8.8   The Standard Error of the Regression Coefficient

The regression equation of y on x can be written

$$y - \bar{y} = b(x - \bar{x}) \tag{8.13}$$

where b is the estimated coefficient of regression of y on x. A further set of observations of x and y would provide an equation which would be different, though perhaps only slightly so, from the first. In other words, the "constants" of equation 8.13, i.e., b, $\bar{x}$ and $\bar{y}$, are derived from a finite random sample and therefore have standard errors.

To find the standard error of b we note that in the formula $b = \frac{s_{xy}}{s_x^2}$ the denominator s_x^2 is the estimated variance of the independent variable x, and the numerator s_{xy} is the estimated covariance of x and y. Consider further samples of n pairs for the *same set of values of the independent variable* x. The variations between samples arise because there are different values of y for any given value of x. The variance of x, s_x^2, remains constant for the samples, but for any given value of x there will be a distribution of y's about the estimated mean value of y. We shall assume that this distribution of y's has the same standard error s_y' for all values of x.

We have then
$$\Sigma d_x d_y = \Sigma(x - \bar{x})(y - \bar{y})$$
$$= \Sigma y(x - \bar{x}) - \bar{y} \cdot \Sigma(x - \bar{x})$$
$$= \Sigma y(x - \bar{x}), \text{ since } \Sigma(x - \bar{x}) \text{ is zero}$$

and in this sum of products the term $(x - \bar{x})$ takes in turn the values $(x_1 - \bar{x})$, $(x_2 - \bar{x})$, ... $(x_n - \bar{x})$, all of which are constants. The y's are independent variables with equal standard errors of s_y'. We therefore have

$$\Sigma d_x \cdot d_y = (n - 1) s_{xy} \text{ or } s_{xy} = \Sigma \frac{(x - \bar{x})}{n - 1} \cdot y$$

to which the result of equation 7.11 can be applied. This gives

$$\text{Var. } (s_{xy}) = \Sigma_1^n \left[\frac{(x - \bar{x})^2}{(n - 1)^2} \cdot \text{Var. } (y_r) \right]$$
$$= \frac{s_y'^2}{(n - 1)^2} \cdot \Sigma(x - \bar{x})^2$$
$$= \frac{s_y'^2}{(n - 1)} \cdot s_x^2$$

since Var. $(y) = s_y'^2$ for every term. Hence

$$S.E. \left(\frac{s_{xy}}{s_x^2} \right) = \frac{1}{s_x^2} \cdot S.E. (s_{xy}) = \frac{1}{s_x^2} \cdot \frac{s_y' \cdot s_x}{\sqrt{n - 1}}$$
$$= \frac{s_y'}{\sqrt{n - 1} \cdot s_x}$$

A more exact argument shows that in this formula the factor $\sqrt{n - 1}$ should be replaced by $\sqrt{n - 2}$ because of the loss of another degree of freedom. It is better therefore to use the form

$$S.E. (b) = \frac{s_y'}{\sqrt{n - 2} \cdot s_x} \tag{8.14}$$

To compute $S.E. (b)$ the new statistic, s_y', the standard error of y for a given value of x is required. It is possible to express s_y' in terms of quantities already known. For a given value of x, say x_r, the deviation of any particular value of y, say y_r, from the estimated mean will be $y_r - y$ (Fig. 52), where $y = b(x_r - \bar{x}) + \bar{y}$

or $\quad y_r - \bar{y} - b(x_r - \bar{x})$. (Fig. 52.)

and therefore $\Sigma(y_{\mathbf{r}} - y)^2 = \Sigma\{\, y_{\mathbf{r}} - \bar{y}) - b\,(x_{\mathbf{r}} - \bar{x})\,\}^2$

$= \Sigma(y_{\mathbf{r}} - \bar{y})^2 - 2b\,.\,\Sigma(y_{\mathbf{r}} - \bar{y})\,(x_{\mathbf{r}} - \bar{x}) + b^2\,.\,\Sigma(x_{\mathbf{r}} - \bar{x})^2$

and, remembering that $\Sigma(y_{\mathbf{r}} - \bar{y})\,(x_{\mathbf{r}} - \bar{x}) = b\,.\,\Sigma(x_{\mathbf{r}} - x)^2$

from the definition of b, we have

$$\Sigma(y_{\mathbf{r}} - y)^2 = \Sigma(y - \bar{y})^2 - b^2\,.\,\Sigma(x_{\mathbf{r}} - \bar{x})^2$$

and hence
$$s_{\mathrm{y}}'^2 = s_{\mathrm{y}}{}^2 - b^2\,.\,s_{\mathrm{x}}{}^2 \tag{8.15}$$

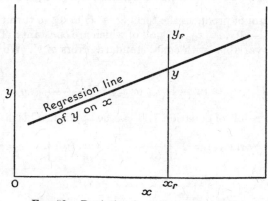

Fig. 52.   Deviation from the regression line.

This equation is sometimes expressed in the form:

(Variance of y about regression) = (Variance of y about the mean) — b^2 . (Variance of x.)

The extended use of the term "Variance" should be noted.

By means of equations 8.14 and 8.15 the standard error of b may be computed directly from quantities which are already familiar. Applying these results to the data of Table XXXI, we have, since

$$s_{\mathrm{x}}^2 = 1{,}760{\cdot}7/(n - 1) = 1{,}760{\cdot}7/477 = 3{\cdot}691$$

$$s_{\mathrm{y}}^2 = 1{,}741{\cdot}8/(n - 1)$$

and $b = 0{\cdot}687$

$$s_{\mathrm{y}}'^2 = [1{,}760{\cdot}7 - (0{\cdot}687)^2 \times 1{,}741{\cdot}8] \div 477$$

$$= (1{,}760{\cdot}7 - 831{\cdot}8)/477$$

$$= 928{\cdot}9/477$$

This gives $s_{\mathrm{y}}' = \sqrt{\dfrac{928{\cdot}9}{477}}$

$$= 1{\cdot}39$$

We then have $S.E.\,(b) = \dfrac{1{\cdot}39}{\sqrt{476 \times 3{\cdot}691}} = 0{\cdot}0332.$

The calculation of the standard error of the coefficient for the regression of x on y is obtained in a similar way. We should, however, require to calculate $\dfrac{s_x'}{\sqrt{n-2} \cdot s_y}$ instead of $\dfrac{s_y'}{\sqrt{n-2} \cdot s_x}$ assuming that all the random errors occur in the values of x.

If both variables are subject to random or experimental errors the formulæ we have used are still applicable to the regression coefficients.

8.9 The Testing of the Significance of a Regression Coefficient

To investigate the significance of an estimated statistic we consider the distribution of the ratio of estimated values of the statistic to its standard error. In the case of the regression coefficient we need to know how the ratio $\dfrac{b}{S.E.\,(b)}$ is distributed. In 1922 R. A. Fisher showed that if the hypothetical value of the regression coefficient was β, then the distribution of the ratio $\dfrac{b-\beta}{S.E.\,(b)}$ was precisely that of the t-distribution described in section 7.6. This distribution closely approximates to the Normal for large samples but for small values of n the difference of the two distributions may be serious.

To test the significance of the difference between the estimated and hypothetical regression coefficients we therefore calculate the ratio $t = \dfrac{b-\beta}{S.E.\,(b)}$. If n is greater than about 20 we use the table of the Normal probability integral, Table XXVI (p. 281), noting that as we are concerned with the absolute value of the difference $(b-\beta)$ the test is two-tailed, and therefore the table reading must be doubled. If n is less than about 20 we use the table giving the significance levels of observed values of t, Table XXX, entering it for $(n-2)$ degrees of freedom where n is the number of observations on which the estimate of b is based. It should be remembered that the significance levels of this table already correspond to the two-tailed test.

Example 1. In the calculation of a regression coefficient for 18 pairs of observations it was found that $b = 1 \cdot 12$ and $S.E.(b) = 0 \cdot 06$. Is the estimate significantly different from the expected value $1 \cdot 00$?

The hypothesis is that the difference between the population value and $1 \cdot 00$ is zero.

$$\text{We have } t = \frac{1 \cdot 12 - 1 \cdot 00}{0 \cdot 06} = 2 \cdot 00$$

Referring to Table XXX and entering it for $(18 - 2) = 16$ degrees of freedom we see that the 5% point of P is $2 \cdot 12$. As the value of t is less than $2 \cdot 12$ the hypothesis is accepted; the coefficient is not significantly different from $1 \cdot 00$.

Example 2. A regression coefficient calculated from 850 pairs of observations was found to be 0·035 with standard error 0·010. Is this regression significantly different from zero?

The hypothesis is that the coefficient is zero.

We have $t = 0·035/0·010 = 3·5$

For so large a sample as 850 we may use the Normal probability Table XXVI. Entering this table for a deviation of 3·5 we find $P = 0·000233$ and therefore $2P = 0·000466$ or less than 0·05%. The probability of the value 0·035 being exceeded is therefore less than 0·1%. The hypothesis must be rejected; the coefficient is significantly different from zero.

EXERCISES XXIX

1. In a bivariate distribution $s_x = 2$, $s_y = 13$, $\Sigma d_x d_y = 270$ and n is 28. Find the regression coefficient and its standard error. Verify that it is significantly different from zero at the 5% level.

2. Verify that for a distribution for which $b = -3·86$, with standard error 1·91, based on 42 pairs of observations, the regression is barely significant at the 5% level.

3. The equation of regression of H on V is found to be $H = 3·6V + 2·5$. The variances of H and V are 4·8 and 0·15 sq. units respectively. Show that the variance of H about the regression is 2·86 sq. units.

4. The coefficient of regression of y on x calculated from 1,040 pairs of observations is found to be 1·027 when the hypothetical value of the coefficient is 1·000. Given that the variances of x and y in the distribution are respectively 3·2 and 7·5 sq. units show that the calculated value of the coefficient is not significantly different from the hypothetical value.

5. On graph paper plot the two distributions A and B. Calculate for each coefficient of regression of y on x and test the coefficient for significance by an accurate test. Verify that for distribution A the calculated value of the coefficient is not significantly different from zero, but that for distribution B the regression coefficient is highly significant.

Distribution A.

x	1	4	4	6	7	7	9	10	10	12
y	11	7	12	9	4	11	8	2	5	6

Distribution B.

x	1	3	4	5	7	8	9	10	11	12
y	11	10	9	8	7	7	6	5	4	3

SUMMARY OF CHAPTER VIII

1. Bivariate distributions may be represented by solid histograms, but more conveniently by scatter diagrams.

2. The curves of regression are the smooth curves passing through the means of the arrays. There are usually two distinct curves.

3. If the regression curves are straight lines they may be determined with reasonable accuracy by plotting the means of the arrays and drawing the lines through them.

4. Using the Principle of Least Squares, i.e., that the sum of the squared deviations is a minimum for the best value, the equation of the line of regression of y on x is found to be

$$y - \bar{y} = \frac{\Sigma d_x d_y}{\Sigma d_x^2} (x - \bar{x}) = \frac{s_{xy}}{s_x^2} (x - \bar{x})$$

where s_{xy} and s_x^2 are the estimates of the covariance of x and y and the variance of x obtained from the data.

5. The covariance, $s_{xy} = \dfrac{1}{(n - 1)} \left\{ \Sigma(x - x_0)(y - y_0) - n \cdot a \cdot b \right\}$

$$= \frac{1}{(n - 1)} \Sigma xy - \frac{n}{n - 1} \cdot \bar{x} \cdot \bar{y}$$

if x_0, y_0, are the working means, and a, b, the deviations of the estimated means $\bar{x}$, $\bar{y}$ from the working means.

6. In computing $\Sigma d_x d_y$ use may be made of the identities:

$$2\Sigma d_x d_y = \Sigma d_x^2 + \Sigma d_y^2 - \Sigma(d_x - d_y)^2$$

$$2\Sigma d_x d_y = \Sigma(d_x + d_y)^2 - \Sigma d_x^2 - \Sigma d_y^2$$

7. The standard error of the regression coefficient, b, is

$$\frac{s_y'}{\sqrt{n - 2} \cdot s_x}$$

where s_y', the standard error of the y's about the regression line, is given by

$$s_y'^2 = s_y^2 - b^2 \cdot s_x^2$$

8. For testing the significance of the regression coefficient we use the fact that the ratio $\dfrac{b}{S.E.\ (b)}$ is distributed as Student's "t-distribution", which closely approaches the Normal for large samples. If n is less than 20 the t-test should be applied.

EXERCISES XXX
ALGEBRAIC

1. Show that for a bivariate distribution of n pairs (x_r, y_r), $r = 1, 2, 3, \ldots n$:

(a) $\bar{x} \cdot \Sigma y_r = \bar{y} \cdot \Sigma x_r$.

(b) $\Sigma(x_r - \bar{x})(y_r - \bar{y}) = \Sigma y_r(x_r - \bar{x}) = \Sigma x_r(y_r - \bar{y})$.
$$= \Sigma x_r y_r - n \cdot \bar{x} \cdot \bar{y}.$$

(c) $\Sigma(x_r + y_r)^2 = (n - 1)\left\{ s_x^2 + 2s_{xy} + s_y^2 \right\} + n(\bar{x} + \bar{y})^2$.

2. If the regression equation of y on x derived from a sample of n pairs (x_r, y_r), $r = 1, 2, 3, \ldots n$, is
$$y - \bar{y} = b \cdot (x - \bar{x})$$
show that the sum of the squares of the deviations $(y_r - \bar{y})$ from this line is $(n - 1)(s_y^2 - b^2 \cdot s_x^2)$.

3. If V denotes the sum of the variances of x and y, sketch bivariate distributions which satisfy the conditions that the covariance is:

(a) negligibly small compared with V,
(b) equal to $0 \cdot 9 V$ approximately,
(c) equal to $-\frac{1}{2}V$ approximately.

4. The scatter diagram of a bivariate distribution is seen to be symmetrical about the ordinate through its mean centre. Show that for this distribution $s_{xy} = 0$, and that the lines of regression are parallel to the x- and y-axis.

NUMERICAL

5. The official estimates of the population of the Argentine at the mid-year for each of the years 1938 to 1947 are, to the nearest 100,000: 141, 143, 145, 147, 151, 153, 156, 158, 160, 161 respectively. Plot these points on a graph together with the calculated trend line. Estimate from the trend line the population at mid-year 1948 and compare it with the official estimate of 16,400,000.

6. Plot the following observed values of x and y. Find the equations of the two regression lines.

x	23	26	28	30	30	32	34	36	40	41
y	134	136	140	129	135	129	125	128	127	123
x	43	45	46	46	48	49	50	53	55	60
y	118	120	122	117	114	117	111	117	107	109

7. The following pairs of observations were noted in experimental work on cosmic rays:

C	14·2	14·9	16·6	18·0	19·3	23·2
R	24·1	20·5	14·0	7·30	5·00	1·47

Taking C as the independent variable find the values of a and b for the equation $\log R = a - b \cdot C$ which best satisfy the given data. Estimate the most probable value of R for $C = 20·7$.

8. Using the data of Table IV (*b*), p. 17, plot the logarithm of the central value of each income group (*x*) against the logarithm of the corresponding column height (*y*), taking the central value of the last group to be 180,000. Calculate the best values of the constants of a linear equation expressing *y* in terms of *x*. Estimate from your equation the comparative frequencies of incomes of £5,000 and £20,000.

9. In the table below *R* denotes the average Bank of England rate, correct to the nearest 0·1%, and *C* the average price of Consols, correct to the nearest integer, for each of the years 1922 to 1946. Find the regression equation of *C* on *R*. Is the regression coefficient significantly different from zero, and if it is, at what level?

R	3·7	3·7	4·0	4·6	5·0	4·7	4·5	5·5	3·4	4·0	3·0	2·0	2·0
C	56	58	57	56	55	55	56	54	56	55	67	74	81

R		2·0	2·0	2·0	2·0	2·5	2·0	2·0	2·0	2·0	2·0	2·0	2·0
C		87	86	76	74	67	72	80	82	81	80	87	95

10. In an experiment in which the growth of duckweed under certain laboratory conditions was measured the following results were obtained. [Quoted by D'Arcy Thompson (1942) in *Growth and Form*; results of W. B. Bottomley.]

Weeks (*t*)	0	1	2	3	4	5	6	7	8
No. of fronds (*n*)	20	30	52	77	135	211	326	550	1,052

Show that the equation of regression of log *n* on *t* is

$$\log n = 0\cdot230t + 1\cdot176.$$

11. Find the equation of the line of regression of toughness (*T*) on % nickel (*N*) for the data of Ex. XXXI, 7, p. 212.

12. Find the equation of the line of regression of wool consumption (*C*) on income (*I*) using the data of Ex. XXXIV, 11, p. 229.

Find the equations of the regression lines of the following bivariate distributions: The values of *x* and *y* are central values of the class intervals.

13.

	95	—	—	—	—	—	—	—	1	1	1
	85	—	—	—	—	—	—	1	3	3	—
	75	—	—	—	—	—	1	3	2	1	1
	65	—	—	—	—	2	1	3	2	—	—
y	55	—	—	—	2	4	3	2	2	1	—
	45	—	—	1	3	5	3	—	1	—	—
	35	—	—	1	4	3	2	—	—	—	—
	25	—	2	3	4	1	—	—	—	—	—
	15	1	2	2	—	—	—	—	—	—	—
	5	—	2	—	—	—	—	—	—	—	—
		5	15	25	35	45	55	65	75	85	95

x

14.

y	28	29	30	31	32	33	34	35	36	37
13	—	—	—	—	1	—	—	—	—	—
12	—	—	1	1	2	2	—	—	—	—
11	1	—	1	2	3	3	2	—	—	—
10	—	1	3	4	5	6	3	2	1	—
9	—	—	1	3	3	4	2	1	—	1
8	—	—	—	2	3	3	4	—	1	—
7	—	—	—	—	1	1	3	2	1	—

x

15.

y	23	25	27	29	31	33	35	37	39	41	43
13	1	—	—	—	—	—	—	—	—	—	—
11	—	1	—	2	—	—	—	—	—	—	—
9	—	2	3	1	1	—	—	—	—	—	—
7	—	—	3	7	5	2	—	—	—	—	—
5	—	—	1	4	8	10	5	2	—	—	—
3	—	—	—	2	3	8	6	4	1	1	—
1	—	—	—	—	1	4	5	3	2	1	—
−1	—	—	—	—	—	—	2	4	3	2	—
−3	—	—	—	—	—	—	—	1	3	—	1
−5	—	—	—	—	—	—	—	—	2	1	1

x

16.

y	17	18	19	20	21	22	23	24	25	26	27
$11\frac{1}{2}$	—	—	—	1	1	2	—	—	—	—	—
$10\frac{1}{2}$	—	1	—	2	3	1	—	—	—	—	—
$9\frac{1}{2}$	—	—	1	1	3	4	3	1	—	—	—
$8\frac{1}{2}$	—	1	—	—	1	2	4	2	—	—	—
$7\frac{1}{2}$	—	—	2	—	2	4	3	3	1	—	—
$6\frac{1}{2}$	1	—	2	2	3	1	5	6	4	2	—
$5\frac{1}{2}$	—	—	1	—	1	—	3	2	3	1	—
$4\frac{1}{2}$	—	—	—	—	1	2	—	1	3	2	1
$3\frac{1}{2}$	—	—	—	—	—	—	1	—	2	1	1
$2\frac{1}{2}$	—	—	—	—	—	—	—	1	—	1	—
$1\frac{1}{2}$	—	—	—	—	—	—	—	2	1	—	—

x

17. (Calculate the line of regression of x on y; find the curve of regression of y on x by plotting the means.)

y	1	2	3	4	5	6	7	8
8	1	1	1	1	1	1	1	1
7	7	6	5	4	3	2	1	—
6	21	15	10	6	3	1	—	—
5	35	20	10	4	1	—	—	—
4	35	15	5	1	—	—	—	—
3	21	6	1	—	—	—	—	—
2	7	1	—	—	—	—	—	—
1	1	—	—	—	—	—	—	—

$$x$$

Examine the significance of the coefficients.

GENERAL

18. Explain what is meant by the "curves of regression" of a bivariate distribution. Describe a graphical method of finding them.

19. Derive the equation of regression of y on x for a bivariate distribution of x and y.

20. Derive an expression for the standard error of a regression coefficient. Explain how the significance of a regression coefficient may be tested.

21. If $y = bx + c$ is the equation of the line of regression of y on x show that the variance of the y-deviations about the line is

(Variance of y) $- b^2$. (Variance of x).

22. Diagrams (a), (b) and (c) show the regression lines of three bivariate distributions, the scales of x and y being equal. What information can be derived about the distributions from these diagrams?

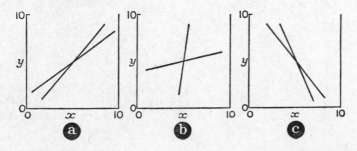

MATHEMATICAL

23. A continuous bivariate distribution has a relative frequency density which is constant over the area enclosed by the ellipse

$$ax^2 + 2hxy + by^2 = 1 \ (h^2 < ab)$$

Show that the regression lines are given by $ax + hy = 0$ and $hx + by = 0$.

24. A continuous bivariate distribution has a relative frequency density $z = k \cdot exp\left[- (ax^2 + 2hxy + by^2) \right]$ where a, h and b are constants such that $h^2 < ab$, and k is such that $\int_{-\infty}^{+\infty} \int_{-\infty}^{+\infty} z\,dx\,dy = 1$ when $-\infty < x < \infty$, $-\infty < y < \infty$. By comparing the function z with the univariate Normal frequency function, show that

(a) when $y = y_1$ the corresponding frequency distribution of x is Normal with mean at hy_1/a,

(b) the curve of regression of x on y is the straight line $ax = hy$.

(The function z defines the frequency surface of a continuous bivariate Normal frequency distribution.)

CHAPTER IX

Correlation

9.1 The Product-Moment Coefficient of Correlation

In Chapter VIII we found that the regression coefficient of y on x is $\dfrac{s_{xy}}{s_x^2}$ and that the regression coefficient of x on y is $\dfrac{s_{xy}}{s_y^2}$. If the two variables are completely independent we find that both these coefficients are zero, or, at least, not significantly different from zero. A low or zero value of the regression coefficients indicates that there is no tendency for particular values of x to be associated linearly with any particular values of y. The size of the covariance s_{xy} therefore gives a measure of the degree of association of the two variables x and y, though this measure is unsatisfactory unless we can find a standard of comparison for it.

If the association of x and y is complete and is exactly linear, we know that the two regression lines will coincide and each regression coefficient will be the reciprocal of the other, so that the product of the regression coefficients in this case will be unity. We have then, for complete and exact linear association

$$\frac{s_{xy}^2}{s_x^2 \cdot s_y^2} = 1$$

and, taking the square root,

$$\frac{s_{xy}}{s_x \cdot s_y} = \pm 1$$

or

$$s_{xy} = \pm \, s_x \cdot s_y$$

Since s_x and s_y are always positive quantities the positive sign is required only when large and small values of x are associated with large and small values of y respectively, so that d_x and d_y always have the same sign. If, however, large and small values of x are associated with small and large values of y respectively, then d_x and d_y are of opposite sign and

$$s_{xy} = - \, s_x \cdot s_y$$

If then we calculate $\dfrac{s_{xy}}{s_x \cdot s_y}$ for any bivariate distribution we shall obtain a number which lies between $+1$ and -1. This number, called the *product-moment coefficient of correlation* is generally denoted

207

by r, and is an estimate of the degree of linear association of the two variables.

Summarising its properties, we have:

$$\text{Coefficient of correlation}, r = \frac{s_{xy}}{s_x \cdot s_y} \qquad (9.1)$$

If $r = +1$, x and y are said to be perfectly *directly* or *positively* correlated; if $r = -1$, x and y are said to be perfectly *inversely* or *negatively* correlated; if $r = 0$, x and y are said to be *uncorrelated*, though this does not mean that they might not be associated in some way other than linearly, e.g., the scatter diagram of Fig. 46 (*d*) shows a fairly close association—about a parabola—but r would be approximately zero.

A value of r lying between 0 and $+1$ indicates (with reservations to be considered later) that the two variables have a tendency to be grouped in a direct or positive linear association, and the greater the value of r the more marked is this tendency. Values of r lying between 0 and -1 indicate similarly that the two variables have a tendency to be grouped in a negative or inverse linear association, high values of the one being associated, on the average, with low values of the other.

The coefficient of correlation, r, is clearly related to the regression coefficients. Since the regression coefficient of y on x is $\dfrac{s_{xy}}{s_x^2}$ we have

$$r = \frac{s_x}{s_y} \cdot b$$

and, similarly,
$$r = \frac{s_y}{s_x} \cdot a \qquad (9.2)$$

where a is the regression coefficient of x on y. It immediately follows that

$$r^2 = ab \qquad (9.3)$$

We also have $s_y'^2 = s_y^2 - b^2 \cdot s_x^2$ from 8.13

and therefore $\quad s_y'^2 = s_y^2 (1 - r^2) \qquad (9.4)$

Since $s_y'^2$ is always positive or zero, $|r| \leqslant 1$, as stated before.

Note that while the regression coefficients b and a have the dimensions "units of y per unit x" and "units of x per unit y" respectively, the correlation coefficient r is dimensionless; it is a pure number.

9.2 Calculation of the Correlation Coefficient

If the two regression coefficients have already been calculated the coefficient of correlation is immediately obtainable from equation

9.3, the sign of r being determined by the sign of $\Sigma d_x d_y$. If, however, the correlation coefficient has to be determined directly from the data the quantities to be calculated are Σd_x^2, Σd_y^2 and $\Sigma d_x d_y$. The calculation of these quantities has already been demonstrated and there is therefore nothing new to be explained in the calculation. For convenience of reference, however, the whole calculation of the coefficient of correlation for ungrouped data, including the arithmetical checks, is set out in Table XXXIV. Since the sole purpose of the table is to show the details of the *method* of calculating r, a set of only 10 pairs of numbers is used, but it is stressed that the result, $r = -0.654$, based on so small a sample, is of doubtful significance; this question will be considered further in a later section of this chapter.

TABLE XXXIV

CALCULATION OF THE PRODUCT-MOMENT CORRELATION COEFFICIENT

x	y	d_x' [60]	d_y' [100]	$d_x'^2$	d'^2	I $d_x' \cdot d_y'$	II $d_x' + d_y'$	II $(d_x' + d_y')^2$
68	0·86	+ 8	−14	64	196	−112	− 6	36
44	0·90	−16	−10	256	100	+160	−26	676
24	1·23	−36	+23	1,296	529	−828	−13	169
82	0·80	+22	−20	484	400	−440	+ 2	4
58	0·99	− 2	− 1	4	1	+ 2	− 3	9
32	1·45	−28	+45	784	2,025	−1,260	+17	289
75	1·05	+15	+ 5	225	25	+ 75	+20	400
66	1·05	+ 6	+ 5	36	25	+ 30	+11	121
67	1·04	+ 7	+ 4	49	16	+ 28	+11	121
46	0·93	−14	− 7	196	49	+ 98	−21	441
Totals		−38	+30	3,394	3,366	−2,247	−8	2,266

Checks. (Columns not shown.)

(a) $\Sigma(d_x' + 1) = -28$; $\Sigma(d_y' + 1) = +40$;

$\Sigma(d_x' + 1)(d_y' + 1) = -2,245.$

$$\Sigma(d_x' + 1)(d_y' + 1) = \Sigma d_x' d_y' + \Sigma d_x' + \Sigma d_y' + N$$
$$= -2,247 + 30 - 38 + 10$$
$$= -2,245 \text{ as required.}$$

(b) $\Sigma(d_x' + 1)^2 = 3,328$

$\Sigma d_x'^2 + 2\Sigma d_x' + N = 3,394 - 76 + 10 = 3,328$, as required.

(c) $\Sigma(d_y' + 1)^2 = 3,436.$

$\Sigma d_y'^2 + 2\Sigma d_y' + N = 3,366 + 60 + 10 = 3,436$, as required.

$$(d) \qquad \Sigma(d_x' + d_y' + 1)^2 = 2{,}260$$

$$\Sigma(d_x' + d_y')^2 + 2\Sigma(d_x' + d_y') + N = 2{,}266 - 16 + 10$$
$$= 2{,}260, \text{ as required.}$$

Calculation

As $N - 1 = 9$, we have,

$$9s_x^2 = 3{,}394 - 10 . (3 \cdot 8^2) = 3{,}394 - 144 = 3{,}250.$$

$$9s_y^2 = 3{,}366 - 10 . (3 \cdot 0^2) = 3{,}366 - 90 = 3{,}276.$$

To find $\Sigma d_x' d_y'$ we can use either column I or column II.

From column I. $\Sigma d_x' . d_y' = - 2{,}247$ directly, but the entries of this column are tedious to calculate if N is large.

From column II. $2\Sigma d_x' . d_y' = \Sigma(d_x' + d_y')^2 - \Sigma d_x'^2 - \Sigma d_y'^2$
$$= 2{,}266 - 3{,}394 - 3{,}366 = - 4{,}494$$

giving $\Sigma d_x' . d_y' = - 2{,}247$ as before, but with the advantage that tables of squares can be used throughout.

Hence $9s_{xy} = - 2{,}247 - 10(- 3 \cdot 8)(3 \cdot 0) = - 2{,}247 + 114 = - 2{,}133$

$$\text{and } r = \frac{s_{xy}}{s_x . s_y} = \frac{- 2{,}133}{\sqrt{3{,}250 \times 3{,}276}} = - 0 \cdot 654.$$

One detail of this calculation of Table XXXIV that may require explanation is that, although the values of y range from $0 \cdot 86$ to $1 \cdot 45$, the decimal points have been ignored and the values of y have been read as though they ranged from 86 to 145, with no correction at any later stage. To explain this let us consider the two cofficients of correlation of distributions A and B, where distribution A is (x_r, y_r), $r = 1, 2, 3, \ldots n$, and distribution B is (kx_r, ly_r), $r = 1, 2, 3, \ldots n$, where k and l are constants, which are both positive or both negative. The coefficient of correlation of distribution B is

then $\dfrac{\Sigma(kd_x . ld_y)}{\sqrt{\Sigma k^2 d_x^2 . \Sigma l^2 d_y^2}}$ which simplifies immediately to $\dfrac{s_{xy}}{s_x . s_y}$ the

coefficient of correlation of distribution A. Therefore in calculating the coefficient of correlation either or both sets of variables can be multiplied by any factors which would simplify the computation. Similarly, any number may be added to or subtracted from the two sets of variables without altering the value of the coefficient.

For grouped data the calculation of the product sum is demonstrated in Table XXXIII; the method of calculating the standard deviations is known.

In arithmetical work of this kind every stage of the calculation should be checked. Where it is possible the check should be independent, but otherwise it is good practice always to estimate mentally the result of each process in the calculation, as well as the main results, and to compare these mental estimates with the actual results. Serious divergencies should be investigated as they arise.

EXERCISES XXXI

1. Plot the following distributions of points on graph paper:

A:
x	0	2	4	6	8	10	12	14	16	18
y	15	16	17	18	19	20	21	22	23	24

B:
x	25	26	27	28	29	30	31	32	33	34
y	30	27	24	21	18	15	12	9	6	3

C:
x	17	19	21	23	25	27	29	31	33	35
y	17	18	19	20	21	22	23	24	25	26

Write down the correlation coefficient of each set. Verify one of your answers by calculation.

2. What are the correlation coefficients of distributions for which:

(i) Regression coefficient of y on x is 2·4 units x/units y; regression coefficient of x on y is 0·15 units y/unit x.

(ii) Regression coefficient of y on x is $-$ 0·32 units x/unit y; regression coefficient of x on y is $-$ 2 units/unit x.

(iii) $\Sigma d_x d_y = 2,000$, $n = 101$, $s_x = 5$, $s_y = 16$.

(iv) $\Sigma d_x d_y = -1,440$, $n = 21$, $s_x = 12$, $s_y = 8$.

(v) $s_y' : s_y = 3 : 5$?

3. Interpret the equation $s_y'^2 = s_y^2 (1 - r^2)$ for distributions in which $s_y' = s_y$, 0 and $\frac{1}{2} s_y$ respectively.

4. Plot the following sets of points on graph paper. In each case make an estimate of the coefficient of correlation from the dot diagram and compare your estimates with the results obtained by calculation.

A:
x	1	3	3	3	4	4	5	5	6	6
y	2	2	4	5	4	6	3	5	5	7

x	7	8	8	9	10	11	11	12	12	13
y	6	5	8	7	9	8	10	9	10	10

B:
x	3	3	4	4	4	4	5	5	5	5
y	6	9	3	5	6	7	5	6	7	8

x	5	6	6	6	6	7	7	7	7	9
y	9	6	7	8	10	4	6	8	9	7

C:
x	3	3	3	4	5	5	6	6	7	8
y	7	8	9	8	6	7	5	6	5	4

x	9	10	11	12	12	13	13	14	15	15
y	5	5	4	5	6	7	8	7	8	9

D:
x	8	9	9	9	10	10	11	11	11	12
y	10	10	9	8	7	8	5	6	7	4

x	12	12	13	13	14	14	15	15	15	16
y	5	6	3	4	2	3	1	2	3	2

5. Show that if r is the coefficient of correlation of a bivariate distribution (x_i, y_i), where $i = 1, 2, 3 \ldots n$, then the coefficient of correlation of the distribution $(x_i + k, y_i + l)$ where $i = 1, 2, 3 \ldots n$, and k, l are constants, is also r.

Find the coefficient of correlation of the following corresponding values of x and y:

x	1,276	1,278	1,273	1,279	1,280	1,278	1,281	1,276	1,278
y	8·21	8·24	8·19	8·24	8·27	8·25	8·29	8·20	8·21

6. In an examination the candidates do two papers in mathematics. The marks of the candidates are set out below: find the coefficient of correlation between the two sets of marks.

Paper I.	29	32	53	47	45	32	70	45	70	53
Paper II.	56	60	72	48	72	35	67	67	75	31

Paper I.	22	18	42	78	42	53	33	78	33	37
Paper II.	44	37	64	98	48	65	72	50	42	43

Paper I.	42	15	45	59	23	42	43	50	32
Paper II.	68	30	27	50	61	62	52	50	51

7. Specimens of similarly treated alloy steels containing various percentages of nickel are tested for toughness with the following results:

Toughness (arbitrary units)

47	50	52	52	54	56	58	59	60	60	62	64	65	66

Percentage of nickel

2·5	2·7	2·8	2·8	2·9	3·2	3·2	3·3	3·4	3·5	3·5	3·6	3·7	3·8

Find the coefficient of correlation between the percentage of nickel and the toughness as measured by the test.

8. Calculate the coefficient of correlation between building activity, as measured by the number of permanent houses completed (denoted by N) and the wholesale price index of building materials (denoted by I) for the United Kingdom from the following data:

	1946		1947		1948	
	N (thousands)	I	N	I	N	I
Jan.			8·0	182	13·7	205
Feb.			3·8	185	14·4	210
Mar.			6·0	185	18·3	210
Apr.	2·1	159	8·7	190	17·1	210
May	2·4	161	10·6	197	17·7	210
June	3·2	162	10·8	197		
July	4·4	171	11·3	198		
Aug.	4·6	172	10·2	199		
Sept.	6·3	177	12·8	200		
Oct.	7·5	177	14·0	204		
Nov.	7·4	177	16·2	204		
Dec.	9·0	177	13·7	204		

(The figures are based on those given in the *U.N. Monthly Bulletin of Statistics, Vol.* II, *No.* 6)

9. Calculate the coefficient of correlation for each of two sets of grouped data given in Tables A and B.

Table A

y	1	2	3	4	5	6	7	8	9	10
10	—	—	—	—	—	—	—	1	—	1
9	—	—	—	—	—	—	1	2	1	—
8	—	—	—	—	—	1	2	4	4	3
7	—	—	—	—	—	3	5	6	3	1
6	—	—	—	1	2	6	8	5	2	1
5	—	—	1	5	7	9	8	4	1	—
4	—	1	3	10	9	8	5	3	1	—
3	2	3	5	8	5	3	2	—	—	—
2	2	4	6	3	2	2	—	—	—	—
1	1	3	4	2	1	—	—	—	—	—

x

Table B

y	1	2	3	4	5	6	7	8	9	10
10	7	3	1	—	—	—	—	—	—	—
9	9	8	5	1	—	—	—	—	—	—
8	5	7	8	6	2	—	—	—	—	—
7	1	3	8	11	6	2	1	—	—	—
6	—	1	3	10	12	8	4	1	—	—
5	—	1	2	7	15	10	7	3	3	—
4	—	—	—	3	7	12	9	5	3	1
3	—	—	—	—	2	7	10	6	2	1
2	—	—	—	—	1	3	5	8	4	3
1	—	—	—	—	—	—	1	4	4	5

x

10. Calculate the product moment correlation coefficient of each of the distributions of Ex. XXVIII, 5, 6, 7, 8, p. 195–6.

9.3 The Significance of the Correlation Coefficient

The methods of testing the significance of correlation coefficients are closely analogous to those used in testing regression coefficients. For large samples and small or moderate values of the coefficient ρ, it is found that the distribution of r approximates to the Normal and is distributed about ρ, the true value of r, with standard error $\dfrac{1 - \rho^2}{\sqrt{n - 1}}$. For values of n greater than 100, $r \simeq \rho$, and the properties of the Normal distribution may therefore be used directly to determine whether a correlation coefficient is significantly different from zero, but should any doubt arise a more accurate test should be applied.

Example I. A coefficient of correlation of 0·21 is obtained from a sample size of 400. Is this correlation significant?

Using the large sample method, the standard error of the coefficient $= \dfrac{1-\rho^2}{\sqrt{n-1}} \simeq \dfrac{1-(0\cdot21)^2}{\sqrt{400}} = 0\cdot048$. Since $r > 4 \times S.E.(r)$ the coefficient is significantly different from zero.

Example 2. A coefficient of correlation of $0\cdot20$ is obtained from a sample size of 100. Is this correlation significant?

Again using the large sample method, we have

$$S.E.(r) \simeq \frac{1-(0\cdot20)^2}{\sqrt{100}} = 0\cdot096$$

The coefficient of correlation is thus only about twice its standard error. The level of significance is doubtful; it should be determined more precisely by means of a more accurate test.

The extent to which the distribution of r deviates from the Normal as the size of the sample from a Normal bivariate population decreases can be seen in Fig. 53, which is based on data derived from F. N. David's "Tables of the Correlation Coefficient". The distribution approaches the Normal, for $\rho = 0\cdot5$, only for the samples in which $n = 100$. For higher values of $|\rho|$ the deviation from the Normal is even more pronounced (Fig. 54). The test already described is therefore only to be used as a rough guide for large samples, i.e., $n > 100$, and with moderate values of r, i.e., $|\rho| < 0\cdot5$.

It is only rarely that samples of 100 or more are available or are practicable to measure. Accurate tests are therefore required for small samples.

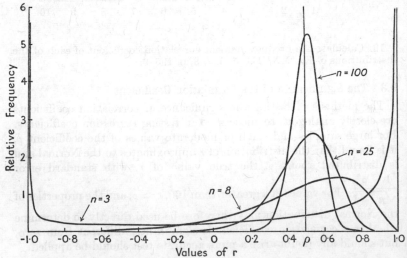

FIG. 53.   Distribution of r for samples of different sizes drawn from a population for which $\rho = 0.5$.

The usual method of approaching a problem of this kind, in which the distribution of the statistic itself does not conform to the Normal or other standard form, is to find a simple function of the statistic which is distributed in a standard form.

The first function of r which we will consider is the ratio $\frac{r}{\sqrt{1 - r^2}} \cdot \sqrt{n - 2}$. It is found that this ratio is distributed exactly in Student's "t-distribution" whatever the size of the sample if $\rho = 0$. To test the significance of a correlation coefficient, r, we calculate

$$t = \frac{r}{\sqrt{1 - r^2}} \cdot \sqrt{n - 2}$$

and locate this value of t in Table XXX, for the appropriate value of $(n - 2)$. The null hypothesis is that the variables are uncorrelated; the value of P corresponding to t as given by the table is the probability that a value of r equal to or greater than the particular value could arise from random sampling of the population from which it was drawn.

Example. The thicknesses of twenty annual rings of a tree and the corresponding annual rainfall were found to be correlated with a coefficient of $+ 0.47$. Is this correlation significant?

For $r = 0.47, n = 20$, we have
$$t = \frac{0.47}{\sqrt{1 - (0.47)^2}} \cdot \sqrt{18} = 2.26$$

The table shows that, for $n - 2 = 18$ degrees of freedom, this value of t corresponds to a value of P lying between 5% and 1%. The correlation

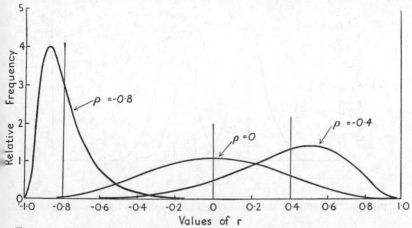

FIG. 54.   Distribution of r obtained from random samples of 10 from populations with various values of ρ.

is therefore significant at the 5% level, i.e., the probability of such a correlation arising from a random sample of the variables is less than 0·05.

We may also need to know whether the coefficient of correlation calculated from a sample of a bivariate universe is significantly different from that derived from another sample or from some hypothetical value. We cannot usually solve this problem by the method we used for regression coefficients because of the transformation we have to apply to r in calculating the ratio t. This difficulty has been solved by Professor R. A. Fisher by means of another transformation. He showed that the function $\frac{1}{2} \log_e \frac{1+r}{1-r}$ denoted by z, has a distribution which approximates very closely to the Normal with a mean $\frac{1}{2} \log_e \frac{1+\rho}{1-\rho}$ and a variance $\frac{1}{(n-3)}$ where n is the size of the sample. The statistic obtained by transforming r into z therefore lends itself readily to operations with which we are familiar.

The effect of the transformation is apparent from Fig. 55 in which the three curves of Fig. 54 are transformed into three curves which are visually indistinguishable from the Normal.

To use the z-transformation (it should not be called the "z-distribution" because this term is reserved for the distribution, also investigated by Fisher, mentioned in section 7.6), to compare an estimate of r with a theoretical value, the difference in the two corresponding values of z is compared with the standard error of z, i.e., with $\frac{1}{\sqrt{n-3}}$

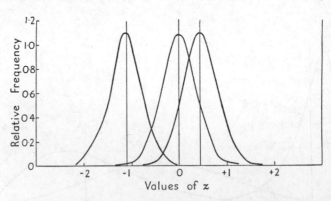

FIG. 55.   The effect of the z-transformation applied to the curves of Fig. 54.

Example. A correlation coefficient of 0·72 is obtained from a sample of 28. Is the coefficient significantly different from 0·80?

For $r = 0.72$, $\quad z = \frac{1}{2} \log_e \dfrac{1 + r}{1 - r}$

$$= \frac{1}{2} (\log_e 1.72 - \log_e 0.28)$$

$$= 0.908$$

(If tables of $\tanh^{-1}x$ are available, $z = \tanh^{-1}r$ directly.)

For $\rho = 0.80$, $\quad \zeta = \frac{1}{2} \log_e \dfrac{1 + \rho}{1 - \rho} = \frac{1}{2} \log_e \dfrac{1.80}{0.20} = 1.099$

Hence $|z - \zeta| = |0.908 - 1.099| = 0.19$

$$S.E. (z) = \frac{1}{\sqrt{n - 3}} = \frac{1}{\sqrt{25}} = 0.2$$

Since the deviation of z is approximately equal to the standard error of z, the value of 0.72 for the correlation coefficient is not significantly different from 0.80, the theoretical value.

To test the significance of the difference of two correlation coefficients derived from two separate samples, we have to compare the difference of the two corresponding values of z with the standard error of that difference remembering that the standard error of the *difference* of two statistical quantities is the square root of the *sum* of their variances. (Chapter VII.)

Example. Correlation coefficients of $- 0.35$ and $- 0.44$ are derived from two samples of 40 and of 50 pairs respectively. Do these coefficients differ significantly?

For $r_1 = - 0.35$, $\quad z_1 = \frac{1}{2} \log_e \dfrac{0.65}{1.35} = - 0.3655$

For $r_2 = - 0.44$, $\quad z_2 = \frac{1}{2} \log_e \dfrac{0.56}{1.44} = - 0.4723$

$$|z_1 - z_2| = 0.1068$$

$$\text{Var.} (z_1 - z_2) = \text{Var.} (z_1) + \text{Var.} (z_2)$$

$$= \frac{1}{40 - 3} + \frac{1}{50 - 3}$$

$$= 0.027 + 0.021 = 0.048$$

$$S.E. (z_1 - z_2) = \sqrt{.048} = 0.22$$

Since $|z_1 - z_2|$ is less than half its standard error the two correlation coefficients are not significantly different, i.e., they could well arise from two random samples from the same population.

The z-transformation can be used very simply to combine, or average, two or more correlation coefficients giving due weight to the sample sizes. Let $z_1, z_2, z_3 \ldots$ be the values of z corresponding to the given coefficients, based on samples of $N_1, N_2, N_3 \ldots$ observations respectively. Then, $\bar{z}$, the value of z corresponding to the required mean coefficient, $\bar{r}$, is the weighted mean of $z_1, z_2, z_3 \ldots$ where the weights are the corresponding variances $N_1 - 3$, $N_2 - 3$, $N_3 - 3$, etc. So that, writing $N_1 - 3 = n_1$, $N_2 - 3 = n_2$, etc., we have

$$\bar{z} (n_1 + n_2 + n_3 + \ldots) = n_1 z_1 + n_2 z_2 + n_3 z_3 - \ldots$$

Then $\bar{z} = \frac{1}{2} \{ \log (1 + \bar{r}) - \log (1 - \bar{r}) \}$ whence $\bar{r}$ can be found directly if conversion tables are available, or otherwise by using the relations

$$r = (e^{2z} - 1) / (e^{2z} + 1)$$

or $r = \tanh z$.

The standard error of $\bar{z}$ will be $\dfrac{1}{\sqrt{n_1 + n_2 + \ldots}}$

Example. Three samples of 20, 25 and 30 pairs drawn from the same population gave correlation coefficients of $0 \cdot 66$, $0 \cdot 68$ and $0 \cdot 63$ respectively. Find the average value of the coefficient and its standard error.

Tabulating the work, we have:

r	N	z	n	nz
0·66	20	0·793	17	13·481
0·68	25	0·829	22	18·238
0·63	30	0·741	27	20·001
			66	51·726

$$\bar{z} = \frac{51 \cdot 726}{66} = 0 \cdot 784$$

Hence $\bar{r} = 0 \cdot 655$ and $S.E. (\bar{r}) = \dfrac{1}{\sqrt{66}} = 0 \cdot 123$

EXERCISES XXXII

1. Using the significance test for large samples, show that the minimum sample sizes for a correlation coefficient of $\pm 0 \cdot 1$ to be significantly different from zero, when the significance requirement is that the coefficient should exceed (*a*) three times, (*b*) twice, its standard error, are approximately 900 and 400 respectively.

2. Use the table of the t-distribution to verify that the minimum values of $|r|$ that are significant at the 5% level for samples of 20, 40 and 80 pairs are $0 \cdot 44$, $0 \cdot 31$ and $0 \cdot 22$ respectively.

3. Find, as precisely as the table of the t-distribution permits, the probability that $|r|$ would be exceeded in a random sample of the same size drawn from a Normal uncorrelated bivariate population, for each of the following cases:

	r	n
(a)	0·27	66
(b)	$-0·38$	27
(c)	$-0·50$	38
(d)	0·51	18

(If the direct conversion tables are not available, note that $\dfrac{r}{\sqrt{1-r^2}} = \tan\theta$

where $\theta = \sin^{-1}r$. E.g., to find the value of $\dfrac{r}{\sqrt{1-r^2}}$ when $r = 0·27$, we have

$\sin^{-1} 0·27 = 15°\ 40'$ and therefore $\dfrac{r}{\sqrt{1-r^2}} = \tan 15°\ 40' = 0·2805$.)

4. A correlation coefficient of 0·30 is obtained from a sample of 40 pairs of observations. Find the probability of this value being exceeded in a random sample of 40 drawn from a Normal uncorrelated bivariate population using (a) the large sample significance test, (b) the t-distribution and (c) the z-transformation. Comment on the three results.

5. Use the z-transformation to test the significance of the following correlation coefficients:

	r	n
(a)	$-0·10$	1,000
(b)	0·30	75
(c)	0·50	10
(d)	$-0·70$	12

(If tables of $\tanh^{-1}x$ are available, use $z = \tanh^{-1}r$.)

6. Are any of the following correlation coefficients, derived from samples of 84 pairs of observations, consistent with the hypothesis that in each case the true correlation coefficient was 0·50? The coefficients are 0·80, 0·60, 0·45 and 0·20.

7. Combine the results of the four tests given below to obtain the average value of the coefficient. It can be assumed that all four samples were drawn from the same Normal population.

	r	n
(a)	0·38	40
(b)	0·42	33
(c)	0·31	36
(d)	0·33	43

8. Observations of a Normally distributed bivariate population are made in sets of 103 pairs and the correlation coefficient of each set is calculated. If the population is known to have a correlation coefficient of 0·33, between what limits would you expect to find (a) 90%, (b) 99% of the correlation coefficients of the sets?

9. Is there a significant difference between correlation coefficients of 0·30 derived from 28 pairs of observations and 0·60 derived from 23 pairs of observations?

10. Two samples, of 13 and 43 pairs, gave correlation coefficients of $-0·23$ and $+0·05$ respectively. Show that this result is not incompatible with the hypothesis that the two samples were drawn from the same Normal bivariate universe. Combine the results and find the average value of the coefficient.

9.4   Coefficient of Rank Correlation

The calculation of the product-moment coefficient of correlation is a laborious arithmetical process even when a calculating machine is available. A method which would yield an approximate value of the coefficient with rather less arithmetic would be useful. The method of *ranking* the data before calculating the coefficient reduces the labour of computation and yields an approximate value of r in most cases.

The *coefficient of rank correlation* is the product-moment coefficient of correlation of the *ranks* of the original data. Thus the five number pairs (87, 63), (22, 48), (33, 46), (72, 51) and (38, 28) are ranked by setting out the two series of numbers and then noting their order of magnitude from the greatest downwards. Applying this operation to the five pairs above we have:

87	1	63	1
22	5	48	3
33	4	46	4
72	2	51	2
38	3	28	5

and obtain the corresponding pairs (1, 1), (5, 3), (4, 4), (2, 2) and (3, 5), which are much simpler to deal with arithmetically than the original pairs.

More generally, in the distribution (x_r, y_r), $r = 1, 2, 3 \ldots n$, the two sets of variables are arranged in descending order. If then x_r is the sth in order or rank of the x's, and y_r is the tth in order or rank of the y's, the pair (x_r, y_r) is replaced by the pair (s, t) and the coefficient of correlation is found for the distribution of pairs like (s, t).

Since the n possible values of both s and t consist of the n integers 1, 2, 3 . . . n, some simplification of the coefficient formula 9.1 is possible.

In the first place the mean of the series 1, 2, 3 . . . n is $\frac{1}{2}(n + 1)$, so that $\bar{s} = \bar{t} = \frac{1}{2}(n + 1)$ and

$$\Sigma d_s^2 = \Sigma d_t^2 = \Sigma_1^n r^2 - n \cdot \frac{1}{4}(n + 1)^2$$

$$= \frac{1}{6}n(n + 1)(2n + 1) - \frac{n}{4}(n + 1)^2$$

$$= \frac{1}{12} \cdot n(n^2 - 1).$$

To find $\Sigma d_s \cdot d_t$ we put $(s - t) = d$, so that

$$\Sigma(s - t)^2 = \Sigma d^2 = \Sigma s^2 + \Sigma t^2 - 2\Sigma s \cdot t$$

giving $$2\Sigma s \cdot t = \Sigma s^2 + \Sigma t^2 - \Sigma d^2$$

$$= 2\Sigma_1^n r^2 - \Sigma d^2.$$

Hence
$$\Sigma d_s . d_t = \Sigma s . t - n . \bar{s} . \bar{t}$$

$$= \Sigma_1^n r^2 - n . \tfrac{1}{4} (n + 1)^2 - \tfrac{1}{2} \Sigma d^2$$

$$= \tfrac{1}{12} . n(n^2 - 1) - \tfrac{1}{2} . \Sigma d^2$$

The coefficient of rank correlation, R, is the value of

$$\frac{\Sigma d_s d_t}{\sqrt{\Sigma d_s{}^2 . \Sigma d_t{}^2}}$$

taken over the ranked pairs.

Hence
$$R = \left\{ \tfrac{1}{12} n(n^2 - 1) - \tfrac{1}{2} \Sigma d^2 \right\} \div \tfrac{1}{12} n(n^2 - 1)$$

$$= 1 - \frac{6 \Sigma d^2}{n(n^2 - 1)} \tag{9.5}$$

If the two ranks are equal in every pair then $\Sigma d^2 = 0$ and $R = +1$ for perfect correlation of ranks. If the two ranks are such that the 1st, 2nd, 3rd . . . of one correspond to the nth, $(n - 1)$th, $(n - 2)$th . . . of the other, then it can be shown that $R = -1$ exactly. The limits of R are therefore the same as those of r, and for intermediate values R may, in general, be taken as an approximation to r.

The tests of significance devised for the product-moment coefficient r are not strictly applicable to the rank coefficient R, and though they are occasionally used, they only give a rough guide even for large samples and must be used with circumspection.

The rank coefficient has the advantage that the data to which it is applied need not be accurate measurements. The two variables or qualities to be compared have only to be placed in order, and this can often be done when exact measurement is impossible, impracticable, or perhaps unnecessary. Thus it is possible to rank depths of colour without requiring some form of graduated scale, and to rank dimensions of objects merely by comparing one with another and arranging them in sequence.

For convenience of reference the complete calculation of the coefficient of rank correlation is shown in Table XXXV in which the data of Table XXXIV are used. It will be noticed that in the ranking of x and y a difficulty occurs because there are two pairs with the same value of y. Since these two values of y would take third and fourth places it is conventional, though not mathematically justifiable, to give both places the average order of the equal values, i.e., $3\tfrac{1}{2}$ in this example. The result of the calculation is that R is -0.52, whereas for the same data the product-moment coefficient is -0.65.

TABLE XXXV

CALCULATION OF THE RANK CORRELATION COEFFICIENT

x	y	s	t	d	d^2
68	0·86	3	9	−6	36
44	0·90	8	8	0	0
24	1·23	10	2	8	64
82	0·80	1	10	−9	81
58	0·99	6	6	0	0
32	1·45	9	1	8	64
75	1·05	2	$3\frac{1}{2}$	$-1\frac{1}{2}$	2·25
66	1·05	5	$3\frac{1}{2}$	$1\frac{1}{2}$	2·25
67	1·04	4	5	−1	1
46	0·93	7	7	0	0
				Total	250·5

$$R = 1 - \frac{6 \Sigma d^2}{n(n^2 - 1)}$$
$$= 1 - \frac{6 \cdot 250 \cdot 5}{10 \times 99}$$
$$= 1 - \frac{1,503}{990}$$
$$= -0 \cdot 52$$

EXERCISES XXXIII

1. Show that in a ranked bivariate distribution in which no ties occur and in which the variables are independent:

(a) $\Sigma(d^2)$ is always even,

(b) there are not more than $\frac{1}{6}(n^3 - n) + 1$ possible values of R.

2. Find the coefficient of ranked correlation for the data of Exercise XXXI, 6, p. 212.

3. The table gives indices of various economic statistics for a selected list of countries at January 1947 (1937 level = 100). The indices are of:

(a) Employment in manufacturing.

(b) Industrial production.

(c) Retail trade.

(d) Quantum of imports.

(e) Quantum of exports.

(f) Market price of industrial shares.

(g) Cost of living.

(h) Wholesale prices.

Country	(a)	(b)	(c)	(d)	(e)	(f)	(g)	(h)
Argentine	142	—	214	113	46	—	165	215
Australia	147	—	167	69	106	145	133	141
Austria	—	46	100	13	16	—	185	—
Belgium	—	84	291	—	—	238	329	311
Bulgaria	—	108	107	43	29	—	627	715
Canada	167	161	174	—	—	87	125	135
Chile	137	144	—	—	—	88	345	261
Czechoslovakia	88	—	—	65	49	—	343	310
Denmark	123	110	—	—	—	130	162	188
France	106	88	—	97	66	1,042	981	874
Hungary	100	—	—	42	22	—	385	403
India	—	—	—	79	80	228	252	290
Ireland	115	102	—	93	64	150	174	204
Netherlands	151	86	168	53	41	181	198	247
Norway	117	109	175	104	68	129	165	168
Poland	—	105	—	118	40	—	13,305	—
South Africa	144	—	—	—	—	—	140	165
Sweden	118	108	—	101	41	154	152	170
Switzerland	128	—	176	120	103	151	155	196
Turkey	—	—	—	66	167	—	348	421
United Kingdom	105	106	126	64	89	142	132	167
U.S.A.	148	163	233	119	250	109	149	164

Find, as far as paired values allow, the coefficient of rank correlation between:

(i) columns (a) and (e)

(ii) columns (b) and (d)

(iii) columns (c) and (h)

(iv) columns (d) and (g)

(v) columns (f) and (g)

(These figures are abstracted from the *U.N. Monthly Bulletin of Statistics*, **2**, 6.)

9.5   The Interpretation of the Correlation Coefficient

There is probably no other statistic which is so freely misused as the coefficient of correlation. It must always be remembered that the coefficient of correlation is merely a measure of the degree to which large and small values of one variable are associated with large and small values of another variable and is nothing more. A high value of the coefficient implies only that large and small values of one variable occur in association with large and small values of the other variable, but this does not imply any other relation between them.

For example, any steadily increasing series of numbers will have a high correlation with any other steadily increasing series of numbers if the two series are put side by side to form a series of pairs. The number of wireless licences annually issued in Great Britain steadily increased during the years 1935 to 1946 except for a slight decrease in the first years of the War. The number of mental defectives notified in England and Wales followed a rather similar course with a slight lag. The figures are set out below:

Year	Wireless Licences (*Millions*)	Mental Defectives notified (*Thousands*)
1935	7·0	86
1936	7·6	88
1937	8·1	92
1938	8·6	96
1939	9·0	99
1940	9·0	101
1941	8·8	101
1942	8·7	98
1943	9·2	98
1944	9·6	100
1945	9·7	102
1946	10·4	102

These two series of figures give the high correlation of $+ 0.91$, a figure which even for as small a sample as 12, is highly significant by the usual tests. It would be wrong, however, to infer without some evidence that a direct casual relation exists between the two, apart from the fact that the number of mental defectives *notified* is a measure not only of mental deficiency, but also of the efficiency of certain administrative processes. Both of the sets of numbers would have a high correlation with any similar set of numbers which show a similar trend such as (*a*) the annual consumption of tobacco over the same period, (b) the numbers 1, 2, 3, 4, 5, 5, 4, 3, 6, 7, 8, 9, (c) the annual total payment of income tax and surtax in almost any consecutive twelve years.

The interpretation of a correlation coefficient requires the greatest care and a knowledge of all the relevant facts. The data used in this chapter to illustrate the methods of calculation are derived from the *Annual Abstract of Statistics*, No. 84. The entries of column *x* of Table XXXIV are the estimated quantities of fruit harvested in this country for the years 1936 to 1945 and are given correct to the nearest 10,000 tons. The entries of column *y* are the ratios (Fruit price index)/(Agricultural products index) for the corresponding years. The data suggest that the quantity of fruit available and its average price are negatively associated, illustrating a well-known economic law. The correlation coefficient would probably have been nearer to −1 had not some Government control of prices been exercised in the later years of the period.

9.6 Historical Note

The fundamental ideas of regression and correlation were first enunciated and applied by Sir Francis Galton in 1886–1888. At that time the coefficients were determined only by graphical methods. The product moment formula was introduced by Karl Pearson in 1896; the rank correlation method by C. Spearman in 1910. R. A. Fisher deduced the distribution of the correlation coefficient for samples drawn from a normal universe in 1914, and later he developed the methods of testing the significance of observed coefficients that have been described in this chapter.

Several aspects of regression and correlation await further investigation. The theory of correlation is based on the assumption that samples are drawn from universes which at least approximate to the Normal form. In practice, however, the correlation coefficient is used with little regard for the form of the distribution; this indiscriminate use awaits theoretical justification. Other measures of correlation and association have been developed in recent years.

SUMMARY OF CHAPTER IX

1. The product-moment coefficient of correlation is estimated from the formula

$$r = \frac{s_{xy}}{s_x \cdot s_y} = \frac{\Sigma d_x \cdot d_y}{\sqrt{\Sigma d_x^2 \cdot \Sigma d_y^2}}$$

It ranges from -1 to $+1$, and is a measure of the degree of linear association of the two variables. If $r = 0$ the two variables are uncorrelated but not necessarily unassociated.

2. The coefficient r is connected with the regression coefficients a (of x on y) and b (of y on x) by the relations:

$$r = \frac{s_y}{s_x} . a \quad ; \quad r = \frac{s_y}{s_x} . b$$

$$r^2 = ab.$$

3. The function $z = \frac{1}{2} \log_e \frac{1 + r}{1 - r} = \tanh r$ has a distribution which approximates very closely to the Normal. It has a mean $\frac{1}{2} \log_e \frac{1 + \rho}{1 - \rho}$ and variance $\frac{1}{n - 3}$, where ρ is the true value of r. This z-transformation, due to R. A. Fisher, provides the simplest means of testing the significance of the correlation coefficient.

4. An approximation to r which is simpler to compute is given by the coefficient of rank correlation, R. The observed values of the variables are replaced by their respective ranks, i.e., their order in the series obtained when the two sets of variables are arranged in descending order of magnitude. R is the product-moment coefficient of the distribution of ranks. It is given by

$$R = 1 - \frac{6\Sigma d^2}{n(n^2 - 1)}$$

where $d =$ difference of rank for any pair of variables.

5. The theory of correlation significance is based on the assumption that the distributions to which it is applied are approximately Normal.

EXERCISES XXXIV

1. Use equations 9.2 and 9.3 to show that the acute angle between the regression lines is $\tan^{-1} \dfrac{1 - ab}{a + b} = \tan^{-1} \dfrac{(1 - r^2)\, \sigma_x \sigma_y}{r(\sigma_x{}^2 + \sigma_y{}^2)}$.

2. Find the coefficient of correlation for normal bivariate distributions of which the regression equations, based on samples of 400 pairs, are:

$$(a) \quad y = -0{\cdot}765x + 18{\cdot}72$$
$$x = -0{\cdot}035y + 6{\cdot}51$$
$$(b) \quad y = 0{\cdot}318x + 0{\cdot}055$$
$$x = 0{\cdot}138y + 0{\cdot}036$$

Examine the significance of each of the correlations.

3. Find the coefficient of correlation for distributions in which

(a) Variance of y = 6·25 sq. units.

Variance of y about regression = 2·25 sq. units.

(b) Standard deviation of x = 3·6 units.

Standard deviation of y = 2·5 units.

Covariance of x and y = − 1·8 sq. units.

(c) Standard deviation of x = 3·0 units.

Variance of y = 1·96 sq. units.

Coefficient of regression of y on x = 0·28 unit x / unit y.

4. Using the large sample formula for the standard error of a correlation coefficient, draw a graph which shows the minimum numerical value of the coefficient that is significant, at the level at which $|r| > 3 \times S.E.(r)$, for samples which range in size from 100 to 2,500.

5. If the ranks 1, 2, 3 . . . n are associated with ranks in exactly the reverse order show that the coefficient of rank correlation is exactly − 1. Consider separately the cases in which $n = 2m$ and $n = 2m + 1$.

6. Show that for n pairs of observations in which no ties occur the number of possible combinations of the paired ranks is $n!$

Examine the probability distribution of the rank coefficient for $n = 2$, 3 and 4 when no ties occur.

7. The *reliability* of a test or examination is sometimes measured by finding the correlation between the two series of marks obtained when duplicate tests are applied to the same students. By finding both the product moment and rank correlation coefficients, calculate in two ways the reliability coefficient of an examination in which the duplicate marks in a trial were:

62	33	55	42	45	87	52	70	32	70
48	49	59	31	59	89	60	55	34	68

45	55	70	60	88	72	53	47	52	17
58	55	73	56	78	77	42	38	50	26

[In calculating the product moment use the relation

$$2\Sigma xy = \Sigma x^2 + \Sigma y^2 - \Sigma(x - y)^2.]$$

8. The counties playing in the cricket championship are given below in the order in which they finished in the 1948 season, together with the order in which they finished in 1947. Find R, the coefficient of rank correlation between these two orders.

1. Glamorgan (9)   7. Warwick   (15)   13. Essex   (11)
2. Surrey   (6)   8. Gloucester (2)   14. Nottingham (12)
3. Middlesex (1)   9. Hampshire   (16)   15. Kent   (4)
4. Yorkshire (8)   10. Worcester   (7)   16. Sussex   (10)
5. Lancashire (3)   11. Leicester   (14)   17. Northants (17)
6. Derbyshire (5)   12. Somerset   (13)

9. The data of the table below were obtained in the U.S.A. during an investigation of the environmental variations of a wild plant. *Daucus curota L.*, by W. D. Baten, (1934). (*Biometrika*, **26**, 443). In the table

x and y denote the number of rays and the number of bracts per inflorescence respectively.

Show that

    (a)   the equation of regression of x on y is $x = 4 \cdot 46 + 4 \cdot 25y$,

    (b)   the coefficient of correlation between x and y is $0 \cdot 59$.

y	12	17	22	27	32	37	42	47	52	57	62	67	72	77	82	87	92	Total
16	—	—	—	—	—	—	—	1	—	—	—	—	—	—	—	—	—	1
15	—	—	—	—	—	—	—	—	—	—	—	—	—	—	—	—	—	0
14	—	—	—	—	—	—	—	—	1	—	1	1	—	1	—	—	—	4
13	—	—	—	—	—	1	—	3	5	10	5	—	1	1	—	—	—	26
12	—	—	—	1	1	2	5	4	7	4	4	6	1	2	2	—	1	40
11	—	—	—	—	—	5	15	23	25	10	10	3	1	—	—	—	—	92
10	—	—	—	—	5	21	34	47	24	15	3	4	—	—	—	—	—	153
9	—	—	—	7	21	51	68	41	29	20	7	7	1	1	—	—	—	253
8	1	2	7	38	54	95	60	29	15	10	3	1	1	1	1	—	—	318
7	—	3	9	21	23	23	10	3	1	—	1	—	—	—	—	—	—	94
6	—	—	4	2	2	1	—	—	—	—	—	—	—	—	—	—	—	9
5	1	5	3	—	—	—	—	1	—	—	—	—	—	—	—	—	—	10
	2	10	23	69	106	199	193	151	107	69	34	22	5	6	3	—	1	1,000

Column heading for x: *(Centre of Class Interval)*

10. In an investigation on the left-right asymmetry of the human head the quantity $(1 - r)$ was used as a measure of the departure from perfect symmetry of the two variables. A condensed table of results is given below. Show that $(1 - r) = 0 \cdot 108$ [Woo (1930), *Biometrika*, **22**, 324].

d_y' (Left)	d_x' (Right) −7	−6	−5	−4	−3	−2	−1	0	1	2	3	4	5	6	7	8	Tota
−8	—	1	—	—	—	—	—	—	—	—	—	—	—	—	—	—	—
−7	2	2	—	—	—	—	—	—	—	—	—	—	—	—	—	—	—
−6	1	2	—	1	—	—	—	—	—	—	—	—	—	—	—	—	—
−5	—	—	3	1	2	1	—	—	—	—	—	—	—	—	—	—	—
−4	—	2	4	14	13	4	—	—	—	—	—	—	—	—	—	—	3
−3	—	—	—	3	17	15	10	1	—	—	—	—	—	—	—	—	4
−2	—	—	—	3	17	38	22	6	1	1	—	—	—	—	—	—	8
−1	—	—	1	1	5	17	50	45	13	5	—	—	—	—	—	—	13
0	—	—	—	—	—	8	26	78	31	19	5	1	—	—	—	—	16
1	—	—	—	—	—	1	4	11	41	31	13	4	—	—	—	—	10
2	—	—	—	—	—	—	2	6	20	46	20	8	2	—	—	—	10
3	—	—	—	—	—	—	—	1	6	27	32	17	5	2	—	—	9
4	—	—	—	—	—	—	—	—	4	4	10	13	12	—	—	—	4
5	—	—	—	—	—	—	—	—	—	2	2	8	11	5	2	—	8
6	—	—	—	—	—	—	—	—	—	—	3	1	5	2	—	—	
7	—	—	—	—	—	—	—	—	—	—	1	—	3	—	2		
	3	7	8	23	54	84	114	148	116	135	82	55	31	15	4	2	8

11. The data of the table given below are from a paper on "Wool in the World Economy", by Blau (1946), (*Journal of the Royal Statistical Society*, **109**, 198). Show that the coefficient of correlation, r, is $0\cdot797$, and the coefficient of rank correlation, R, is $0\cdot86$.

	Average wool consumption per head. (1 *lb. clean*)	*Average real income per head.* (*International units*)
United Kingdom	5·27	1,069
New Zealand	4·65	1,202
Australia	4·63	980
Belgium	4·55	600
Sweden	3·55	653
France	3·52	684
Switzerland	3·22	1,018
Argentina	3·00	1,000
Germany	2·87	646
U.S.A.	2·66	1,381
Czechoslovakia	2·04	455
Jugoslavia	1·74	330
Japan	1·26	353
Italy	1·22	343
Hungary	1·12	359
Poland	0·99	352
U.S.S.R.	0·87	320
South Africa	0·83	276
India	0·20	200
China	0·10	100–120

12. Find the coefficient of correlation for the bivariate distribution of the table given below, which gives Johanssen's measurements of the corresponding lengths and breadths of beans. [Quoted by Pretorius (1930), *Biometrika*, **22**, 110.]

x and y denote the lengths and breadths of the beans respectively. The measurements are in millimetres; the central value of the class interval is given in each case.

y	17	16½	16	15½	15	14½	14	13½	13	12½	12	11½	11	10½	10	9½	Totals
	—	2	—	—	3	—	—	—	—	—	—	—	—	—	—	—	5
	4	8	17	19	—	—	—	—	—	—	—	—	—	—	—	—	48
	2	23	101	156	93	23	2	—	—	—	—	—	—	—	—	—	400
	—	18	105	494	574	227	56	9	—	—	—	—	—	—	—	—	1,483
	—	4	44	375	956	913	362	73	12	3	—	—	—	—	—	—	2,742
	—	—	7	81	385	871	794	330	89	19	3	—	—	—	—	—	2,579
	—	—	1	4	65	236	469	361	175	55	27	4	—	—	—	—	1,397
	—	—	—	—	6	23	91	137	124	78	37	22	11	—	1	—	530
	—	—	—	—	—	1	13	18	28	35	25	32	11	6	1	—	170
	—	—	—	—	—	—	—	1	9	8	21	12	13	7	1	—	72
	—	—	—	—	—	—	—	—	—	—	2	—	1	4	3	—	10
	—	—	—	—	—	—	—	—	—	1	—	—	—	1	1	1	4
Totals	6	55	275	1,129	2,082	2,294	1,787	929	437	199	115	70	36	18	7	1	9,440

13. Using the table of the t-distribution draw graphs which show the minimum values of $|r|$ that are significant at the 1% and 5% levels for samples ranging in size from 10 pairs to 100 pairs.

14. Summarise the methods that may be used to test the significance of correlation coefficients; note carefully the limitations of each method.

15. Derive the formula of Spearman's coefficient of rank correlation. What are the advantages and disadvantages of this coefficient compared with the product-moment coefficient?

16. Briefly explain the advantages that follow from Fisher's "z-transformation" of the product-moment correlation coefficient. Describe how this transformation can be used to combine the results of several samples drawn from the same bivariate universe.

17. Devise a coefficient based on rank which gives a measure of the change of order that can take place in any ordered class, e.g., a football league table. The coefficient should be easy to compute and simple to interpret.
Modify the coefficient to reflect that an interchange of first and second places is more noteworthy than a change of second and third places, etc.

18. Examine the detailed results of any general examination that are available to determine which single subject gives results which are most closely correlated with the combined result, equal weight being given to all subjects. (Use the rank correlation coefficient.)

19. Collect data on the height and weight of friends and colleagues (at least 20) and then find the product moment coefficient of correlation between

    (a) height and weight
    (b) height and $\sqrt[3]{\text{weight}}$

Comment on your results.

20. Briefly explain the difference between the ideas of *regression* and *correlation*. Are *uncorrelated* variables necessarily *unassociated*?

21. Calculate the product moment correlation coefficient of each of the distributions of Ex. XXX, Nos. 13, 14, 15, 16, 17. Test the coefficients for significance at the 5% level.

CHAPTER X
Goodness of Fit and Contingency Tables

10.1 Goodness of Fit

In Chapter VII tests were described which decided whether the mean or standard deviation of a sample conformed to some hypothesis. For example, if the hypothesis was that the population mean was μ and a sample of n gave a sample mean and standard deviation $\bar{x}$ and s the test involved calculating $t = \dfrac{\bar{x} - \mu}{s/\sqrt{n}}$ based on $(n - 1)$ degrees of freedom and determining the significance of the result. Again if the test was to decide whether two populations had the same standard deviation and samples of n_1 and n_2 were taken which gave standard deviations s_1 and s_2 then the test was based on $z = \frac{1}{2} \log_e s_1^2/s_2^2$.

In this chapter a test will be described which answers a much more general question than those discussed in Chapter VII. The purpose of this test is to decide whether in a sample the frequencies of the results, that is the number of results occurring in each class interval, *taken as a whole* can reasonably be considered to be in accordance with some specified law of distribution. An example will make this more clear. Table XXXVI shows the (fictitious) results obtained from rolling a die 600 times. If the die were unbiased the expected distribution of scores would be 100 of each. Is it reasonable to suppose on the basis of this experiment that the die is unbiased, so that each face has an equal chance of turning up?

TABLE XXXVI
SIX HUNDRED THROWS OF A DIE (FICTITIOUS RESULTS)

Score	1	2	3	4	5	6	Total
Observed frequency (n)	200	50	50	50	50	200	600
Theoretical frequency (ν)	100	100	100	100	100	100	600

The mean score of the observed results is given by $\frac{1}{600}$ [1 × 200 + 2 × 50 + 3 × 50 + 4 × 50 + 5 × 50 + 6 × 200] = $\frac{1}{600}$ × 2100 = 3·5, and this is the same as the theoretical mean score. However, despite this coincidence, a glance at the Table shows that the

231

observed results are very far from those which would be expected if the die were not biased. There are twice as many scores of 1 and 6 as would be expected, and most people would refuse to believe that this result could be obtained by chance.

This artificial example was devised to emphasise the point that it is the discrepancies between observed and theoretical class frequencies which are being studied. Table XXXVII shows the results of an experiment in which a die was thrown 300 times. In this chapter n will be taken to denote observed frequencies and ν the theoretical frequencies. The differences $(\nu - n)$ are also shown in Table XXXVII.

TABLE XXXVII

THREE HUNDRED THROWS OF A DIE (ACTUAL DATA)

Score	1	2	3	4	5	6	Total
Observed frequencies (n)	41	62	49	53	37	58	300
Theoretical frequencies (ν)	50	50	50	50	50	50	300
Differences $(\nu - n)$	9	−12	1	−3	13	−8	

Here it is much more difficult to decide by inspection whether the observed frequencies, taken as a whole, are significantly different from the theoretical frequencies. The question is how can the significance of the result be established on the hypothesis that the die is unbiased?

THE χ^2 TEST. The answer to this question is given by a statistical test discovered about 1900 by Karl Pearson. He called the test the χ^2 (pronounced "kye squared") test. The application of the test is very easy to learn and involves an idea which has already been introduced to readers of this book: this is *the number of degrees of freedom*, a number closely associated with the number of frequency groups involved.

CALCULATION OF χ^2. There is a wide range of problems to which the test can be applied and examples of these will be given in this chapter. The calculation of χ^2 is always the same. If n_r ($r = 1, 2, \ldots s$) denote the observed frequencies in s class intervals and ν_r ($r = 1, 2, \ldots s$) denote the corresponding frequencies based on some specified hypothetical distribution, then χ^2 is defined as the sum

$$\chi^2 = \Sigma_1^s \frac{(\nu_r - n_r)^2}{\nu_r}$$

That is to say, the difference between observed and theoretical frequencies in each group is squared and the result is divided by the theoretical frequency for that group, and the result is summed over all groups. The calculation for Table XXXVII is set out in Table XXXVIII.

TABLE XXXVIII

THREE HUNDRED THROWS OF A DIE. CALCULATION OF χ^2

Score	n_s	ν_s	$\nu_s - n_s$	$\dfrac{(\nu_s - n_s)^2}{\nu_s}$
1	41	50	9	1·62
2	62	50	−12	2·88
3	49	50	1	0·02
4	53	50	−3	0·18
5	37	50	13	3·38
6	58	50	−8	1·28
Totals	300	300	0	9·36 ($= \chi^2$)

The calculation is carried out in this way because it provides a simple routine with a subsidiary check. $\Sigma(\nu_s - n_s)$ should always be zero, since $\Sigma\nu_s = \Sigma n_s$. The term $\dfrac{(\nu_s - n_s)^2}{\nu_s}$ is formed by dividing the square of the entry in the fourth column by that in the third (e.g., $9^2/50 = 1\cdot62$). The sum of the 5th column gives χ^2; in this example $\chi^2 = 9\cdot36$.

Since the difference $(\nu_s - n_s)$ occurs in χ^2 as a square, it is obvious that any discrepancy between the observed class frequencies and the corresponding theoretical frequencies will serve to increase χ^2. Whether the difference $(\nu_s - n_s)$ is positive or negative it will add to the value of χ^2. In this way it can be seen that χ^2 does provide an overall measure of the individual differences between observed and theoretical frequencies. If χ^2 is calculated for the results in Table XXXVI the value is many times larger, namely $\chi^2 = 300$, and this confirms the common-sense view that the fictitious figures in Table XXXVI are much more suggestive of bias than those in Table XXXVII. There still remains the question of how to obtain the exact significance of χ^2.

DEGREES OF FREEDOM. The calculation of the significance of χ^2 involves a number f, which denotes the number of degrees of freedom used in calculating χ^2. Suppose a sample consists of data grouped into s classes. The hypothesis states that the class frequencies are those which would be obtained if the data obeyed a certain law of distribution such as for example the Normal or Binomial laws.

Now, in determining the law of distribution it may be necessary to calculate *from the sample* one or more statistics to specify the distribution. Let us suppose there are r such statistics. Then f is defined by the equation $f = s - r$. The conception of "degrees of freedom" is difficult to get hold of at first. The reader is advised to study the examples which follow. The determination of f is described carefully in each one and with a little practice the reader will become familiar with the idea.

THE χ^2 TABLE. The final stage in the calculation of χ^2 involves the use of Table XXXIX. The table consists of values of χ^2 arranged

TABLE XXXIX
PERCENTAGE POINTS OF THE χ^2 DISTRIBUTION

f \ $P\%$	99	97·5	95	90	50	10	5	2·5	1
1	0·0	0·0	0·0	0·0	0·5	2·7	3·8	5·0	6·6
2	0·0	0·1	0·1	0·2	1·4	4·6	6·0	7·4	9·2
3	0·1	0·2	0·4	0·6	2·4	6·3	7·8	9·3	11·3
4	0·3	0·5	0·7	1·1	3·4	7·8	9·5	11·1	13·3
5	0·6	0·8	1·1	1·6	4·4	9·2	11·1	12·8	15·1
6	0·9	1·2	1·6	2·2	5·3	10·6	12·6	14·4	16·8
7	1·2	1·7	2·2	2·8	6·3	12·0	14·1	16·0	18·5
8	1·6	2·2	2·7	3·5	7·3	13·4	15·5	17·5	20·1
9	2·1	2·7	3·3	4·2	8·3	14·7	16·9	19·0	21·7
10	2·6	3·2	3·9	4·9	9·3	16·0	18·3	20·5	23·2
11	3·1	3·8	4·6	5·6	10·3	17·3	19·7	21·9	24·7
12	3·6	4·4	5·2	6·3	11·3	18·5	21·0	23·3	26·2
13	4·1	5·0	5·9	7·0	12·3	19·8	22·4	24·7	27·7
14	4·7	5·6	6·6	7·8	13·3	21·1	23·7	26·1	29·1
15	5·2	6·3	7·3	8·5	14·3	22·3	25·0	27·5	30·6
16	5·8	6·9	8·0	9·3	15·3	23·5	26·3	28·8	32·0
17	6·4	7·6	8·7	10·1	16·3	24·8	27·6	30·2	33·4
18	7·0	8·2	9·4	10·9	17·3	26·0	28·9	31·5	34·8
19	7·6	8·9	10·1	11·7	18·3	27·2	30·1	32·9	36·2
20	8·3	9·6	10·9	12·4	19·3	28·4	31·4	34·2	37·6
21	8·9	10·3	11·6	13·2	20·3	29·6	32·7	35·5	38·9
22	9·5	11·0	12·3	14·0	21·3	30·8	33·9	36·8	40·3
23	10·2	11·7	13·1	14·8	22·3	32·0	35·2	38·1	41·6
24	10·9	12·4	13·8	15·7	23·3	33·2	36·4	39·4	43·0
25	11·5	13·1	14·6	16·5	24·3	34·4	37·7	40·6	44·3
26	12·2	13·8	15·4	17·3	25·3	35·6	38·9	41·9	45·6
27	12·9	14·6	16·2	18·1	26·3	36·7	40·1	43·2	47·0
28	13·6	15·3	16·9	18·9	27·3	37·9	41·3	44·5	48·3
29	14·3	16·0	17·7	19·8	28·3	39·1	42·6	45·7	49·6
30	15·0	16·8	18·5	20·6	29·3	40·3	43·8	47·0	50·9

in rows corresponding to a value of f and in columns corresponding to a value of P. P denotes the probability that a value of χ^2 as big as or bigger than that observed can be obtained by random sampling if the hypothesis is correct. A large value of P, e.g., $P > 0{\cdot}05$ would incline us to accept the hypothesis and a small value concerning the hypothetical distribution of P, e.g., $P < 0{\cdot}05$ or $P < 0{\cdot}01$ would incline us to reject it. It should be observed that this test is a single tail test. This is because interest is concentrated on the chance of getting a value of χ^2 very much larger than the expected value.

Example 1. Test the significance of the value of χ^2 obtained from Table XXXVII.

CALCULATION OF f. The number of classes is 6, so that $s = 6$. The hypothesis asserts that on the average an equal number of results should be obtained in each class. There is one restriction, namely that the total of the theoretical frequencies should be the same as the total of the observed frequencies in the sample. This corresponds to one statistic calculated from the sample and therefore $r = 1$, so that

$$f = s - r = 6 - 1 = 5.$$

In Table XXXIX the value of χ^2 for $f = 5$ which lies on the 5% level of significance, is given by $\chi^2 = 11{\cdot}1$. The observed value ($9{\cdot}36$) is less than this, so that we conclude that the result is not significant of any real departure from the hypothesis that the die is unbiased: if the hypothesis is true the result could quite reasonably have occurred by chance.

For the fictitious example in Table XXXVI the value of $\chi^2 = 300$. Table XXXIX shows that for $f = 5$, $\chi^2 = 20{\cdot}5$ is below the 1% level of significance. The observed value, $\chi^2 = 300$ is very much greater than this and is clearly highly significant. This confirms the common-sense view of the results: in the one case, we should be prepared to accept the view that the die is unbiased; in the other case we should emphatically reject it.

Example 2. Four different makes of machine tool were tried at the same time over a period of some months and the number of recorded breakages for each type were 18, 12, 17, 15. Are there real differences between them in respect of breakage?

The hypothesis here is that there is no difference between the four types. There are altogether 62 recorded breakages, so that on the average the number of breakages for each type of tool would be $15\frac{1}{2}$, if the hypothesis were correct. (Half a breakage may seem fanciful, but it should not present any difficulty: $15\frac{1}{2}$ is an average figure in the same way that $3\frac{1}{2}$ is the average score in throwing a die.)

Here $s = 4$, and the only use made of the sample is to ensure that the total number of theoretical breakages agrees with the sample total of 62. Therefore, $r = 1$ and $f = 3$.

The calculation of χ^2 is set out in the usual tabular form:

Type of tool	n_s	ν_s	$\nu_s - n_s$	$\dfrac{(\nu_s - n_s)^2}{\nu_s}$
A	18	15·5	−2·5	0·40
B	12	15·5	3·5	0·79
C	17	15·5	−1·5	0·15
D	15	15·5	0·5	0·02
Total	62	62	0	1·36 ($= \chi^2$)

The 5% value of χ^2 for $f = 3$ is 7·8; the hypothesis is not rejected and this result is not significant of any real differences between the machine tools in respect of breakage.

Example 3. In Table I, page 9, the results are given of a card drawing experiment. The theoretical frequencies shown in the table were calculated on the hypothesis that any sample of three cards is equally likely. What is the significance of the experimental results?

In applying the χ^2 test an important restriction must be made. No class frequency should be less than 10, otherwise the test becomes inaccurate. When a class frequency is less than 10, it should be combined with an adjacent class. For this reason, classes corresponding to $x = 6, 7$ and $x = 26, 27$ have been combined in the following table.

x	n_s	ν_s	$\nu_s - n_s$	$\dfrac{(\nu_s - n_s)^2}{\nu_s}$
6 and 7	8	10	2	0·40
8	10	10	0	0·00
9	22	15	−7	3·27
10	12	20	8	3·20
11	19	25	6	1·44
12	45	35	−10	2·86
13	36	40	4	0·40
14	50	45	−5	0·56
15	54	50	−4	0·32
16	53	50	−3	0·18
17	51	50	−1	0·02
18	43	50	7	0·98
19	44	45	1	0·02
20	40	40	0	0·00
21	30	35	5	0·71
22	24	25	1	0·04
23	16	20	4	0·80
24	17	15	−2	0·27
25	11	10	−1	0·10
26 and 27	15	10	−5	2·50
Totals	600	600	0	18·07 ($= \chi^2$)

There are 20 classes and one statistic, namely the total 600, has been calculated from the sample, so that $f = 20 - 1 = 19$. Therefore $\chi^2 = 18 \cdot 07$, $f = 19$. From Table XXXIX the 5% level of χ^2 is $30 \cdot 1$, and therefore the result is not significant.

If the result had been significant it would have indicated that the samples of cards were not true random samples and that there must have been some bias in shuffling the cards or selecting the samples.

Example 4. In a biochemical experiment 20 insects were put into each of 100 jars and were subjected to a fumigant. After three hours the number of living insects in each jar was counted. The distribution is shown. Can this distribution be fitted by a Binomial distribution?

More specifically, is it reasonable to suppose that the probability of an insect being alive after three hours is the same for all insects and equal to p, say, so that the probability of having r survivors in a particular jar is $^{20}C_r p^r (1 - p)^{20-r}$? If this is true the expected number of jars having r survivors will be $100 \, ^{20}C_r \, p^r \, (1 - p)^{20-r}$

No. insects alive, x,	0	1	2	3	4	5	6	7	8	9	Total
No. of jars, n,	3	8	11	15	16	14	12	11	9	1	100

The total number of insects subjected to the poison was $20 \times 100 = 2,000$ and of these the number of survivors was $\Sigma nx = 439$.

If every insect had an equal chance of surviving, then that chance is given by $p = \dfrac{439}{2,000} = 0 \cdot 2195$. Therefore, if a Binomial distribution fits the data it will be

$$100 (0 \cdot 7805 + 0 \cdot 2195)^{20},$$

and the theoretical frequencies will be given by the expansion of this namely $100 (0 \cdot 7805)^{20}$, $100 \times 20 (0 \cdot 7805)^{19} (0 \cdot 2195)$, etc. These theoretical frequencies are shown in Table XL together with the calculation of χ^2.

TABLE XL

CALCULATION OF χ^2. BIOLOGICAL DATA

x	n_8		ν_8		$\nu_8 - n_8$	$\dfrac{(\nu_8 - n_8)^2}{\nu_8}$
0	3 ⎫		0·7 ⎫			
1	8 ⎬ 22		4·0 ⎬ 15·3		−6·7	2·93
2	11 ⎭		10·6 ⎭			
3	15		17·8		2·8	0·44
4	16		21·3		5·3	1·32
5	14		19·2		5·2	1·41
6	12		13·5		1·5	0·17
7	11 ⎫		7·6 ⎫			
8	9 ⎪		3·5 ⎪			
9	1 ⎬ 21		1·3 ⎬ 12·9		−8·1	5·09
10	0 ⎪		0·4 ⎪			
11	0 ⎭		0·1 ⎭			
Totals	100		100		0	11·36 ($= \chi^2$)

Note that classes with frequencies less than 10 have been combined with adjacent classes.

After grouping the data to ensure that no class contains less than 10, there are 6 frequency classes left, so that $s = 6$. In this example two statistics have been calculated from the sample: the total, 100, and the estimated value of p which was found to be 0·2195. In this case $r = 2$ and $f = s - r$ = 4. For $f = 4$, the 5% value of χ^2 is 9·5, and therefore the result is significant. In other words, the Binomial distribution does not give an adequate fit to the observed data.

Example 5.   A list of wars of modern civilisation (Prof. Quincey Wright *A Study of War,* 1942) provides the following data for the years A.D. 1500 to 1931:

No. of outbreaks in the year	0	1	2	3	4	5	Total
No. of such years	223	142	48	15	4	0	432

Fit a Poisson distribution to the data and test for goodness of fit.

The mean number a of outbreaks per year is given by $432a = [0 \times 223 +1 \times 142 + .. + 4 \times 0]$ so that $a = 299/432 = 0·69$. The theoretical frequencies can be calculated from the Poisson chart in the following way.

No. of outbreaks X	Proportion of outbreaks not less than X $P(x \geqslant X)$	Proportion of exactly X outbreaks $P(X) = P(x \geqslant X) - P(x \geqslant X + 1)$	Theoretical frequency $432\,P(X)$
0	1·00	0·53	229
1	0·47	0·35	151
2	0·12	0·08	35
3	0·04	0·035	15
4	0·005	0·005	2
>4	0·000		
Totals		1·000	432

By this method the theoretical frequencies have been calculated using the Poisson chart and care must be taken to get as accurate a reading as possible. An alternative and more accurate method would be to calculate successive values of the Poisson frequencies given by the expression

$$p = 432e^{-0·69}\,(0·69)^x/x!$$

x	p
0	216·7 [$= 432e^{-0·69}$]
1	149·5 [$= 216·7 \times 0·69$]
2	51·5 [$= 149·5 \times (0·69/2)$]
3	11·8 [$= 51·5 \times (0·69/3)$]
4	2·0 [$= 11·8 \times (0·69/4)$]
Total	431·5

The terms in brackets show how the results may be obtained by successive multiplications without too much work. The total is not exactly 432 as it should be, owing to small errors of rounding off. The discrepancy is not important but to bring the observed and theoretical totals into line 216·7, 149·5 and 11·8 will be rounded up and 51·5 will be rounded down to make the observed and theoretical totals exactly equal. This arbitrary procedure could be avoided by carrying the calculations to more places of decimals, but this is not really necessary.

To calculate χ^2, classes $x = 3, 4$ must be combined:

x	n_8	v_8	$v_8 - n_8$	$\dfrac{(v_8 - n_8)^2}{v_8}$
0	223	217	−6	0·17
1	142	150	8	0·43
2	48	51	3	0·18
3 and over	19	14	−5	1·79
Totals	432	432	0	2·57 ($= \chi^2$)

There are four classes used in the calculation of χ^2. Two statistics, namely the total and the mean, a, have been calculated from the observed data and therefore the number of degrees of freedom is given by $f = 4 - 2 = 2$. For $f = 2$, the 5% value of χ^2 is 6·0, and therefore the calculated value is not significant and the Poisson distribution gives a satisfactory fit to the data.

Example 6. Table XXIII, p. 115, gives the distribution of heights of adult males. The mean and standard deviation calculated from the data are

$$\bar{x} = 67·52,$$

$$s = 2·57.$$

Calculate the theoretical class frequencies given by the Normal distribution with the same mean and standard deviation, and test for goodness of fit.

As described in section 6.1, the class limits are $56\frac{15}{8}$, $57\frac{15}{8}$, $58\frac{15}{8}$, and so on. To obtain the theoretical frequencies corresponding to each class value, it will be necessary to calculate the areas of the normal curve within each pair of class limits ($56\frac{15}{8}$–$57\frac{15}{8}$, $57\frac{15}{8}$–$58\frac{15}{8}$, etc.) and then to multiply the areas by the total frequency 8,585. The area of the theoretical Normal curve corresponding to a particular class must equal the area of the histogram on the same class interval as base.

In Chapter VI it was sufficient for the purpose of that chapter to assume that the class limits were exactly 57, 58 . . ., etc. On this assumption the mean was found to be 67·52 ins. In the process of calculating the theoretical Normal frequencies it is important to use the correct class limits. The correct value for the mean is therefore less than 67·52 by $\frac{1}{16}$

$$\text{or } x = 67\cdot52 - 0\cdot06 = 67\cdot46 \text{ ins.}$$

The value of the standard deviation is unaltered so that $s = 2\cdot57$ ins.

The calculation of a theoretical class frequency will be shown in detail for one interval $(57\frac{15}{16}-58\frac{15}{16})$ and then the work will be completed in tabular form.

Theoretical frequency in class $(56\frac{15}{16}-57\frac{15}{16})$

To find the area to the right of the ordinate at $x = 56\frac{15}{16}$ calculate d where

$$d = \frac{x - \bar{x}}{s} = \frac{(57 - \frac{1}{16}) - (67\cdot52 - \frac{1}{16})}{s}$$

$$= \frac{57 - 67\cdot52}{2\cdot57} = -\frac{10\cdot52}{2\cdot57} = -4\cdot093$$

$$P(d \geqslant -4\cdot09) = 1\cdot0000$$

Since $P(d \geqslant -D) = 1 - P(d \geqslant D)$. See Fig. 38.)

For the area to the right of the ordinate at $x = 57\frac{15}{16}$

$$d = \frac{58 - 67\cdot52}{2\cdot57} = -3\cdot704$$

and $P(d \geqslant -3\cdot70) = 0\cdot9999$

The area between these class limits is therefore

$$1\cdot0000 - 0\cdot9999 = 0\cdot0001,$$

and the required theoretical frequency is given by

$$= 8{,}585 \times 0\cdot0001 = 0\cdot9$$

The work can be done most conveniently in tabular form and is greatly simplified if use is made of the fact that successive values of d differ by $\frac{1}{s} = \frac{1}{2\cdot57}$, since x increases by steps of 1. For example, $-4\cdot09 + \frac{1}{2\cdot57} = -4\cdot09 + 0\cdot389 = -3\cdot704$.

$x + \frac{1}{16}$	$D = \dfrac{x - \bar{x}}{s}$	$P(d \geqslant D)$	Area in cells A	Theoretical frequencies $\nu s = 8{,}585\,A$
57	−4·093	1·0000	0·0001	1
58	−3·704	0·9999	0·0004	3
59	−3·315	0·9995	0·0013	11
60	−2·926	0·9982	0·0038	33
61	−2·537	0·9944	0·0103	88
62	−2·148	0·9841	0·0234	201
63	−1·759	0·9607	0·0460	395
64	−1·370	0·9147	0·0780	670
65	−0·981	0·8367	0·1136	975
66	−0·592	0·7231	0·1426	1,224
67	−0·203	0·5805	0·1542	1,324
68	+0·186	0·4263	0·1437	1,234
69	0·575	0·2826	0·1131	971
70	0·964	0·1695	0·0815	700
71	1·353	0·0880	0·0473	406
72	1·742	0·0407	0·0241	207
73	2·131	0·0166	0·0107	92
74	2·520	0·0059	0·0041	35
75	2·909	0·0018	0·0013	11
76	3·298	0·0005	0·0004	3
77	3·687	0·0001	0·0001	1
78	4·076	0·0000	0·0000	0
79	4·465	0·0000		
		Totals	1·0000	8,585

There are some points about the construction of the table which should be remembered:

(1) The second column is calculated by working out the leading entry − 4·10, and then adding $\frac{1}{s} = 0·389$ to obtain the next entry, and repeating the addition for each successive entry. In this way, 0·389 is added 22 times. Had $\frac{1}{s}$ been written down to four figures it would have been 0·3891. There is therefore an accumulative error of + 0·0001 which, multiplied by 22, becomes + 0·0022. Thus, the last entry in the column should be 4·467. This is a small error and does not materially affect the results. If the results were affected, $\frac{1}{s}$ should be calculated to four decimal places.

(2) The column $P(d \geqslant D)$ is read directly from Table XXVI. Simple interpolation is used where it is necessary.

(3) The area in each cell is obtained by successive subtractions in the preceeding column. Thus $0 \cdot 0001 = 1 \cdot 0000 - 0 \cdot 9999$; $0 \cdot 0004 = 0 \cdot 9999 - 0 \cdot 9995$; $0 \cdot 0012 = 0 \cdot 9995 - 0 \cdot 9983$, and so on.

(4) In this example, the sum of the theoretical frequencies happens to come to 8,585. It might have been 8,584 or 8,586 due to small rounding off errors in the individual frequencies and would not be very serious. It is permissible if necessary to adjust the total by altering one or more of the larger frequencies (for example, at $x = 67\frac{15}{16}$).

It remains now to calculate χ^2 in the usual way, noting that some classes in each tail have to be grouped together.

$x + \frac{1}{16}$	n_8	ν_8	$\nu_8 - n_8$	$\dfrac{(\nu_8 - n_8)^2}{\nu_8}$
59 and less	20	15	-5	1·67
60	41	33	-8	1·94
61	83	88	5	0·28
62	169	201	32	5·09
63	394	395	1	0·00
64	669	670	1	0·00
65	990	975	-15	0·23
66	1,223	1,224	1	0·00
67	1,329	1,324	-5	0·02
68	1,230	1,234	4	0·01
69	1,063	971	-92	8·72
70	646	700	54	4·17
71	392	406	14	0·48
72	202	207	5	0·12
73	79	92	13	1·84
74	32	35	3	0·26
75 and over	23	15	-8	4·27
Totals	8,585	8,585	0	29·10 ($= \chi^2$)

The number of classes used in the calculation of χ^2 is 17. There were three statistics calculated from the observed data to fit the theoretical distribution, namely the total frequency (8,585), the mean and the standard deviation.

$$\text{Therefore,} f = 17 - 3 = 14.$$

From the table of χ^2, the 5% significance level for $f = 14$ is 23·7 and the 1% value is 29·1. The calculated result is therefore just not significant at the 1% level but it is significant at the 5% level. The Normal curve appears to give only a moderately satisfactory fit to the observed data.

EXERCISES XXXV

1. Four coins were tossed simultaneously and the number of heads occurring at each throw was noted. This was repeated 240 times with the following results:

No. of heads	0	1	2	3	4	Total
No. of throws	13	64	85	58	20	240

On the assumption that all the coins have an equal chance of coming down heads or tails, calculate the theoretical distribution from the Binomial expansion of $240(\frac{1}{2} + \frac{1}{2})^4$. Test the results for goodness of fit.

2. Carry out the experiment described in Ex. 1. (Use more throws than 240 if it is convenient) and test the results for goodness of fit on the same assumption.

3. Table XVIII, on page 97 gives the observed and theoretical results of an experiment in drawing marbles. Test the results for goodness of fit. (Treat classes $x = 5, 6, 7$ and 8 as one group.)

4. Test the goodness of fit of the calculated Poisson frequencies to the data of Ex. XVI, 5.

5. The following table shows the number of accidents to 647 women working on H.E. shells in 5 weeks and also the theoretical distribution given by (a) the Poisson, (b) Negative Binomial distributions.

No. accidents	Observed frequency	Theoretical (Poisson)	Theoretical (Negative Binomial)
0	447	405	441
1	132	189	140
2	42	45	45
3	21	7	14
4	3	1	5
5	2	0	2
Totals	647	647	647

Test these distributions for goodness of fit given the fact that the mean and total were calculated in order to fit the Poisson distribution while the mean, standard deviation and total were calculated to fit the negative Binomial.

6. The following data shows suicides of women in eight German states during fourteen years (Bortkiewicz, 1898):

No. of suicides in a State per year	0	1	2	3	4	5	6	7	8	9	10	Total
Observed frequency	9	19	17	20	15	11	8	2	3	5	3	112

Fit a Poisson distribution to the data, and show that the theoretical frequencies are:

No. of suicides	0	1	2	3	4	5	6
Theoretical frequency	3·5	12·1	21·0	24·3	21·1	14·6	8·5

No. of suicides	7	8	9	10	Total
Theoretical frequency	4·2	1·8	0·7	0·2	112·0

Combining groups 0 and 1, and groups 6 and over, show that the fit is not satisfactory.

7. The following table shows the distribution of digits chosen at random from the London Telephone Directory. Show that it is unlikely to have arisen from a population in which all digits occurred equally frequently.

Digit	0	1	2	3	4	5	6	7	8	9	Total
Frequency	1,026	1,107	997	966	1,075	933	1,107	972	964	853	10,000

8. Mendel obtained the following frequencies for different kinds of seeds in crosses from plants with round yellow seeds and wrinkled green seeds. Round and yellow, 315; wrinkled and yellow, 101; round and green, 108; wrinkled and green, 32. The Mendelian theory of inheritance states that the frequencies should be in the ratio 9 : 3 : 3 : 1. Test the hypothesis by calculating χ^2.

9. Twelve dice were thrown and a 5 or 6 was counted as a success. The number of successes in each throw was noted. This experiment was repeated 26,306 times (Weldon's data) with the following results:

No. of successes	Observed frequency	No. of successes	Observed frequency
0	185	6	3,067
1	1,149	7	1,331
2	3,265	8	403
3	5,475	9	105
4	6,114	10	18
5	5,194		
		Total	26,306

Does the Binomial expansion $26,306 \left(\frac{2}{3} + \frac{1}{3}\right)^{12}$ give a satisfactory fit?

10. In Ex. 9 calculate p, the chance of a success from the data. Does the Binomial expansion $26,306 (p + q)^{12}$ give a satisfactory fit?

11. In a practical examination in physics, 352 candidates determined a value for the gravitational constant g, using an ordinary pendulum. Fit a Normal curve to the data and test for goodness of fit.

Mid-class value	31·5	31·6	31·7	31·8	31·9	32·0	32·1
Observed frequency	3	8	17	24	42	61	78

Mid-class value	32·2	32·3	32·4	32·5	32·6	Total
Observed frequency	56	31	21	9	2	352

12. The records of an insurance company provided the following results for a selected class of policy holders:

Age in years	Deaths in each age group	Age in years	Deaths in each age group
0 –	2	45 –	51
5 –	0	50 –	29
10 –	4	55 –	18
15 –	15	60 –	11
20 –	21	65 –	7
25 –	84	70 –	3
30 –	96	75 –	2
35 –	82	80 –	1
40 –	48		
		Total	474

Fit a Normal distribution to the data and test for goodness of fit.

10.2 Contingency Tables

Sometimes data are best presented in the form of a contingency table. If a contingency table consists of m rows and n columns, it is then called an $m \times n$ contingency table. An illustration of a 4×3 contingency table is given by the following investigation. Four hundred and ninety-two candidates for scientific posts gave particulars of their university degrees and their hobbies. The degrees were in either maths, chemistry or physics, and the hobbies could be classified roughly as music, craftswork, reading or drama. Every candidate therefore represents one degree and one hobby, and the data can be presented concisely in a table, as follows:

	Maths.	Chemistry	Physics	Totals
Music	24	83	17	124
Craftswork	11	62	28	101
Reading	32	121	34	187
Drama	10	26	44	80
Totals	77	292	123	492

The totals of the rows show the number of candidates who expressed a preference for each hobby, and the column totals show the number with each type of degree. The sum of the row totals and the sum of the column totals are, of course, each equal to the total number of candidates. The table shows readily the division of hobbies and degrees amongst the different candidates. For example, 24 with mathematical degrees liked music, 121 with chemistry degrees liked reading, and so on.

The following questions may arise when examining this table. The proportion of mathematical candidates is $77/492 = 0.16$, while in that group of candidates who have music as their hobby the proportion of mathematical candidates is $24/124 = 0.19$. Does this indicate that music lovers are more likely to have mathematical degrees than people interested in other hobbies? Again, the proportion of those candidates who prefer reading is $187/492 = 0.38$, while the proportion of those candidates with physics degrees who prefer reading is $34/123 = 0.28$. Does this indicate that physicists are less likely to be fond of reading than those with other degrees? If such tendencies do exist, there is said to be an *association* between degrees and hobbies. The table of χ^2 can be used to test the significance of the association.

THE CALCULATION OF THEORETICAL FREQUENCIES IN THE CONTINGENCY TABLE ON THE ASSUMPTION OF NO ASSOCIATION. Imagine the 492 candidates as a sample from a large population. Then the probability of obtaining a mathematical candidate is estimated by $77/492$. Again, the probability of obtaining a musical candidate is $124/492$. Therefore, if these two probabilities are independent, the chance of getting a candidate who has a mathematical degree and whose hobby is music is $\dfrac{77}{492} \times \dfrac{124}{492}$. The point about independence should be carefully noted. It means that the fact of a candidate having a mathematical degree has no influence on his chance of having music as a hobby, and vice versa. Finally, if the probability of a musical and mathematical candidate is $\dfrac{77}{492} \times \dfrac{124}{492}$, then the expected number in a sample of 492 is $492 \times \dfrac{77}{492} \times \dfrac{124}{492} = \dfrac{77 \times 124}{492}$

$= 19.4$. All the other cells in the contingency table can be filled in with theoretical frequencies in the same way.

CONTINGENCY TABLE.   THEORETICAL FREQUENCIES

	Mathematics	Chemistry	Physics	Total
Music	$\dfrac{77 \times 124}{492} = 19.4$	$\dfrac{292 \times 124}{492} = 73.6$	$\dfrac{123 \times 124}{492} = 31.0$	124
Craftswork	$\dfrac{77 \times 101}{492} = 15.8$	$\dfrac{292 \times 101}{492} = 59.9$	$\dfrac{123 \times 101}{492} = 25.3$	101
Reading	$\dfrac{77 \times 187}{492} = 29.3$	$\dfrac{292 \times 187}{492} = 111.0$	$\dfrac{123 \times 187}{492} = 46.7$	187
Drama	$\dfrac{77 \times 80}{492} = 12.5$	$\dfrac{292 \times 80}{492} = 47.5$	$\dfrac{123 \times 80}{492} = 20.0$	80
Totals	77	292	123	492

It remains now to calculate χ^2 in the usual way:

n_s	ν_s	$\nu_s - n_s$	$\dfrac{(\nu_s - n_s)^2}{\nu_s}$
24	19·4	− 4·6	1·09
83	73·6	− 9·4	1·20
17	31·0	14·0	6·32
11	15·8	4·8	1·46
62	59·9	− 2·1	0·07
28	25·3	− 2·7	0·29
32	29·3	− 2·7	0·25
121	111·0	−10·0	0·90
34	46·7	12·7	3·45
10	12·5	2·5	0·50
26	47·5	21·5	9·73
44	20·0	−24·0	28·80
Totals	492	492	54·06 $(= \chi^2)$

CALCULATION OF f, THE NUMBER OF DEGREES OF FREEDOM FOR A $m \times n$ CONTINGENCY TABLE. In the example we are considering, there are 4×3 frequency groups and, therefore, $s = 12$. The theoretical contingency table was constructed so that the row totals, the column totals and the grand total remained unaltered. It might appear therefore that $(4 + 3 + 1)$ statistics are calculated from the sample, but this is not the case. If the grand total and any three row totals are known, the fourth row total is also known, since it is the difference between the grand total and the other three. For example, knowing that the grand total is 492 and that three of the row totals are 124, 101 and 187, the remaining row total is clearly $492 - 124 - 101 - 187 = 80$. Similarly, the number of column totals which need to be known together with the grand total is 2. Therefore, the essential information from the sample is embodied in three row totals, two column totals and one grand total, so that $r = 3 + 2 + 1 = 6$.

Therefore $f = s - r = 6$.

A very simple result appears for the general case. For a $m \times n$ table, the number of frequency groups is $s = mn$. To construct the theoretical contingency table $(m - 1)$ row totals, $(n - 1)$ column totals and the grand total must be known, so that

$$r = (m - 1) + (n - 1) + 1 = m + n - 1, \text{ and } f = s - r =$$
$$mn - m - n + 1 = (m - 1)(n - 1).$$

Therefore, the number of degrees of freedom for a $m \times n$ table is given by $f = (m - 1)(n - 1)$. In the example considered, $\chi^2 = 54·06$ and $f = (4 - 1)(3 - 1) = 6$.

The 1% level of χ^2 for six degrees of freedom is 16·8 and therefore the result is highly significant and we conclude that the two criteria of classification are not independent. Having established the significance of the result, it is easy to see that the two major contributions to χ^2 come from the Physics-Drama group (28·80) and the Chemistry-Drama group (9·73).

Example 1.   The following data shows the effect of vitamin B deficiency on the sex-ratio of the offspring of rats. Is the effect significant?

	Males	Females	*Totals*
Vitamin B deficient	123	153	276
Vitamin B sufficient	145	150	295
Totals	268	303	571

This is an example of a 2 × 2 table. The theoretical frequencies on the assumption of independence are given by the ratios $\dfrac{268 \times 276}{571}$, etc.:

	Males	Females	*Totals*
Vitamin B deficient	$\dfrac{268 \times 276}{571} = 129\cdot5$	$\dfrac{303 \times 276}{571} = 146\cdot5$	276
Vitamin B sufficient	$\dfrac{268 \times 295}{571} = 138\cdot5$	$\dfrac{303 \times 295}{571} = 156\cdot5$	295
Totals	268	303	571

It will be observed that, having calculated one theoretical frequency, the others can be filled in by subtraction from row and column totals. Thus, having calculated $\dfrac{268 \times 276}{571} = 129\cdot5$, the others are given by $276 - 129\cdot5 = 146\cdot5$; $268 - 129\cdot5 = 138\cdot5$, and $295 - 138\cdot5 = 303 - 146\cdot5 = 156\cdot5$.

χ^2 can be calculated in the usual way:

n_s	v_s	$v_s - n_s$	$\dfrac{(v_s - n_s)^2}{v_s}$
123	129·5	+6·5	0·33
153	146·5	−6·5	0·29
145	138·5	−6·5	0·31
150	156·5	+6·5	0·27
Totals 571	571	0	1·20 $(= \chi^2)$

Here $f = (2 - 1)(2 - 1) = 1$.

The 5% value of χ^2 for one degree of freedom is 3·8 and therefore the result is not significant. There is no evidence of association between vitamin B deficiency and sex of rats' offspring.

Example 2. The following tables gives the numbers of boys and girls whose hair colour falls into five different groups. Is there any evidence of association between hair colour and sex?

	Fair	Red	Medium	Dark	Jet Black	*Totals*
Boys	592	119	849	504	36	2,100
Girls	544	97	677	451	14	1,783
Totals	1,136	216	1,526	955	50	3,883

This is an example of a $2 \times n$ contingency table. The theoretical frequencies can be calculated most easily by working out $\dfrac{1,136 \times 2,100}{3,883} =$ 614·4, and then subtracting it from 1,136, to give 521·6. These are the two theoretical frequencies for the "Fair" column. This is repeated for the other columns and the calculation of χ^2 shows the results.

Hair colour	Sex	n_s	v_s	$v_s - n_s$	$\dfrac{(v_s - n_s)^2}{v_s}$
Fair	{ Boys	592	614·4	+22·4	0·82
	Girls	544	521·6	−22·4	0·96
Red	{ Boys	119	116·8	− 2·2	0·04
	Girls	97	99·2	+ 2·2	0·05
Medium	{ Boys	849	825·3	−23·7	0·68
	Girls	677	700·7	+23·7	0·80
Dark	{ Boys	504	516·5	+12·5	0·30
	Girls	451	438·5	−12·5	0·36
Jet Black	{ Boys	36	27·0	− 9·0	3·00
	Girls	14	23·0	+ 9·0	3·52
	Totals	3,883		0	10·53 (= χ^2)

$$f = (2 - 1)(5 - 1) = 4.$$

The 5% value of χ^2 is 9·5, and the 1% value is 13·3, so the result is significant on the 5% level. We may conclude that there is evidence of association between sex and hair colour, particularly as regards "Jet Black" hair which appears to be associated with boys rather than with girls.

SUMMARY OF CHAPTER X

1. If n_r denote the observed frequencies in s class intervals ($r = 1$, $2 \ldots s$) and v_r denote the corresponding frequencies based on some specified hypothetical distribution then χ^2 is defined as

$$\chi^2 = \Sigma_1^s \frac{(v_r - n_r)^2}{v_r}$$

2. The null hypothesis is that the specified hypothetical distribution can account for the observed class frequencies. If χ^2 is large this implies that the differences between the observed and theoretical class frequencies in some or all of the intervals are large and the null hypothesis may be rejected.

3. If r statistics have been calculated to specify the hypothetical distribution and there are s class intervals then the number of degrees of freedom is given by $f = s - r$.

Table XXXIX gives values of χ^2 arranged in rows corresponding to values of f and in columns corresponding to the probability of a value of χ^2 as big or bigger than the entry in the table.

4. In a $m \times n$ contingency table the number of degrees of freedom is given by $f = (m - 1)(n - 1)$.

EXERCISES XXXVI

1. (Greenwood and Yule's data for typhoid.)

	Attacked	Not attacked	*Totals*
Inoculated	56	6,759	6,815
Not inoculated	272	11,396	11,668
Totals	328	18,155	18,483

Determine whether or not typhoid attack is independent of inoculation.

2. Show that for the contingency table of the general type:

	A	Not-A	*Totals*
B	a	b	a + b
Not-B	c	d	c + d
Totals	a + c	b + d	a + b + c + d

$$\chi^2 = \frac{(ad - bc)^2 (a + b + c + d)}{(a + b)(c + d)(a + c)(b + d)}$$

Check the value of χ^2 in Ex. 1 by using this expression.

3. (Brownlee's data on severity of smallpox attack.) For 1,689 cases of smallpox the severity of attack was noted as "very severe, severe, moderate or light", and the number of years which had elapsed since vaccination was also recorded. The data is shown in the following table. Determine whether there is any association between severity of attack and years elapsed since vaccination.

Severity of Attack

Years since Vaccination	Very severe	Severe	Moderate	Light	*Totals*
0–25	43	120	176	148	487
25–45	184	299	268	181	932
over 45	46	48	33	28	155
Unvaccinated	65	41	7	2	115
Totals	338	508	484	359	1,689

4. The numbers of fiction and non-fiction books issued by a library on six days of a week are given below. Is there any evidence that the proportion of fiction to non-fiction is associated with the day of the week?

	Mon.	Tues.	Wed.	Thurs.	Fri.	Sat.	*Totals*
Fiction	813	1,238	1,823	673	721	2,634	7,902
Non-Fiction	87	149	165	72	98	438	1,009
Totals	900	1,387	1,988	745	819	3,072	8,911

5. Sulphate content of boiler water may have some effect on the cracking of boiler plates. Test the following data which was collected to examine this possibility.

SO_4 (p.p.m.)	0	200	400	600
Uncracked	37	43	26	44
Cracked	12	30	19	15

(Weir, *Trans. A.S.M.E.*, April 1948.)

6. Test the following data to see if there is a significant association between the origin of the accident and the year.

Accidents due to Gassing by Carbon Monoxide

	1941	1942	1943
At blast furnaces	24	20	19
At gas producers	28	34	41
At gas works and coke ovens	26	26	10
In distribution and use of gas	80	108	123
Miscellaneous sources	68	51	32
Totals	226	239	225

(M. of Labour, *Memo. on CO Poisoning*, 1945.)

7. The following data was collected to determine whether the age of divers working in caissons had any effect on the number who were injured by exposure to compressed air. What is your conclusion?

Ages	Number of men examined and passed	Number of men taken ill
15–20	55	0
20–25	145	15
25–30	152	37
30–35	91	19
35–40	61	14
40–45	38	10
45–50	5	3

Hill & Greenwood. *Proc. Roy. Soc., Series B, Vol.* 80 (1908), *p.* 13.

CHAPTER XI
Planning Statistical Experiments

11.1 Experimental Design

Experiments are carried out in order to test the validity of a hypothesis or to estimate the magnitude of an effect. The physician who suspects that some hitherto untried drug will have a beneficial effect in the treatment of a disease will, if he is scientifically trained, frame his enquiry in terms of some suitable hypothesis and will then design an experiment to test this hypothesis. Claims of advances in our knowledge of natural phenomena are not readily allowed by scientists until the evidence has been subjected to a penetrating examination. Every detail of the experiment will be scrupulously examined by critics who are eager to expose any fault in the experiment which may invalidate the conclusions. Indeed, in some cases this attitude of scepticism may be carried too far. R. A. Fisher says: "The other type of criticism to which experimental results are exposed is that the experiment itself was ill-designed, or, of course, badly executed. If we suppose that the experimenter did what he intended to do, both of these points come down to the question of the *design*, or the logical structure of the experiment. This type of criticism is usually made by what I might call a heavy weight *authority*. Prolonged experience, or at least the long possession of a scientific reputation, is almost a prerequisite for this line of attack. Technical details are seldom in evidence. The authoritative assertion 'His *controls* are *totally* inadequate' must have temporarily discredited many a promising line of work."*

The inadequacy of controls is now perhaps a less frequent source of error than it used to be. The type of oversight which can occur is illustrated by the following example. In an experiment to determine the lethality of a fumigant against grain weevils fumigant No. 3 gave a mortality of 85% compared with 68% for a standard fumigant under supposedly similar experimental conditions. This showed an apparent improvement of 17%. It was discovered, however, that the weevils subjected to fumigant No. 3 were of a different generation from the weevils which had been tested with the standard fumigant. This immediately cast doubt on the result of the experiment since the two sets of weevils would be quite likely to have different characteristic resistances to the fumigants. When the experiment was

---

* FISHER, R. A. *The Design of Experiments* (Edinburgh, 1946), *p*. 2.

repeated on a single generation of grain weevils the results gave a mortality of 78% for fumigant No. 3 and 70% for the standard fumigant—a very much smaller improvement in favour of the new fumigant.

Another example of inadequate experimental design is the case of the farmer who wanted to compare the different effects of two fertilisers on the yield of wheat. To do this he dressed one half of a twenty-acre field with fertiliser A and the other half with fertiliser B, sowed his wheat and measured the respective yields at harvest time The fault here lies in the fact that over such a large field there are almost certain to be considerable variations in the natural fertility of the soil. There may be a fertility gradient, or increase in fertility, from one half of the field to the other and, if this is so, any difference in the two yields will not be due to differences between the fertilisers alone. The experiment, as it is designed, provides no means of estimating and allowing for such a fertility gradient in the comparison between the two fertilisers. Another incidental weakness in this design is that with only one measurement for each fertiliser there is no way of calculating the significance of any observed difference. An adequate design for this experiment will be described in a later section of this chapter under the heading of Latin Squares. It would be a useful exercise for the reader to consider now, before reading that section, how he would design the experiment.

The remainder of this chapter will deal with one or two experimental designs which occur frequently in statistical work. A full treatment of the statistical analysis of these designs is beyond the scope of this book, but some indication is given of how the data can be treated.

11.2   Comparison in Pairs

The advantage to be gained by careful experimental design is very well illustrated by the device of arrangement in pairs. The method can best be described by means of an actual experiment. When metal coated pipes are buried underground, they are subject to corrosion. An engineer wanted to discover whether there was any difference in the effects of corrosion on (1) lead coated steel pipe, and (2) bare steel pipe. To do this, twenty pairs of pipes were buried, each pair being buried in a characteristic type of soil. One member of each pair was lead coated steel pipe, while the other was bare steel pipe. The following results were obtained:

Soil type	Corrosion of lead coated steel pipe (x)	Corrosion of bare steel pipe (y)
A	17	13
B	12	26
C	15	23
D	22	21
E	3	8
F	2	10
G	5	16
H	11	14
I	18	9
J	22	24
K	17	26
L	12	16
M	11	17
N	16	21
O	11	13
P	21	19
Q	19	32
R	18	20
S	23	12
T	20	27

$\bar{x}$, the average corrosion for the lead coated pipe, is 14·75, while $\bar{y}$ is 18·35. Carrying out the test for the significance of the difference of two means described in Chapter VII, we have:

$$\bar{y} - \bar{x} = 3·60$$

$$\Sigma(x - \bar{x})^2 = 743·75 \qquad \Sigma(y - \bar{y})^2 = 842·55$$

$$s^2 = \frac{\Sigma(x - \bar{x})^2 + \Sigma(y - \bar{y})^2}{n_1 + n_2 - 2} = \frac{1586·30}{38}$$

$$= 41·745$$

$$s^2\left(\frac{1}{n_1} + \frac{1}{n_2}\right) = \frac{s^2}{10} = 4·1745$$

Therefore standard deviation $(\bar{y} - \bar{x}) = \sqrt{4·1745} = 2·04$

$$d = \frac{\bar{y} - \bar{x}}{\text{Standard error of } (\bar{y} - \bar{x})} = \frac{3·60}{2·04} = 1·76$$

Since t is based on 38 degrees of freedom it will be sufficient to use the Normal probability table to find the significance level of the result.

The null hypothesis is that $\bar{x} = \bar{y}$. From Table XXVI, we find that $P(d \geqslant 1·76) = 0·078$. In other words, if the average corrosion of the two types of pipe were the same there would be a chance of 8 in 100 of obtaining the observed result. This is too large to be significant on the 5% level.

However, in this example it is possible to take advantage of the experimental design which will allow a slightly different statistical analysis to be applied to the results. The two pipes in each pair are exposed to the same soil type, so that any difference between the corrosions of members of a pair will be entirely due, apart from random error, to a difference in the resistance to corrosion of the two types of pipe. The twenty differences which can be calculated from the experimental data are therefore all direct measures of the difference in corrosion effect.

Soil type	Difference in corrosion effect ($d = y - x$)	Soil type	Difference in corrosion effect ($d = y - x$)
A	−4	K	9
B	14	L	4
C	8	M	6
D	−1	N	5
E	5	O	2
F	8	P	−2
G	11	Q	13
H	3	R	2
I	−9	S	−11
J	2	T	7

It is now possible to test whether these differences constitute a random sample from a population with zero mean. In other words, the null hypothesis, as before, states that no real difference in corrosion effect actually exists. This is tested in the usual way:

$$\bar{d} = 3 \cdot 60$$

$$\Sigma(d - \bar{d})^2 = 830 \cdot 8$$

$$s^2 = \frac{830 \cdot 8}{19} = 43 \cdot 726$$

$$\frac{s^2}{20} = 2 \cdot 1863$$

Therefore the standard error of $\bar{d} = \sqrt{2 \cdot 1863} = 1 \cdot 48$

$t = \dfrac{3 \cdot 60}{1 \cdot 48} = 2 \cdot 43$ based on 19 degrees of freedom and the

$P(t \geqslant 2 \cdot 43) = 0 \cdot 025$ or $2\frac{1}{2}\%$ (Table XXX).

This result indicates that there is a real difference between the corrosion of the two types of pipe. The reason for the different results obtained by these two methods of analysis is not hard to find. A glance at the original data shows that the different types of soil vary considerably in the amount of corrosion they produce. For example, soil type D produced a high corrosion in both types of pipe, whereas soil E had a relatively small effect. Now the standard error of $\bar{y} - \bar{x}$, calculated by the first method, includes this variation between soil types, whereas in the second method of analysis it has been eliminated by dealing with the differences between pairs. It has been pointed out that these differences are direct measures of the difference in corrosion for the two pipes, into which the variable effect of different types of soil does not enter.

This can be put in another way. Any measurement of corrosion can be expressed as the sum of three parts: (1) a part due to the soil type, which naturally varies from soil to soil, (2) a part due to the type of pipe coating, and (3) a random variation.

Thus, for soil type A, we can express this:

$$x_A = T_A + P_x + E_{Ax} \; ; \; y_A = T_A + P_y + E_{Ay}$$

where:

x_A and y_A are the corrosions for soil type A,

T_A is the part due to the soil type,

P_x and P_y are the parts due to the type of pipe coating,

E_{Ax} and E_{Ay} are the random errors.

Similar expressions can be written down for the other soil types; thus:

$$x_B = T_B + P_x + E_{Bx}; \; y_B = T_B + P_y + E_{By}.$$

Now the calculation of the standard error of $\bar{y} - \bar{x}$, based on the variances s_x^2 and s_y^2, must include the variation between the different soil types T_A, T_B, etc., and it is easy to see that this component of the variation can be eliminated by the second method of analysis which only treats differences, since:

$$d_A = y_A - x_A = P_y - P_x + (E_{Ay} - E_{Ax}),$$
$$d_B = y_B - x_B = P_y - P_x + (E_{By} - E_{Bx}),$$
$$\text{etc.}$$

The variance s_d^2 is based, therefore, only on the random errors of the measurements and any actual difference between the effects of the two types of coating and so, in general, can be expected to be smaller than the variance calculated by the first method. The experimental design which arranges the pipes in pairs allows this fact to be used in testing the significance of the difference between the two types of pipe coating.

Mathematical Note. Two sets of results (x, y) are collected in pairs:

x_1	y_1	$d_1 = x_1 - y_1$
x_2	y_2	$d_2 = x_2 - y_2$
.	.	. .
.	.	. .
.	.	. .
x_n	y_n	$d_n = x_n - y_n$

The mean difference is $\bar{d} = \bar{x} - \bar{y}$,

$$\text{since } d = \frac{1}{n} \sum_{r=1}^{n} d_r = \frac{1}{n} \sum_{r=1}^{n} (x_r - y_r)$$

$$= \frac{1}{n} \sum_{r=1}^{n} x_r - \frac{1}{n} \sum_{r=1}^{n} y_r$$

$$= \bar{x} - \bar{y}$$

It has been shown that the standard error of the mean difference can be calculated in two ways.

Method 1.

$$s^2 = \frac{\Sigma(x - \bar{x})^2 + \Sigma(y - \bar{y})^2}{2n - 2}$$

$$= \frac{\Sigma x^2 + \Sigma y^2 - \frac{1}{n}[(\Sigma x)^2 + (\Sigma y)^2]}{2(n - 1)}$$

Let s_1^2 denote the variance of the difference between the means calculated by the first method.

Then

$$s_1^2 = s^2\left(\frac{1}{n} + \frac{1}{n}\right) = \frac{2s^2}{n}$$

$$= \frac{\Sigma x^2 + \Sigma y^2 - \frac{1}{n}[(\Sigma x)^2 + (\Sigma y)^2]}{n(n - 1)}$$

Method 2. Let s_2^2 denote the variance of the mean difference calculated by the second method.

$$s_2^2 = \frac{s^2}{n}$$

where

$$s^2 = \frac{\Sigma(d - \bar{d})^2}{n - 1} = \frac{\Sigma d^2 - \frac{1}{n}(\Sigma d)^2}{n - 1}$$

$$= \frac{1}{n-1}\left[\Sigma(x - y)^2 - \frac{1}{n}\left\{\Sigma(x - y)\right\}^2\right]$$

After some reduction this gives

$$s_2^2 = \frac{1}{n(n-1)}\left[\Sigma x^2 + \Sigma y^2 - \frac{1}{n}(\Sigma x)^2 - \frac{1}{n}(\Sigma y)^2 - 2\left\{\Sigma xy - \frac{1}{n}(\Sigma x)(\Sigma y)\right\}\right]$$

$$= s_1^2 - \frac{2}{n(n-1)}\Sigma(x - \bar{x})(y - \bar{y})$$

$$= s_1^2 - \frac{2}{n}\frac{\Sigma(x-\bar{x})(y-\bar{y})}{\sqrt{\Sigma(x-\bar{x})^2 \Sigma(y-\bar{y})^2}}\sqrt{\frac{\Sigma(x-\bar{x})^2}{n-1} \cdot \frac{\Sigma(y-\bar{y})^2}{n-1}}$$

$$= s_1^2 - \frac{2}{n}r s_x s_y \tag{11.1}$$

where s_x and s_y are the sample standard deviations of x and y respectively, and r is the coefficient of correlation between x and y.

When r is positive equation 11.1 shows that s_2 is less than s_1 so that the second method gives a better chance of detecting a significant difference. When $r = 0$ the results of the two methods are equivalent. The deliberate design of an experiment so that results can be paired is a method which sometimes gives a positive correlation between the variables.

EXERCISES XXXVII

1. The total absence per month expressed as a percentage in two factories is as follows:

Month	Jan.	Feb.	March	April	May	June
Factory A	12	8	9	7	4	5
Factory B	15	10	9	8	3	6

Month	July	Aug.	Sept.	Oct.	Nov.	Dec.
Factory A	8	7	3	4	2	6
Factory B	8	9	5	3	3	11

Is there any reason to suppose that the rates of absenteeism at the two factories differ? Treat the monthly readings as pairs.

2. The acidity of a standard solution is measured by fifteen persons, each of whom makes two determinations using two different indicators. Test for the significance of the difference between the means, using both methods of analysis and stating the significance level in each case.

Indicator I	11·5	11·2	12·1	12·6	10·9	10·0	11·5	13·0
Indicator II	11·7	11·4	12·3	12·8	11·8	11·5	11·4	12·8

Indicator I		11·5	10·4	11·0	12·0	11·0	11·8	12·1
Indicator II		12·7	11·2	11·5	12·2	11·6	11·2	12·6

3. Two yields of dressed grain in bushels per acre are shown for twelve years, each year's yield coming from two different plots. Determine the significance of the difference in the means by both methods.

Year	Plot A	Plot B	Year	Plot A	Plot B
1955	29·62	33·00	1961	33·75	34·94
1956	32·38	36·91	1962	43·44	35·88
1957	43·75	44·84	1963	55·56	53·66
1958	37·56	38·94	1964	51·06	45·78
1959	30·00	34·66	1965	44·06	40·22
1960	32·62	27·72	1966	32·50	29·91

4. Using the data of Ex. 11.2, calculate $\dfrac{2}{n}rs_x s_y$ and verify the relationship:

$$s_2^2 = s_1^2 - \frac{2}{n}rs_x s_y$$

11.3 Difference Between Several Means

In Chapter VII we examined the problem of the significance of the difference between two means. The more general problem is to determine whether a group of means differ significantly amongst themselves. This is usually solved by a statistical calculation known as "analysis of variance". For the purpose of this book, however, a more elementary and less accurate test will be described which depends on the distribution of the range.

THE STANDARDISED RANGE. The range of a sample has been defined in Chapter III as the difference between the extreme values of the variable. If a random sample of n, taken from a Normal population with standard deviation σ, has a range R_n, then R_n/σ is known as the *standardised range*. If a large number of samples of n are taken the values of the standardised range will form a statistical distribution from which the significance of any observed result can be calculated. Table XLI shows, for different values of n, the values of R_n/σ which there is a 1% chance of exceeding.

TABLE XLI

n	2	3	4	5	6	7	8	9	10	11	12	16	2
The 1% value of R_n/σ	3·64	4·12	4·40	4·60	4·76	4·88	4·99	5·08	5·16	5·23	5·29	5·50	5·

Thus if a random sample of five is chosen from a normal population there is a chance of 1% that the standardised range will exceed 4·60.

Example 1. A random sample of seven has a range of 15·2. Is this consistent with the hypothesis that the sample is drawn from a normal population which has a standard deviation 2·8?

Here $n = 7$,

$R_7/\sigma = 5·4$.

On the hypothesis, Table XLI shows that there is a 1% chance of R_7/σ exceeding 4·88 so that the observed result is certainly significant on the 1% level and the hypothesis is rejected. The sample appears to be more variable than would be expected.

Example 2. Mica plates for wireless condensers are cut to a prescribed thickness by an automatic machine. The standard deviation for the thickness is alleged to be 0·0032 in. Four plates picked at random have the following thicknesses, 0·134 in., 0·130 in., 0·136 in., 0·147 in. What conclusion can be drawn?

$$R_4 = 0.147 - 0.130 = 0.017.$$

$$R_4/\sigma = \frac{0.017}{0.0032} = 5.3$$

For $n = 4$, the 1% point of R_4/σ is 4·40. There is evidence therefore that the thickness of the mica plates is more variable than would be represented by a standard deviation of 0·0032 in.

THE ANALYSIS FOR SEVERAL MEANS. The following data represents the breaking strength of starch films. There are six varieties of starch and ten results for each variety.

Breaking Strength (grams)

	Wheat Starch	Rice Starch	Dasheen Starch	Canna Starch	Corn Starch	Potato Starch
	496	557	380	792	398	983
	280	561	371	611	593	950
	213	520	430	863	306	1,050
	382	505	485	835	336	873
	269	604	465	941	400	1,233
	672	523	395	710	416	866
	314	532	436	622	393	924
	292	545	402	818	605	1,660
	311	619	389	990	857	748
	326	548	419	941	710	897
Mean	355·5	551·4	417·2	812·3	501·4	1,018·4

There is considerable variation within each starch group. It remains to decide whether the observed variation between the different means is due to this intrinsic variability of the results, or whether the mean breaking strengths of the different starches differ significantly between themselves.

The first step is to calculate an estimate s^2 of σ^2, the variance of the breaking strengths. Six separate estimates of σ^2 can be obtained from the variance within each of the groups and a pooled estimate of σ^2 is then obtained by taking the mean of these.

For example, for the wheat starch group

$$\Sigma x = 3,555,$$

$$\Sigma x^2 = 1,426,511,$$

$$\Sigma(x - \bar{x})^2 = \Sigma x^2 - \frac{(\Sigma x)^2}{10} = 162,708.$$

Estimate of $\sigma^2 = \frac{1}{9} \Sigma(x - \bar{x})^2 = 18,079$, and similarly for the other five groups.

Starch type	Estimate of σ^2
Wheat	18,079
Rice	1,314
Dasheen	1,382
Canna	17,271
Corn	32,738
Potato	67,308
Mean	23,015

Therefore $E(\sigma^2) = 23,015$.

Now, each of the six means is based on ten results so the estimate of the variance of the means is given by:

$$s_m^2 = \frac{23,015}{10} = 2,301 \cdot 5,$$

or $s_m = 48 \cdot 0$.

The test can now be carried out. The means constitute a sample of six from a population whose estimated standard deviation is $48 \cdot 0$.

$R_6 = $ range of group means $= 1,018 \cdot 4 - 355 \cdot 5 = 662 \cdot 9$,

so that $R_6/s_m = 662 \cdot 9/48 \cdot 0 = 13 \cdot 8$.

But, from Table XLI, the 1% significance level corresponds to $R_6/s_m = 4 \cdot 76$, so that variation between the means is highly significant.

The steps of the calculation are recapitulated as follows:

(a) Calculate the mean and variance for each group.

(b) Obtain the best estimate of the variance by calculating $E(\sigma^2)$ from the average of the group variances.

(c) Obtain s_m^2 by dividing $E(\sigma^2)$ by the number of results in each group and hence obtain s_m.

(d) Determine R_6, the range of the means and calculate R_6/s_m.

(e) Compare this with the appropriate 1% value in Table XLI.

EXERCISES XXXVIII

1. The percentage moisture content is determined from ten samples for each of four different soils. Is there a significant difference between the soils?

Soil A	Soil B	Soil C	Soil D
12·8	8·1	9·8	16·4
13·4	10·3	10·6	8·2
11·2	4·2	9·1	15·1
11·6	7·8	4·3	10·4
9·4	5·6	11·2	7·8
10·3	8·1	11·6	9·2
14·1	12·7	8·3	12·6
11·9	6·8	8·9	11·0
10·5	6·9	9·2	8·0
10·4	6·4	6·4	9·8

2. In the manufacture of glass, the quality of the glass is measured by the mean number of "seed" per unit area of glass. The following results were obtained for three makes of glass. Is there any significant difference between makes?

Make I	Make II	Make III
47	100	61
55	93	62
35	56	60
78	113	93
33	128	29
52	36	80
21	49	97
31	25	54

3. The B.T.U. values of twelve specimens of fuel gas are estimated by five check tests on each gas. Is there any evidence of a significant difference between the specimens?

Specimen	I	II	III	IV	V	VI
	533	540	528	526	537	512
	537	532	526	528	549	526
	546	549	536	519	538	518
	535	545	534	530	541	520
	538	541	533	526	540	515

Specimen	VII	VIII	IX	X	XI	XII
	531	552	519	538	513	519
	528	538	537	519	538	541
	540	548	521	527	526	536
	538	542	528	528	531	528
	536	556	532	531	527	533

11.4 Latin Squares

This is a form of experimental design which has been used a great deal in agricultural experimental work and which has applications in other types of statistical investigation. Consider an experiment in which the effects of four different fertilisers on the yield of wheat is to be tested. The field on which the experiment is carried out is divided into sixteen similar plots, which are then treated with fertilisers A, B, C and D, as shown in Fig. 56.

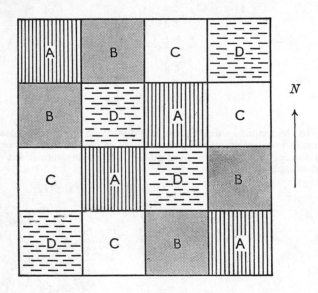

Fig. 56.   A 4 × 4 Latin square.

Each fertiliser is used only once in each row and in each column. The advantage of this design, which is only one of many possible designs, is that it enables any fertility gradients in the field to be eliminated in the comparison of the effects of the four fertilisers on the yield of wheat. For example, each row is treated equally with all fertilisers so that, if no fertility gradient existed in the north-south direction, the mean yield from all four rows should be the same within the limits of experimental error. If any significant differences between the rows are observed they can be eliminated before the final estimate of the significance of the treatments is carried out. A possible fertility gradient in the east-west direction can be eliminated by adjusting the columns in the same way.

Consider the following set of (fictitious) results:

A 50	B 49	C 63	D 92
B 36	D 59	A 60	C 68
C 39	A 46	D 66	B 57
D 46	C 40	B 40	A 62

First of all, without making any adjustments for possible fertility gradients, calculate the mean yields and variances for the four fertilisers.

	A	B	C	D
	50	49	63	92
	60	36	68	59
	46	57	39	66
	62	40	40	46
Means	54·50	45·50	52·50	65·75
Variances	59·67	88·33	229·67	374·92

To test whether the fertilisers differ significantly, calculate according to equation 11.3, the pooled estimate of σ^2

$$= \tfrac{1}{4}\,(59\!\cdot\!67 + 88\!\cdot\!33 + 229\!\cdot\!67 + 374\!\cdot\!92),$$

$$= 188\!\cdot\!15$$

s_m^2, the corresponding estimate of the variance of the mean is given by

$$s_m^2 = \frac{188 \cdot 15}{4} = 47 \cdot 04,$$

or $s_m = 6 \cdot 9$

Now, $R_4 = 65 \cdot 75 - 45 \cdot 50 = 20 \cdot 25,$

and so $R_4/s_m = 2 \cdot 9$

The 1% value of R_n/s_m for $n = 4$ is $4 \cdot 40$, so the observed result is not significant on the 1% level of significance.

This method of analysis, however, neglects the experimental design which allows the effects of possible fertility gradients to be eliminated in the following way. Calculate the mean yield for each row and column and also the mean yield over the whole field.

	Col. 1	Col. 2	Col. 3	Col. 4	Means of Rows
Row 1	A 50	B 49	C 63	D 92	63·50
Row 2	B 36	D 59	A 60	C 68	55·75
Row 3	C 39	A 46	D 66	B 57	52·00
Row 4	D 46	C 40	B 40	A 62	47·00
Means of Columns	42·75	48·50	57·25	69·75	54·56

The results show that, although each row and each column represent equally all four fertilisers, there is a considerable difference in row and column means both up and across the field. This is presumably due to variable fertility over the field. To remove this effect, it is only necessary to make the means of the rows and the columns the same as the field mean by adjusting the results in the field. For example, the first row mean 63·50 exceeds the field mean 54·56 by 8·94. Therefore, subtract 8·94 from each result in row 1. In the same way, subtract 1·19 from each result in row 2, add 2·56 to each result in row 3, and 7·56 to each result in row 4. For the columns, add 11·81, 6·06, − 2·69 and − 15·19 to results in columns 1, 2, 3 and 4 respectively.

When this has been done, the adjusted yields are:

A 52·87	B 46·12	C 51·37	D 67·87
B 46·62	D 63·87	A 56·12	C 51·62
C 53·37	A 54·62	D 65·87	B 44·37
D 65·37	C 53·62	B 44·87	A 54·37

The reader can verify that the row and column averages are now the same as the field average.

Now repeat the calculation of the mean yield and variances for the four fertilisers.

	A	B	C	D
	52·87	46·12	51·37	67·87
	56·12	46·62	51·62	63·87
	54·62	44·37	53·37	65·87
	54·37	44·87	53·62	65·37
Mean	54·50	45·50	52·50	65·75
Variances	1·77	1·11	1·36	2·73

The pooled estimate of the variance of a single yield is given by

$$\tfrac{1}{4}(1\cdot77 + 1\cdot11 + 1\cdot36 + 2\cdot73) = 1\cdot74$$

and the estimate of the variance of a mean of four yields is

$$s_m^2 = \frac{1\cdot74}{4} = 0\cdot435, \text{ and } s_m = 0\cdot66.$$

Therefore, $R_4/s_m = \dfrac{20\cdot25}{0\cdot66} = 30\cdot7.$

This result is highly significant so that it is safe to conclude that there is a real difference in the effects of the fertilisers.

Example. Five different grades of plastic material A, B, C, D and E are tested to find whether they show any difference in surface smoothness after being worked by machine. Five machines and five operators are used for the test, and five samples of each plastic are tested, and the operators and machines are distributed amongst the grades so that one operator, one machine and one grade are only associated once. The arrangement with the corresponding results are shown with operator and machine means.

			Operator			
Machine	1	2	3	4	5	*Mean*
1	A 7	B 14	C 17	D 14	E 16	13·6
2	C 9	A 11	D 16	E 10	B 12	11·6
3	E 9	C 14	B 15	A 7	D 14	11·8
4	B 10	D 16	E 18	C 14	A 14	14·4
5	D 14	E 16	A 16	B 15	C 16	15·4
Mean	9·8	14·2	16·4	12·0	14·4	13·4

The operator and machine differences are removed by adjusting the results so that the row and column means are the same as the grand mean, 13·4.

			Operator		
Machine	1	2	3	4	5
1	A 10·4	B 13·0	C 13·8	D 15·2	E 14·8
2	C 14·4	A 12·0	D 14·8	E 13·2	B 12·8
3	E 14·2	C 14·8	B 13·6	A 10·0	D 14·6
4	B 12·6	D 14·2	E 14·0	C 14·4	A 12·0
5	D 15·6	E 13·2	A 11·0	B 14·4	C 13·0

Calculate the means and variances for the five grades of plastic:

	A	B	C	D	E
	10·4	13·0	13·8	15·2	14·8
	12·0	12·8	14·4	14·8	13·2
	10·0	13·6	14·8	14·6	14·2
	12·0	12·6	14·4	14·2	14·0
	11·0	14·4	13·0	15·6	13·2
Mean	11·1	13·3	14·1	14·9	13·9
Variance	0·84	0·54	0·49	0·29	0·48

Then $\frac{1}{5}$ (0·84 + 0·54 + 0·49 + 0·29 + 0·48)

$$= 0·53$$

$$s_m^2 = \frac{0·53}{5} = 0·106$$

and $s_m = 0·33$

$$R_5 = 14·9 - 11·1 = 13·8,$$

and $R_5/s_m = 13·8/0·33 = 41·8$.

This result is highly significant and we can conclude that there are real differences between the grades of plastic in respect of surface smoothness.

EXERCISES XXXIX

1. Perform algebraically the operation of equalising column and row means on the 4 × 4 Latin square given below, and hence show that the means for the four treatments remain unaltered.

A x_{11}	B x_{12}	C x_{13}	D x_{14}
B x_{21}	A x_{22}	D x_{23}	C x_{24}
C x_{31}	D x_{32}	A x_{33}	B x_{34}
D x_{41}	C x_{42}	B x_{43}	A x_{44}

2. If x_{rc} is the experimental result in the rth row and cth column of a Latin square, and if $\bar{x}_r$, $\bar{x}_c$ are the means of the rth row and cth column respectively and $\bar{x}$ is the grand mean, show that the process of equalising the means of rows and columns is equivalent to calculating

$$x_{rc} - \bar{x}_r - \bar{x}_c + 2\bar{x} \text{ for all values of } c \text{ and } r.$$

3. Write down four different 5×5 Latin squares. (There are 161,280 different 5×5 Latin squares.)

4. The following results were obtained in a texile experiment to compare the effects of "sizing" treatments, A, B, C and D, on the number of warps breaking per hour. The two factors whose effects are to be eliminated are the loom and time. Is the difference between the treatments significant?
(Tippett.)

Loom

Period	1	2	3	4
1	A 54	B 29	C 71	D 44
2	B 59	A 22	D 100	C 22
3	C 40	D 38	B 79	A 31
4	D 83	C 29	A 100	B 27

5. The results of six types of fertilisers on the yield of potatoes, using a 6×6 Latin square design, are given below. Eliminate any apparent fertility gradient effects and estimate whether the fertilisers produce significantly different effects. (Fisher.)

E 633	B 527	F 652	A 390	C 504	D 416
B 489	C 475	D 415	E 488	F 571	A 282
A 384	E 481	C 483	B 422	D 334	F 646
F 620	D 448	E 505	C 439	A 323	B 384
D 452	A 432	B 411	F 617	E 594	C 466
C 500	F 505	A 259	D 366	B 326	E 420

6. Four men were employed in collecting beetles in a field and they were assigned to set areas in the field in Latin Square form. The arrangement is shown with the result. Do the men show any significant difference in the number of beetles they collected?

D 1,127	B 1,331	A 628	C 430
C 658	A 635	D 969	B 758
B 869	D 794	C 560	A 411
A 523	C 490	B 213	D 517

(Geoffrey Beall, *Biometrika*, **30**, 422.)

11.5 Factorial Design

When the effect of varying a single factor is measured, much care is usually devoted to keeping all other possible factors constant, so that any variations in the results of the experiment can be directly attributed to the factor which is being altered. For example, in

K

determining how the volume of a gas varies with the pressure the experiment is carried out at a constant temperature, since it is known that the temperature is also a factor which affects the volume. In some fields of research, such as biology, sociology and agriculture it is by no means always possible to ensure that all but one factor remains unaltered throughout an experiment. In such cases the experimental design can sometimes be arranged so that the effect of any factors considered irrelevant may be estimated from the analysis. This is known as *balancing*. In the experiment on the corrosion of underground pipes, the coating of the pipe was the factor whose effect was being measured and the other irrelevant factor, namely the type of soil, was eliminated by pairing the results. Again, in the agricultural experiment on fertilisers the varying soil fertility was the irrelevant factor and it was eliminated by using a Latin square design.

In experiments where the effects of varying more than one factor are to be determined, it is not correct to assume that the best procedure is to vary each factor one at a time. The reason for this will appear in the following discussion of a chemical experiment.

A chemical material is prepared by adding one component to another at a steady feed rate. The mixture is stirred and kept at a constant temperature. It is proposed to investigate how altering the three factors, feed rate (F), stirrer speed (S) and temperature (T) affects the amount of material produced. This is to be done by trying two levels of each factor, namely two different feed rates F_1 and F_2, two stirrer speeds S_1 and S_2 and two temperatures T_1 and T_2.

Now there are exactly eight different ways in which these three factors can be associated at each level:

$$F_1 S_1 T_1 \qquad\qquad F_2 S_1 T_1$$
$$F_1 S_2 T_1 \qquad\qquad F_2 S_2 T_1$$
$$F_1 S_1 T_2 \qquad\qquad F_2 S_1 T_2$$
$$F_1 S_2 T_2 \qquad\qquad F_2 S_2 T_2$$

Eight determinations are made and the weight of material produced is measured for each association of factor levels. Denote the weight of material by small letters so that, for example, the weight of compound made by the association of F_1, S_1 and T_1 is $f_1 s_1 t_1$. These eight results can now be arranged in pairs in three different ways to give an estimate of the effect of each of the three factors.

Thus the effect of F is measured by the average of

$$(f_1 s_1 t_1 - f_2 s_1 t_1),$$
$$(f_1 s_2 t_1 - f_2 s_2 t_1),$$
$$(f_1 s_1 t_2 - f_2 s_1 t_2),$$
$$(f_1 s_2 t_2 - f_2 s_2 t_2),$$

Similarly, the effects of S and T are measured by the averages of

$$(f_1 s_1 t_1 - f_1 s_2 t_1), \text{ and } (f_1 s_1 t_1 - f_1 s_1 t_2),$$
$$(f_2 s_1 t_1 - f_2 s_2 t_1), \qquad (f_2 s_1 t_1 - f_2 s_1 t_2),$$
$$(f_1 s_1 t_2 - f_1 s_2 t_2), \qquad (f_1 s_2 t_1 - f_1 s_2 t_2),$$
$$(f_2 s_1 t_2 - f_2 s_2 t_2), \qquad (f_2 s_2 t_1 - f_2 s_2 t_2), \text{ respectively.}$$

It should be noted that the measurement of each effect is based on eight results, four at each factor level.

Suppose that, instead of adopting this factorial design, the method of varying the factors one at a time was used. Then, to determine the effect of varying F with equivalent precision, it would be necessary to keep S and T constant while eight experiments were carried out, four at the F_1 level and four at the F_2 level. To determine the effect of S, another eight experiments would be required, this time keeping F and T constant. Finally, a third set of eight experiments would be necessary to determine the effect of T. Altogether, twenty-four experimental determinations would be required, whereas by using a factorial design eight determinations are sufficient to obtain the estimates of the effects with equivalent precision. This economy in experimental effort is an important advantage of the factorial design.

Example. In the chemical experiment just described the following eight results were obtained:

$$f_1 s_1 t_1 = 3 \cdot 6 \qquad f_2 s_1 t_1 = 1 \cdot 0$$
$$f_1 s_2 t_1 = 4 \cdot 2 \qquad f_2 s_2 t_1 = 1 \cdot 5$$
$$f_1 s_1 t_2 = 3 \cdot 3 \qquad f_2 s_1 t_2 = 1 \cdot 7$$
$$f_1 s_2 t_2 = 4 \cdot 6 \qquad f_2 s_2 t_2 = 1 \cdot 9$$

Effect of varying F:

$$3 \cdot 6 - 1 \cdot 0 = 2 \cdot 6$$
$$4 \cdot 2 - 1 \cdot 5 = 2 \cdot 7$$
$$3 \cdot 3 - 1 \cdot 7 = 1 \cdot 6$$
$$4 \cdot 6 - 1 \cdot 9 = 2 \cdot 7$$

Total	9·6
Mean	2·40

Effect of varying S:

$$3 \cdot 6 - 4 \cdot 2 = -0 \cdot 6$$
$$3 \cdot 3 - 4 \cdot 6 = -1 \cdot 3$$
$$1 \cdot 0 - 1 \cdot 5 = -0 \cdot 5$$
$$1 \cdot 7 - 1 \cdot 9 = -0 \cdot 2$$

Total	-2·6
Mean	-0·65

Effect of varying T:

$$3\cdot6 - 3\cdot3 = 0\cdot3$$
$$4\cdot2 - 4\cdot6 = -0\cdot4$$
$$1\cdot0 - 1\cdot7 = -0\cdot7$$
$$1\cdot5 - 1\cdot9 = -0\cdot4$$

$$\text{Total} \quad -1\cdot2$$
$$\text{Mean} \quad -0\cdot30$$

The statistical analysis of factorial designs demands a rather more advanced treatment than can be given in this book and so the question of the significance of these results will not be discussed. Some of the advantages of the factorial design can, however, be appreciated without entering into the subtleties of the further analysis.

INTERACTIONS. In addition to providing equivalent accuracy for less effort the factorial design also gives information about effects which cannot be obtained from the "single factor at a time" treatment. Consider the following question. Does the effect of varying the F factor depend on the level of the S factor? In statistical language, is there an *interaction* between F and S?

To decide this, write down the means of the pairs $(f_1\,s_1\,t_1, f_1\,s_1\,t_2)$, $(f_1\,s_2\,t_1, f_1\,s_2\,t_2)$, $(f_2\,s_1\,t_1, f_2\,s_2\,t_2)$, $(f_2\,s_2\,t_1, f_2\,s_2\,t_2)$ and denote the result of averaging the T factor by $\bar t$. This gives the following results.

$$f_1\,s_1\,\bar t = 3\cdot45, f_2\,s_1\,\bar t = 1\cdot35,$$
$$f_1\,s_2\,\bar t = 4\cdot40, f_2\,s_2\,\bar t = 1\cdot70.$$

Now the effects of altering F when factor S is at the S_1 and S_2 levels respectively are

$$f_1\,s_1\,\bar t - f_2\,s_1\,\bar t = 2\cdot10 \quad (S_1),$$
$$\text{and } f_1\,s_2\,\bar t - f_2\,s_2\,\bar t = 2\cdot70 \quad (S_2).$$

These two effects differ and this difference, $2\cdot70 - 2\cdot10 = 0\cdot60$, is a measure of the interaction.

This illustrates another advantage of the factorial design, since in experimental work it is often important to know when the effects of one factor vary with changes in other factors. It is not possible by varying only one factor at a time to obtain any estimate of interactions.

EXERCISES XL

1. Show that in the chemical experiment the eight different combinations of three factors at two levels are given by the terms in the expansion of $(F_1 + F_2)(S_1 + S_2)(T_1 + T_2)$.

2. In an experiment two factors A and B are tested at two levels. Write down the four possible combinations of factor levels. Using small letters to denote the results of the experiments, write down the expressions for the mean effects of varying A and B.

3. In Example 11.3, calculate the $F \times T$ interaction, averaging S, and the $S \times T$ interaction, averaging F.

4. The effect of the presence or absence of three fertilisers on the yield of potatoes was tested. The factors were

Sulphate of ammonia (N)	*Sulphate of potash* (K)	*Dung* (D)
None: $\quad N_1$	None: $\quad K_1$	None: $\quad D_1$
0·45 cwt./acre: N_2	1·12 cwt./acre: K_2	8 tons/acre: D_2

The following results were obtained.

Yield in tons/acre

$N_1K_1D_1$	$N_2K_1D_1$	$N_1K_2D_1$	$N_2K_2D_1$	$N_1K_1D_2$	$N_2K_1D_2$	$N_1K_2D_2$	$N_2K_2D_2$
2·84	2·85	7·49	8·06	8·59	9·35	11·20	12·10

Estimate the effects of the three fertilisers and also the three interactions, $N \times K$, $K \times D$ and $N \times D$. (Yates.)

5. Four factors A, B C and D are each tested at two levels. Write down the sixteen different associations of factor levels.

SUMMARY OF CHAPTER XI

1. In the design of an experiment to compare the effect of two treatments there may be an advantage if the results can be grouped in pairs and the analysis is carried out on the differences between each pair of results.

2. If a random sample of n has a range R_n then R_n/σ is known as the *standardised range*. Table XLI gives the 1% points of the standardised range for values of n.

3. To determine whether a group of means differ significantly amongst themselves:

   (*a*) Calculate the mean and variance for each group.

   (*b*) Obtain the best estimate of the variance by calculating $E(\sigma^2)$ from the average of the group variances.

   (*c*) Obtain s_m^2, the variance of the group means by dividing $E(\sigma^2)$ by the number of results in each group.

   (*d*) Determine R_n the range of the means and calculate R_n/s_m.

   (*e*) Compare this with the appropriate 1% value in Table XLI.

4. Two other examples of experimental design are the Latin square and factorial design.

CHAPTER XII

Mathematical Appendix

12.1 Probability Density and Distribution Functions

If we write the equation of the normal curve (Section 6.3) in the form

$$f(x) = \frac{1}{\sigma\sqrt{2\pi}}\, e^{-x^2/2\sigma^2}$$

then $f(x)$ is called the *probability density function* (pdf) of the normal probability distribution. The right-hand side expresses the *probability density* at any point x—not the *probability* which, at a point, is strictly zero. As a probability density can be only positive or zero and as the total probability must be unity, it is necessary to state the range of the variable. For the normal probability distribution we write

$$f(x) = \frac{1}{\sigma\sqrt{2\pi}}\, e^{-x^2/2\sigma^2}, \quad (-\infty < x < \infty)$$

Corresponding to the cumulative frequency curve (Section 6.3) there is a cumulative probability function

$$F(x = X) = \frac{1}{\sigma\sqrt{2\pi}} \int_{-\infty}^{X} e^{-x^2/\sigma^2}\, dx, \quad (-\infty < x < \infty).$$

This function $F(x = X)$, often written more shortly as $F(x)$, is called the *probability distribution function* (Df). As X increases from the lower to the upper limit of the range of x, i.e. from $-\infty$ to $+\infty$ in the case of the normal distribution, so the value of $F(x)$ increases monotonically from 0 to 1.

Clearly, $f(x)$ and $F(x)$ are related. If $F(x)$ is everywhere differentiable over the specified range of x, then

$$\frac{dF(x)}{dx} = F'(x) = f(x) \quad \text{and} \quad \int_{x_1}^{x_1} f(x)\, dx = F(x_2) - F(x_1)$$

The use of these two functions simplifies the analysis of continuous probability distributions.

Example 1. If a pdf has the form $kx(a - x)$, $(0 \leqslant x \leqslant a)$, where k is a constant, what is its Df?

276

The constant k is determined by means of the equation which states that the total probability must be unity:

$$F(x = a) = \int_0^a kx(a - x)\, dx = 1$$

This yields $\quad k\left[\tfrac{1}{2}ax^2 - \tfrac{1}{3}x^3\right]_0^a = 1 \text{ or } k = 6/a^3$

So $F(x = X) = \dfrac{6}{a^3}(\tfrac{1}{2}aX^2 - \tfrac{1}{3}X^3) = X^2(3a - 2X)/a^3, \quad (0 \leqslant X \leqslant a).$

(Sketch the graphs of the two functions).

Example 2. The resistances of mass-produced resistors of nominal resistance ω ohms are normally distributed with mean ω ohms and standard deviation $\omega/10$ ohms. A special selection is made of resistors whose resistances lie within 10% of the nominal value ω.

What is the pdf of the truncated normal distribution of selected resistances?

What percentage of the selected resistors have resistances within 1% of the nominal value?

Here $\qquad f(x) = \dfrac{k}{\sigma\sqrt{2\pi}}\, e^{-(x-\mu)^2/2\sigma^2}$

where $\sigma = \omega/10$, $\mu = \omega$ and k is a constant which makes $f(x)$ a proper pdf for the range $0.9\,\omega$ to $1.1\,\omega$.

Referring to Table XXVI, we see that at the upper limit

$$D = (x - \mu)/\sigma = (1.1\omega - 1.0\omega)/0.1\omega = 1.0$$

for which the entry is 0.1587. The area under the central part of the truncated normal distribution is therefore

$$1 - 2 \times 0.1587 = 0.6826$$

and so $k = 1/0.6826$. Hence

$$f(x) = \dfrac{1}{0.6826} \cdot \dfrac{10}{\omega\sqrt{2\pi}} \exp\{-50(x - \omega)^2/\omega^2\}, \quad (0.9\omega \leqslant x \leqslant 1.1\omega)$$

For ease of reference to normal probability tables there is no point in simplifying this expression further.

The fraction of resistors having resistances within 1% of ω is therefore $F(x = 1.01\omega) - F(x = 0.99\omega)$ and for $D = 0.1$ the entry in Table XXVI is 0.4602. Hence the required percentage is

$$\dfrac{100}{0.6826}(1 - 2 \times 0.4602) = 11.6\%$$

Example 3. The random variable x has the pdf e^{-x}, $(0 \leqslant x < \infty)$.

What is the pdf of the distribution of values of x greater than a, $(0 \leqslant a < \infty)$?

Since
$$f(x) = e^{-x}, \quad (0 \leqslant x < \infty)$$

and
$$\int e^{-x} \, dx = -e^{-x}, \quad \text{we have} \quad \int_a^\infty e^{-x} \, dx = e^{-a}.$$

The pdf of the new distribution is therefore
$$f_1(x) = e^{-x}/e^{-a} \quad (a \leqslant x < \infty)$$
$$\geqslant e^{-x+a}, \quad (a \leqslant x < \infty)$$

If we put $x - a = y$, so that $dx = dy$, we have
$$\int_a^\infty e^{-x+a} \, dx = \int_0^\infty e^{-y} \, dy, \quad (a \leqslant x < \infty, 0 \leqslant y < \infty)$$

The pdf of the random variable y is therefore
$$e^{-y}, \quad (0 \leqslant y < \infty)$$

which is of precisely the same form as that of x.

12.2 Change of Variable

Sometimes the following position arises: If the pdf of a continuous random variable is $f(x)$, what is the pdf of some specified function of x such as, for example, x^2 or $\sqrt{x}$ or $\log x$?

The technique involves the change of the variable of an integral and so the change must be made with due consideration of the behaviour of the two variables over their ranges.

Example 1. If x is normally distributed with zero mean and unit s.d., what is the pdf of $u = x^2$.

Here
$$f(x) = \frac{1}{\sqrt{2\pi}} e^{-x^2/2}, \quad (-\infty < x < \infty)$$

and
$$u = x^2, \quad (0 \leqslant u < \infty)$$

since u cannot be negative. Hence
$$F(x) = \frac{1}{\sqrt{2\pi}} \int e^{-x^2/2} \, dx, \quad (-\infty < x < \infty)$$
$$= \frac{2}{\sqrt{2\pi}} \int e^{-x^2/2} \, dx, \quad (0 \leqslant x < \infty)$$
$$F_1(u) = \frac{2}{\sqrt{2\pi}} \int e^{-u/2} \tfrac{1}{2} u^{-1/2} \, du, \quad (0 \leqslant u < \infty)$$
$$= \frac{1}{\sqrt{2\pi}} \int e^{-u/2} u^{-1/2} \, du, \quad (0 \leqslant u < \infty).$$

So the pdf of u is $\quad \dfrac{1}{\sqrt{2\pi}} e^{-u/2} u^{-1/2} = f_1(u)$

When u is near zero, $e^{-u/2} \approx 1$, but $u^{-\frac{1}{2}} \to \infty$ as $u \to 0$.

Hence the graph of $f_1(u)$ tends to infinity as u tends to zero and tends to zero as u tends to infinity.

12.3 Expectation

Let $\phi(x)$ be a function, such as x^2 or e^x, of the random variable x which has the continuous pdf $f(x)$ and which ranges from a to b.

The *expectation* or *expected value* of $\phi(x)$, written $E[\phi(x)]$, is defined as the mean value of $\phi(x)$ as x assumes all possible values of x, i.e. values of x lying between a and b duly weighted according to the corresponding probability density.

So
$$E[\phi(x)] = \int_a^b \phi(x)\, f(x)\, dx$$

Consider some particular cases. When $\phi(x) = x$ we have

$$E[x] = \int_a^b x f(x) = \mu$$

where μ is the mean of the distribution of x, i.e. the mean value of x duly weighted according to the corresponding value of $f(x)$.

When $\quad \phi(x) = x^2$, then

$$E[x^2] = \int_a^b x^2 f(x)\, dx$$

$$= \mu_2', \text{ the second moment } about\ the\ origin.$$

The use of expectation also provides a means of establishing the properties of a random variable z which is a function of two or more random variables.

Let $z = x + y$ where y is a second random variable with pdf $g(y)$. If x and y are independent, then the probability that x falls in the interval $x + dx$ when y falls in the interval $y + dy$ is $f(x)\, dx\, dy$.

Then, assuming that the relevant limits are understood,

$$E[x \pm y] = \iint (x \pm y) f(x)\, g(y)\, dx\, dy$$

$$= \iint x f(x)\, g(y)\, dx\, dy \pm \iint y f(x)\, g(y)\, dx\, dy$$

$$= \int x f(x)\, dx \pm \int y g(y)\, dy = E[x] \pm E[y].$$

By putting $y = u \pm v$, we have
$$E[u \pm v] = E[u] \pm E[v] = E[y]$$

and so $E[x \pm y] = E[x \pm u \pm v] = E[x] \pm E[u] \pm E[v]$

Thus the rule can be extended to any number of independent variables. We can then write

$$E[\Sigma x] = \Sigma E[x] \tag{1}$$

If a and b are constants we also have

$$E[ax + by] = a\, E[x] + b\, E[y] \tag{2}$$

Rules (1) and (2) can be shown to be valid even if the variables are not independent.

Now let $z = xy$. We then have

$$E[xy] = \int\int xy\, f(x)\, g(x)\, dx\, dy$$

$$= \int xf(x)\, dx \int y f(y)\, dy$$

$$= E[x]\, E[y] \tag{3}$$

but this result is valid *only if* x and y are independent, so enabling the double integral to be split into the product.

The covariance of x and y is $E[(x - \mu_1)(y - \mu_2)]$ where $\mu_1 = E[x]$ and $\mu_2 = E[y]$, the two means. So

$$E[(x - \mu_1)(y - \mu_2)] = E[xy - \mu_1 y - \mu_2 x + \mu_1\mu_2]$$
$$= E[xy] - \mu_1\, E[y] - \mu_2\, E[x] + \mu_1\mu_2$$
$$= E[x]\, E[y] - \mu_1\mu_2 - \mu_2\mu_1 + \mu_1\mu_2$$

which, if x and y are independent, reduces to zero.

Let $z = (ax \pm by)^2$. Then

$$E[z] = E[a^2x^2 \pm 2abxy + b^2y^2]$$
$$= a^2\, E[x^2] \pm 2ab\, E[xy] + b^2\, E[y^2]$$
$$= a^2\, E[x^2] \pm 2ab\, E[x]\, E[y] + b^2\, E[y^2] \tag{4}$$

if x and y are independent.

This and related results have already been derived by other methods in Section 7.6. But we can also use expectation to justify the use of the divisor $(n - 1)$ in estimating the s.d. of a population from a sample of size n by means of the formula

$$s^2 = \Sigma(x_r - \bar{x})^2/(n - 1)$$

Consider one single term of the summation, $x_r - \bar{x}$.

Put

$$x_r - \bar{x} = x_r - \Sigma x_r/n$$
$$= (nx_r - \Sigma x_r)/n$$
$$= (- x_1 - x_2 \ldots + \overline{n - 1}\, x_r \ldots -x_n)/n$$
$$= (\overline{\mu - x_1} + \overline{\mu - x_2} \ldots + (n - 1)(x_r - \mu) \ldots + \overline{\mu - x_n})/n \tag{5}$$

where $\mu = E[x]$, the mean.

We then have

$$E[u - x_1] = E[u - x_2] = E[u - x_r] \ldots, \text{etc.}$$

each equal to zero since each of the sample values is drawn at random from the whole population and independently of all others. Similarly,

$$E[(\mu - x_1)^2] = E[(\mu - x_2)^2] = \ldots = E[(\mu - x_r)^2] = \sigma^2$$

where σ is the s.d. and

$$E[(\mu - x_1)(\mu - x_2)] = E[(\mu - x_2)(\mu - x_3)] = \ldots = 0$$

since $x_1, x_2, x_3, \ldots$ are independent.

The expectation of the square of expression (5) is therefore

$$\{(n - 1)\sigma^2 + (n - 1)^2\sigma^2\}/n^2 = (n - 1)\sigma^2/n$$

But in the formula for s^2 there are n such terms each of which has the same expectation.

So $E[\Sigma(x_r - \bar{x})^2] = n(n - 1)\sigma^2/n = (n - 1)\sigma^2$ and the unbiased estimate of σ^2 is given by dividing $\Sigma(x_r - \bar{x})^2$ by $(n - 1)$ rather than by n.

12.4 Functions of two independent variables

Though the use of expectation provides the mean and variance of a sum or difference of two independent random variables, it does not yield the pdf of the new variable.

Consider two independent random variables, x and y, with pdf's $f(x)$ and $g(y)$ respectively. Let z be a function of x and y which varies monotonically with x as y is fixed and monotonically with y as x is fixed. To find the pdf of z, we first express one of the variables, say x, in terms of y and z meanwhile holding y fixed. We thus obtain the joint distribution of z and y. The pdf of z is then obtained by 'integrating out' the remaining variable y.

For example, let the variables x and y both be normal variates with zero mean and unit s.d. and consider the pdf of $z = x/y$. The new random variable z is thus the result of dividing a sample value of x by a sample value of y and its distribution is the resultant of all possible divisions of that kind. So here we have

$$f(x) = \frac{1}{\sqrt{2\pi}} e^{-x^2/2}, \quad (-\infty < x < \infty)$$

$$f(y) = \frac{1}{\sqrt{2\pi}} e^{-y^2/2}, \quad (-\infty < y < \infty)$$

and $z = x/y$.

We now put $x = yz$ and temporarily hold y fixed so that $\dfrac{\partial x}{\partial z} = |y|$, noting that z ranges from $-\infty$ to $+\infty$ as x ranges from $-\infty$ to $+\infty$ for a given $|y|$. The joint distribution of y and z is then

$$\frac{1}{\sqrt{2\pi}} e^{-y^2 z^2/2} |y| \frac{1}{\sqrt{2\pi}} e^{-y^2/2}, \quad (-\infty < y < \infty)$$

So
$$h(z) = \int_{-\infty}^{\infty} \frac{1}{2\pi} e^{-y^2(1+z^2)/2} |y|\, dy$$

$$= \frac{1}{\pi} \int_{0}^{\infty} e^{-y^2(1+z^2)/2}\, y\, dy.$$

Substitute $y(1 + z^2)^{\frac{1}{2}} = u$, $dy(1 + z^2)^{\frac{1}{2}} = du$.

Then $h(z) = \frac{1}{\pi} \cdot \frac{1}{1+z^2} \int_{0}^{\infty} e^{-u^2/2}\, du$

$$= \frac{1}{\pi} \frac{1}{1+z^2} \left[e^{-u^2/2} \right]_{0}^{\infty} = \frac{1}{\pi} \cdot \frac{1}{1+z^2}, \quad (-\infty < z < \infty)$$

which is the pdf of a Cauchy distribution (Section 6.8).

Example. If x and y are random variables both drawn from normal distributions with zero mean and unit s.d., find the pdf of

$$r = (x^2 + y^2)^{\frac{1}{2}}$$

In Section 12.2 we have already shown that if $x^2 = u$,

$$f_1(u) = \frac{1}{\sqrt{2\pi}} e^{-u/2}\, u^{-\frac{1}{2}}$$

Let $y^2 = v$, so that $f_1(v) = \frac{1}{\sqrt{2\pi}} e^{-v/2}\, v^{-\frac{1}{2}}$ $(0 \leqslant v < \infty)$ and put

$u + v = x^2 + y^2 = w$.

Then $u = w - v$ and $\dfrac{\partial u}{\partial w} = 1$. The joint distribution of w and v is

$$\frac{1}{\sqrt{2\pi}} e^{-(w-v)/2} (w-v)^{-\frac{1}{2}} \cdot 1 \cdot \frac{1}{\sqrt{2\pi}} e^{-v/2}\, v^{-\frac{1}{2}}, \quad (0 \leqslant v \leqslant w).$$

Note that v cannot exceed w, so the range of v is 0 to w.

Then
$$g(w) = \frac{e^{-w/2}}{2\pi} \int_{0}^{w} \frac{dv}{\sqrt{v(w - v)}}, \quad (0 \leqslant w < \infty)$$

$$= \tfrac{1}{2} e^{-w/2} \text{ as the value of the integral is } \pi.$$

Now put $w = r^2$. For this substitution we write

$$G(w) = \int \tfrac{1}{2} e^{-w/2}\, dw, \quad (0 \leqslant w < \infty)$$

and, putting $w = r^2$, $dw = 2r\,dr$.

$$G_1(r) = \int \tfrac{1}{2}e^{-r^2/2}\,2r\,dr, \quad (0 \leqslant r < \infty)$$

$$= \int e^{-r^2/2}\,r\,dr.$$

The required pdf is therefore $r\,e^{-r^2/2}$, $(0 \leqslant r < \infty)$.

Distributions whose pdf's are reducible to this form are sometimes known as Rayleigh distributions. They can arise in the study of noise. The graph of this function rises from zero, when $r = 0$, to a maximum, $e^{-\frac{1}{2}}$ when $r = 1$, and then fades away towards zero again as r tends to infinity.

12.5　Gamma functions and probability distributions

The gamma function, $\Gamma(n)$, arises frequently in probability theory; we have already met some simple examples in this Appendix. The function can be defined as

$$\Gamma(n) = \int_0^\infty x^{n-1}\,e^{-x}\,dx, \quad (n > 0).$$

For $n > 2$ the graph of the function touches the x-axis at the origin, rises to a maximum at $x = n - 1$ and then falls, more slowly, as x increases, to converge asymptotically to the x-axis again. For $n > 0$ the area under the graph is always finite.

Usually in probability theory the values of n are integral or half integral. Integrating $\Gamma(n)$ by parts in succession it is easily shown that

$$\Gamma(n) = (n - 1)\,\Gamma(n - 1)$$
$$= (n - 1)(n - 2)\,\Gamma(n - 2) \quad \text{and so on,}$$
$$= (n - 1)(n - 2)\ldots 1\,\Gamma(1) \quad \text{if } n \text{ is integral}$$

As $\qquad \Gamma(1) = \displaystyle\int_0^\infty e^{-x}\,dx = 1, \qquad$ we therefore have

$$\Gamma(n) = (n - 1)!$$

For example, $\displaystyle\int_0^\infty x^3\,e^{-x}\,dx = \Gamma(4) = 3! = 6$

It can also be shown that $\Gamma(\tfrac{1}{2}) = \sqrt{\pi}$ so that, for example,

$$\int_0^\infty x^{3/2}\,e^{-x}\,dx = \Gamma(\tfrac{5}{2}) = \tfrac{3}{2}\cdot\tfrac{1}{2}\cdot\Gamma(\tfrac{1}{2}) = 3\sqrt{\pi}/4$$

Functions related to the Normal pdf such as $x^r\,e^{-x^2/2}$ can be integrated by substituting

$$x^2 = 2z, \quad x = \sqrt{2z}, \quad dx = dz/\sqrt{2z}.$$

For example,

$$\int_{-\infty}^{\infty} \frac{1}{\sqrt{2\pi}} x^6 e^{-x^2/2} dx = \frac{2}{\sqrt{2\pi}} \int_0^{\infty} x^6 \, e^{-x^2/2} \, dx, \text{ since the function is even,}$$

$$= \frac{2}{\sqrt{2\pi}} \int_0^{\infty} (2z)^3 e^{-z} z^{-\frac{1}{2}} \frac{1}{\sqrt{2}} \, dz, \text{ on substituting,}$$

$$= \frac{8}{\sqrt{\pi}} \int_0^{\infty} z^{5/2} \, e^{-z} \, dz$$

$$= \frac{8}{\sqrt{\pi}} \Gamma(\tfrac{7}{2}) = \frac{8}{\sqrt{\pi}} \cdot \tfrac{5}{2} \cdot \tfrac{3}{2} \cdot \tfrac{1}{2} \sqrt{\pi} = 15.$$

If the limits of the integral are not 0 or ∞, the numerical value can be found either by expanding the integral as a series or more directly from tables of the 'incomplete' gamma function.

A random variable whose Df is a gamma function is said to have a gamma distribution or to be a Γ-variate. If x is a Γ-variate, its Df and pdf would be

$$F(x = X) = \frac{1}{\Gamma(n)} \int x^{n-1} e^{-x} \, dx, \quad (0 \leqslant x < \infty),$$

$$f(x) = \frac{1}{\Gamma(n)} x^{n-1} \, e^{-x}, \quad (0 \leqslant x < \infty),$$

the factor $1/\Gamma(n)$ being required to make the total area under the graph, i.e. the total probability, equal to unity.

The mean of the distribution, μ, is given by

$$\mu = \frac{1}{\Gamma(n)} \int_0^{\infty} x \cdot x^{n-1} \, e^{-x} \, dx$$

$$= \frac{1}{\Gamma(n)} \int_0^{\infty} x^n e^{-x} \, dx = \frac{\Gamma(n+1)}{\Gamma(n)} = n.$$

The second moment about the origin is, similarly,

$$\frac{\Gamma(n+2)}{\Gamma(n)} = n(n+1)$$

and so the variance is $n(n+1) - n^2 = n$.

Example. Show that if x is a unit Normal variate, then $\tfrac{1}{2}x^2$ is a Γ-variate.

In Section 12.2, $u = x^2$ was shown to have the Df

$$F(u) = \frac{1}{\sqrt{2\pi}} \int_0^{\infty} e^{-u/2} \, u^{-\frac{1}{2}} \, du, \quad (0 \geqslant u < \infty)$$

By substituting $u/2 = v = \frac{1}{2}x^2$, $du = 2dv$ we have

$$F_1(v) = \frac{1}{\sqrt{2\pi}} \int e^{-v} \frac{1}{\sqrt{2v}} 2dv, \quad (0 \leqslant v < \infty)$$

$$= \frac{1}{\sqrt{\pi}} \int v^{-\frac{1}{2}} e^{-v} dv, \quad (0 \leqslant v < \infty)$$

which is the Df of the Γ-variate with parameter $n = \frac{1}{2}$.

12.6 The negative exponential distribution

The simplest of the gamma distributions is that for which $n = 1$. The Γ-function then reduces to

$$\int e^{-x} dx, \quad (0 \leqslant x < \infty)$$

As $\Gamma(1) = 1$, $\qquad e^{-x}, \quad (0 \leqslant x < \infty)$

is the pdf in proper form of the negative exponential distribution.

The graph of this pdf has the value 1 when $x = 0$ and then falls ever more slowly towards the x-axis as x increases to infinity.

The negative exponential distribution frequently arises in the consideration of the intervals between successive events which occur at random in time or space. It therefore has practical applications in traffic control, notably in telephone traffic, and in queuing problems.

Consider the following problem: A radio-active tracer emits particles at random instants but at an overall average rate of a per sec. What is the pdf of t, the time interval between successive emissions?

The number of particles, x, emitted in fixed time intervals will be a Poisson variate. Consider time intervals t/n. The average number emitted during this interval will be at/n. So from the Poisson series

$$e^{-at/n} \left\{ 1 + \frac{at}{n} + \frac{1}{2!}\left(\frac{at}{n}\right)^3 + \ldots \frac{1}{r!}\left(\frac{at}{n}\right)^r + \ldots \right.$$

we can say that

$$P(x = 0) = e^{-at/n}$$

$$P(x = 1) = e^{-at/n} at/n, \text{ etc.}$$

So the probability of the occurrence of $(n - 1)$ successive intervals in which *no* particle is emitted followed by an nth interval in which a particle *is* emitted is

$$(e^{-at/n})^{n-1} e^{-at/n} at/n = ae^{-at} t/n.$$

This is therefore the probability that the event will occur in the interval between $t - \Delta t$ and t where $\Delta t = t/n$. So

$$F(t) - F(t - \Delta t) = ae^{-at} \Delta t$$

where $F(t)$ is the Df of the variate t. As $n \to \infty$

$$\frac{F(t) - F(t - \Delta t)}{\Delta t} \to \frac{dF(t)}{dt} = f(t) = ae^{-at} \quad (0 \leqslant t < \infty)$$

which is the pdf of the required distribution.

We have, for the mean,

$$\mu = E[t] = \int_0^\infty at \, e^{-at} \, dt$$

which may be integrated by parts or alternatively, by putting $at = x$, $dt = dx/a$, giving

$$\mu = \int_0^\infty xe^{-x} \frac{dx}{a} = \frac{1}{a} \int_0^\infty x \, e^{-x} \, dx = \frac{1}{a} \Gamma(2) = \frac{1}{a}$$

Example. A certain plant is distributed at random over a field with an average density of a per square metre. A line is laid across the field and the occurrence of a plant whose centre is within 5 cm. of the line is noted. The distance, x, between successive occurrences is measured. What is the expected distribution of x?

In effect the line marks out a strip 10 cm. wide. The average number of plants per metre length of strip will be $a/10$. The pdf of the required distribution will therefore be $\dfrac{a}{10} e^{-ax/10}$ if x is measured in metres.

The mean distance between plants along the strip will be $10/a$ metres. The s.d. of x will also be $10/a$ metres. If the plants are randomly distributed one would therefore expect to find, for any practical distribution of x, that $\bar{x} = s$ approximately. However, if the plant tends to occur in scattered clusters, one would expect higher frequencies of relatively small and of relatively large values of x than the negative exponential distribution predicts. We should then expect to find $\bar{x} < s$.

Reliability

If the failure of a component of an electrical or a mechanical system can be regarded as a random event, as it can after the initial and 'running-in' period of testing has been completed, the negative exponential distribution can be applied to the analysis of the reliability of the system.

On the assumption that the failure occurs at random in time; the pdf of the distribution of failure times is given by

$$f(t) = ae^{-at}, \quad (0 \leqslant t < \infty),$$

where $1/a$ is the mean time to failure.

The corresponding distribution function of t is

$$F(t = T) = \int_0^T ae^{-at} \, dt = \left[-e^{-at} \right]_0^T$$
$$= 1 - e^{-aT}, \quad (0 \leqslant T < \infty).$$

This is the probability that the component will fail within time T. It is therefore a measure of the unreliability of the component. The probability that the component will *not* fail within time T is

$$1 - (1 - e^{-aT}) = e^{-aT}, \quad (0 \leqslant T < \infty)$$

And so, if we are considering a component C with mean time to failure $1/a$ we define

$$R(C) = e^{-aT}$$

as a measure of the *reliability* of the component,
and

$$Q(C) = 1 - e^{-aT}$$

as a measure of its *unreliability*.

Components in series

If components are linked in series, like a chain, it is assumed that the whole series fails when any one of its components fails.

Consider a system which consists of two components, C_1 and C_2, in series and for which

$$R(C_1) = e^{-a_1t}, \quad R(C_2) = e^{-a_2t}, \quad (0 \leqslant t < \infty).$$

The probability that both survive time t is

$$e^{-a_1t} e^{-a_2t} = e^{-(a_1+a_2)t}$$

Similarly, for a chain of n components in series, the probability that the whole system survives time t is

$$R_s(t) = R(C_1) . R(C_2) \ldots R(C_n)$$
$$= e^{-(a_1+a_2+ \ldots +a_n)t} \tag{1}$$

If the n components are similar and can therefore be assumed to have equal failure rates

$$R_s(t) = e^{-nat} \tag{2}$$

These expressions for $R_s(t)$ are known as the *product law of reliability for components in series*.

The mean of the distribution

$$f(t) = ae^{-at}, \quad (0 \leqslant t < \infty),$$

as we have seen, is $1/a$. The constant a is a measure of the failure rate of the component and $1/a$ is a measure of the mean time between failures assuming that as components of the system fail they are immediately replaced by similar new components. For a system of n components in series we have

$$a_s = a_1 + a_2 + \ldots + a_n$$

where a_s is the failure rate of the system. If t_r is the mean time of failure corresponding to a_r, we therefore have

$$1/t_s = \Sigma(1/t_r)$$

When all the components are similar with mean time to failure $\bar{t}$, then

$$1/\bar{t}_s = n/\bar{t}$$

or $$\bar{t}_s = \bar{t}/n \quad .$$

Thus the reliability of a system of components in series also conforms with the negative exponential law but the failure rate of the system is the sum of the failure rates of its components i.e. the expected life to failure to a system of components in series is less than that of any of its components. For example, a system of four similar components in series, each with a failure rate of 2·8 per 1000 hours, would have an expected failure rate of $4 \times 2 \cdot 8 = 11 \cdot 2$ per 1000 hours and a mean time to failure of $1000/11 \cdot 2 = 90 \cdot 2$ hours.

Components in parallel

If all the components are in parallel it is assumed that the system functions until every component has failed. Clearly, the expectation of life of a system of two or more components in parallel is greater than that of any of its components.

For two components, C_1 and C_2, the probability that *both fail* within time t is

$$Q_p(t) = (1 - e^{-a_1 t})(1 - e^{-a_2 t}) = Q(C_1) . Q(C_2) \tag{3}$$

This law, which can obviously be extended to any number of components in the same parallel set, is known as the *product law of unreliability for components in parallel*.

The probability that both components survive time t is

$$1 - Q_p(t) = R_p(t) = 1 - Q(C_1) . Q(C_2)$$

If the system consists of n similar components in parallel, then the probability that the system survives time t is

$$R_p(t) = 1 - \{Q/C)\}^n = 1 - (1 - e^{-at})^n$$

and the probability that the system fails within time t is

$$Q_p(t) = (1 - e^{-at})^n, \quad (0 \leqslant t < \infty).$$

As $Q_p(t = 0) = 0$ and $Q_p(\infty) = 1$, $Q_p(t)$ is a proper Df and its pdf, $f(t)$, is given by differentiating it with respect to t. So

$$Q_p'(t) = f(t) = nae^{-at}(1 - e^{-at})^{n-1}$$

This equation states the probability density of failure at time t. The life expectation or mean time to failure is

$$\bar{t}_n = \int_0^\infty t f(t)\, dt = na \int_0^\infty e^{-at}(1 - e^{-at})^{n-1}\, dt.$$

The integral is evaluated by expanding the binomial and integrating term by term. After putting in the limits it yields

$$\bar{t}_n = \frac{1}{a}\left\{ {}^nC_1 - \frac{1}{2} . {}^nC_2 + \frac{1}{3} . {}^nC_3 \cdots \left(-1\right)^n \frac{1}{n} . {}^nC_n \right\}$$

For various values of n, we have

$$t_1 = \frac{1}{a}, \text{ as expected for a single component, } t_1 \pm t,$$

$$t_2 = \frac{1}{a}\left(2 - \frac{1}{2}\right) = \frac{1}{a}\left(1 + \frac{1}{2}\right) = t\left(1 + \frac{1}{2}\right).$$

This result shows that by putting two similar components in parallel the expected life of the parallel system is 150% that of the single component. For $n = 3$

$$t_3 = \frac{1}{a}\left(1 + \frac{1}{2} + \frac{1}{3}\right) = t\left(1 + \frac{1}{2} + \frac{1}{3}\right)$$

and for n components in parallel the expression above can be shown by induction to reduce to

$$t_n = \frac{1}{a}\left(1 + \frac{1}{2} + \frac{1}{3} + \ldots + \frac{1}{n}\right) \text{ or } t\left(1 + \frac{1}{2} + \frac{1}{3} + \ldots + \frac{1}{n}\right)$$

in contrast to the result $t_n = t/n$ for n components in series.

It can be seen, however, that the addition of components to a parallel set is rewarded by diminishing returns. The mean life of a single component is extended by 50% for the cost of one additional component of the same type, by a further 33% by the addition of a third component and by further 25%, 20% ... by further additions. This is not surprising. If the n components originally have equal expectations of life, the time to failure of the system is the time to failure of the last of the n components to fail, i.e. the expected time is the expected mean value of the *largest* (and in a series system, the *smallest*) of a set of n random samples drawn from the probability distribution of the life of a single component.

Other distributions used in reliability analysis

The negative exponential distribution applies only to systems which have a *constant* rate of failure or decay. Such a rule may apply in practice to simple components such as transistors and other relatively simple solid-state devices. But many components in practical use are themselves complex systems of sub-components each with its own implicit failure rate. So constant rates of failure are by no means universal. More flexible laws readily adapted to empirical failure-rates are therefore needed. The most widely used distribution in reliability analysis is a modified form of the Γ-distribution.

$$f(t) = \frac{1}{\Gamma(n)} t^{n-1} e^{-t} \quad (0 \leqslant t < \infty)$$

in which the variable t is replaced by at^b where a and b are parameters determined by empirical analysis of the relevant data. Such distributions, known as Weibull distributions, are very flexible. The values of the three parameters—a, b and n—can be varied to fit a very wide range of practical failure characteristics. The values of the parameters are usually found by graphical methods using logarithmic scales.

Example 1. A mechanized system consists of six components of which A_1, A_2, similar components in parallel, are connected in series with the single component B and then with the three similar components C_1, C_2, C_3 which are in parallel with each other. The failure rates of A, B and C are 2·4, 1·1 and 3·3 per 1,000 hours respectively. Find the expected time to failure of the system.

For the two A's in parallel

$$\frac{1}{a_s} = \frac{1}{a}\left(1 + \frac{1}{2}\right)$$

so that $a_s = 2a/3 = 1·6$ per 1,000 hours.

For the three C's in parallel

$$\frac{1}{c_s} = \frac{1}{c}\left(1 + \frac{1}{2} + \frac{1}{3}\right)$$

so that $C_s = bc/11 = 1·8$ for 1,000 hours.

For the series ABC, the sum of the component rates is

$$1·6 + 1·1 + 3·3 = 6·0 \text{ failures per 1,000 hours}$$

The expected time to failure of the system is therefore $1,000/6·0 = 166·7$ hours.

Example 2. A mechanical system comprises components A in parallel which are in series with one component B. The failure rates of A and B components are 4·5 and 2·0 per 1,000 hours. How many components A would have to be put in parallel to equalize the failure of the system from A and B failures?

For the n components A in parallel,

$$\frac{1}{a_s} = \frac{1}{4·5}\left(1 + \frac{1}{2} + \frac{1}{3} + \ldots + \frac{1}{n}\right) = \frac{1}{2·0}$$

and so it is required to solve this equation for n. This is most easily done by adding successive terms of the reciprocal series until the required value is attained.

Thus the sums of 2, 3, 4 . . . terms are successively 1·5, 1·833, 2·083 and 2·283. The factor required is $4·5/2·0 = 2·25$, which is most closely attained where $n = 5$. Five components A in parallel are therefore required.

12.7 Beta functions and distributions

The beta function, which involves two parameters, also arises frequently in probability theory. It can be defined as

$$B(m, n) = \int_0^1 x^{m-1} (1 - x)^{n-1} dx, \quad (m > 0, n > 0),$$

$$= 2 \int_0^{\pi/2} \sin^{2m-1} \theta \cos^{2n-1} \theta$$

It can be shown that the B-function is related to the Γ-function thus:

$$B(m, n) = \frac{\Gamma(m) \, \Gamma(n)}{\Gamma(m + n)} = B(n, m)$$

and so can be evaluated easily if n and m are integral values.

For example:

$$B(4, 3) = \int_0^1 x^3 (1 - x)^2 dx = \frac{\Gamma(4) \, \Gamma(3)}{\Gamma(7)} = \frac{3.2.1.2.1}{6.5.4.3.2.1} = \frac{1}{60}$$

or

$$\int_0^{\pi/2} \sin^4 \theta \cos^3 \theta \, d\theta = \tfrac{1}{2} B(5/2, 2) = \tfrac{1}{2} \frac{\Gamma(\tfrac{5}{2}) \, \Gamma(2)}{\Gamma(\tfrac{9}{2})}$$

$$= \frac{\tfrac{1}{2} \cdot \tfrac{3}{2} \cdot \tfrac{1}{2} \cdot \sqrt{\pi} . 1}{\tfrac{7}{2} \cdot \tfrac{5}{2} \cdot \tfrac{3}{2} \cdot \tfrac{1}{2} \sqrt{\pi}} = \tfrac{8}{35}$$

If the limits of the integral involve intermediate values of x, tables of the 'incomplete' B-function are available.

In general, for values of m and n greater than 3, the graphs of the beta functions touch the x-axis at 0 and at 1 and rise to a maximum when $x = (m - 1)/((m + n - 2)$.

A linear transformation can convert the range, normally from 0 to 1, into that between any two other points with finite abscissae.

For the function

$$f(x) = k x^{m-1} (1 - x)^{n-1}, \quad (0 \leqslant x \leqslant 1), (m > 0, n > 0)$$

to be a proper pdf, the constant k must ensure that the total area under the graph is unity. So $k = 1/B(m, n)$.

Hence $f(x)$ is the pdf of a beta distribution if

$$f(x) = \frac{1}{B/m, n)} x^{m-1} (1 - x)^{n-1}, \quad (0 \leqslant x \leqslant 1), (m > 0, n > 0).$$

Example 1. Find the mean and variance of the $B(m, n)$ probability distribution.

We have $\quad \mu = \dfrac{1}{B(m, n)} \displaystyle\int_0^1 x \, x^{m-1} (1 - x)^{n-1} dx$

$$= \frac{B(m + 1, n)}{B(m, n)} = \frac{m}{m + n}$$

Similarly we have

$$\mu_2' = \frac{1}{B(m, n)} \int_0^1 x^2 \, x^{m-1} (1 - x)^{n-1} dx$$

$$= \frac{B(m+2, n)}{B(m, n)} = \frac{m(m+1)}{(m+n)(m+n+1)}$$

giving
$$\mu_2 = \sigma^2 = \mu_2' - \mu^2 = \frac{mn}{(m+n)^2 (m+n+1)}$$

Example 2. If x and y are gamma variates with parameters m and n respectively, show that $z = x + y$ is also a gamma variate and that it has the parameter $(m + n)$.

Here
$$f(x) = \frac{1}{\Gamma(m)} x^{m-1} e^{-x}, \quad (0 \leqslant x < \infty),$$

and
$$f(y) = \frac{1}{\Gamma(n)} y^{n-1} e^{-x}, \quad (0 \leqslant y < \infty).$$

Putting $y = z - x$, $\left| \dfrac{dy}{dz} \right| = 1$, we have for the joint probability of z and x,

$$\frac{1}{\Gamma(n)} (z-x)^{n-1} e^{-(z-x)} \frac{1}{\Gamma(m)} x^{m-1} e^{-x}, \quad (0 \leqslant x \leqslant z, 0 \leqslant z < \infty).$$

So
$$f(z) = \frac{1}{\Gamma(m)\Gamma(n)} e^{-z} \int_0^z (z-x)^{n-1} x^{m-1} \, dx$$

In the integral put $x/z = w$, $(0 \leqslant w \leqslant 1)$,
so that
$$dx = z \, dw.$$

The integral then becomes

$$\int z^{m+n-1} (1-w)^{n-1} w^{m-1} \, dw$$

$$= z^{m+n-1} B(n, m) = z^{m+n-1} \frac{\Gamma(n)\Gamma(m)}{\Gamma(m+n)}$$

and so
$$f(z) = \frac{1}{\Gamma(m+n)} z^{m+n-1} e^{-z}, \quad (0 \leqslant z < \infty),$$

which is the pdf of a gamma variate with parameter $(m + n)$.

12.8 Moment Generating Functions

Consider the expectation of $e^{\theta x}$ where x is a random variate and θ is an arbitrary parameter. If the pdf of the variate is $f(x)$, $(a \leqslant x \leqslant b)$ then

$$E[e^{\theta x}] = \int_a^b e^{\theta x} f(x) \, dx \qquad (1)$$

If this integral exists, x can be 'integrated out' and $E[e^{\theta x}]$ becomes a function of θ only. It is called the *moment generating function* (mgf) of the variate or distribution and is denoted by $M[\theta, x]$ or by $M[\theta]$ if there is no ambiguity.

For example, if $f(x) = \dfrac{1}{\Gamma(n)} x^{n-1} e^{-x}, \quad (0 \leqslant x < \infty)$

then
$$E[e^{\theta x}] = \frac{1}{\Gamma(n)} \int_0^\infty e^{\theta x} x^{n-1} e^{-x} dx$$

$$= \frac{1}{\Gamma(n)} \int_0^\infty e^{-x(1-\theta)} x^{n-1} dx$$

This integral exists, i.e. its value is finite, if $0 \leqslant \theta < 1$. Substituting $x(1 - \theta) = y$, $dx(1 - \theta) = dy$, we have

$$E[e^{\theta x}] = \frac{1}{\Gamma(n)} \cdot \frac{1}{(1 - \theta)^n} \int_0^\infty e^{-y} y^{n-1} dy, \quad (0 \leqslant y < \infty)$$

$$= (1 - \theta)^{-n} \text{ since the integral is } \Gamma(n)$$

$$= M[\theta] \text{ for the } \Gamma\text{-variate with parameter } n.$$

Every pdf has its unique mgf. For example, only Γ-variates have mgf's of the form $(1 - \theta)^{-n}$. So if a probability distribution is known to have the mgf $(1 - \theta)^{-3}$, the pdf of the distribution is $x^2 e^{-x}/\Gamma(3)$, $(0 \leqslant x < \infty)$, i.e. the Γ-variate with $n = 3$.

Properties of the mgf. As θ is a parameter independent of x, we have,

from
$$M[\theta, x] = \int_a^b e^{\theta x} f(x) dx, \quad (a \leqslant x \leqslant b) \tag{1}$$

$$\frac{\partial^k M[\theta, x]}{\partial \theta^k} = \int_a^b e^{\theta x} x^k f(x) dx$$

Putting θ now equal to zero,

$$\frac{\partial^k M[\theta, x]}{\partial \theta^k} \bigg|_{\theta=0} = \int_b^a x^k f(x) dx = \mu'_k$$

where μ'_k is the kth moment about the origin.

Thus, if $M[\theta] = (1 - \theta)^{-n}$,

$$\frac{\partial^k M[\theta]}{\partial \theta^k} = n(n + 1) \ldots (n + k - 1)(1 - \theta)^{-n-k}$$

and, when $\theta = 0$,

$$\mu'_k = (n + k - 1)!/(n - 1)!$$

Thus, for the Γ-variate with parameter n, and putting $k = 1$ and then $k = 2$,

$$\mu = \mu'_1 = n \quad \text{and} \quad \mu'_2 = n(n + 1)$$

as we have already seen.

Alternatively, the exponential in equation (1) can be expressed as an infinite series. We then have

$$M[\theta, x] = \int_a^b (1 + \theta x + \frac{\theta^2}{2!} x^2 + \ldots + \frac{\theta^4}{k!} x^4 + \ldots) f(x) \, dx$$

and, integrating term by term,

$$M[\theta, x] = \int_a^b f(x) \, dx + \theta \int_a^b x f(x) \, dx + \frac{\theta^2}{2!} \int_a^b x^2 f(x) \, dx + \ldots$$

$$+ \frac{\theta^k}{4!} \int_a^b x^k f(x) \, dx + \ldots$$

$$= 1 + \theta \mu + \frac{\theta^2}{2!} \mu_2' + \ldots + \frac{\theta^k}{k!} \mu_k' + \ldots \quad (2)$$

which explains why $M[\theta, x]$ is called a moment generating function.

If the distribution of x is symmetrical and the mean is taken as origin, then $\mu = 0$ and all higher moments of odd order will also be zero. In such a case $M[\theta]$ will be an even function of θ, such as some function of θ^2. For example, if $f(x)$ is the normal pdf,

$$f(x) = \frac{1}{\sigma \sqrt{2\pi}} e^{-x^2/2\sigma^2}, \quad (-\infty < x < \infty),$$

it can easily be shown that $M[\theta, x] = e^{\frac{1}{2}\theta^2\sigma^2}$. The expansion of this function as an exponential series yields:

$$e^{\frac{1}{2}\theta^2\sigma^2} = 1 + \frac{1}{2}\theta^2\sigma^2 + \frac{1}{2!}\left(\frac{\theta^2\sigma^2}{2}\right)^2 + \ldots + \frac{1}{k!}\left(\frac{\theta^2\sigma^2}{2}\right)^k + \ldots$$

$$= 1 + \frac{\theta^2}{2!} \sigma^2 + \frac{\theta^4}{4!} \cdot 3\sigma^4 + \ldots + \frac{\theta^{2k}}{(2k)!} \frac{(2k)!}{k!} \frac{\sigma^{2k}}{2^k} + \ldots$$

Comparison of the coefficients of powers of θ with those of equation (2) verifies that all central moments of odd order are zero and that

$$\mu_2 = \sigma^2, \quad \mu_4 = 3\sigma^4, \quad \text{and } \mu_{2k} = \frac{(2k)!}{k!2^k} \sigma^{2k}$$

Two measures involving moments are sometimes useful in estimating the shape of the graph of a pdf. The dimensionless function

$$\gamma = \frac{\mu_3}{(\mu_2)^{3/2}}$$

is a measure of the skewness of the graph. For a graph which is symmetrical about the origin, $\mu_3 = 0$ and therefore $\gamma = 0$. If γ is positive or negative the graph is correspondingly positively or negatively skew.

The second dimensionless function

$$\beta = \frac{\mu_4}{(\mu_2)^2} - 3$$

compares the 'peakiness' of the graph with that of a normal distribution graph. For a normal graph, $\beta = 0$. If β is positive the graph is flatter than the normal; if β is negative the graph is more 'peaky' than the normal. These functions β and γ implicitly compare, of course, the graphs of variates standardized to equal standard deviations of the same scale.

For example, it can be shown that, for the Binomial distribution,

$$\mu_3 = npq(q - p) \quad \text{and} \quad \mu_4 = 3n^2p^2q^2 + npq(1 - 6pq)$$

We already know that $\mu_2 = npq$. So $\gamma = (q - p)/(npq)^{\frac{1}{2}}$ and $\beta = (1 - 6pq)/npq$. It can therefore be seen that $\gamma = 0$ when $q = p = \frac{1}{2}$ and that $\gamma \longrightarrow 0$ as $n \longrightarrow \infty$ even if $p \neq q$, i.e. the Binomial distribution becomes more nearly symmetrical as n increases. It can also be seen that $\beta \longrightarrow 0$ as $n \longrightarrow 0$, so the Binomial distribution tends towards the normal as $n \longrightarrow \infty$.

If $\phi(x)$ is a function of the random variate x, then

$$M[\theta, \phi(x)] = \int_a^b e^{\theta\phi(x)} f(x)\, dx, \quad (a \leqslant x \leqslant b).$$

It is the expected value of $e^{\theta\phi(x)}$ when x ranges, duly weighted, over the pdf $f(x)$. For example, if c and d are constants,

$$M[\theta, cx] = \int e^{\theta cx} f(x)\, dx = M[c\theta, x],$$

$$M[\theta, x + d] = \int e^{\theta(x + d)} f(x)\, dx = e^{\theta d} M[\theta, x]$$

so that

$$M[\theta, (x - \mu)/\sigma] = e^{-\theta\mu} M[\theta/\sigma, x].$$

These properties make it possible to derive $M[\theta]$ for linear transformations of the variate. For example, as the mgf of the normal variate $(0, 1)$ is $e^{\frac{1}{2}\theta^2}$, the mgf of the normal variate (μ, σ) is $M[\theta, \sigma x + \mu]$ $= e^{\frac{1}{2}\theta^2\sigma^2 + \theta\mu}$. The mgf $e^{8\theta^2 + 6\theta}$ is therefore that of the normal variate $(6 \cdot 0, 4 \cdot 0)$.

If $\phi(x)$ is not linear in x, the mgf $M[\theta, \phi(n)]$ cannot be simply related to $M[\theta, x]$ but the mgf of $\phi(x)$ may still be useful. For example, if $\phi(x)$ is x^2 and x is the normal variate $(0, 1)$ then

$$E[e^{\theta x^2}] = M[\theta, x^2] = \frac{1}{\sqrt{2\pi}} \int_{-\infty}^{\infty} e^{\theta x^2} e^{-x^2/2}\, dx$$

On substituting $x(1 - 2\theta) = t$, the integral reduces to the required mgf, $(1 - 2\theta)^{-\frac{1}{2}}$. This is recognized as of the basic form $(1 - \theta)^{-\frac{1}{2}}$, which is the mgf of a Γ-variate, say v, with parameter $\frac{1}{2}$, but the coefficient of 2 implies that the variate is $\frac{1}{2}v$. The Df of this function is therefore

$$F\left(\frac{v}{2}\right) = \frac{1}{\sqrt{\pi}}\int \left(\frac{v}{2}\right)^{-\frac{1}{2}} e^{-v/2} d\left(\frac{v}{2}\right), \quad \left(0 \leqslant \frac{v}{2} < \infty\right)$$

which is equivalent to

$$F_1(v) = \frac{1}{\sqrt{2\pi}}\int v^{-\frac{1}{2}} e^{-v/2} \, dv, \quad (0 \leqslant v < \infty)$$

as obtained more directly in Section 12.2.

If $z = x + y$, where x and y are random variates with known pdf's, then

$$M[\theta, z] = M[\theta, x + y] = \iint e^{\theta(x+y)} f(x) f(y) \, dx \, dy.$$

If x and y are independent this double integral can be expressed as

$$\int e^{\theta x} f(x) \, dx \int e^{\theta y} f(y) \, dy = M[\theta, x] M[\theta, y].$$

The mgf of the sum of two independent variates is therefore equal to the product of the mgf's of the two variates. If x_1 and x_2 are random variates with the same distribution, then

$$M[\theta, x_1 + x_2] = \{M[\theta, x]\}^2$$

These results can obviously be extended to sums of any finite number of independent variates. Thus, for $\bar{x} = \Sigma x_r / n$

$$M[\theta, \bar{x}] = M[\theta, \Sigma x_r / n] = \{M[\theta/n, x]\}^n$$

Applying these results to the normal variate (μ, σ) we have

$$M[\theta, x] = \exp(\tfrac{1}{2}\theta^2 \sigma^2 + \theta\mu)$$

and so

$$M[\theta, \Sigma x_r] = \exp\{(\tfrac{1}{2}\theta^2\sigma^2 + \theta\mu)n\} = \exp(\tfrac{1}{2}n\theta^2\sigma^2 + n\theta\mu).$$

As a function of θ, this last exponential is of the same form as the mgf of a normal variate but its mean, the coefficient of θ, is $n\mu$ and its standard deviation, derived from the coefficient of θ^2, is $\sigma\sqrt{n}$. We therefore conclude that the sum of n normal variates (μ, σ) is also a normal variate $(n\mu, \sigma\sqrt{n})$.

Similarly, for $\bar{x}$, when θ/n is also substituted for θ,

$$M[\theta, \bar{x}] = \exp\left[\left\{\frac{1}{2}\left(\frac{\theta}{n}\right)^2 \sigma^2 + \frac{\theta}{n}\mu\right\}n\right]$$

$$= \exp\left\{\frac{1}{2}\frac{\theta^2}{n}\sigma^2 + \theta\mu\right\}$$

which is the mgf of the normal variate $(\mu, \sigma/\sqrt{n})$.

Example 1. Find the pdf of the χ^2-distribution.

The χ^2-distribution for n degrees of freedom is defined by

$$\chi^2 = x_1{}^2 + x_2{}^2 + \ldots + x_r{}^2 + \ldots + x_n{}^2$$

where the x_r are independent normal variates $(0, 1)$.

We have already shown that the mgf of a single squared normal variate $(0, 1)$ is $(1 - 2\theta)^{-\frac{1}{2}}$. The mgf of the sum of n independent similar variates is therefore $(1 - 2\theta)^{-n/2}$. As this is the mgf of a variate which is half a Γ-variate of parameter $\frac{1}{2}n$, we have for the corresponding Df:

$$F(\tfrac{1}{2}\chi^2) = \frac{1}{\Gamma(\frac{1}{2}n)} \int (\tfrac{1}{2}\chi^2)^{\frac{1}{2}n-1} e^{-\frac{1}{2}\chi^2} d(\tfrac{1}{2}\chi^2), \quad (0 \leqslant \tfrac{1}{2}\chi^2 < \infty)$$

which is equivalent to

$$F_1(\chi^2) = \frac{1}{\Gamma(\frac{1}{2}n)} \frac{1}{2^{n/2}} \int (\chi^2)^{\frac{1}{2}n-1} e^{-\chi^2/2} d(\chi^2), \quad (0 \leqslant \chi^2 < \infty)$$

The required pdf is therefore

$$f_1(\chi^2) = \frac{(\chi^2)^{\frac{1}{2}n-1} e^{-\chi^2/2}}{\Gamma(\frac{1}{2}n)2^{n/2}} \quad (0 \leqslant \chi^2 < \infty)$$

but it is easier to remember that $\frac{1}{2}\chi^2$ is a Γ-variate of parameter $\frac{1}{2}n$.

Example 2. If $t = (\bar{x} - \mu)/\sigma$ where $\bar{x}$ is the mean of n independent random variates x with mean μ and s.d. σ, show that the pdf of t tends to the normal $(0, 1)$ as $n \to \infty$.

This, the Central Limit Theorem, is valid only if σ exists, i.e. if σ is not infinite.

Since no generality is lost by transferring the origin of coordinates to the mean of x, so that $\mu = 0$, we can then expand $M[\theta, x]$ as the following series:

$$M[\theta, x] = 1 + \frac{\theta^2}{2!} \sigma^2 + \frac{\theta^3}{3!} \mu_3 + \ldots$$

and t can now be written as $\bar{x}\sqrt{n}/\sigma$. So

$$M[\theta, t] = M[\theta, \bar{x}\sqrt{n}/\sigma] = M[\theta, \Sigma x_r/\sigma\sqrt{n}]$$

$$= \{M[\theta/\sigma\sqrt{n}, x]\}^n$$

Hence $\log M[\theta, t] = n \log M\left[\dfrac{\theta}{\sigma\sqrt{n}}, x\right]$

Substituting $\theta/\sigma\sqrt{n}$ for θ in the above series, we have

$$\log M[\theta, t] = n \log \left[1 + \frac{\theta^2\sigma^2}{\sigma^2 n 2!} + o\left(\frac{\theta}{\sqrt{n}}\right)^3\right]$$

$$= n \log \left[1 + \frac{\theta^2}{2n} + o\left(\frac{\theta}{\sqrt{n}}\right)^3\right].$$

Since $\log (1 + x) = x - \dfrac{x^2}{2} + \dfrac{x^3}{3} + \ldots$, for $0 < x < 1$, the above

logarithm, for θ sufficiently small, can also be expressed as a series. So

$$\log M[\theta, t] = n\left[\frac{\theta^2}{2n} + o\left(\frac{\theta}{\sqrt{n}}\right)^3\right]$$

$$= \frac{\theta^2}{2} + o\left(\frac{\theta^3}{\sqrt{n}}\right)$$

Hence, as $n \to \infty$, $\log M[\theta, t] \to \tfrac{1}{2}\theta^2$, i.e. $M[\theta, t] \to e^{\frac{1}{2}\theta x^2}$ which is the mgf of the normal variate $(0, 1)$.

This theorem justifies the widespread use of normal distribution techniques, especially with large samples, even if the samples are drawn from populations which are either non-normal or not well defined. We have already shown that the means of samples from normal distributions are also normally distributed: the theorem shows that even though the sampled population is of any form, so long as the s.d. of the population is finite, then the means of samples are distributed in a form which tends to the normal as the sample size increases.

A disadvantage of the mgf is that it offers no systematic method of recovering the pdf of the variate from an unknown form of $M[\theta]$. This problem is solved by the use of *characteristic functions* in which the real parameter θ is replaced by a complex parameter $i\omega$. Characteristic functions have properties similar to those of mgf's except that, in addition, the pdf can (in principle) be recovered from them—but only by the use of complex functions beyond the scope of this book.

12.9   The Normal Distribution in Two or Three Dimensions

If the co-ordinates (x, y) of a point P in a plane are both normal variates $(0, \sigma)$, what are the probability distributions of $r = OP$ and of r^2, where O is the origin of co-ordinates?

The joint probability that P lies in the rectangle bounded by x, $x + dx$ and y, $y + dy$ is

$$\frac{1}{\sigma\sqrt{2\pi}} e^{-x^2/2\sigma^2} dx \, \frac{1}{\sigma\sqrt{2\pi}} e^{-y^2/2\sigma^2} dy = \frac{1}{2\pi\sigma^2} e^{-(x^2 + y^2)/2\sigma^2} dx \, dy$$

The probability density within this elementary rectangle is therefore $\dfrac{1}{2\pi\sigma^2} e^{-r^2/2\sigma^2}$, where $r^2 = x^2 + y^2$, and is a function of r only. It is therefore constant within the ring bounded by r and $r + dr$. Hence we can write, for the ring of radius r and $r + dr$,

$$dF(r) = \frac{1}{2\pi\sigma^2} e^{-r^2/2\sigma^2} 2\pi r \, dr, \quad (0 \leqslant r < \infty),$$

$$= \frac{1}{\sigma^2} r \, e^{-r^2/2\sigma^2}$$

So $\quad F(r = R) = \int_0^R \frac{r}{\sigma^2} e^{-r^2/2\sigma^2} \, dr = 1 - e^{-R^2/2\sigma^2}$

and $\qquad f(r) = \frac{r}{\sigma^2} e^{-r^2/2\sigma^2}, \quad (0 \leqslant r < \infty).$

The probability that $r \geqslant R$ is $1 - F(r = R) = e^{-R^2/2\sigma^2}$. The above results relate to the distribution of $r = (x^2 + y^2)^{\frac{1}{2}}$. For the distribution of $u = r^2$, $du = 2r \, dr$, we have

$$dF_1(u) = \frac{1}{2\sigma^2} e^{-u/2\sigma^2} \, du$$

and $\qquad f_1(u) = \frac{1}{2\sigma^2} e^{-u/2\sigma^2}, \quad (0 \leqslant u \leqslant \infty).$

Putting $u/\sigma^2 = \chi^2$, these results are of course identical with those for χ^2 with two degrees of freedom. These particular distributions, sometimes known as Rayleigh distributions, have already been derived in Section 12.4.

The distribution $r = OP$ for three dimensions, when P has the co-ordinates (x, y, z), each of which is a normal variate $(0, 1)$, can be obtained similarly by showing that the probability density is constant within the spherical shells centred at 0. The results are then

$$f(r) = \sqrt{\frac{2}{\pi}} \frac{r^2}{\sigma^3} e^{r^2/2\sigma^2}, \quad (0 \leqslant r < \infty),$$

and $\qquad f_1(u) = \frac{1}{\sqrt{2\pi}} \frac{u^{\frac{1}{2}}}{\sigma^3} e^{-u/2\sigma^2}, \quad (0 \leqslant u < \infty).$

These are known as Maxwell distributions. In a Maxwellian gas (of molecules, neutrons or electrons) the velocities of the particles are normal variates, with $\sigma^2 = kT/m$, where k is Boltzman's constant, T is the absolute temperature and m is the mass of the particle.

Finally, the method can be extended to n dimensions. The volume of a hyperspherical shell is taken to be $nkr^{n-1} \, dr$ and the value of the numerical constant k can be obtained from the fact that the total probability must be unity. The resulting distribution is of course that of χ^2 for n degree of freedom.

The success of the method depends on the fact that, when the co-ordinates of the point P are normal variates, the joint probabilities are of the form $\exp(-\Sigma x_r^2) = e^{-r^2}$ and so depend only on r. The method is therefo re not generally applicable.

12.10 Discrete Distributions

In this section it will be assumed that x is a discrete variate which takes the integral values $0, 1, 2, \ldots$ with specified probabilities. For example, the binomial distribution is defined by

$$p(x = k) = {}^nC_k p^k q^{n-k}$$

where p is constant, $0 < p < 1$, and $q = 1 - p$. (Section 5.3.)

As with the mgf's of continuous variates, the mgf of a discrete variate is defined as $E[e^{\theta x}]$. For the above binomial variate we therefore have

$$M[\theta, x] = \sum_{k=0}^{n} {}^nC_k e^{\theta k} p^k q^{n-k}$$

$$= \sum_{k=0}^{n} {}^nC_k (pe^{\theta})^k q^{n-k}$$

$$= (q + pe^{\theta})^n$$

This result shows that the binomial variate can be regarded as the sum of n binomial variates each of which has the mgf $(q + pe^{\theta})$ a variate which has only two values, 0 and 1, with $P(x = 0) = q$ and $P(x = 1) = p$. It is also clear that the sum of two binomial variates of parameters (n_1, p) (n_2, p) is a third binomial variate of parameter $(n_1 + n_2, p)$.

However, the mgf's of discrete distributions are sometimes cumbersome to manipulate and a simpler alternative is available.

This alternative function, the series *generating function* (gf) is defined for x, the binomial variate (n, p), thus:

$$g(t, x) = \sum_{k=0}^{n} {}^nC_k (pt)^k q^{n-k} = (q + pt)^n$$

Here t is again an arbitrary parameter and the function itself, denoted by $g(t, x)$, or by $g(t)$ when there is no ambiguity, is again expressible as a series. But in this series the coefficients of ascending powers of t are $a_0 = P(x = 0)$, $a_1 = P(x = 1) \ldots a_n = P(x = n)$.

To examine the properties of generating functions consider the general case of the infinite series

$$g(t) = a_0 + a_1 t + a_2 t^2 + \ldots + a_k t^k + \ldots$$

where $0 \leqslant a_k \leqslant 1$ for all k, $0 \leqslant k < \infty$ and $0 < t = 1$. If $|t| < 1$, such a series converges, since if $a_k = 1$ for all k, it becomes the geometric series with parameter t and a sum to infinity of $1/(1 - t)$. We also have $g(1) = \Sigma a_x = 1$, the total probability.

Differentiating $g(t)$ with respect to t, we have

$$g'(t) = a_0 . 0 + a_1 . 1 + a_2 . 2t + \ldots + a_k . k t^{k-1} + \ldots$$

$$= \sum_{k=0}^{\infty} a_k . k, \quad \text{when } t = 1$$

$$= \mu.$$

Hence $g'(t) \mid_{t=1} = \mu$.

Multiplying $g'(t)$ by t and differentiating again we have, on putting $t = 1$,

$$g'(t) + g''(t) = \mu_2'$$

Thus, for the binomial,

$$g'(t) = np(q + pt)^{n-1}$$
$$g''(t) = n(n - 1)p^2 (q + pt)^{n-2}$$

so that $\mu = np$, and $\mu_2 = \mu_2' - \mu^2 = npq$, as we have already seen in Section 5.4.

If the two random variates x and y have gf's $g_1(t)$ and $g_2(t)$ where

$$g_1(t) = a_0 + a_1 t + \ldots + a_k t^k + \ldots$$
$$g_2(t) = b_0 + b_1 t + \ldots + b_k t^k + \ldots$$

then

$$g_1(t) . g_2(t) = a_0 b_0 + (a_1 b_0 + a_0 b_1)t + (a_2 b_0 + a_1 b_1 + a_0 b_2)t^2 + \ldots$$
$$+ (a_k b_0 + a_{k-1} b_1 + \ldots + a_1 b_{k-1} + a_0 b_k)t^k + \ldots$$
$$= h(t), \text{ let us say.}$$

The coefficient of t^k in $h(t)$ is $P(z = x + y = k)$ since, as x takes the decreasing values $k, k - 1 \ldots 1, 0$, y must take the increasing values $0, 1, \ldots k - 1, k$ when $x + y = k$.

The series $h(t)$ is called the *convolution* of the series $g_1(t)$ and $g_2(t)$.

Thus if x and y are discrete random variates whose probability generating functions are $g_1(t)$ and $g_2(t)$, then the probability generating function of $z = x + y$ is $h(t)$ where $h(t)$ is the convolution of $g_1(t)$ and $g_2(t)$, usually written $g_1(t)*g_2(t)$.

The variate of the Poisson distribution (Section 5.5) is defined by

$$P(x = k) = e^{-a} a^k / a!, \quad (0 \leqslant k < \infty),$$

So

$$g(t, x) = \sum_{k=0}^{\infty} e^{-a}(at)^k / a! = e^{-a} . e^{at} = e^{-a(1-t)}.$$

The moments of the Poisson variate are easily found since $g'(t) = a$, $g''(t) = a^2$, $g'''(t) = a^3$, and so on.

For the sum of two Poisson variates x and y, with parameters a and b respectively, we have, putting $z = x + y$

$$h(t, z) = g_1(t, x)* g_2(t, y) = e^{-(a+b)(x+y)} = e^{-(a+b)z}$$

which is the gf of a Poisson variate with parameter $(a + b)$.

The variate of the geometric distribution is defined by

$$P(x = k) = q^k p, \quad (0 \leqslant k < \infty)$$

where p is a constant, $0 < p < 1$, and $q = (1 - ps)$. The successive terms of the distribution as $k = 0, 1, 2, \ldots$ in sequence form a geometric series with factor q. The distribution arises from 'Bernouilli trials', i.e. in successive trials with constant probabilities of success or failure; k is the number of failures that occur before the first success is achieved.

The gf of the geometric distribution is

$$g(t, x) = \sum_{k=0}^{\infty} p(qt)^k = p/(1 - qt)$$

from which $\mu = q/p$ and $\mu_2 = q/p^2$ can easily be derived. For example, in a table of random digits the occurrences of any specified digit, say 7, are separated by occurrences of other digits. The probability of 'success' at any one 'trial' is $1/10$, so the number of 'failures' which occur before a 7 arises is a geometric variate with $p = 1/10$, $q = 9/10$. In this case, therefore, the mean number of failures is 9 and the variance is 90. But note that the most probable number of failures is 0 and that the probabilities decline very slowly from the first and greatest term.

If we are interested in the number of trials which precede the nth success, there will be $(n-1)$ preceding successes accompanied by

$$S_n = x_1 + x_2 + \ldots + x_r + \ldots + x_n$$

failures, where the x_r are independent geometric variates with the same parameter p. The gf of the probability distribution of S_n is therefore

$$g(S_n, t) = \{p/(1 - qt)\}^{n^*}$$

which is the n-fold convolution of the geometric distribution. In the binomial expansion of this function the coefficient of t^k is

$$p^n \cdot \frac{n(n + 1) \ldots (n + k - 1)}{1.2.3 \ldots k} q^k = \frac{(n + k - 1)!}{n!k!} p^n q^k$$

We therefore have for the distribution of S_n, i.e. the number of failures preceding the kth success,

$$P(S_n = k) = {}^{n+k-1}C_k p^n q^k, \quad (0 \leqslant k < \infty)$$

This is known as *Pascal's distribution*. It can be seen that the geometric distribution is a particular case, with $n = 1$, of this more general distribution. Pascal's distribution is, in turn, a particular case, with integral exponent n, of the more general negative binomial *distribution* in which n need not be an integer.

By differentiating $g(S_n)$ with respect to t and applying the rates established earlier in this section it can readily be shown that the mean of the negative binomial variate is nq/p and its variance nq/p^2.

Example. The number of candidates from a certain school who take a higher examination in pure mathematics is a Poisson variate with mean a. The probability that any candidate passes the examination is p, a constant. What is the probability distribution of the number of passes per examination?

If n candidates take one of the examinations, then the number of passes, r, is the binomial variate

$$P(x = r) = {}^nC_r q^{n-r} p^r, \quad (0 \leqslant r \leqslant n)$$

where n is the Poisson variate

$$P(y = n) = e^{-a} a^n n! \quad (0 \leqslant n < \infty)$$

Hence the probability that in any one examination r candidates pass is

$$P(N = r) = \sum_{n=r}^{\infty} {}^nC_r q^{n-r} p^r e^{-a} a^n/n!$$

$$= e^{-a} p^r \sum_{n=r}^{\infty} \frac{n!}{(n-r)! r!} q^{n-r} \frac{a^r a^{n-r}}{n!}$$

$$= e^{-a} \frac{(ap)^r}{r!} \sum_{n=r}^{\infty} \frac{(aq)^{n-r}}{(n-r)!}$$

$$= e^{-a} \frac{(ap)^r}{r!} e^{aq}$$

$$= e^{-ap} (ap)^r/r!, \quad (0 \leqslant r < \infty)$$

The numbers of passes per examination is therefore a Poisson variate with mean ap.

In terms of generating functions we could have written for the Poisson variate y,

$$g_1(t_1, Y) = e^{-a(1-t_1)}$$

As each candidate is subjected to a binomial chance of success, p, or failure, q, for which

$$g_2(t, X) = q + pt$$

we now substitute $q + pt$ for t_1 and obtain for the gf of the distribution sought,

$$g(t, N) = e^{-a(1-q-pt)} = e^{-ap(1-t)}$$

which is the gf of a Poisson variate with mean ap as found above.

12.11 Final comment

The preceding pages of this Appendix offer an introduction to a

L

few of the techniques that can be applied to problems in probability theory. The exercises that follow will demonstrate that some of the techniques described are convenient to use on some forms of distribution and on some types of problem but are not suitable for others. It will become apparent that it is useful to acquire a wide range of techniques, including some beyond the scope of this book, to learn both their uses and their limitations, and so to have at command the tool most suitable for each probability problem that arises.

EXERCISES XLI

The notations and abbreviations used in the following exercises are those used in the Mathematical Appendix.

1. If $f(-x) = f(x)$ for all values of the variate x, $(-\infty < x < \infty)$, show that $F(-x) = 1 - F(x)$.

2. Find the variance of the truncated Cauchy distribution which has the pdf $f(x) = k/(1 + x^2)$, $(-a \leqslant x \leqslant a)$ and show that as $a \to \infty$ so the variance tends to infinity also.

3. Independent random samples are taken of a variate with pdf $f(x)$ and Df $F(x)$, $(a \leqslant x \leqslant b)$. If n such sample values are arranged in order of increasing magnitude—$x_1, x_2, \ldots, x_r, \ldots, x_n$—show that the pdf of the variate x_r is

$$k\{F(x^r)\}^{r-1}f(x_r)\{1 - F(x_r)\}^{n-r}, \quad (a \leqslant x \leqslant b)$$

where $k = n!/(r - 1)!(n - r)!$

4. If in Ex. 3, $f(x) = 1/b$, $(0 \leqslant x \leqslant b)$ and $n = 3$, show that the pdfs of x_1, x_2 and x_3 are respectively

$$3(b - x_1)^2/a^3, \quad 6x_2(b - x_2)/b^3 \quad \text{and} \quad 3x_3^2/b^3, \quad (0 \leqslant x \leqslant b).$$

Sketch the graphs of these three functions.

5. Put $x_n - x_1 = R$, the range, in Ex. 3 and show that

$$f(R) = c\int_a^{b-R} f(x)\{F(x + R) - F(x)\}^{n-2}f(x + R)\,dx, \quad (0 \leqslant R \leqslant b),$$

where $c = n!/(n - 2)!$
Show also that, for the data of Ex. 4, R and x_2 are similarly distributed.

6. If x is uniformly distributed from $-a$ to $+a$, show that
   (i) for $y = |x|$, $f(y) = 1/a$, $(0 \leqslant y \leqslant a)$, and that
   (ii) for $z = x^2$, $f_1(z) = 2z^{-\frac{1}{2}}/a$, $(0 \leqslant z \leqslant a^2)$.

7. If θ is uniformly distributed from $-\frac{1}{2}\pi$ to $+\frac{1}{2}\pi$, show that
   (i) $x = \tan \theta$ is a Cauchy variate, and that
   (ii) $y = \sin \theta$ has the pdf $\dfrac{1}{\pi}(1 - y^2)^{-\frac{1}{2}}$, $(-1 \leqslant y \leqslant 1)$.

8. If $f(t) = 6t/(1 + t^4)$, $(0 \leqslant t \leqslant \infty)$, show that t and $u = 1/t$ are similarly distributed.

9. Show that if $F(x)$ is the Df of a variate x, $(0 \leqslant x > \infty)$, then the variate $y = F(x)$, $(0 \leqslant y < 1)$, is rectangular.

MATHEMATICAL APPENDIX

10. In a Maxwellian gas the distribution of molecular speeds, v, at any instant is given by

$$f(v) = \left(\frac{2}{\pi}\right)^{\frac{1}{2}} \sigma^3 v^2 \exp\left(-v^2/2\sigma^2\right), \quad (0 \leqslant v < \infty),$$

where $\sigma^2 = kT/m$. Show that the distribution of molecular energies, $E = \frac{1}{2}mv^2$, is given by

$$f_1(E) = \frac{2}{\sqrt{\pi}} E^{\frac{1}{2}}(kT)^{3/2} \exp\left(-E/kT\right), \quad (0 \leqslant E < \infty).$$

11. If x is a variate with pdf $f(x)$ and b is an arbitrary constant, show that

  (i) $E[(x - b)]$ is a minimum when b is the median,

  (ii) $E[(x - b)^2]$ is a minimum when b is the mean.

12. If x_1 and x_2 are independent random samples from the same distribution, show that $E[(x_1 - x_2)^2] = 2\sigma^2$.

13. If x is a normal variate (μ, σ), show that

$$E[x^3] = 3\sigma^2\mu + \mu^3$$

14. If $f(x) = 1/\pi$, $(0 \leqslant x \leqslant \pi)$, show that

  (i) $E[\sin x] = 2/\pi$, and

  (ii) $E[\sin^2 x] = 1/2$.

15. If x_1, x_2 and x_3 are independent random samples from the normal distribution (θ, σ) and if

$$u = x_1 + kx_2 \quad \text{and} \quad v = x_1 + kx_3,$$

show that $E[uv] = \sigma^2$, that $E[u^2] = E[v^2] = (1 + k^2)\sigma^2$, and hence that the expected correlation of u and v is $1/(1 + k^2)$.

16. If $f(x) = e^{-x}$ and $f(y) = e^{-y}$, $(0 \leqslant x, y < \infty)$, show that the pdf of the variate $z = x/y$ is $1/(1 + z)^2$, $(0 \leqslant z < \infty)$. Show also that the mean of this variate does not exist.

17. If $g(w) = \frac{1}{2}e^{-w/2}$ and $p(t) = (\pi t e^t)^{-\frac{1}{2}}$, $(0 \leqslant w, t < \infty)$, show that the pdf of the variate $s = w + t$ is

$$(2\pi)^{-\frac{1}{2}}s^{\frac{1}{2}}e^{-s/2}.$$

18. Using the method of Section 12.3 show that the difference of two normal variates $(0, \sigma_1)$ and $(0, \sigma_2)$ is also a normal variate $[0, (\sigma_1^2 + \sigma_2^2)^{\frac{1}{2}}]$.

19. If x_1 and x_2 are two independent random observations of the Cauchy variate which has the pdf $f(x) = 1/\pi(1 + x^2)$, $(-\infty < x < \infty)$, show that the mean value $\mu = \frac{1}{2}(x_1 + x_2)$ has the same distribution as x.

20. If x and y are independent Γ-variates with parameters m and n respectively, show that $z = x + y$ is a Γ-variate also, but with parameter $(m + n)$.

21. Sketch the graphs of $f(x) = x^{n-1}e^{-x}/\Gamma(n)$, $(0 \leqslant x < \infty)$, for $n = \frac{1}{2}, 1, 1\frac{1}{2}, 2, 3$ and 4. Mark their means and modes.

22. If $f(v) = \frac{1}{\sqrt{\pi}} v^{-\frac{1}{2}} e^{-v}$, $(0 \leqslant v < \infty)$, find the distributions $\pm\sqrt{v}$ and of $|\sqrt{v}|$.

23. Show that the mean and variance of the Weibull distribution

$$f(t) = 2at \exp\left(-at^2\right), \quad (0 \leqslant t < \infty)$$

are $\frac{1}{2}(\pi/a)^{\frac{1}{2}}$ and $\left(1 - \frac{\pi}{4}\right)/a$ respectively.

24. If $\Gamma(a,n) = \dfrac{1}{\Gamma(n)} \displaystyle\int_a^\infty x^{n-1} e^{-x}\, dx$, show that

$$\Gamma(a,\, n) = \frac{1}{\Gamma(n)} a^{n-1} e^{-a} + \Gamma(a,\, n-1)$$
$$= e^{-a}\left[\frac{a^{n-1}}{(n-1)!} + \frac{a^{n-2}}{(n-2)!} + \cdots + \frac{a^2}{2!} + a + 1 \right].$$

Use this result to verify, by use of the Poisson chart (p. 110), that $\Gamma(5, 7) = 1 - 0.25 = 0.75$.

25. Fisher has shown that, for $n > 15$, a $\Gamma(n)$ variate x can be transformed, approximately, to a Normal variate $(\sqrt{4n - 1},\, 1)$ by putting $y = 2\sqrt{x}$. Use this approximation to estimate the 90% confidence limits for the Γ-variate with $n = 20$. (12·0, 29·4.)

26. The Laplace distribution has the pdf

$$f(x) = \tfrac{1}{2} a e^{-a|x|}, \quad (-\infty < x < \infty).$$

Sketch the graphs of e^{-ax} and of $e^{-a|x|}$, and verify that the variance of the Laplace variate is $2/a^2$.

27. Three similar components, each with a mean failure rate a, are connected to form (i) a series system, (ii) a parallel system. Find $P(t > 1/a)$, the probability that the system survives longer than $1/a$, for each of the two systems. (0·05, 0·75.) (Use Ex. 4.)

28. Calculate the expected time to failure of a system of 5 components, $AB(CC)B$, in which the C's are in parallel. The mean failure rates of A, B and C are 1·6, 1·8 and 2·4 per 1,000 hours respectively. (147 hours.)

29. Components X and Y, with mean failure rates of 1·2 and 1·8 per 1,000 hours respectively, are put in series to form a system XY. To reduce the mean failure rate of the system, further components of the same type can be put in parallel with each other to form a system such as $(XXX..X)(YYY..Y)$. Find the smallest number of components which will reduce the mean failure rate of the system to less than 1 per 1,000 hours.

30. A component has a mean life of 600 hours. What are the 90% confidence limits (45% on each side of the mean) within which you would expect the life of the component to lie? (25·5 hrs., 1,500 hours.)

31. By substituting $F(x) = y$ in the pdf of x_r (Ex. 3) show that
$$k = n/B(r - 1,\, n - r) = n!/(r - 1)!(n - r)!$$

32. Sketch the graphs of the B-variates with
$$f(x) = x^{m-1}(1 - x)^{n-1}/B(m, n) \quad (0 \leqslant x \leqslant 1)$$
for which (m, n) takes the values $(1, 1)$, $(2, 1)$, $(\tfrac{1}{2}, \tfrac{1}{2})$, $(1, 3)$, $(2, 2)$, $(3, 1)$ and $(5, 5)$.

33. The F-distribution for $(2m, 2n)$ d.f. has the pdf
$$\frac{kF^{m-1}}{(n + mF)^{m+n}}, \quad (0 \leqslant F < \infty)$$

Show that the substitution $x = mF/(n + mF)$ transforms the $F(2m, 2n)$ variate into a $B(m, n)$ variate.

34. Use integration by parts to show that the incomplete B-function
$$60\int_0^p t^3(1 - t)^2\, dt = 15p^4q^2 + 6p^5q + p^6, \quad (q = 1 - p).$$

Generalize this result to show how sums of terms of the binomial distribution can be found by reference to tables of the incomplete B-function.

35. Verify that $\quad \mu_3 = \mu_3' - 3\mu\mu_2' + 2\mu^3$

and that $\qquad\qquad \mu_4 = \mu_4' - 4\mu\mu_3' + 6\mu^2\mu_2' - 3\mu^4$

Show that if the distribution is symmetrical about its mean, μ, then

$$\mu_4 = \mu_4' - 6\mu^2\mu_2 - \mu^4$$

36. Show that any linear function of n independent Normal variates is also a Normal variate.

37. Show that the mgf of the continuous variate with the pdf

$$f(x) = 1/2a, \quad (a \leqslant x \leqslant a)$$

is $(\sinh a\theta)/a\theta$. Expand this function as a power series and thus show that $\mu_2 = a^2/3$ and $\mu_{2k} = a^{2k}/(2k + 1)$.

38. Show that the mgf of the distribution of $\bar{x}_n$, the mean of samples of n drawn from the distribution of Ex. 37, is

$$\left\{ \frac{\sinh (a\theta/n)}{a\theta/n} \right\}^n$$

Consider the behaviour of this function as $n \longrightarrow \infty$ and show that the variate $\sqrt{3}\bar{x}_n/a$ tends towards the unit normal variate $(0, 1)$ as $n \longrightarrow \infty$.

39. The *cumulant function* $K[\theta, x]$ is defined as $\log M[\theta, x]$. The coefficients, κ_r, $(r = 1, 2, 3, \ldots)$ of $\theta^r/r!$ in the series expansion of $K[\theta, x]$ are called cumulants.

Verify that for the normal variate (μ, σ), $\kappa_1 = \mu$, $\kappa_2 = \sigma^2$, and $\kappa_r = 0$ for all $r > 2$.

40. Show that, in general,

$$\kappa_1 = \mu, \quad \kappa_2 = \sigma^2, \quad \kappa_3 = \mu_3 \quad \text{and} \quad \kappa_4 = \mu_4 - 3\sigma^2.$$

[After showing that $\kappa_1 = \mu$, transfer the origin of coordinates to the mean, thus simplifying the power series expansion of $M[\theta, x]$. Then use the series expansion of $\log (1 - x)$.]

Hence show that the first four moments of the $\Gamma(n)$ variate about its mean are n, n, $2n$ and $6n + 3n^2$. Show that the $\Gamma(n)$ variate tends towards the Normal as $n \longrightarrow \infty$.

41. If x is a Gaussian variate $(0, 1)$ and y is a Γ-variate with parameter $\frac{1}{2}$, show that the variates $\frac{1}{2}x^2$ and y both have the same mgf. Hence derive the pdf's of the variates $u = (x_1^2 + x_2^2)^{\frac{1}{2}}$ and $v = (x_1^2 + x_2^2 + x_3^2)$ where x_1, x_2 and x_3 are independent random samples of x.

42. Use the χ^2-table to estimate the percentage of the molecules in a Maxwellian gas which, at any instant, have an energy 8 or more times the mean energy ($0 \cdot 75\%$ approx.).

43. If x and y are independent random variates with the same pdf, $f(x)$, show that it is not *generally* true that the variate $Z = X + Y$ is of the same form as X and Y.

44. The coordinates (x, y) of a point in a plane are random variates. If $f(x) = \frac{1}{2}ce^{-c|x|}$ and $f(y) = \frac{1}{2}ce^{-c|y|}$, $(-\infty < x, y < \infty)$, find the contours of equal probability density. Given that the median of the $\Gamma(2)$ function is $2 \cdot 674$ locate an inner area in which the probability of the point falling is $\frac{1}{2}$. (The square with corners at $(\pm 2 \cdot 674/c, \pm 2 \cdot 674/c)$.)

45. Pressurized paint sprayers aimed at a point 0 on a flat surface are found to produce a circular distribution of droplets with a density proportional to $re^{-r^2/2\sigma^2}$ at radius r. Two sprayers, one with dispersion σ_1 and loaded with red paint, and one with dispersion σ_2 and loaded with blue paint, are aimed at the same point. Equal quantities of paint are sprayed. Show that the area which is predominantly red is

$$4\pi\sigma_1{}^2 \log k/(k^2 - 1)$$

where $\qquad k = \sigma_2/\sigma_1 \quad$ and $\quad \sigma_2 > \sigma_1$

46. A generator of random binary digits is set to produce sequences of the form

$$S = X_1 + X_2 + \ldots + X_r + \ldots + X_n$$

where $P(X_r = 1) = p$, $P(X_r = 0) = q$, $p + q = 1$, and n is constant. Find the probability distribution of S. Then find its first four moments and discuss the behaviour of the distribution as $n \rightarrow \infty$.

47. A counter records the numbers of 0's that precede the occurrence of each 1 in a long sequence S. (Ex. 46.) Assuming that each digit produced is independent of its predecessor, find the distribution of the variate x and calculate its mean and variance.

If it were suspected that the digits were 'sticking' slightly, so that $P(X_{r+1} = X_r) = p + \alpha$ when $X_r = 1$ and $q + \alpha$ when $X_r = 0$, what difference would be made to the proportions of 0's and 1's generated? What difference would be made to the frequency of changes, from 0 to 1 or from 1 to 0? $(q/p; \{q - (p - q)\alpha\}/\{p + (p - q)\alpha\}; pq/(pq - \alpha).$

48. What is the distribution of S (Ex. 46) when n is a Poisson variate with mean r? (Poisson variate with mean pr.)

49. The number of currants in a bun of a certain type is a Poisson variate with a mean of α currants per bun. But n different types of bun have different mean numbers of currants. If buns with mean α_r occur with probability p_r, show that the probability of finding k currants in a bun selected at random from the universe of buns is

$$P(x = k) = \sum_{r=0}^{\infty} p_r\, e^{-\alpha_r} \frac{(\alpha_r)^k}{k!}$$

Find the mean and variance of this distribution.

50. A coin-operated machine gives either a ticket for a coin of value 1D or a ticket plus change of 1D for a coin of value 2D. Consider S, the initial store of coins of value 1D, which, it is hoped, will enable the machine to sell 1,600 tickets without failing to give change as required. What initial value of S would reduce the probability of 'failure' to 5% or less when p = probability of change being needed? $(80\sqrt{pq})$.

Miscellaneous Exercises

Group 1

1. The mean of 25 independent measurements is 1·326 with s.d. 0·015. Is this mean significantly different from the value of 1·333 predicted by theory?

($t = 2.33$, 24 d.f.; significant at 5% level.)

2. Show that, for the following data, $\bar{x} = s^2$:

x	0	1	2	3	4
$f(x)$	45	36	14	4	1

Verify that the frequencies above conform closely with those of a Poisson distribution with mean 0·80.

($\bar{x} = s^2 = 0.80$.)

3. Equal batches of similar electronic circuits assembled from their components by eight different operatives working independently are tested. The rejects are counted:

Operative	A	B	C	D	E	F	G	H
Rejects	10	13	4	8	11	16	8	10

On the basis of these figures it is asserted that 'C' is obviously more skilled than F. Question this assertion.

($\chi^2 = 9.0$; 7 d.f.; not significant at 5% level.)

4. If x_1 and x_2 are two independent random samples from a population with mean μ and s.d. σ, write down the mean and standard deviation of $z = x_1 - x_2$.

Group 2

1. If 100 pennies are thrown on to the floor and the number of 'heads' is counted what is the probability that exactly 50 'heads' will be found? Use Stirling's approximation: $n! \approx (2\pi n)^{\frac{1}{2}} (n/e)^n$,

to express the result numerically.

(0·0798.)

2. For the following data calculate the line of regression of y on x and determine whether its slope is significantly different (5% level) from 0·750

x	0	1	2	3	4	5
y	0·7	1·2	1·9	3·0	3·4	4·2

($y = 0.720x - 0.600$, $t = 1.5$, 4 d.f.; not significant.)

3. The critical dimension of a machine-produced component is 5·00 cm $\pm$ 0·02 cm. Components outside these limits are rejected at a loss to the manufacturer of 6d. per reject. The machine is capable of being set to produce exactly the average dimension of 5·00 cm with standard deviation 0·016 cm. At a cost of 1d. per component the standard deviation can be reduced to 0·008 cm. Should the improvement be made?

(Yes. For 10,000 components the additional cost is 10,000d. but the saving on rejects is 12,300d.)

4. For moderately asymmetrical distributions the relationship
Mean − Mode = 3(Mean − Median) is approximately true.
Illustrate this for the following data

x:	1	2	3	4	5	6	7
f:	2	8	27	20	15	12	7

(Mean = 3·5; mode = 3·0; median = 3·3.)

Group 3

1. During design work to reduce the input current to a circuit for a given power output, five tests were made on a modified version of the standard circuit. The standard circuit gave an output of 1 watt for an input current of 0·165 amp. The modified circuit gave 1 watt output for 0·160, 0·163, 0·162, 0·161 and 0·159 amp. inputs.

Is the improvement significant at the 5% level?
($t = 5·7$ with 4 d.f.: the 5% point (one-tail) is 2·13. The result is significant at the 5% level.)

2. How many currents per bun should the baker allow on average if the probability that a bun contains at least one currant is to be (a) 95%, (b) 99%, (c) 99·9%?

((a) 3·0   (b) 4·6   (c) 7·0)

3. The following table (*J. Amer. Med. Ass.*, 166 1294, 1958) shows the numbers of deaths for various causes in a sample of about 12,000 men.

Cause of death	Smokers	Non-smokers
Accidents	363	277
Heart disease	4,593	2,930
Cancer	1,460	789
Lung disease (not cancer)	231	107
All other diseases	*669*	*451*
Man-years exposure ('000)	382	285

Does this support the hypothesis that incidence of the causes of death is unaffected by smoking?

($\chi^2 = 121$ d.f. 5. The null hypothesis is rejected.)

4. Two departments A and B were merged to form a single department. The numbers, means and standard deviations of the ages of individuals in the separate departments were:

	A	B
Number	20	30
Mean	45	50
Standard deviation	10	6

Calculate the mean age and the standard distribution of the ages of the combined department.
(48 : 8·2)

Group 4

1. (a) The results of a well-designed experiment which is carefully repeated four times are +0·00014, −0·00004, +0·00007 and 0·00003. Is the mean of these four results significantly different from zero at the 5% level?
(b) The results of some rough tests repeated four times are +140,

-40, $+70$ and $+30$. Is the mean of these four results significantly different from zero at the 5% level?

Comment on your conclusions.

(In both cases, $t = 1.325$, $3d.f.$: neither is significant. Only the relative magnitudes of the results is relevant.)

2. A moving point P has coordinates (x, y). It moves in steps: at each step y increases by one unit, and x either *increases* or *decreases* one unit with equal probability. If P begins at the origin, where is it after n steps? Trace 10 such steps using random digits (odd and even) or by tossing a coin.

(The point will be at (cx, ny) with probability given by the coefficient of x^c in the expansion of $(\frac{1}{2})^n(x + \frac{1}{x})^n$.)

3. The 'mean deviation from the mean' of a Gaussian distribution is 3.05 units. What is the standard deviation of the distribution?

($s = (\frac{1}{2}\pi)^{\frac{1}{2}}$ m.d. $= 1.253 \times 3.05 = 3.82$ units.)

4. Verify for the distribution $f(x) = xe^{-x}(0 < x < \infty)$ that

Mean $-$ Mode $= 3$(Mean $-$ Median) approximately

(Use: root of $2(1 + x) = e^x$ is $x = 1.7$.)

Group 5

1. A mass production process has a 2% level of defectives. After modifying the process, an ineffective batch of 100 items is found to contain 6 defectives. Does this result support a claim that the modification has adversely affected the mass-production process?

(Yes. P(No. of defectives $\geqslant 6$) $= 0.019$: result is significant at 0.1% level.)

2. Two variables x and y are known to be related by an equation of the form $y = a.10^{bx}$, where a and b are constants.

Experimental values of y for specified values of x are found to be

x	3.00	4.00	5.00	6.00	7.00
y	1.64	2.18	2.91	3.90	5.20

Estimate the values of a and b from the line of regression of $\log y$ on x.

($a = 1.226$, $b = 0.125$.)

3. It is known that 8% of the marks obtained in a large-scale examination equal or exceed 85 and that 30% equal or are less than 35. Assuming that the marks are normally distributed estimate the mean and upper and lower quartiles of the distribution.

(48.6, 66.1, 31.1.)

4. The regression coefficients of y on x and x on y, estimated from a sample of 18, are 3.00 and 0.16 respectively. Calculate the correlation coefficient of x and y. Use Students' 't-distribution' to determine whether it is significantly different from zero.

(0.7; $t = 4$; highly significant.)

Group 6

1. The results of 64 determinations of the strength of a magnetic field yield $\bar{x} = 0.1810$ units with $\Sigma(x - \bar{x})^2 = 0.000063$ units². Is this result significantly different (at the 5% level) from an earlier determination which gave the field strength to be 0.1814 units?

($t = 3.2$, which is significant.)

2. An electronic noise generator is designed to print out random sequences of the binary digits 0 and 1 with $P(0) = p$ and $P(1) = q$, where $p + q = 1$.

(a) What is the probability that a run of k 0's will occur?

(b) What is the average length of run, if runs of both 0's and 1's are counted?

$(p^k q; (p^2 + q^2)/pq.)$

3. Refer to Ex. XXXVI.2 and find the formula for χ^2 for the particular case in which the contingency table can be expressed as:

	A	Not-A
B	$a + x$	$a - x$
Not-B	$a - x$	$a + x$

Then find the values of x which correspond to the 5% and the 1% points of ψ^2 when (i) $a = 100$, (ii) $a = 1000$.

((i) 9·8, 31·0   (ii) 14·0, 44·4.)

4. The following table is taken from the Royal College of Physicians' Report on Smoking and Health.

Death rates from all causes per 1000 per year

Age	Non-smokers	Smokers : Cigarettes per day		
		1–14	15–24	25+
35–44	1·1	1·56	1·55	4·41
45–54	3·7	5·56	7·18	10·19
55–64	12·0	17·69	20·37	25·57
65–74	31·7	47·10	42·09	59·82

Rewrite this table to show the risk of dying for each decade, as fractions, all with numerator 1, e.g. 1·1 rate corresponds to 1 in 90, 31·7 rate corresponds to 1 in 3. Comment on the fact that the difference between smokers and non-smokers is greater at younger ages.

Group 7

1. At a motorway checkpoint the number of cars passing, from midnight to 0070 hours, is 60 per hour and the rate is constant. Calculate the probability of exactly 4 cars passing in 10 minutes.

$(10^{-4} \times 0.454; 0.97).$

2. Annual consumption of a basic chemical over a 7-year period has been

Year	1	2	3	4	5	6	7
Consumption	500	565	620	700	791	890	975

The underlying growth mechanism is believed to be $y = a(l + i)^t$ where y is consumption, t is the year $(1, 2, \ldots)$ and i is the compound interest growth rate. Estimate a and i and also the consumption at $t = 10$. $\Sigma \log y = 5.924; \Sigma t \log y = 25.066).$

(0·6506; 11·2%; 1380.)

3. The standard errors of the means of two samples, sizes 16 and 9, are 2·0 and 4·0. Calculate the population variances and determine whether they differ significantly.

(64, 144; not significant at 10% level.)

4. Sketch the graph of the Cauchy distribution (p. 136) and find the area under the curve between $x = -t$ and $x = t$.

Find the values of t for which the area is (a) 0·5, (b) 0·1. Check that your values correspond to the 50% and 10% points of the t-distribution for $f = 1$.

Group 8

1. The following results A and B were obtained alternately using two different techniques:

A	1·32	1·35	1·36	1·31
B	1·35	1·34	1·39	1·36

Are the results significantly different at the 5% level?

($t = 2·0$, 3 d.f.: the 5% point is 3·2 and so the differences are not significant.)

2. Ten particles are distributed at random among ten cells. What is the probability that each cell contains precisely one particle?

($10!/10^{10}$.)

3. Records kept at Teddington over 14 years from 1954 to 1967 show the following incidence of rainy days according to the day of the week.

	Number of rainy days
Sunday	316
Monday	296
Tuesday	313
Wednesday	325
Thursday	350
Friday	320
Saturday	328
	2,248

Is this evidence that some days of the week are more subject to rain than others?

(No. $\chi^2 = 5·0$; 6 d.f.)

4. The diameter of a spindle must not exceed 1·015 inches or be less than 1·003 inches. In a production run all spindles are checked automatically on a go no-go gauge. 16·6% are oversize and 33% undersize. Assume that the distribution of spindle diameters is Normal. Calculate the mean and standard deviation.

(1·0067″; 0·0085″.)

Group 9

1. Thin sheets of a new dielectric material are found to have 'weak spots' distributed at random over their surface areas. If the average number of weak spots is 0·6 per 25 cm², estimate:

(a) The probability of at least one weak spot in one area of 25 cm².
(b) The probability that an area of 10 cm² selected at random is free of weak spots.
(c) The area which has a 50/50 chance of having no weak spot.

((a) 0·022, (b) 0·79, (c) 28·9 cm².)

2. The index of retail prices for the last five years has been:

Year	Index
1963	100·0
1964	103·3
1965	108·2
1966	112·5
1967	115·1

When will the index have doubled to 200 if the growth rate is assumed to be at (a) simple (b) compound interest.

((a) 1988; (b) 1982.)

3. Copper rods (mean length 10·0 cm., s.d. 0·12 cm) are pushed into plastic sleeves (mean length 9·0 cm., s.d. 0·15 cm) so that, on average, 1·00 cm of rod protrudes from its sleeve. What proportion of such rods would conform with the specification that the protruded length be 1·05 ± 0·15 cm?

(55%)

4. For the distribution

$$f(x) = 6x \, (1 - x) \qquad 0 < x < 1$$
$$= 0 \qquad \text{all other } x$$

show that $\mu = \frac{1}{2}$ and $\sigma^2 = 1/20$.

Group 10

1. It is suspected that difference of ambient temperature may be affecting the results of an experiment. With the ambient temperature 'hot', the results were:

$$3·45, 3·49, 3·51, 3·47. \quad \text{Mean}: 3·48$$

With the ambient temperature 'cold', the results were:

$$3·51, 3·52, 3·56, 3·49, 3·48, 3·50. \quad \text{Mean}: 3·51$$

Are the means of these two sets of results significantly different at the 5% level?

($t = 1·7$, 8 d.f.: not significant.)

2. A 'full house' in poker is a hand of five cards in which 2 have the same face value and 3 have the same face value different from the pair (e.g. AA 10 10 10). A player observes over a 1000 independent hands that he drew 8 that were 'full house'. Is this consistent with the theoretical expectation.

(Pr. 'full house' = 0·0014; highly significant).

3. A coin is spun 10 times. Calculate accurately the probability of obtaining 7 or more heads and compare your answer with the approximation given by the Normal distribution.

(0·1719; $\mu = 5$, $\sigma = \sqrt{10}/2$, 0·1714.)

4. Analyse the significance of the effects of treatments in the Latin Square design.

A 21	B 21	C 30
B 27	C 23	A 23
C 33	A 17	B 28

($R_3/S_m = 21$; highly significant difference between treatments. Adjusted means (A, B, C,) = (20·4, 25·4, 28·7))

Group 11

1. Measurements taken before and after one adjustment to the measuring instrument are:

Before   9·5   9·5 9·7   9·6 9·4 9·3
After   9·7 10·0 9·6 10·0 9·9 9·6 9·8 9·8

Show that the means of these two sets of results are just significantly different at the 5% level

($t = 2·4$, 12 d.f.)

2. The number of aircraft arriving at an airport during operational hours is a Poisson variate with a mean of 2·0 per 5-minute interval. What is the probability.
(a) That at least one aircraft arrives in the next 10 minutes?
(b) That none arrives in the next 25 minutes?

($1 - e^{-4} = 0·982$; $e^{-10} = -0·000045$.)

3. The number of emissions from a weak radioactive source for a 100 separate seconds give the following results:

No. emissions/sec.   0   1   2   3 4 5 : T
No. of seconds   22 35 24 13 5 1 : 100

Find the mean number of emissions per second and verify that the figures conform with a Poisson distribution by applying a χ^2 test. Comment on the goodness of fit.
(Mean: 1·47 emissions/sec.
        distribution: 23, 34, 25, 12, (4, 1, 1,)
   $\chi^2 = 0·19$, 4 d.f.)

4. If x, y, and z are independent normal random variates all with zero means and variances σ^2, then corr $(x + y, y + z) = \frac{1}{2}$.
Show that var $(x + y) =$ var $(x + z) = 2\sigma^2$

Group 12

1. Theory predicts a change of 1% in the value of a physical constant under certain conditions. But the best experimental determinations under these conditions are normally distributed with a standard deviation of 5%. How may independent results are needed to establish the possible 1% differences at the 5% significance level?

(At best 100, taking $t = 2·0$ for 5%)

2. $P(t)$ is the probability that a hand of 13 cards drawn at random from a pack of 52 cards contains exactly t cards of a specified suit. Write down an expression for $P(t)$ and show that

$P(t + 1)/P(t) = (13 - t)^2/(t + 1)(27 + t)$

The distribution of 3400 hands by number of a specified suit held, was found to be: (Karl Pearson, 1924, Biometrika 16,172.)

Number of specified suit	Observed number of hands
0	35
1	280
2	696
3	937
4	851
5	444
6	115
7	21
8 & over	11
	3400

Given that $3400\, P(0) = 43 \cdot 486$ calculate the theoretical frequencies $3400\, P(1)$, $3400\, P(2)$ etc.

($^{13}C_t \; ^{39}C_{13-t}/^{52}C_{13}$; $272 \cdot 19$, $699 \cdot 92$ etc.)

3. A large set of examination marks is found to be normally distributed with mean $47 \cdot 5$ and standard deviation $12 \cdot 4$. Using normal probability paper show how this set of marks can be standardized to have a normal distribution with mean $50 \cdot 0$ and standard deviation $15 \cdot 0$.

Find the standardized marks (to the nearest integer) corresponding to 20, 40, 60 and 80 in the original set.

(17, 41, 65, 89.)

4. Find the mean and standard error of the following experimental results:

$$14 \cdot 17 \quad 14 \cdot 20 \quad 14 \cdot 19 \quad 14 \cdot 21 \quad 14 \cdot 18$$

Assuming that the results are normally distributed, express the 95% confidence limits of the mean values.

($\bar{x} = 14 \cdot 190 \pm 0 \cdot 014$.)

Group 13

1. If x and y are Poisson variates with means a and b respectively, show that $z = x + y$ is a Poisson variate with mean $(a + b)$. A mass-produced component may be defective in length or in diameter; these defects are independent. It is found that batches of equal size have, on average, one item defective in length and two defective in diameter. Find the probability that any given batch has 4 or more *items* with (a) defective length, (b) defective diameter, (c) either defect.

((a) $0 \cdot 02$, (b) $0 \cdot 143$, (c) $0 \cdot 353$.)

2. The diameters of mass-produced pins are normally distributed (mean, $1 \cdot 000''$, s.d. $0 \cdot 001''$) and the diameters of mass-produced sockets are also normally distributed (mean, $1 \cdot 001''$, s.d. $0 \cdot 002''$). The pins and sockets are available in equal numbers. What proportion of the pins could be matched to sockets to give $0 \cdot 001''$ clearance?

($70 \cdot 6\%$)

3. Data x are arranged in k groups of n items.

x_{11}	x_{21}	x_{k1}
x_{12}	x_{22}	x_{k2}
:	:	:
x_{1n}	x_{2n}	x_{kn}

Group Means $\quad \bar{x}_1 \qquad \bar{x}_2 \qquad \bar{x}_k$

Grand Mean $= \Sigma x_{ij}/nk = \bar{x}$

Prove the identity

$$\sum_{ij}(x_{ij} - \bar{x})^2 = \sum_{ij}(x_{ij} - \bar{x}_i)^2 + n\sum_{i}(\bar{x}_i - \bar{x})^2$$

Us this relationship to calculate $E(\sigma^2)$ for

$$\sum_{ij}(x_{ij} - \bar{x})^2 = 4{,}491{,}664$$

and

$$\sum_{i}(\bar{x}_i - \bar{x})^2 = 324{,}884.$$

4. Research work on a process to increase the strength of glass reveals that increase of mean strength is accompanied by an increase in variability. If the coefficient of variation is 0·25 what mean strength must be achieved to ensure that not more than 5% of the specimens of strengthened glass fall below 40 p.s.i. Assume that the results are Normally distributed. (68 p.s.i.).

Group 14

1. Are the means of the results in sets A and B below significantly different at the 5% level?

| Set A | 782 | 778 | 783 | 777 | 780 | |
| Set B | 780 | 783 | 786 | 783 | 784 | 782 |

($t = 2·19, f = 9$; not significant at 5% level.)

2. A mass production assembly contains 10 A-components and 15 B-components. The failure probabilities of A and B are 0·01 and 0·005 respectively. What is the probability of an assembly failure? At a cost of 1/- per component the A-component failure probability can be reduced to 0·005. Is this increased cost worth while if the cost of correcting a defective assembly is £10 per assembly.

(0·160; No. Increased cost per 1000 assemblies is £500 but saving in correction cost is only £430.)

3. The number of new strikes per week in British heavy industry has been recorded by Kendall for the years 1948–1959 (*J.R. Statist. Soc.*, Series A, *124*, 9, 1961). Show that the Poisson distribution describes the results.

Number of Strikes started/week	Number of weeks
0	252
1	229
2	109
3	28
4	8

(Mean $= 0·9$; $\chi^2 = 0·7$, 3 d.f.; not significant.)

4. A factorial design with factors a, b, c, each tested at two levels gave the following results. Estimate the main effects of the three factors.

$a_1b_1c_1$	$a_2b_1c_1$	$a_1b_2c_1$	$a_2b_2c_1$	$a_1b_1c_2$	$a_2b_1c_2$	$a_1b_2c_2$	$a_2b_2c_2$
8	8	21	24	27	25	32	35

($a, b, c, = 1·3, 14·7, 14·5$.)

Group 15

1. It is suspected that one of the components of an electronics device is inadequately screened. An improved screen is designed and readings of the output of the device are taken with the original and the improved screens being used alternately. The results are:

Original screen: 18·5   18·4   18·5   18·6
Improved screen: 18·7   18·4   18·9   18·8

Do these figures support the hypothesis that the output has been affected by the improved screen?

($t = 1·4$, 3 d.f.—which is not significant. The hypothesis is not supported.)

2. The U.K. consumption and production of a chemical over 5 years are:

Year (t)	1	2	3	4	5
Consumption (c)	80	82	87	91	93
Production (p)	50	54	62	68	75

The shortfall is made up by imports. Assuming that both consumption and production increase at constant annual compound interest rates, in what year will production overtake consumption if these rates are maintained?

(Year 9.   Use $\Sigma \log c = 4·684$, $t \log c = 14·227$, $\Sigma \log p = 3·931$, $\Sigma t \log p = 12·246$.)

3. In a large-scale examination the marks of Maths I and Maths II are normally distributed with means 45 and 52 and with s.d.'s 12 and 10 respectively. What should be the two pass marks which fail the bottom fifth on each paper? Show that 81 on Maths I is a better mark than 81 on Maths II.

($35, 44$; $81 = \bar{x}_1 + 3·0s_1 = \bar{x}_2 + 2·9s_2$.)

4. Errors $E(x)$ in measurements x of radiation intensity are distributed according to the law $E(x) = E_0 \log_2 x/1$. For n such measurements show that the value of I which makes $\Delta^2 = \overset{n}{\Sigma}[E(x_r)]^2$ a minimum is $I = (x_1 x_2 \ldots x_n) 1/n$

$\left(\text{Consider } \dfrac{\delta\Delta^2}{\delta I} = 0.\right)$

Group 16

1. It is suspected that the results of an experiment in electronics are affected by changes in atmospheric humidity. On a dry day 4 results were found: 12·5, 12·4, 12·5, 12·6, with mean 12·5; on a humid day 6 results were found: 12·8, 12·5, 12·7, 12·8, 12·6, 12·8, with mean 12·7. Do the results support the hypothesis that the change of humidity has affected the results?

($t = 2·76$, 8 d.f.—which is significant at the 5% level: the hypothesis is supported.)

2. Five cards are drawn from a pack of 52. Find the chance that the hand contains exactly two cards of the same face value. Find the chance of drawing a pair at least twice in 10 games.

($^{13}C_4 \times 4^4 \times {}^4C_2/^{52}C_5 = 0·4224$; $0·2857$.)

3. If three out of five arts students read economics or history in their first year, show that in a random sample of 12 the chance that 10 or more read economics or history is $0·0834$. What result is obtained if the Normal distribution approximation to the binomial is used?

($\mu = 7·2$, $\sigma = 6/2/5$, $P = 0·0877$.)

4. The correlation coefficient calculated from 80 results is 0·25. Use (i) Fisher's z-transformation, and (ii) Student's t-distribution to determine the significance level of this result on the assumption that the true correlation is zero.

((i) 0·0512; (ii) 0·0500.)

Answers to Exercises in Part Two

Exercises XXII (p. 149)

1. (*a*) There is no difference in weight; (*b*) boys are heavier than girls. Girls weigh 1 lb. more than boys. **2.** (e). **3.** The appropriate null hypothesis is that the average age is 38. The average age is 45. **4.** The null hypothesis is not true, yet the experiment by chance gives a result which does not lead to the rejection of the null hypothesis. **5.** The higher level of significance would be used for the less plausible hypothesis. **7.** The appropriate null hypothesis is that there is no difference in quality. From the expansion of $(\frac{1}{2} + \frac{1}{2})^8$ the observed result is not significant at the 5% level. $P = 7\%$. **8.** Yes. $P = 3.8\%$.

Exercises XXIII (p. 152)

2. No. **3.** Yes. **4.** Yes, $P = 0.3620$. **7.** (*a*) No, (*b*) Yes. **8.** (*a*) 6, (*b*) 8, (*c*) 11.

Exercises XXIV (p. 157)

1. $m = 7.67995$; $s = 6.75$; $m_n = 7.67995$, $sn = 2.86$; $s/\sqrt{n} = 3.37$ **2.** $m = 15.2$ min.; $s = 0.56$ min. **3.** 15. **4.** 13.5 lbs.

Exercises XXV (p. 161)

2. The time T.

Exercises XXVI (p. 174)

1. Not sig.; not sig.; sig. at 5% level; sig. at 1% level. **2.** 0.16, 0.45, 1.15, 3.26 ($t = 2.02$). **3.** $m = 1.63$, $s = 2.04$, $t = 3.11$. Sig. at 5%. **4.** $t = 8.7$. Highly sig. **5.** $t = 10$. **6.** Not sig. **7.** $F_{(25, 33)} = 1.37$; not sig. at 10% level. **8.** $t = 4.4$. Sig. on 5%, not on 1%. **9.** $t = 0.79$. Not sig. **10.** $t = 0.2$. Not sig. **11.** $s_1^2/s_2^2 = 1.95$. Not sig. **12.** 3.65 ± 0.14; ± 0.19; ± 0.35; ± 0.77. **13.** 17.86 ± 0.93. **14.** (*a*) 68.5446 ± 0.1348, 67.4345 ± 0.0636. (*b*) 1.1081 ± 0.1514. **15** (*a*) 1.30 and 4.75 (*b*) 1.72 and 2.40. **16.** A 6.25 and 11.13; B 7.49 and 29.46. **17.** 1.31 and 9.26 are 95% confidence limits of σ^2.

Exercises XXVII (p. 184)

4. 2.4, 4.9.

Exercises XXVIII (p. 195)

In 1–4 the equations are expressed in the form $y - \bar{y} = b(x - \bar{x})$ so that the values of $\bar{x}$ and $\bar{y}$ can be checked.
1. (*a*) $y - 14.3 = 1.62(x - 6.6)$; 8.5; 18.2. (*b*) $y - 10.9 = - 2.95 (x - 6.3)$; 17.7; $- 3.0$. **2.** $y - 389 = 1.10(x - 368)$. **3.** $y - 237 = 1.147(T - 5.5)$ where $T =$ (Year No. $- 1930$). **4.** $y - 24.65 = 1.58 (T - 9.5)$ where $T =$ (Year No. $- 1930$). **5.** $y = 0.69x + 0.82$; $x = 0.91y + 0.96$. **6.** $y = - 0.48x + 5.96$; $x = - 1.37y + 10.2$. **7.** $y = 2.37x - 40.3$; $x = 0.079y + 20.4$. **8.** $y = 0.030x + 0.644$; $x = 8.91y + 11.6$.

Exercises XXIX (p. 200)

1. $b = 2 \cdot 5$, S.E.$(b) = 6/\sqrt{26} = 1 \cdot 18$. **5.** $t(A) = 2 \cdot 4$, just. sig.; $t(B) = 14$, highly sig.

Exercises XXX (p. 202)

5. $y = 2 \cdot 382x + 138 \cdot 4$ where $x = $ (Year No. $- 1937$); 16,460,000.
6. $y = - 0 \cdot 840x + 157 \cdot 14$; $x = - 1 \cdot 053y + 170 \cdot 14$. **7.** $\log_{10} R = 3 \cdot 369 - 0 \cdot 1379C$; $C = 20 \cdot 7$; $R = 3 \cdot 27$. **8.** $y = 5 \cdot 995 - 2 \cdot 883x$; 9,555, 880.
9. $C = 98 \cdot 93 - 9 \cdot 735 R$. Yes; highly sig. **11.** $T = 14 \cdot 28 N + 11 \cdot 90$.
12. $C = 0 \cdot 00342 I + 0 \cdot 324$. **13.** $y = 0 \cdot 827x + 8 \cdot 54$; $x = 0 \cdot 823y + 9 \cdot 18$.
14. $y = - 0 \cdot 729x + 33 \cdot 3$; $x = - 0 \cdot 989y + 42 \cdot 0$. **15.** $y = - 0 \cdot 717x + 27 \cdot 5$; $x = - 0 \cdot 939y + 36 \cdot 44$. **16.** $y = - 0 \cdot 561x + 19 \cdot 7$; $x = - 0 \cdot 474y + 25 \cdot 8$. **17.** $x = - 0 \cdot 474y + 19 \cdot 4$.

Exercises XXXI (p. 211)

1. A, 1; B, $- 1$; C, 1. **2.** (i) $0 \cdot 6$; (ii) $- 0 \cdot 8$; (iii) $0 \cdot 25$; (iv) $- 0 \cdot 75$;
(v) $\pm 0 \cdot 8$. **3.** Uncorrelated; perfectly corr.; partially corr. **4.** A, $0 \cdot 909$;
B, $0 \cdot 145$; C, $- 0 \cdot 0079$; D, $- 0 \cdot 948$. **5.** $0 \cdot 901$. **6.** $0 \cdot 480$. **7.** $0 \cdot 991$. **8.**
$0 \cdot 937$. **9.** A, $0 \cdot 757$; B, $0 \cdot 873$. **10.** (i) $0 \cdot 792$; (ii) $- 0 \cdot 812$; (iii) $0 \cdot 434$.
(iv) $0 \cdot 519$.

Exercises XXXII (p. 218)

3. (a) Between $0 \cdot 025$ and $0 \cdot 05$; (b) $0 \cdot 05$; (c) between $0 \cdot 01$ and $0 \cdot 05$;
(d) about $0 \cdot 01$. **4.** (a) $r/$S.E.$(r) = 2 \cdot 05$; $P = 2 \cdot 02\%$. (b) $t = 1 \cdot 94$; $P = \frac{1}{2} \times 6 \cdot 2 = 3 \cdot 1\%$. (The t-table is 2-tailed.) (c) $z = 1 \cdot 83$; $P = 3 \cdot 4\%$.
5. (a) $0 \cdot 16\%$; (b) $1 \cdot 1\%$; (c) $14 \cdot 6\%$; (d) $0 \cdot 93\%$. **6.** Yes, $0 \cdot 60$ and $0 \cdot 45$.
7. $0 \cdot 36$. **8.** $0 \cdot 18 - 0 \cdot 56$; $0 \cdot 09 - 0 \cdot 69$. **9.** $t = 1 \cdot 28$; not sig. **10.** $t = 0 \cdot 80$;
not sig.; $r = 0 \cdot 087$.

Exercises XXXIII (p. 222)

1. (a) Consider $\Sigma d^2 = \Sigma s^2 + \Sigma t^2 - 2\Sigma st$. (b) Consider the number of possible even values of Σd^2. **2.** $R = 0 \cdot 2775$. **3.** (i) $0 \cdot 27$; (ii) $0 \cdot 62$;
(iii) $0 \cdot 04$; (iv) $- 0 \cdot 76$; (v) $0 \cdot 53$.

Exercises XXXIV (p. 226)

2. $- 0 \cdot 164$; $0 \cdot 209$; both sig. ($t = 3 \cdot 23$, $4 \cdot 11$). **3.** (a) $\pm 0 \cdot 8$; (b) $- 0 \cdot 2$,
(c) $0 \cdot 6$. **6.** $n = 2$, $R = 1 (p = \frac{1}{2})$ or $- 1(p = \frac{1}{2})$. $n = 3$, $R = 1(\frac{1}{8})$, $\frac{1}{2}(\frac{3}{8})$,
$- \frac{1}{2}(\frac{3}{8})$, $- 1(\frac{1}{8})$. $n = 4$ $R = \pm 1(1/24)$, $\pm 0 \cdot 8 (\frac{1}{8})$, $\pm 0 \cdot 6(1/24)$, $\pm 0 \cdot 4(\frac{1}{8})$;
$\pm 0 \cdot 2(1/12)$, $0(1/12)$. **7.** $r = 0 \cdot 886$; $R = 0 \cdot 756$. **8.** $R = 0 \cdot 463$. **11.** $r = 0 \cdot 793$; $R = 0 \cdot 858$. **12.** $r = 0 \cdot 754$. **21.** $0 \cdot 825$; $- 0 \cdot 849$; $- 0 \cdot 823$; $- 0 \cdot 516$;
$0 \cdot 474$. All highly sig.

Exercises XXXV (p. 243)

1. $\chi^2 = 2 \cdot 546$, $f = 4$. Not sig. **3.** $\chi^2 = 1 \cdot 098$, $f = 4$. Not sig. **4.** $\chi^2 = 0 \cdot 065$, $f = 3 - 2 = 1$. Not sig. **5.** Poisson; $\chi^2 = 25 \cdot 77$, $f = 3 - 2 = 1$.
Highly sig. Negative Binomial: $\chi^2 = 1 \cdot 93$; $f = 4 - 3 = 1$. Not sig.
6. $\chi^2 = 16 \cdot 07$, $f = 6 - 2 = 4$. Between $0 \cdot 5\%$ and $0 \cdot 1\%$. **7.** $\chi^2 = 58 \cdot 54$,
$f = 9$. Highly sig. **8.** $\chi^2 = 0 \cdot 470$, $f = 4 - 1 = 3$. Not sig. **9.** $\chi^2 = 36$,
$f = 11 - 1 = 10$. Highly sig. **10.** $\chi^2 = 8 \cdot 2$, $f = 11 - 2 = 9$. Not sig.
11. 3, 10, 22, 40, 56, 67, 61, 46, 27, 13, 5, 2. $\chi^2 = 26 \cdot 10$, $f = 9 - 3 = 6$
$P < 0 \cdot 1\%$. **12.** (1, 3, 9, 19), 35, 55, 71, 78, 72, 57, 38, 21, (10, 4, 1, 0, 0).
$\chi^2 = 50 \cdot 1$; $f = 10 - 3 = 7$. Highly sig.

Exercises XXXVI (p. 250)

1. $\chi^2 = 56, f = 1$. Highly sig. **3.** $\chi^2 = 193, f = 3 \times 3 = 9$. Highly sig. **4.** $\chi^2 = 49\cdot2, f = 5$. Highly sig. **6.** $\chi^2 = 34\cdot22, f = 8$. Highly sig. **7** $\chi^2 = 15\cdot8, f = 4$. $0\cdot1\% \leqslant P \leqslant 0\cdot5\%$.

Exercises XXXVII (p. 259)

1. $t = 2\cdot53$, $\nu = 11$, $P \simeq 2\frac{1}{2}\%$. **2.** 1st method, $t = 1\cdot58$, $\nu = 28$, $P \simeq 10\%$. 2nd method, $t = 2\cdot9$, $\nu = 14$, $P \simeq 1\%$. **4.** $0\cdot0464$.

Exercises XXXVIII (p. 263)

1. $R_4/s = 1\cdot66$. No sig. difference. **2.** $R_3/s = 1\cdot73$. No sig. difference. **3.** $R_{12}/s = 1\cdot41$. No sig. difference.

Exercises XXXIX (p. 269)

4. $R_4/s = 11\cdot2$. Highly sig. **5.** $R_6/s = 19\cdot72$. Highly sig. **6.** $R_4/s = 4\cdot54$. Just sig. at 1% level.

Exercises XL (p. 274)

2. $(A_1 + A_2)(B_1 + B_2)$; $a_1 b_1$, $a_1 b_2$, $a_2 b_1$, $a_2 b_2$. Varying a: $\frac{1}{2}(a_1 b_1 - a_2 b_2 + a_1 b_2 - a_2 b_2)$. Varying b: $\frac{1}{2}(a_1 b_1 - a_1 b_2 + a_2 b_1 - a_2 b_2)$. **3.** $F \times T$, $0\cdot50$; $S \times T$, $0\cdot20$. **4.** N, $- 0\cdot180$; K, $- 3\cdot805$; D, $- 5\cdot00$. $K \times D$, $- 2\cdot25$; $N \times D$, $0\cdot22$; $K \times N$, $1\cdot11$. **5.** Expansion of $(A_1 + A_2)(B_1 + B_2)(C_1 + C_2)(D_1 + D_2)$.

Appendix—Tables and Charts

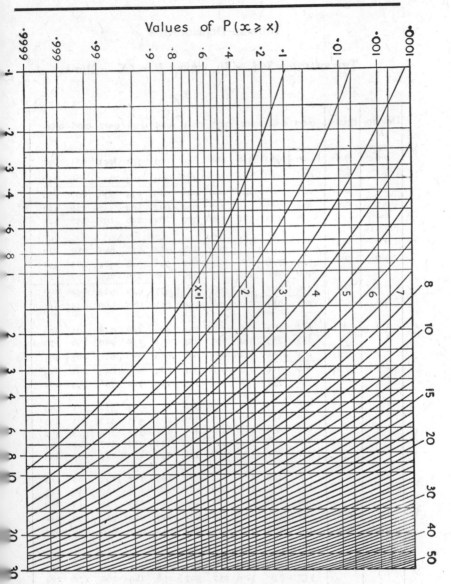

Values of $P(x \geqslant x)$

The Poisson summation chart

TABLE XXVI

NORMAL DISTRIBUTION

THE FRACTION $P(d \geqslant D)$, WHERE $D = (X - \mu)/\sigma$

Deviate D	Prefix	0·00	0·01	0·02	0·03	0·04	0·05	0·06	0·07	0·08	0·09
0·0	0·5	000	960	920	880	840	801	761	721	681	641
0·1	0·4	602	562	522	483	443	404	364	325	286	247
0·2	0·4	207	168	129	090	052	013	974	936	897	859
0·3	0·3	821	783	745	707	669	632	594	557	520	483
0·4		446	409	372	336	300	264	228	192	156	121
0·5	0·3	085	050	015	981	946	912	877	843	810	776
0·6	0·2	743	709	676	643	611	578	546	514	483	451
0·7		420	389	358	327	296	266	236	206	177	148
0·8	0·2	119	090	061	033	005	977	949	922	894	867
0·9	0·1	841	814	788	762	736	711	685	660	635	611
1·0		587	563	539	515	492	469	446	423	401	379
1·1		357	335	314	292	271	251	230	210	190	170
1·2	0·1	151	131	112	093	075	056	038	020	003	985
1·3	0·0	968	951	934	918	901	885	869	853	838	823
1·4		808	793	778	764	749	735	721	708	694	681
1·5		668	655	643	630	618	606	594	582	571	559
1·6		548	537	526	516	505	495	485	475	465	455
1·7		446	436	427	418	409	401	392	384	375	367
1·8		359	351	344	336	329	322	314	307	301	294
1·9		287	281	274	268	262	256	250	244	239	233
2·0		228	222	217	212	207	202	197	192	188	183
2·1		179	174	170	166	162	158	154	150	146	143
2·2		139	136	132	129	125	122	119	116	113	110
2·3	0·0	107	104	102	990	964	939	914	889	866	842
2·4	0·00	820	798	776	755	734	714	695	676	657	639
2·5		621	604	587	570	554	539	523	508	494	480
2·6		466	453	440	427	414	402	391	379	368	357
2·7		347	336	326	317	307	298	289	280	272	264
2·8		256	248	240	233	226	219	212	205	199	193
2·9	0·00	187	181	175	169	164	159	154	149	144	140

TABLE XXVI—*continued.*

Deviate (D)	Proportion of Whole Area (P)	Deviate (D)	Proportion of Whole Area (P)	Deviate (D)	Proportion of Whole Area (P)	Deviate (D)	Proportion of Whole Area (P)
3·0	·00 135	3·5	·000 233	4·0	·0^4 317	4·5	·0^6 340
3·1	·000 968	3·6	·000 159	4·1	·0^4 207	4·6	·0^6 211
3·2	·000 687	3·7	·000 108	4·2	·0^4 133	4·7	·0^6 130
3·3	·000 483	3·8	·0^4 723	4·3	·0^4 085	4·8	·0^6 793
3·4	·000 337	3·9	·0^4 481	4·4	·0^4 054	4·9	·0^6 479
						5·0	·0^6 287

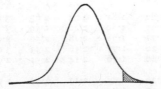

The illustration shows the Normal curve. The shaded area is a fraction, P, of the whole area, where P is given in the table.

The entries refer to positive values of the argument, D. For negative values of D, write the complements of the entries, i.e., $1 - P$. The lines on the table indicate when the prefix changes.

EXAMPLES

(a) $D = 0.84$. The prefix is 0·2 and the entry is 005, so that $P(d \geqslant 0.84) = 0.2005$. (b) $D = 0.85$. The prefix is now 0·1 and the entry is 977, so that $P(d \geqslant 0.85) = 0.1977$. (c) $D = -2.37$. The tabulated value for $D = + 2.37$ is 0.00889 and since D is negative $P(d \geqslant -2.37) = 1 - 0.00889 = 0.99111$. (d) $D = 1.26$. The area outside $\pm D$ is $2P(d \geqslant D) = 2 \times 0.2077 = 0.4154$. (e) $D = 4.2$. The tabulated value is $P(d \geqslant 4.2) = 0.0000267$.

TABLE XXX

Percentage Points of the t-Distribution

f	$P(\%)$							
	50	25	10	5	2·5	1	0·5	0·1
1	1·00	2·41	6·31	12·7	25·5	63·7	127	637
2	·816	1·60	2·92	4·30	6·21	9·92	14·1	31·6
3	·765	1·42	2·35	3·18	4·18	5·84	7·45	12·9
4	·741	1·34	2·13	2·78	3·50	4·60	5·60	8·61
5	·727	1·30	2·01	2·57	3·16	4·03	4·77	6·86
6	·718	1·27	1·94	2·45	2·97	3·71	4·32	5·96
7	·711	1·25	1·89	2·36	2·84	3·50	4·03	5·40
8	·706	1·24	1·86	2·31	2·75	3·36	3·83	5·04
9	·703	1·23	1·83	2·26	2·68	3·25	3·69	4·78
10	·700	1·22	1·81	2·23	2·63	3·17	3·58	4·59
11	·698	1·21	1·80	2·20	2·59	3·11	3·50	4·44
12	·695	1·21	1·78	2·18	2·56	3·05	3·43	4·32
13	·694	1·20	1·77	2·16	2·53	3·01	3·37	4·22
14	·692	1·20	1·76	2·14	2·51	2·98	3·33	4·14
15	·691	1·20	1·75	2·13	2·49	2·95	3·29	4·07
16	·690	1·19	1·75	2·12	2·47	2·92	3·25	4·01
17	·689	1·19	1·74	2·11	2·46	2·90	3·22	3·96
18	·688	1·19	1·73	2·10	2·44	2·88	3·20	3·92
19	·688	1·19	1·73	2·09	2·43	2·86	3·17	3·88
20	·687	1·18	1·72	2·09	2·42	2·85	3·15	3·85
21	·686	1·18	1·72	2·08	2·41	2·83	3·14	3·82
22	·686	1·18	1·72	2·07	2·41	2·82	3·12	3·79
23	·685	1·18	1·71	2·07	2·40	2·81	3·10	3·77
24	·685	1·18	1·71	2·06	2·39	2·80	3·09	3·74
25	·684	1·18	1·71	2·06	2·38	2·79	3·08	3·72
26	·684	1·18	1·71	2·06	2·38	2·78	3·07	3·71
27	·684	1·18	1·70	2·05	2·37	2·77	3·06	3·69
28	·683	1·17	1·70	2·05	2·37	2·76	3·05	3·67
29	·683	1·17	1·70	2·05	2·36	2·76	3·04	3·66
30	·683	1·17	1·70	2·04	2·36	2·75	3·03	3·65
40	·681	1·17	1·68	2·02	2·33	2·70	2·97	3·55
60	·679	1·16	1·67	2·00	2·30	2·66	2·91	3·46
120	·677	1·16	1·66	1·98	2·27	2·62	2·86	3·37
∞	·674	1·15	1·64	1·96	2·24	2·58	2·81	3·29

The appearance of the t-curve is similar to that of the Normal curve. The quantity P is the area under the two tails of the t-curve. P is therefore the probability that $|t|$, the absolute value of t, will exceed the tabular entry.

f is the number of degrees of freedom.

(a) Let $\mu = 32\cdot4$, sample size $n = 15$, $\bar{x} = 31\cdot3$ and $s = 1\cdot55$. Then $s/\sqrt{n} = 0\cdot40$; $t = (32\cdot4 - 31\cdot3)/0\cdot40 = 2\cdot75$; and $f = 15 - 1 = 14$. This value of t lies between the 5% and 1% values of P for $f = 14$ and is therefore significant. (b) Let $\bar{x}_1 = 0\cdot326$, $\bar{x}_2 = 0\cdot501$, $s_1 = 0\cdot182$, $s_2 = 0\cdot164$, $n_1 = 4$, $n_2 = 6$. Then $s^2 = [(n_1 - 1)s_1^2 + (n_2 - 1)s_2^2]/(n_1 + n_2 - 2) = 0\cdot0292$, $s^2\left(\dfrac{1}{n_1} + \dfrac{1}{n_2}\right) = 0\cdot0122$, $s\sqrt{\left(\dfrac{1}{n_1} + \dfrac{1}{n_2}\right)} = 0\cdot11$, $t = (0\cdot501 - 0\cdot326)/0\cdot11 = 1\cdot59$ and $f = 4 + 6 - 2 = 8$. The 5% tabular entry at $f = 8$ is $2\cdot31$ and so this value of t is not significant.

TABLE XXXIX

PERCENTAGE POINTS OF THE χ^2 DISTRIBUTION

$P\%$ / J	99	97·5	95	90	50	10	5	2·5	1
1	0·0	0·0	0·0	0·0	0·5	2·7	3·8	5·0	6·6
2	0·0	0·1	0·1	0·2	1·4	4·6	6·0	7·4	9·2
3	0·1	0·2	0·4	0·6	2·4	6·3	7·8	9·3	11·3
4	0·3	0·5	0·7	1·1	3·4	7·8	9·5	11·1	13·3
5	0·6	0·8	1·1	1·6	4·4	9·2	11·1	12·8	15·1
6	0·9	1·2	1·6	2·2	5·3	10·6	12·6	14·4	16·8
7	1·2	1·7	2·2	2·8	6·3	12·0	14·1	16·0	18·5
8	1·6	2·2	2·7	3·5	7·3	13·4	15·5	17·5	20·1
9	2·1	2·7	3·3	4·2	8·3	14·7	16·9	19·0	21·7
10	2·6	3·2	3·9	4·9	9·3	16·0	18·3	20·5	23·2
11	3·1	3·8	4·6	5·6	10·3	17·3	19·7	21·9	24·7
12	3·6	4·4	5·2	6·3	11·3	18·5	21·0	23·3	26·2
13	4·1	5·0	5·9	7·0	12·3	19·8	22·4	24·7	27·7
14	4·7	5·6	6·6	7·8	13·3	21·1	23·7	26·1	29·1
15	5·2	6·3	7·3	8·5	14·3	22·3	25·0	27·5	30·6
16	5·8	6·9	8·0	9·3	15·3	23·5	26·3	28·8	32·0
17	6·4	7·6	8·7	10·1	16·3	24·8	27·6	30·2	33·4
18	7·0	8·2	9·4	10·9	17·3	26·0	28·9	31·5	34·8
19	7·6	8·9	10·1	11·7	18·3	27·2	30·1	32·9	36·2
20	8·3	9·6	10·9	12·4	19·3	28·4	31·4	34·2	37·6
21	8·9	10·3	11·6	13·2	20·3	29·6	32·7	35·5	38·9
22	9·5	11·0	12·3	14·0	21·3	30·8	33·9	36·8	40·3
23	10·2	11·7	13·1	14·8	22·3	32·0	35·2	38·1	41·6
24	10·9	12·4	13·8	15·7	23·3	33·2	36·4	39·4	43·0
25	11·5	13·1	14·6	16·5	24·3	34·4	37·7	40·6	44·3
26	12·2	13·8	15·4	17·3	25·3	35·6	38·9	41·9	45·6
27	12·9	14·6	16·2	18·1	26·3	36·7	40·1	43·2	47·0
28	13·6	15·3	16·9	18·9	27·3	37·9	41·3	44·5	48·3
29	14·3	16·0	17·7	19·8	28·3	39·1	42·6	45·7	49·6
30	15·0	16·8	18·5	20·6	29·3	40·3	43·8	47·0	50·9

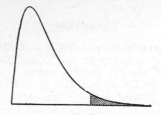

The illustration shows the χ^2 curve for $f = 3$. The shaded area is a fraction, P, of the whole area where P is given in the table.

f is the number of degrees of freedom.

When $f > 30$ it is approximately true that

$$\sqrt{(2 \chi^2)} - \sqrt{(2f - 1)}$$

is normally distributed with unit standard deviation. The probability for χ^2 corresponds to a single tail of the Normal curve.

EXAMPLES

(a) Let $\chi^2 = 15\cdot2$, $f = 12$. This value of χ^2 lies between the 50% and 10% points and is not significant. (b) Let $\chi^2 = 45\cdot0$, $f = 24$. This value of χ^2 lies between the 1% and 0·1% points and is therefore significant. (c) Let $\chi^2 = 126$, $f = 110$. Then $D = \sqrt{252} - \sqrt{219} = 15\cdot87 - 14\cdot80 = 1\cdot07$. From Table XXVI, for $D = 1\cdot07$, $P = 14\cdot23\%$. χ^2 is therefore not significant.

TABLE XLII
F-DISTRIBUTION: UPPER 5% POINTS

f_2 \ f_1	5	6	7	8	9	10	12	15	20	30	60	∞
5	5·1	5·0	4·9	4·8	4·8	4·7	4·7	4·6	4·6	4·5	4·4	4·4
6	4·4	4·3	4·2	4·1	4·1	4·1	4·0	3·9	3·9	3·8	3·7	3·7
7	4·0	3·9	3·8	3·7	3·7	3·6	3·6	3·5	3·4	3·4	3·3	3·2
8	3·7	3·6	3·5	3·4	3·4	3·3	3·3	3·2	3·2	3·1	3·0	2·9
9	3·5	3·4	3·3	3·2	3·2	3·1	3·1	3·0	2·9	2·9	2·8	2·7
10	3·3	3·2	3·1	3·1	3·0	3·0	2·9	2·8	2·8	2·7	2·6	2·5
11	3·2	3·1	3·0	2·9	2·9	2·9	2·8	2·7	2·6	2·6	2·5	2·4
12	3·1	3·0	2·9	2·8	2·8	2·8	2·7	2·6	2·5	2·5	2·4	2·3
13	3·0	2·9	2·8	2·8	2·7	2·7	2·6	2·5	2·5	2·4	2·3	2·2
14	3·0	2·8	2·8	2·7	2·6	2·6	2·5	2·5	2·4	2·3	2·2	2·1
15	2·9	2·8	2·7	2·6	2·6	2·5	2·5	2·4	2·3	2·2	2·2	2·1
16	2·9	2·7	2·7	2·6	2·5	2·5	2·4	2·4	2·3	2·2	2·1	2·0
17	2·8	2·7	2·6	2·5	2·5	2·4	2·4	2·3	2·2	2·1	2·1	2·0
18	2·8	2·7	2·6	2·5	2·5	2·4	2·3	2·3	2·2	2·1	2·0	2·0
19	2·7	2·6	2·5	2·5	2·4	2·4	2·3	2·2	2·2	2·1	2·0	1·9
20	2·7	2·6	2·5	2·4	2·4	2·3	2·3	2·2	2·1	2·0	1·9	1·8
21	2·7	2·6	2·5	2·4	2·4	2·3	2·3	2·2	2·1	2·0	1·9	1·8
22	2·7	2·5	2·5	2·4	2·3	2·3	2·2	2·2	2·1	2·0	1·9	1·8
23	2·6	2·5	2·4	2·4	2·3	2·3	2·2	2·1	2·0	2·0	1·9	1·8
24	2·6	2·5	2·4	2·4	2·3	2·3	2·2	2·1	2·0	1·9	1·8	1·7
25	2·6	2·5	2·4	2·3	2·3	2·2	2·2	2·1	2·0	1·9	1·8	1·7
26	2·6	2·5	2·4	2·3	2·3	2·2	2·1	2·1	2·0	1·9	1·8	1·7
27	2·6	2·5	2·4	2·3	2·3	2·2	2·1	2·1	2·0	1·9	1·8	1·7
28	2·6	2·4	2·4	2·3	2·2	2·2	2·1	2·0	2·0	1·9	1·8	1·7
29	2·5	2·4	2·3	2·3	2·2	2·2	2·1	2·0	1·9	1·9	1·8	1·6
30	2·5	2·4	2·3	2·3	2·2	2·2	2·1	2·0	1·9	1·8	1·7	1·6
40	2·4	2·3	2·2	2·2	2·1	2·1	2·0	1·9	1·8	1·7	1·6	1·5
60	2·4	2·3	2·2	2·1	2·0	2·0	1·9	1·8	1·7	1·6	1·5	1·4
120	2·3	2·2	2·1	2·0	2·0	1·9	1·8	1·8	1·7	1·6	1·4	1·3
∞	2·2	2·1	2·0	1·9	1·9	1·8	1·8	1·7	1·6	1·5	1·3	1·0

For $f_1 > 10$ interpolate using $60/f_1$
For $f_2 > 30$ interpolate using $120/f_2$

TABLE XLIII

F-DISTRIBUTION: UPPER 1% POINTS

f_2 \ f_1	5	6	7	8	9	10	12	15	20	30	60	∞
5	11·0	10·7	10·5	10·3	10·2	10·1	9·9	9·7	9·6	9·4	9·2	9·0
6	8·7	8·5	8·3	8·1	8·0	7·8	7·7	7·6	7·4	7·2	7·1	6·9
7	7·4	7·2	7·0	6·8	6·7	6·6	6·5	6·3	6·2	6·0	5·8	5·6
8	6·6	6·4	6·2	6·0	5·9	5·8	5·7	5·5	5·4	5·2	5·0	4·9
9	6·1	5·8	5·6	5·5	5·4	5·3	5·1	5·0	4·8	4·6	4·5	4·3
10	5·6	5·4	5·2	5·1	4·9	4·8	4·7	4·6	4·4	4·2	4·1	3·9
11	5·3	5·1	4·9	4·7	4·6	4·5	4·4	4·3	4·1	3·9	3·8	3·6
12	5·1	4·8	4·6	4·5	4·4	4·3	4·2	4·0	3·9	3·7	3·5	3·4
13	4·9	4·6	4·4	4·3	4·2	4·1	4·0	3·8	3·7	3·5	3·3	3·2
14	4·7	4·5	4·3	4·1	4·0	3·9	3·8	3·7	3·5	3·3	3·2	3·0
15	4·6	4·3	4·1	4·0	3·9	3·8	3·7	3·5	3·4	3·2	3·0	2·9
16	4·4	4·2	4·0	3·9	3·8	3·7	3·6	3·4	3·3	3·1	2·9	2·8
17	4·3	4·1	3·9	3·8	3·7	3·6	3·5	3·3	3·2	3·0	2·8	2·7
18	4·2	4·0	3·8	3·7	3·6	3·5	3·4	3·2	3·1	2·9	2·7	2·6
19	4·2	3·9	3·8	3·6	3·5	3·4	3·3	3·2	3·0	2·8	2·7	2·5
20	4·1	3·9	3·7	3·6	3·5	3·4	3·2	3·1	2·9	2·8	2·6	2·4
21	4·0	3·8	3·6	3·5	3·4	3·3	3·2	3·0	2·9	2·7	2·5	2·4
22	4·0	3·8	3·6	3·5	3·3	3·3	3·1	3·0	2·8	2·7	2·5	2·3
23	3·9	3·7	3·5	3·4	3·3	3·2	3·1	2·9	2·8	2·6	2·4	2·3
24	3·9	3·7	3·5	3·4	3·3	3·2	3·0	2·9	2·7	2·6	2·4	2·2
25	3·9	3·6	3·5	3·3	3·2	3·1	3·0	2·9	2·7	2·5	2·4	2·2
26	3·8	3·6	3·4	3·3	3·2	3·1	3·0	2·8	2·7	2·5	2·3	2·1
27	3·8	3·6	3·4	3·3	3·1	3·1	2·9	2·8	2·6	2·5	2·3	2·1
28	3·8	3·5	3·4	3·2	3·1	3·0	2·9	2·8	2·6	2·4	2·3	2·1
29	3·7	3·5	3·3	3·2	3·1	3·0	2·9	2·7	2·6	2·4	2·2	2·0
30	3·7	3·5	3·3	3·2	3·1	3·0	2·8	2·7	2·5	2·4	2·2	2·0
40	3·5	3·3	3·1	3·0	2·9	2·8	2·7	2·5	2·4	2·2	2·0	1·8
60	3·3	3·1	3·0	2·8	2·7	2·6	2·5	2·4	2·2	2·0	1·8	1·6
120	3·2	3·0	2·8	2·7	2·6	2·5	2·3	2·2	2·0	1·9	1·7	1·4
∞	3·0	2·8	2·6	2·5	2·4	2·3	2·2	2·0	1·9	1·7	1·5	1·0

For $f_1 > 10$ interpolate using $60/f_1$
For $f_2 > 30$ interpolate using $120/f_2$

Index

331

Notes on
the Teaching of
Statistics in Schools

With a Foreword by

PROFESSOR E. S. PEARSON, C.B.E., M.A., D.SC.
Department of Statistics, University College, London.

This book supplies all the guidance needed for the teaching of elementary Statistics. It is based on the recommendations of the Report of the Teaching Committee of the Royal Statistical Society, of which Mr. Brookes is a member.

It suggests methods of introducing the simpler statistical ideas and problems to pupils as part of their general education, together with a series of connected notes which are designed to prove useful in teaching for the papers or questions set in the subject by the various examining boards.

Professor Pearson says in his Foreword:
"It seems to me to provide an admirable account of how one teacher would approach these basic statistical concepts: variation, correlation, probability, sampling; how he would make his pupils collect the data by which to clothe these concepts with reality; and how he would use the results to encourage a critical and inquiring attitude of mind."